Transformations

Feminist thought has made an important mark on the social and political life of the twentieth century. But in the wake of this and other wider social transformations, can it be said that feminism's project is now obsolete? *Transformations* argues for its continued relevance.

Refusing to accept the notion that transformation of gender relations has simply taken place, or that feminism is inherently transformative, this book examines the place of feminism in contemporary life. With contributions from some important current feminist thinkers, *Transformations* traces both the shifts in thinking that have allowed feminism to arrive at its present point and the way that feminist agendas have progressed in line with wider social developments. The authors engage in current debates as diverse as globalisation, technoscience, embodiment and performativity, taking feminism in fresh directions, mapping new territory and suggesting alternative possibilities.

This book will be essential reading for students and scholars working in the areas of Gender Studies and Women's Studies.

Sara Ahmed is Co-Director of the Institute for Women's Studies at Lancaster University; **Jane Kilby** is Lecturer in Sociology at Salford University; **Celia Lury** is Reader in Sociology at Goldsmiths College, University of London; **Maureen McNeil** is Reader in the Institute for Women's Studies, Lancaster University; and **Beverley Skeggs** is Chair of Sociology at Manchester University.

Transformations: Thinking Through Feminism
Edited by:
Maureen McNeil
Institute of Women's Studies, Lancaster University
Lynne Pearce
Department of English, Lancaster University
Beverley Skeggs
Department of Sociology, Manchester University

Other books in the series include:

Strange Encounters
Embodied Others in Post-Coloniality
Sara Ahmed

Feminism and Autobiography
Texts, Theories, Methods
Edited by Tess Cosslett, Celia Lury and Penny Summerfield

Advertising and Consumer Citizenship
Gender, Images and Rights
Anne M. Cronin

Mothering the Self
Mothers, Daughters, Subjects
Stephanie Lawler

Transformations

Thinking Through Feminism

**Edited by Sara Ahmed,
Jane Kilby, Celia Lury,
Maureen McNeil and
Beverley Skeggs**

London and New York

First published 2000
by Routledge
11 New Fetter Lane, London EC4P 4EE

Simultaneously published in the USA and Canada
by Routledge
29 West 35th Street, New York, NY 10001

Routledge is an imprint of the Taylor & Francis Group

Typeset in Baskerville by Taylor & Francis Books Ltd
Printed and bound in Great Britain by TJ International Ltd,
Padstow, Cornwall

British Library Cataloguing in Publication Data
A catalogue record for this book is available from the British Library

Library of Congress Cataloging in Publication Data
Thinking through feminism / [edited by] Sara Ahmed ... [et al.].
p. cm. – (Transformations)
Includes bibliographical references and index.
1. Feminism–Congresses. 2. Feminist theory–Congresses. 3. Women's
studies–Congresses. I. Ahmed, Sara. II. Series.

HQ1106 .T55 2000
305.42–dc21

00-032845

ISBN 0–415–22066–1 (hbk)
ISBN 0–415–22067–X (pbk)

Contents

List of illustrations   ix
Notes on contributors   xi
Series editors' preface   xv
Acknowledgements   xvii
Permissions   xix

Introduction: thinking through feminism   **1**
SARA AHMED, JANE KILBY, CELIA LURY, MAUREEN MCNEIL
AND BEVERLEY SKEGGS

PART I
The rhetorical affects of feminism   **25**

Introduction   **27**
BEVERLEY SKEGGS

1 **The subject of true feeling: pain, privacy and politics**   **33**
LAUREN BERLANT

2 **Shaming theory, thinking dis-connections: feminism and
reconciliation**   **48**
ELSPETH PROBYN

3 **Owned suffering: thinking the feminist political
imagination with Simone de Beauvoir and Richard Wright**   **61**
VIKKI BELL

4 **Unifying forces: rhetorical reflections on a
   pro-choice image**   77
   KARYN SANDLOS

5 **Luce Irigaray's sexuate rights and the politics of
   performativity**   92
   PENELOPE DEUTSCHER

**PART II
Boundaries and connections**   109

Introduction   111
SARA AHMED

6 **Claiming transformation: travel notes with pictures**   119
   GAYATRI CHAKRAVORTY SPIVAK

7 **From politics of identity to politics of complexity:
   a possible research agenda for feminist politics/movements
   across time and space**   131
   NGAI-LING SUM

8 **Operatic karaoke and the pitfalls of identity politics:
   a translated performance**   145
   SNEJA GUNEW

9 **Crossing boundaries: rethinking/teaching identity**   159
   GAIL CHING-LIANG LOW

**PART III
Knowledges and disciplines**   173

Introduction   175
MAUREEN MCNEIL

10 **Forays of a philosophical feminist: sexual difference, genealogy, teleology** 182
JOANNA HODGE

11 **Philosophy and the feminist imagination** 196
JEAN GRIMSHAW

12 **Still telling it like it is?: problems of feminist truth claims** 207
CAROLINE RAMAZANOGLU AND JANET HOLLAND

13 **Techno-triumphalism, techno-tourism, American dreams and feminism** 221
MAUREEN MCNEIL

14 **Nuclear families: women's narratives of the making of the atomic bomb** 235
CAROL WOLKOWITZ

PART IV
Subject matters 251

Introduction 253
JANE KILBY AND CELIA LURY

15 **Objects of innovation: post-occupational reflexivity and re-traditionalisations of gender** 259
LISA ADKINS

16 **Consumerism and 'compulsory individuality': women, will and potential** 273
ANNE M. CRONIN

17 **Reframing pregnant embodiment** 288
IMOGEN TYLER

18 **Monsters, marvels and metaphysics:
    beyond the powers of horror**   303
    MARGRIT SHILDRICK

19 **Belonging and unbelonging: transformations of memory
    in the photographs of Virginia Woolf**   316
    MAGGIE HUMM

    Index   332

Illustrations

4.1	Gerri Santoro	78
6.1	'Wolfensohn among the Girls'	120
6.2	A Bangladeshi model and cultural icon turned entrepreneur	125
6.3	A West Bengali boy contemplating an image of the goddess Durga and her family	127
18.1	The Monster of Cracow	306
18.2	The Monster of Ravenna	310
19.1	Woolf's mother and father, with Woolf in the background, Talland House 1892	318
19.2	The composer Ethel Smyth	321
19.3	William Plomer, Vita Nicolson and Charles Siepmann	322

Contributors

Lisa Adkins is a Lecturer in Sociology at the University of Manchester. Her research interests are in the areas of social theory, feminist theory, sexuality, gender, and economy. Publications include *Gendered Work*, *Sexualizing the Social* and *Sex, Sensibility and the Gendered Body*. Recent articles have been published in *Theory, Culture and Society* and *Economy and Society*. She is currently completing a book called *Revisions: Towards a Feminist Sociology of Late Modernity*, which considers theories of identity transformation in relation to gender and sexuality, to be published by the Open University Press.

Sara Ahmed is Co-Director with Jackie Stacey of the Institute for Women's Studies at Lancaster University. Her first book, *Differences That Matter: Feminist Theory and Postmodernism*, was published by Cambridge University Press in 1998, and she has since published *Strange Encounters: Embodied Others in Post-Coloniality*, also in the Transformations series (2000).

Vikki Bell is Senior Lecturer in the Sociology Department, Goldsmiths College, University of London. Her first book was entitled *Interrogating Incest: Feminism, Foucault and the Law* (Routledge 1993) and her second book is *Feminist Imagination: Genealogies in Feminist Theory* (Sage 2000). She has also written several articles on various aspects of the work of Foucault, feminist theory and philosophy and is an editor of the journal *Theory, Culture and Society*.

Lauren Berlant is Professor of English and Director of the Center for Gender Studies at the University of Chicago. She is author of *The Queen of America Goes to Washington City: Essays in Sex and Citizenship* (Duke 1997) and editor of *Intimacy* (Chicago 2000), as well as co-editor of *Critical Inquiry*.

Anne M. Cronin is a lecturer in Culture, Media and Communication and Sociology at Lancaster University and her research interests are advertising, consumerism and feminist cultural theory. Her book, *Advertising and Consumer Citizenship: Gender, Images and Rights*, is forthcoming in the Transformations series (Routledge 2000).

Penelope Deutscher is Senior Lecturer in the Department of Philosophy at the Australian National University. She is the author of *Yielding Gender:*

Feminism, Deconstruction and the History of Philosophy (Routledge 1997), and co-editor, with Kelly Oliver, of *Enigmas: Essays on Sarah Kofman* (Cornell University Press 1999).

Jean Grimshaw taught Philosophy and Women's Studies at the University of the West of England, Bristol, until 1999. She is the author of *Feminist Philosophers: Women's Perspectives on Philosophical Traditions* (Wheatsheaf 1986), and co-editor with Jane Arthurs of *Women's Bodies: Discipline and Transgression* (Cassell 1999). In addition she has published many articles on feminism and philosophy. She is a member of the editorial collective of *Radical Philosophy* and the editorial board of *Women's Philosophy Review*.

Sneja Gunew has taught for over twenty-five years at various universities in England, Australia and Canada. She has published widely on multicultural, postcolonial and feminist critical theory and is currently Professor of English and Women's Studies at the University of British Columbia, Canada. She has edited (with Anna Yeatman) *Feminism and the Politics of Difference* (Allen and Unwin 1993) and (with Fazal Rizvi) *Culture, Difference and the Arts* (Allen and Unwin 1994). Her most recent book is *Framing Marginality: Multicultural Literary Studies* (Melbourne University Press 1994). Her current work is in comparative multiculturalism and in diasporic literatures and their intersections with national and global cultural formations using theoretical frameworks deriving from postcolonialism and critical multicultural theory.

Joanna Hodge is Professor in Philosophy at Manchester Metropolitan University and author of *Heidegger and Ethics* (Routledge 1995). She is a regular contributor to *Women's Philosophy Review*.

Janet Holland is a Professor in Sociology and Director of the Social Science Research Centre at South Bank University, London. Her research interests are wide and cluster around gender relations, sexuality, youth and youth values, and feminist methodology. Publications include *Identity and Diversity* and *Debates and Issues in Feminist Research and Pedagogy*, both edited with Maud Blair and published by Multilingual Matters and the Open University 1995; *Sexual Cultures*, edited with Jeffrey Weeks, and *Sex, Sensibility and the Gendered Body*, edited with Lisa Adkins, both published by Macmillan 1996; *The Male in the Head* (with Caroline Ramazanoglu, Sue Sharpe and Rachel Thomson), Tufnell Press 1998; and *Making Space: Citizenship and Others in Schools* (with Tuula Gordon and Elina Lahelma), Macmillan 1999.

Maggie Humm is Professor of Women's Studies at the University of East London and author of ten books in the area of feminist theory, including *Border Traffic: Strategies of Contemporary Women Writers* (Manchester University Press 1991), the best-selling *Feminisms* (Harvester Wheatsheaf 1992), *The Dicti- onary of Feminist Theory* (Harvester Wheatsheaf 1995) and *Feminism and Film* (Edinburgh University Press 1997). Her chapter here is part of a longer study of modernist womens' 'marginalia' for *Borderline:*

Women Writers and Modernist Aesthetics, Edinburgh University Press (forthcoming).

Jane Kilby is a Lecturer in Sociology at Salford University. She has recently completed her PhD on testimony, witnessing and sexual trauma.

Gail Ching-Liang Low has taught at the University of Southampton, the University of East Anglia, the Open University, Staffordshire University and the University of Dundee. Currently she teaches postcolonial, contemporary British and American literature and film at the University of Dundee. She is the author of *White Skins/Black Masks: Representation and Colonialism* (Routledge 1996) and is currently working on pedagogy and canon formation in the institutional transformation of 'Commonwealth' to 'Postcolonial' in Britain.

Celia Lury was a Co-Director of the Institute for Women's Studies between 1994 and 1997. She has since taken up a lectureship in Sociology at Goldsmiths College, University of London. Her publications include *Cultural Rights* (Routledge 1993) , *Consumer Culture* (Polity Press 1996) and *Prosthetic Culture* (Routledge 1998).

Maureen McNeil is Reader in Women's Studies at Lancaster University and was Director of the Institute for Women's Studies from 1997 to 2000. Her publications include: *Under the Banner of Science: Erasmus Darwin and His Age* (Manchester University Press 1987), *Gender and Expertise* (Free Association Books 1987), and with I. Varcoe and S. Yearley (eds) *The New Reproductive Technologies* (Macmillan 1990). She has also published and done research on: foetal alcohol syndrome, 'crack babies', teaching cultural studies, feminism and pedagogy, feminism and Foucault, and gender relations in the history of science. She is currently working on a book on the cultural studies of technoscience.

Elspeth Probyn is Associate Professor of Gender Studies at the University of Sydney. She is the author of numerous articles on feminism and queer theory as well as *Sexing the Self* (Routledge 1993), *Sexy Bodies* (edited with Elizabeth Gross, Routledge 1995), *Outside Belongings* (Routledge 1996) and *Carnal Appetites: Food Sex Identities* (Routledge 2000).

Caroline Ramazanoglu is a former Reader in Sociology at Goldsmiths College University of London. Her interests include feminist sociology and methodology and, currently, problems of analysing white power (*Why Whiteness Matters* (with Brenda Lewis), funded by the Leverhulme Trust). Publications include (as editor) *Up Against Foucault: Explorations of Some Tensions between Foucault and Feminism* (Routledge 1993); (with Janet Holland, Sue Sharpe, and Rachel Thomson) *The Male in the Head: Young People, Heterosexuality and Power* (Tufnell Press 1998); and 'Where Lyotard Leaves Feminism and Where Feminists Leave Lyotard', in C. Rojek and B. Turner *Forget Lyotard* (Routledge 1998).

Karyn Sandlos is a Doctoral Candidate in the Department of Education at York University, Toronto, Ontario, Canada.

Margrit Shildrick is Research Fellow in Humanities and Social Sciences at Staffordshire University, and holds honorary research fellowships at the Universities of Liverpool and Lancaster. She is the author of *Leaky Bodies and Boundaries: Feminism, Postmodernism and (Bio)ethics* (1997 Routledge), and the co-editor of *Vital Signs: Feminist Reconfigurations of the Bio/logical Body* (1998 Edinburgh University Press), and of *Feminist Theory and the Body: A Reader* (1999 Edinburgh University Press).

Beverley Skeggs was a Reader in Women's Studies at Lancaster until 1998, as well as Co-Director between 1994 and 1997. She has since taken up a Chair in Sociology at Manchester University. She is the Director of an ESRC funded project on Violence, Sexuality and Space and is the author of *Formations of Class and Gender: Becoming Respectable* (Sage 1997).

Gayatri Chakravorty Spivak is Avalon Foundation Professor in the Humanities at Columbia University and author of numerous books on post-colonialism, deconstruction and trans-national cultural studies, including *The Post-Colonial Critic* (Routledge 1990), *Outside in the Teaching Machine* (Routledge 1993), *A Critique of Postcolonial Reason* (Harvard University Press 1999) and *Imperatives to Reimagine the Planet* (Passagen Verlag 2000).

Ngai-Ling Sum is the Simon Research Fellow at the International Centre for Labour Studies, University of Manchester. She has research interests in the political economy of East Asia and trans-border issues. Her most recent publications include articles in *Economy and Society*, *New Political Economy* and *Emergo*. She also has various book chapters on the global–regional–local dynamics of 'Greater China'; three new kinds of orientalism and trans-border identities; and regional strategies and identities of East Asian newly industrializing countries. Her current research interest is 'cultural political economy', which examines the interrelationship between the 'cultural turn' and the study of 'political economy' as a set of methods and a field of study.

Imogen Tyler is a Lecturer in the Institute for Cultural Research at Lancaster University. She has another chapter on pregnant embodiment forthcoming in Ahmed, S. and Stacey, J. (eds) *Thinking Through the Skin* (Routledge 2001). She is currently working on a book project on the theme of Narcissism

Carol Wolkowitz is a Lecturer in Sociology at the University of Warwick. She is co-author of the recent *Glossary of Feminist Theory* (with Sonya Andermahr and Terry Lovell) (Arnold 1997) and co-author of several publications on homeworking. She is currently writing a book looking at gender, embodiment and the labour process.

Series editors' preface

The transition to the twenty-first century has brought with it much assessment of change and extensive evaluation of the prospects for transformation. This volume constitutes an exciting collection of reflections about how feminism may *figure* and *figure in* such assessments.

As the flagship of this series, *Transformations* sallies into stormy waters: its contributors venture to *think through feminism*, despite late-twentieth-century uncertainties, dismissals and disavowals (including those focused on feminism). There is no smooth sailing here, as the contributors encounter, for example, the unsettlings associated with poststructuralism and postmodernism; the turbulence of identity politics; the instabilities of deconstruction; the changes encompassed in globalisation; the restructuring of flexible production and designer consumerism. Moreover, mapping direction is not easy for those who (as is the case with many of these authors) are sceptical about 'progress', reject 'origins' and problematise 'home'.

Their navigation has them looking in many directions. In some chapters, contemporary political and social controversies (e.g. the politics of 'reconciliation' in Australia; social practices linked to forms of sentimentality in the USA) come into focus. In others, they are looking over their feminist shoulders (e.g. at Virginia Woolf's photography, at Simone de Beauvoir's relationship with Richard Wright, at women's involvement in the production of nuclear bombs, at the use of images in abortion campaigns, at the history of feminist analyses of technoscience) or around them at feminist relationships to academic disciplines (philosophy), political traditions (rights claims) and language and communication (through metaphor). They turn their attention to the Beijing Conference on Women, to international telecommunication conferences, to poetic and other forms of artistic performance, to the teaching of now almost 'classic' post-colonial novels. They critically scrutinise the horizons of poststructuralism, new forms of consumerism, the representations of pregnant embodiment and the monstrous in the West, as well as reconfigurations of the organisation of labour globally.

The efforts of these twenty-four feminist scholars (amongst whom are some well-known intellectuals as well as new voices) yield a complex yet rich panorama of possibilities for feminist thinking. In and through its different explorations, this volume collectively, but non-complacently, declares feminist theory alive and well. It thinks the conjunction of feminism and transformations in sometimes troubling, definitely contestable, but always challenging and interesting, ways.

Maureen McNeil
Lynne Pearce

Acknowledgements

We would like to express our thanks to colleagues and students who worked in the Institute for Women's Studies, Lancaster University, during the period of the preparation for and holding of the Transformations conference and the production of this volume. We have all benefited greatly from the collective and generous research culture that makes the Institute for Women's Studies such a special place to work.

Our appreciation also goes to all those who attended the Transformations conference, and to the contributors to this volume for allowing us to bring together such interesting work.

In particular, we would like to thank Deborah Bors, Janet Hartley, Cathie Holt and Imogen Tyler for helping smooth out some of the difficulties in the compiling of this volume, as well as Alison Easton, Anne-Marie Fortier, Mimi Sheller and Jackie Stacey for taking time to read and comment on a draft of the introduction.

And finally, our thanks to Lynne Pearce, Mari Shullaw and Routledge's anonymous reader for guidance on the editing of this book.

Permissions

The authors and publishers would like to thank the following for granting permission to reproduce material in this work:

The Harvard Theatre Collection, The Houghton Library, Cambridge, Massachusetts, USA, for the photographs of Virginia Woolf's mother and father with Woolf in the background; of Ethel Smyth; and of William Plomer, Vita Nicolson and Charles Siepmann.

Kalo Baran Laha for the photograph of a Bengali boy looking at the image of Durga and her family.

Ms. magazine for the reproduction of 'She Had a Name, She Had a Family, She was Leona's sister Gerri' from *Ms.* magazine vol. 6, no. 3.

Every effort has been made to contact copyright holders for their permission to reprint material in this book. The publishers would be grateful to hear from any copyright holder who is not here acknowledged and will undertake to rectify any errors or omissions in future editions of this book.

Introduction

Thinking through feminism

Sara Ahmed, Jane Kilby, Celia Lury,
Maureen McNeil and Beverley Skeggs

'Transformations' is a magical concept, alluding to change, disguise, life, growth, power, agency. But if … contemporary feminism is and wants to be transformative, then it would also seem now to be in a moment of eddying quiet, not stagnant but anticipating a new tide, some new directions, new questions.

Bronwen Levy (1999)

The question of transformations

The desire for transformation animates feminist praxis. As a politics seeking radical redress, feminism is driven by an imperative for change. In this sense, the hope for transformation calls feminism into multiple and diverse existence. Contemporary feminism is imbricated in ideas of and expectations for transformation. Differences and conflicts within feminism, or between feminisms,[1] relate not only to what transformations are called for, but also to how we understand what 'it' is that we are seeking to transform. For contemporary feminists, the certainty associated with the *object-ive* of transformation seems lost (at least temporarily) or brought into question. Indeed, in this volume, questions are being asked about the nature of transformation as an *object* of feminism because there is – and has been – a general questioning of the status of *objects* (and subjects) in feminism. Recently this questioning has been applied to 'women' as the 'object of study' in Women's Studies.[2]

So if we begin with the question, 'To what extent have gender relations been transformed by and through feminist demands for transformation?', we might also need to ask: 'Which transformations? Where are they? Who are the subjects of such transformations? And what are its objects?' The question of transformation is bound up with issues of power and authorisation – in each instance in which transformation is claimed, we could ask: '*Who* is calling for this transformation?', 'from *where* are they speaking?', and 'what are the *effects* of making this claim?' Following from this, this volume is an attempt not to claim transformation, but to ask what are the effects of the different ways feminists have made and might make claims for transformation.

Large questions about transformation and specific issues pertaining to the relationship between Women's Studies and transformation propelled the production of this book and the conference with which it is linked, and which shared the same name.[3] Initially, as organisers, we conceived of the conference as an event which would, in part, register the passing of a period of significant transformation in our place of work and which would provide, at the same time, an opportunity to think about possibilities for the future. This occurred at a particular moment in the formation of Women's Studies as an institutional space for feminism at Lancaster University, a moment preceded by a sequence of changes: rapid expansion, threatened restructuring, merging and demise, then another period of expansion with new appointments, consolidated by the award of research funding and transformation into a research Institute, with a corresponding title change (from 'Centre'). During this period we had little time to reflect upon the forms of feminism possible or desirable in the institutional space we were involved in creating.[4] Hence the conference was, amongst other things, an occasion for reflection about our local situation in a broader context.

Of course, as conference organisers, and as co-editors of this volume of papers, each of us inhabits Women's Studies differently. While we all came together at Lancaster University, we arrived here at different moments (in the 1980s and 1990s, in the institution, in our lives), having taken different routes, in terms of life journeys as well as educational ones. In getting here, in getting together, we have all travelled from different national 'homes' (Australia, Canada, the UK), from different disciplinary 'homes' (Cultural Studies, Critical Theory, English Literature, Sociology) and from different categorical locations (we have different types and quantities of economic, social, cultural and symbolic capital from our prior positionings). In arriving here, we also have different relationships to the Institute – for example and most obviously, some of us are, or have been, directors; others are junior lecturers or postgraduate students. We are also of different ages, and different generations of feminism, although age and generation do not, of course, map on to one another directly. For these and many other reasons, organising a conference to mark the forming of the Institute meant different things for each of us, and took us to and from different places. The history of the Institute is precisely, then, a history of multiple journeys, of moving between places and between disciplines. As a form of collectivity, this Institute (like any other equivalent unit) is premised on both the shared experiences of being 'here' at a particular time, but also on fluidity, multiplicity and movement which includes (in our case, at least) moments of painful collision.

The expansion and consolidation realised in the forming of the Institute for Women's Studies at Lancaster University not surprisingly has not eliminated the problems and insecurities endemic to Women's Studies in the UK and elsewhere. Indeed, the decision to take the relationship between feminism and transformations as the theme of the conference (and subsequently of this book) also reflected our concerns about broader institutional insecurities surrounding Women's Studies within the UK, and in some other national settings. In the mid- to late 1990s, falling student recruitment in undergraduate degree programmes, and the shifts in higher education towards a model of learning as narrowly vocational, privatised and something that can be 'bought' (into) by consumers, precipitated something of a crisis for Women's Studies. In this climate of uncertainty, it seemed imperative to reflect upon the different forms feminism can take within and beyond the academy. We felt that it would be valuable to provide an occasion in which conversations could take place about the futures of feminism with others who were similarly concerned with the prospects for feminist knowledge production both inside and outside the academy. This volume is, in this sense, the product of reflections and conversations about the different possibilities of transformation for feminism, and of different articulations of what might be involved in posing questions about the potential transformation of feminism.

While the conference marked a certain moment in the history of the Institute for Women's Studies at Lancaster University and growing concern about the future of Women's Studies (in the UK and possibly elsewhere), it also provided us (and we hope, other participants) with an opportunity to consider, critically and collectively, how we *can* think through and with feminism more generally. Much feminist research and teaching that was being done at Lancaster University and elsewhere had emerged through attacks on foundationalism that not only undermined the transparency of the objects of traditional disciplines (such as History or Sociology), but also the very certainty about which places could be occupied in the name of feminism. In some sense, we wanted to ask what it meant to identify a place as feminist, when the very term 'feminism' is not taken as an object whose meaning or referent is fully secured. Indeed, the conference allowed us to reflect on what it does and does not mean to create a 'feminist space' or a space in which feminists can speak to each other about how we might set political agendas as we face the new millennium. Somewhat inevitably in these circumstances, feminism was not simply the object of shared reflection at the conference, nor was it just the focus of questions about which we and others talked. As an *object* for discussion, feminism slipped in and out of focus: even disappearing, on occasion. What emerged instead, both from the conference and from this book, were explorations of possibilities for thinking through feminism.

The conference allowed us to rethink not just the relationship between Women's Studies and the politics of location and boundary making, but also *the ethics of address*. That is, the conference was for us an occasion to consider what might be 'better' ways of encountering others, of speaking and of hearing, and of responding to difference and disagreement. This event generated reflections on what it means for feminists to take responsibility for the boundaries we inevitably create and for feminists to think ethically. The conference precipitated thinking about how we can relate to, speak with and hear each other as feminists in a way which does justice to the differences between us, whilst keeping lines of communication open. This sometimes involved confronting the prospect of surprising connections and alliances. Nevertheless, we also recognised that this may depend on a recognition of the limits of those possibilities, that is, on the acknowledgement that connections cannot always be made, or that, when they are made, they remain fragile and precarious.

Inevitably, in the process of organising the conference and editing this volume, we have sometimes experienced difficulties in dealing with difference and conflict. A shared *desire* to find ways of dealing with such differences which did not silence or exclude some voices at the expense of others, or which did not assume everyone could speak together (a fantasy of inclusion which often conceals its own exclusions), although it was imperfectly realised, kept us going. We tried to put into effect what Elspeth Probyn identifies in this volume as an 'ethics of antagonism', articulating our differences, confronting our investments and positioning, listening, learning and struggling. This has forced us to question the assumptions of our different feminist trajectories and to recognise the very different positions from which we speak. While *Transformations* is a volume which poses questions for and to feminism, it has simultaneously been a space in which we have lived and have worked together in all our differences. In this way we have found that thinking feminism through the concept of transformation has transformed us in many and surprising ways.

In this introduction we attempt to think through feminism by posing the question of transformation in four stages. First, we reflect on the awkward temporal implications of the very concept of 'transformation' in relation to how we can think the histories and futures of feminism. Second, we examine the way in which Women's Studies and feminism emerged within the institutional spaces of the academy, as sites of transformation, but with political effects that could not always be known in advance. Third, we discuss the need for feminism to constantly question its own political agendas in response to transformations that have been unexpected or surprising. Finally, we reflect on how the question of transformation is not simply one posed *by feminism*, but also a question which can be posed *to feminism*: we consider how feminism itself must constantly be challenged and transformed by the conflicts and divisions between women who identify with it. Questioning feminism by thinking through transformations is also about reflecting on *how* feminism becomes mobilised as a politics and how 'we' can understand the *investments* that make it possible to speak of feminism as a 'we' at all. Asking questions about the possibility for 'better' feminist knowledge, without invoking assumptions of progress; raising critical questions, without becoming detached observers; and being reflexive, without becoming self-absorbed, are some of the ambitions that have helped shape the production of this volume.

Thinking transformations in times of change

The project of this book (and of the conference from which it derived) was to appraise and rethink the prospects for transformation engendered by the politics of feminism. The attempt to realise this goal made us aware that the late twentieth century has been a difficult time to think about transformation. Our efforts to identify some forms of this difficulty, as we indicate in this section, carried us both beyond and back into feminism.

Somewhat ironically, recent social, political and intellectual transformations seem to have left many of us without a vocabulary or framework for discussing transformation. For those who felt uneasy about the gendered nature of the heroic model of revolution, the 'fall' of Eastern European governments and the discrediting of their Marxist underpinnings have confirmed the limitations of this particular rhetoric of change. Furthermore, in the 1980s and 1990s post-modernist and feminist critiques of science and modernist epistemology brought grand narratives and assumptions about progress into disrepute (Harding 1986; Haraway 1991; Lyotard 1989). Meanwhile, the recent labelling of mainstream political agendas as 'new' across Europe makes others wary of what seems to be a repackaging of normative conservatism. In addition, although evolutionary frameworks have recently gained considerable currency in the fields of economics and psychology, the fact that they are fashionable makes some (although not all) feminists suspicious. In this case, the invocation of 'nature' and the patriarchal lineage of Darwinian theory can render evolutionary metaphors problematic for many feminists. The challenges and suspicions aroused from these different quarters coalesce and leave many wondering: how do we/can we even think transformation now?

Moreover, in their everyday lives many feminists (and others) in the Western/Northern world feel uncertainty and ambivalence about transforma-tion. We live in a world of perpetual, continuous change and yet many of us feel there has been little significant transformation: states of change seem both commonplace and ephemeral. To some extent this is a matter of life speeding up with the development of late twentieth-century information and communication technologies. Technological innovation is a feature of contemporary competitive capitalism that guarantees that we are always dealing with change and with the promise of transformed workplaces and homes, and even transformed lives and identities. While the Microsoft entrepreneur Bill Gates and others make millions from technological innovation and its promise, for most people direct experience of positive transformation through technological innovation is rather illusory and elusive.

Nevertheless, the technological world is not the only realm in which feminists have experienced and noticed change. If we could imagine a feminist ghost or 'sleeping beauty/ugly' (invoking the traditions of feminist alternative fairly tales) waking up now, after over thirty years in the recent phase of feminist struggle: what might she make of our world? Reading some of the headlines in the Anglo-speaking press, she might think that she has woken up in feminist heaven: 'The traditional family is being destroyed'; 'Lesbians make better parents'; 'Babies are being cloned'; 'Women take over the work-place'; 'Women sweep into the [British] House of Commons'; 'Girls triumph over boys in schools'. Yet it does not feel to many of us that gender relations have been transformed. In some spheres, such as child care and housework, change is hard to find; in others, the implications of the changes that have been realised are unclear.

Uncertainty about how to evaluate change is heightened by confusion and uncertainty outside and within feminism about what transformations feminists have realised. The proverbial finger is often pointed at feminists as the perpetra-tors of negative changes: '*they* have taken our jobs', '*they* have destroyed the family', '*they* have spoiled our fun'. Even harder to grapple with is the fact that it is inevitably the case that feminists have fought for changes which, when realised, turn out to be dubious or only partial solutions. In the UK, the election of 120 female Members of Parliament, following the overthrow of the Conservative government in the spring of 1997 with the election of New Labour, has not been a straightforwardly uplifting transformation. So, for example, despite the promise of this change, only one woman MP opposed recent punitive legislation attacking lone mothers. The shift from woman-attacking Thatcherism to the incorporation of some women within the modernised Labour government has by no means realised feminist party-political transformation in the UK. In this and other contexts, the need for constant reassessment of the assumptions, goals, priorities, orientations and all the other paraphernalia of transformation emerges as both a constant and an urgent feminist priority.

Such reassessment also involves reconsidering the status of feminism's own narratives of transformation. The espousal of feminism involves a belief in the possibility of a better future, if not in utopia.[5] Yet such a belief requires a questioning of our understanding of history, not only through a questioning of who or what should be the subjects of and for history, but also through a rethinking of how we, as feminists, relate to the past. Thus feminist projects involve the process of *re-membering* themselves in order to understand how aspects of the past may enter into the future without either destructive repetition or denial of those features of the past which such projects might be designed to leave behind. This re-membering involves challenging the terms not only of 'progress' but also of inheritance and evolution, of nostalgia and of sentiment. It means paying attention to the unavoidable gaps between memory and discourse, between the past and the present, and between individual and collective narratives of transformation.

Invoking caution in the modes of feminist construction of the history of our own movement is, in effect, our call for more attention to feminist uses of 'our own' history. Caution is required, for example, when we evoke particular histories of feminism in order to demonstrate the difficulties of achieving political transformation in the present. We advocate care so as not to 'fix' such histories within the parameters of our critiques (although of course a certain closure is inevitable). Assumptions are often made about the political errors of past feminism in order to construct a narrative of a transformed or transforming politics. This is clear, for example, in the feminist work that has reduced past feminisms (in particular, radical feminism) to essentialism in order then to inscribe itself as having overcome that 'political error'.[6] While we as editors and the contributors to this volume certainly engage with the difficulties of doing feminism in the present, in different sites, we are wary of narratives that imagine 'us' as having 'overcome' the belief in identity and essentialism, as if they could be simply overcome and, more importantly, as if past feminisms could be reduced to such beliefs. Indeed, rather than establishing the terms of analysis in this way, rethinking the temporality of feminism can be a point of entry for thinking about alternative futures for feminism. Among the various forms of feminism, then, 'past feminisms' deserve a hearing, a hearing which does not suspend critique (the notion of judgement is implicit in the concept of hearing, at least in its juridical use) but which does allow for 'past ideas' to be heard again – in effect, to be heard anew. Moreover without such a responsive and responsible listening to voices of the past, contemporary feminism could fail to do justice to its inheritance and/or miss the opportunity to witness its own errors, failures, and exclusions in the present.

As the contributions to this volume variously show, the feminist belief in future possibilities involves rethinking histories of our relations to the body, to sensory perception, to knowing and to politics. Thinking through feminism is thus an invitation to re-member and re-*imagine* (Cornell 1993). So for example, in a chapter exploring the visual memories of Virginia Woolf's photographic collection, Maggie Humm uses Lichtenberg-Ettinger's concept of the matrixial as a means to re-imagine a maternal legacy. This and other work of imagination allows an opening or fissure in the past, through which we may realise a different future.

Stepping back from particular examples and issues, we would observe that it has been extraordinarily difficult for feminists to conduct open debate about change and transformation in late capitalist societies in the late twentieth century. Any disagreement or contestation is seized upon as a sign of open warfare or the failure of feminism. This is not only a problem of the media, in Britain and North America for example, being unsympathetic to feminism (although that is an issue); it is also about the difficulty in making social and political space for open debate about change. Moreover, the emotional charge and multiple, sometimes conflicting, investments around many important issues, inevitable though they are, make this even harder. In this context, our hope is that this collection might encourage a reflective assessment of some of the changes realised in, through and around feminism, saying, in effect: 'Look what we've done!' 'Did we/do we want this?' 'Is that all there is?' 'How has this happened?' 'Should or shouldn't this be different?' The contributors to this volume have been, in many different ways, *wonder*-ing about what has and hasn't been realised in the name of feminism. Our task is precisely to *wonder* about transformations as a task of thinking through feminism. Such *wonder*-ing requires excursions into the different possibilities for feminism as transformative politics.

Transforming the academy

As a set of acts which challenge sedimented structures and forms of power, such as the international and domestic divisions of labour, legal statutes on violence and popular representations of Women's bodies, feminism manifests itself as a transformative practice. Through political and theoretical interventions, strategies and tactics which disrupt and agitate, feminist activity is designed to embody its own future object so that it becomes the subject of transformation. Institutional politics, education, labour relations and social welfare in late capitalist societies have all, in some ways, been transformed by feminism. While there are contemporary rhetorics hailing both a 'backlash' culture and a 'post-feminist' era, both notions testify to the impact of feminism. In this respect, we can understand feminism as a transformative politics.

Certainly, within the academy, feminist knowledges and pedagogy emerge as sites of transformation: they begin with the premises that traditional disciplines must be transformed if they are to address women, and that women cannot be added into existing fields of knowledge without a transformation in the construction of these domains (Spender 1981; de Groot and Maynard 1993; Cosslett, Easton and Summerfield 1996). Hence, Women's Studies requires a transformation in the academy in order to come into existence as a (cross)discipline, as it simultaneously seeks to transform the knowledges embedded in the designation and reification of disciplines. Indeed, feminist researchers and teachers have pressed against the limits of 'their' disciplines by asking troubling questions about gender relations, and in so doing, have transformed the formations of knowledge and the classifications that are involved in the demarcation of the 'object' of any discipline, whether it be 'the canon' in English or Literary Studies (Showalter 1989), or 'society' in Sociology (Smith 1987, 1988), or 'history' in History. For example, feminists have challenged the very notion of history and historical truth by asking the apparently simple question: 'Where were the women?' Such a question has led to a rethinking of how history is produced and written: rather than history being understood as the neutral recording of the past, it has been theorised as always written from a particular position, as interpretative and mediated rather than descriptive, as located and partial rather than universal (Scott 1988; Hall 1992).

The specific questions asked by feminists about ways of knowing in the academy have involved, then, a redefinition of what constitutes knowledge itself. Yet the development of Women's Studies in the academy has been a long and contradictory struggle. From early in the recent phase of the Women's movement, the 'ivory tower', associated as it is with patriarchal privilege, has been scrutinised as a problematic feminist location (Evans 1982). Critical questions have continually been raised about the dangers of institutionalisation, of distancing from other sites of feminist activity and of implication in the disempowering hierarchies of class and 'race' endemic in academic institutions. More specifically, Women's and Gender Studies as specific and identifiable sites of feminist intervention in higher education have generated their own problems and sometimes been disappointing locales for feminists determined to challenge power relations (McNeil 1992; Skeggs 1995b; Brown 1997; Martin 1998). Thus, we and many other feminists have come to acknowledge that while Women's Studies might require transformation in order to exist, the changes it effects are unpredictable, and not always or only progressive. We may need to reflect on the contradictory effects of inhabiting different institutional spaces (in this case, an academic one); such inhabitance may both enable and foreclose transformations.

The relationship between feminism and the 'discipline of disciplines' – philosophy – has also been the subject of much debate (Gatens 1982; Holland 1990). Feminists have suggested that the question of sexual difference is unthinkable through the traditional forms of philosophy insofar as the apparent gender neutrality of philosophical language is predicated on an elided masculinity. The double and troubling relationship between feminism and philosophy is the object of Joanna Hodge's chapter in this volume. She asks how feminism can inherit otherwise given that the teleological narratives informing the discipline of philosophy are about masculine inheritance. Her desire for a matrilineal inheritance in philosophy leads to her proposal of other possible ways of doing philosophy, which involve an engagement with, rather than withdrawal from, the discipline itself. Jean Grimshaw pursues transformations in a different way, through an examination of the role of metaphor within philosophy. She shows that the contexts of utterance within disciplines are not fully stable or regulated: transformation is a possibility that cannot be foreclosed by the disciplining of knowledge. By posing questions of sexual difference and/in relation to philosophy, both authors call for a philosophical feminism, rather than a feminist philosophy – a philosophical feminism which imagines how philosophy can inherit and be written or spoken otherwise. In this sense, the critique of the discipline of philosophy is about opening a space in which feminism can enter the dialogue about what is philosophy and about how philosophy should be written or spoken.

More generally, reflection on the relationship between feminism and traditional ways of knowing must see feminism as in itself *implicated in what it seeks to transform*. The ramifications of this implication in traditional knowledges are discussed by both Maureen McNeil and Carol Wolkowitz in relation to technoscience. In both chapters, the authors suggest that the possibility of transformative feminist knowledges depends on a recognition of the impossibility of any 'pure' position 'outside' of traditional, 'masculine' knowledges and domains. In short, they acknowledge that there is no 'outside' of 'the master's house' (Lorde 1984). If feminism is not outside that which it seeks to transform, then we need to think about the location from which feminists can see and know. Such exploration, rather than a positing of feminist vantage points, may also serve to complicate what it might mean to be 'inside' a discipline. Hence, feminists have also recognised that many of the knowledge formations, such as philosophy or technoscience, that have been identified as 'masculine', cannot be reduced to this critique: such knowledges are complex, contradictory and unstable. Indeed, it is the very opposition between 'inside' and 'outside' that is brought into question by the precariousness of feminist positions.

One mode of feminism seeks to transform traditional ways of theorising, understanding and explaining the world by pointing to the transformations already at work in such traditions. Such a process of making trouble, by locating trouble that already exists in social and knowledge formations, is evident in some feminist work on subjectivity. For example, in this volume, Imogen Tyler examines how philosophical models of the subject are predicated on a singularity that cannot deal with women's subjectivity in general, and with women's bodily transitions (particularly in pregnancy) in particular. Likewise, Margrit Shildrick examines how the traditional model of the autonomous and rational subject is predicated upon masculinity, and an exclusion of monstrosity. In both cases, the call for a transformation in our understanding of subjectivity – through making visible the lived experience of pregnancy or the figure of the monstrous – also offers different readings of the modern, masculine subject as troubled *by that which it has apparently excluded*. Such feminist work unsettles masculine domains, by thinking through what is unthought within those domains. These transformations engendered by feminists do not come from the outside, but are brought to the surface by feminist critiques.

Feminism has also had a productive and troubling relationship to other intellectual traditions that have emerged through a critique of the founding subject of modernity. The debates between feminism and Marxism (Campioni and Gross 1983; Nye 1988), feminism and psychoanalysis (Mitchell 1974; Gallop 1982; Rose 1988), feminism and deconstruction (Elam 1994), feminism and poststructuralism (Weedon 1987) and on feminism and postmodernism (Morris 1988; Flax 1990) have engendered alternative ways of thinking, not only about gender relations, but also (to designate but a few topics that could be cited) about the relationships between political economy and culture, the nature of subjectivity, desire, language, narrative, discourse and ethics. Such encounters have not simply involved adding gender (and, by implication, feminism) to these critical traditions. Although feminism might share, for example, a suspicion of meta-narratives that has been defined as crucial to postmodernism (Lyotard 1989), this does not mean that feminism can be incorporated within postmodernism (Nicholson 1990; Ahmed 1998). As Caroline Ramazanoglu and Janet Holland point out in their contribution to this volume, the specificity of feminist concerns about gender hierarchy might also enable a critical reflection on the limits of postmodern epistemology. Feminism, with a double-edged critique of both modernity *and* its critics, may also unsettle simple dichotomies between the modern and the postmodern, universalism and relativism, and the global and the local.

Nevertheless, although feminism may unsettle the domains it inhabits, the consequences of this unsettling in the academy and in the world more generally are not predictable. While feminist teachers and researchers are clearly producing work which presupposes the intimacy of knowledge and power, and theory and practice, the difficulty of translating what is produced within the academy into broader political transformation cannot be underestimated. However, we would contend that such difficulties should not be used to discourage the continuation of feminist exploration of thinking and working towards transformation. Ironically, it is precisely the gap between the knowledges produced, and the political outcomes that are envisaged, that may open up the possibility of transformations that are, in the present, unthinkable.

Responding to transformations

In the late 1960s, feminism was sculpted through engagement with wider political struggles – including 'third world' struggles against colonial regimes and their legacies, in Africa and Latin America, the 'Cultural Revolution' in China, the Civil Rights and the Black Power movements in the USA, the agitation against the Vietnam War and student protests in North America and Britain. These involvements had formative effects on the organisation of the women's movement and the emergence of feminism in different regions from the late 1960s (O'Sullivan 1982). The relationship between feminist and other political struggles, in part, can be understood as a shared commitment to praxis – to building ways of understanding the world that do not simply encourage or enable change, but constitute change, in and of themselves. Certainly, revolutionary feminists of the early period of the recent feminist movement were emphatic about their desire for transformation. They were not alone: liberal feminists also sought change, even if their vision was one that did not challenge the institutions in which everyday life was embedded. In Britain, from a 1970s movement with specific demands for equal pay for equal work, equal educational provision, free 24-hour nurseries, abortion on demand, free contraception, a woman's right to control her own fertility and to define her own sexuality, feminism has become more dispersed, and characterised by diverse claims, from many different places, couched with considerable auto-critique.

We see this diversification as a measure of both feminist influence and success. This fragmentation has a long history as different women have recognised themselves differently as 'women' and have identified different needs and, in some cases, made different demands as feminists. In this respect, feminism is not one set of struggles: it has mobilised different women in different times and places, who are all seeking transformations, but who are not necessarily seeking the same thing, nor even necessarily responding to the same situation. So any attempt to conjure *a* history of feminism in relationship to the question of transformation must fail. The use of the term 'feminism', when considered in this light, is effectively the making of a rhetorical statement which identifies a political interest, in relation not simply to 'women', but to the multiply determined bodies, spaces and histories 'women' assume and occupy. Indeed, we may need to recognise how difficult it is for some to inhabit the category 'feminism' for, as Griffin (1989) argues, it is not a unitary category with identifiable boundaries and a consistent set of ideas. Moreover, this difficulty is compounded by the fact that the word 'feminism' is not put to work exclusively by and for feminists. So, for example, we need to reflect on the impact of various media campaigns and representations that have stigmatised the word feminism, or endorsed certain 'faces of feminism' as acceptable, at the expense of others. The impossibility of a final definition of 'feminism' is indicative of the fact that the 'ownership' of the term feminism is itself part of a broader, ongoing political struggle.

Often, the very transformations that feminism has called for have themselves created complication. This is perhaps at its clearest if we consider the fate of one of feminism's defining projects identified by the slogan 'the personal is political'. For many women, feminism was (and is) an affective/effective politics precisely because it engenders social change via strategies which resignify the personal and its relationships to bodies, spaces and discourses. This has involved disrupting taboos governing the distinction between those who may and may not speak, between the speakable and unspeakable. The 'discovery of a (feminist) voice' or, more precisely, the realisation of the power to speak by many women in and through feminism, has generated, and continues to generate, powerful 'before and after' narratives for women who testify to everyday trauma and suffering. Moreover, such personal narratives of change create an important temporal horizon for feminism, even if, for feminism writ large, the 'after' remains a yet-to-be-arrived-at future. Feminism can thus operate as an interpretative strategy, in which past events are reconceptualised and given a different context and, by extension, alternative futures can be conceived and lived. As a distinctly feminist narrative *form*, then, 'the personal is political' has been, is and will remain significant as a call for transformation.

Yet not all transformations in the relationship between the personal and political, or between the private and the public, have been welcomed by feminism. Lauren Berlant, in her contribution to this volume, points to how the public space of politics has been personalised through a discourse of sentimentality, particularly in the USA. She highlights some of the problematic consequences of such personalisation, including the seductive power of forms of empathy and identification (such as trauma) which work to elide or conceal social antagonisms. In the light of Berlant's arguments, we can also see a potential collusion between liberal, capitalist forms of mass entertainment and individualist therapies, and the feminist emphasis on the importance of the personal. Moreover, as O' Sullivan (1982) notes, the space of the private was (and remains) difficult to conceptualise and rework. The translation of 'the personal as political' into dominant feminist narratives has not been straightforwardly democratising. All too often the 'private' and the 'public' have been substituted for the 'personal' and 'political', with confusion arising as social and cultural spaces have been simultaneously broken down and re-established. Moreover, private spheres, as some feminists have noted, may become the focus for legislation, without transforming power relations. So, for example, while the family can be demonstrated to be both a public and potentially dangerous space, it has nevertheless been designated and privileged as a zone for heterosexual intimacy. Thus, when US legislation guarantees a private space for heterosexuals, it effectively legislates lesbians and gay men as 'the public' (Berlant 1998). The feminist slogan, 'the personal is political', while enabling some important transformations, may have to be reformulated to deal with the complexity of the relationships between public and private, and with specific forms of social differentiation and hierarchisation that operate through the regulation of these spaces. We are suggesting that in every context feminists must address the questions: Whose private? Whose public? Whose personal? Whose political? In this and other instances, thinking of the transformations embedded within feminism as a political practice involves facing the challenges of unpredictable outcomes and unexpected take-ups of the transformations we advocate.

Furthermore, the words, rhetoric and arguments made by different feminisms are inevitably subject to processes of reiteration. In a sense we are arguing that, if feminism is to be/become a transformative politics, then it might need to refuse to (re)present itself as programmatic, *as having an object which can always be successfully translated into a final end or outcome.* Of course, it is instructively paradoxical that our very call for feminism not to be programmatic can make use of programmatic language. We need to reflect on our language here, which is still making a claim for *how feminism should be*, even if we are destabilising what it means 'to be' a feminist, and which is still setting an agenda, even if this is not regarded as immutable or hedged in precise expectations about a final outcome. Hence, we also contend that, although the relation between feminism and its objects is complicated and contingent, it remains impossible (and we would add, undesirable), to think through feminism without identifying desires, priorities and agendas. To assume that we are not setting agendas would be to conceal the agendas we are setting. So the issue here is not *whether* feminists advance programmes for social change, but *how* we set agendas, and whether we allow our agendas to be questioned by the very transformations that are made in our name. What we are calling for, in the contingency of this present moment, is a space in which we can speak of our uncertainties about what are or should be feminist agendas, rather than assuming that such uncertainty necessarily involves a loss or failure of collectivity.

As some of the contributors to this volume contend, the conditions for feminist attention are always changing with the emergence of new institutional spaces, social and political formations and activities. We feel that our desire to transform gender relations must be accompanied by some recognition that gender relations may already be undergoing transformations, and that these transformations are not only about gender. Indeed, gender itself is no longer a privileged category in some feminist work: this is a reflection of the ways in which gender and other categories such as 'race' and class have been shown to be mutually constitutive (hooks 1989; Pettman 1992; Brewer 1993). Thus, some feminists are drawing attention to recent specific changes in the international division of labour, to eruptions of global conflict, and to concomitant shifts in forms of sexism, racism, classism and heterosexism. For example, in her chapter in this volume, Gayatri Chakravorty Spivak demonstrates how recent attempts to telecommunicate the 'third world' produce a new form of gendered colonialism, in which 'third world' women are constructed as objects of information and knowledge exchange. Likewise, Sneja Gunew examines the potential effects on feminism of new forms of racism which emphasise cultural, rather than biological, difference. These contributions to this volume highlight the importance of feminists being vigilant about the perpetual reconfiguration of institutions, bodies, temporalities and categories.

As well as recognising that some transformations in gender relations may be problematic for feminism, we also recognise how easily 'transformation' can itself become a buzz word for conservative politics and thus that not all calls for transformation are progressive. For example, flexible capitalism, modern forms of consumerism or what Celia Lury (1998), amongst others, has called 'prosthetic culture', may themselves use the discourse of transformation to produce a subject who can re-produce existing power relations. Lisa Adkins's chapter illustrates this as she shows that the emphasis on reflexivity in the labour market –

the apparent opening up of labour structures and work practices – actually allows the re-traditionalisation of gender relations. Indeed, when coupled with a negative model of freedom (freedom from), a politics which calls for transformation can easily support a neo-liberal denial of the existence and significance of power relations. Anne M. Cronin's contribution points to the problems in the way in which consumerist calls for 'transformation' can be used to conceal relationships of inclusion and exclusion. Both authors urge caution in dealing with claims of and for transformation that do not pay attention to the processes of inclusion, exclusion and differentiation and which enable only some to generate the potential for agency.

To respond to such claims for transformations requires that feminists make distinctions amongst and judgements about them. In this sense, feminism does not transcend the normative issues implicit in formulating criteria for judgements. We might need to ask: How do we distinguish between better and worse transformations? What criteria are appropriate in deciding which transformations we should welcome as feminists and about which we should be sceptical? As Caroline Ramazanoglu and Janet Holland make clear in their contribution to this volume, we need to find criteria for justifying and validating feminist political knowledge claims. Yet, to suggest that feminism does not transcend the normative, is not to suggest that there is a set of norms which are inherently feminist and which will allow 'us' to adjudicate between the maze of different routes afforded by contemporary transformations. Rather, the need to respond to recent transformations and calls for transformation demands that we debate what criteria we should use to make such judgements. In this sense, we must *make* decisions precisely because the political implications of transformations are not fully determined. Yet we still need to *justify* the decisions we make and the directions we might take. As Nancy Fraser has argued, the need for justification exists precisely because truth does not exist as an automatic ground or reference point for any position (1989: 181). Forms of politics which can adjudicate between transformations thus involve perpetually rejustifying their own grounds of existence: we need to make decisions about which direction we might wish to take, and to act on those decisions, given the absence of any 'automatic ground' for feminist positions.

Transforming feminism?

Questions about transformation are not only posed *by* feminism, but they can also be posed *to* feminism. This is particularly the case in considering the specific investments, attachments and impulses charging contemporary desire for political change. There have been for some time now powerful critiques of feminism by feminists focused on the limits of identity politics and its associated boundary marking (see Fuss 1990; Butler 1996). Feminists who are critical of identity politics have recently tried to explain why and how feminists become *invested* in certain forms of political resistance. So, for example, rather than critiquing the assumption that women 'have' an identity as 'women', or that feminism should overcome the strictures of identity (assuming that such an overcoming was possible), feminists are beginning to think through how politicised identities are lived, felt and practised, and more precisely what animates the desire for a politics of identity. Moreover, feminists have asked who has (and hence who does not have) the possibility of claiming an identity (see Skeggs 1997; Fraser 1999).

Hence, some of the contributors to this volume have joined other feminists in the investigation of investment in specific political identities. So, in her chapter, Vikki Bell argues that identity politics is driven by the pain inflicted through social injustices. Bell draws on and echoes Wendy Brown's (1995) analysis of identity politics in which she argues that feminism is grounded in 'a wounded attachment' to the trauma and suffering associated with systems of inequality (which she developed from Nietzsche's concept of *ressentiment*). Consequently, and seemingly paradoxically, according to Brown, feminism must retain and reproduce the pain of marginalisation in order to maintain itself as a political project. This leads Brown to ask provocatively:

> What are the particular constituents – specific to our time yet roughly generic for a diverse spectrum of identities – of identity's desire for recognition that seem as often to breed a politics of recrimination and rancour, of culturally dispersed paralysis and suffering, a tendency to reproach power rather than aspire to it, to disdain freedom rather than practice it? In short, where do the historically and culturally specific elements of politicized identity's investments in itself, and especially in its own history of suffering, come into conflict with the need to give up these investments, to engage in something of a 'forgetting' of this history, in the pursuit of an emancipatory democratic project?
>
> (Brown 1995: 202)

Brown contends that the injuries, insults and agonies embodied in the politicised subject become a necessary fetish for the gaining of visibility and credibility in late modernity (Taylor 1994; Fraser 1995). The subject, in effect, is what she feels, and she desires recognition of her pain as her primary identity. According to Brown, as a result of this complete identification with pain, the politicised subject is either unable or unwilling to break its hold or envision a less self-absorbing and retributive politics.

Critiques such as Brown's are not simply a call for feminists to overcome all claims to identity or for recognition, but rather they call for reflection on the limits such claims may place on the potential for transformation. If we are too invested in certain categories and versions of ourselves, then it becomes difficult to escape or change them. Nevertheless, feminism can not simply do away with or even forget the categories that are produced in institutional spaces and everyday life (such as woman/female/feminine/women). Instead, we maintain that we need to analyse and understand the (psychic and social) investment in them.

Our call for such an investigation might seem to imply that it is 'categories'

themselves that feminists must transform. Does such a call run the risk of cultivating idealism? We think that this is not necessarily the case, if categories are
considered as not merely linguistic, but rather as material, as produced and
reproduced through practices embedded in relationships of power. The determination of *categorical distinctions* (such as gender, class and race), we would argue,
involves cultural, political and economic processes. Indeed, we contend that it is
precisely the denial of the emergence of categories from material relationships of
power which fetishises them. For example, it is the separation of the category
'woman' from the social relationships of gender that allows the term 'woman' to
accrue essential attributes. We are suggesting here that categories can only be the
site of transformation through analysing the social relationships which their
fetishisation conceals, rather than repeating that concealment by assuming we
can overcome the categories themselves.

Recently feminists have posed many questions about identity, including how it
operates and why it is felt to be so crucial. Yet we would also contend that such
questioning could be extended to include: How does a sense of injustice come to
be felt (owned) as such and can it be felt differently? What conjunctures between
a mobilisation of feeling, a sense of identity, and political action can be envisaged? If identity is *felt* as belonging to an individual or group, then it necessarily
operates in the realm of the corporeal and sensible as well as the intelligible. Not
only can we think about the conceptual frameworks which are implicated in our
agendas, but we may also consider how those agendas may privilege certain
forms of sensory perception over others. Traditionally, Western feminist thought
has been based on a 'scopic economy', which has been a means of *making visible*
that which was previously hidden. Invoking such a framework is about staking a claim
for a future location in which one can be seen, and hence known. This process is
potentially dangerous as it runs the risk of surveillance. In fact, the ambition to
be seen begs questions about who is *being seen by which gaze and by whose eye/'I'*.
Furthermore, the desire *to be seen* may be problematic insofar as it assumes that
the political subject is already constituted (it hence holds in place *the subject* as the
subject *of* transformation rather than subject *to* transformation).

Against this background, we and other feminists have asked: How else can we
theorise the impulse to politics? So, Elspeth Probyn examines in this volume the
role of feelings in the mobilisation of political acts, and in the creation of a space
in which connections can be made. Rather than assuming identity or difference,
we can ask how such feelings already allow the production of unlikely moments
of alliance formation, how they may shape objects, gestures, and name the very
possibility of being touched and heard by others. As Probyn indicates, alliances
and connections may be the affect of surprise: they are about being moved to
different places.

If the impulse to politics is intimately bound up with the realm of the affective, then we may pursue different ways of mobilising the senses and ways of
'making sense' of ourselves, other people and other things. For example, rather
than attempt to either assume or transform the epistemological autonomy and
privilege given to sight, we might explore the implications of foregrounding

listening. Listening is traditionally associated with a certain modesty of intentionality. In fact, it is related to the Latin word for 'obey', *obaudire*, which means 'to listen from below' (Erwin Strauss, quoted in Levin 1989: 12). Moreover, unlike the conventional attributes of seeing, listening is associated with humility *and* vulnerability, in part because ears cannot be willed shut against sound. From this perspective, listening is a form of engagement which physically does not yield to subjective mastery and distance. The relationship between the subject of hearing and its ungraspable 'object' of sound could be invoked to reconfigure the traditional relationship of distance deemed to hold between the knowing (political) agent and that which underwrites or is the 'object' of her inquiry. As Sneja Gunew suggests in her chapter in this volume, joining a voice to a body complicates what we see, potentially disturbing the terms of cultural difference and revising the possibilities for an ethics of recognition. This shift highlights questions not about who is seen, or even who is speaking, but about how can 'we' hear otherwise. Such exploration can allow us to question how the 'we' of feminism may come to life through new ways of hearing 'other' women.

However, as feminist writers largely critical of a political project based on liberal theories of 'giving voice', 'dialogue' or 'conversation' have argued, even when those in power actually assume a position of listening and say 'I hear you', such utterances can mean quite the opposite. As this counter example suggests, it would be undesirable to privilege one sense as inherently feminist. Assuming that feminism involves a particular way of being in the world may privilege a certain kind of 'able' body – whether it is the one that *can* see, or the one that *can* hear, or the one that *can* move easily through space. Instead, we propose more attention to how feminism has been mobilised, in particular times and places, through the deployment of different senses, feelings, concepts and thoughts. To question feminism, then, is to question the *effects* of that deployment, to ask how it has worked, for whom it has worked, and whether we could think, feel or imagine other ways of 'doing' feminism. Here, posing the question of transformation to feminism involves considering how feminists have and are *producing* its object, or producing multiple objects and figures, through the deployment and articulation of feelings and categories. In this way, we begin to think of 'identity' as an effect of the deployment of feminist strategies, tactics and rhetoric, rather than its origin or cause. We can consider how feminism has been mobilised, in particular times and places, through the deployment of different senses, feelings, concepts and thoughts.

One familiar deployment of feminism has been through the invocation of standpoint. We would suggest that a responsible feminism is one that *takes* a standpoint rather than *has* or *owns* a standpoint (since the latter claims assume privilege as the consequence of occupying a categorical position). As Bar-On (1993) argues, claiming to have a standpoint is all too often a way of asserting authoritative knowledge claims against others, rather than with others. Such claims can be a way of closing down possibilities for alliances. In contrast, taking a standpoint without assuming the knowledge it generates as an object for a set of possessive rights, means (or can mean) using knowledge claims with a responsibility for ourselves and others. At the very least, such an orientation involves a recognition of the structural situatedness and historical specificity of all knowledge (see Haraway 1991; Crosby 1992). Of course, 'taking' a stand-point does not necessarily involve overcoming the problems of authorisation. The political effects of different claims to knowledge are always dependent on the contexts in which they are made.

If feminism does not have or own a standpoint, and if it lacks a fixed subject (women) and final goals, what might this mean for different forms of activism? In this volume, authors attempt to theorise feminist activism in a way which does not take the object of feminism for granted. For example, Karyn Sandlos examines how particular images become emblematic of feminist political campaigns, while Penelope Deutscher reconsiders how the appeal to social justice can be thought as performative.[7] The concept of the performative, which has become key in recent feminist scholarship, is used here to think about how a politics that does not take the status of its object for granted *can work*. Indeed, as Gail Ching-Liang Low points out in her contribution to this volume, the absence of any reference to women's collective identity may make possible ways of activating a collective politics. Low advocates work towards collective affiliations. Rather than assuming that collectivity is the foundation of our political work, the implication is that it is precisely the work itself which might make possible a 'we'. Low calls for the production of collective political affiliations which do not erase class and other positionings in their recognition of gender, but which pay close attention to how categories are re-produced, used and how they constitute and disrupt each other (see also McClintock 1995; Skeggs 1997).

One way of analysing how feminist claims and categories are put to work, and called into question, is to consider rights discourse. By calling for 'women's rights', feminists from Mary Wollstonecraft (1983 [1792]) onwards have to some extent challenged and transformed the concept of abstract and universal rights. If the concept of rights has to be extended and specified to include women's rights, then its status as universal is called into question. Rather than rights being intrinsic, they are shown to be historically produced and defined along exclusive and partial criteria. Furthermore, the notion of rights is productive of the very process of group differentiation, whereby the legitimate subject of rights (who is proper, and has property) is already the subject of a demarcated, stratified social group which excludes others. Within a classical liberal framework, 'rights' defined 'men' as a group (a 'fraternity') which excluded women, through the very act of constituting that group as a universal. As Iris Marian Young (1990) has stressed,

> rights are not fruitfully conceived as possessions. Rights are relationships not things, they are institutionally defined rules specifying what people can do in relation to one another. Rights refer to doing rather than having, to social relationships that enable or constrain action.
>
> (1990: 23)

Awareness of the necessary exclusions implicit in the 'rights' tradition has pulled many feminists away from the representation of women's rights as intrinsically given and exhaustible. In this respect, we and other feminists have no illusions that the conjoining of 'women' and 'right' would lead to an absolute and closed programme for action. Women's rights cannot simply be assigned as the proper and only object for feminist activity, precisely because they do not precede their articulation in specific contexts: the event of citing women's rights is always an active process of marking out new sites and boundaries. This is demonstrated by Ngai-Ling Sum in her chapter in this volume. Sum discusses how a liberal rhetoric of 'women's rights' as 'universal rights' functioned, in the United Nations Conference for Women in Beijing (1995), to conceal how the definition of both 'women' and 'rights' was predicated on the exclusion of Black or 'third world' women. As she illustrates, while the citing of 'women's rights' serves to demonstrate the boundaries that established 'human rights', it may also serve to establish its own boundaries. The citing of women's rights thus constitutes, rather than re-presents, a political subject. In a related contribution to this book, Penelope Deutscher examines how Irigaray's call to rights implies the impossibility of simply 'having' any.

The concern with feminist activism should also involve reflection on the different spaces and places in which feminist action takes place. In other words, if feminism makes, rather than describes, its object, then how can feminists deal with differences between localities and locations in a globalised world? Tackling this question may require a form of *unlearning* the privilege to set the agendas for feminism *and* involve forms of learning to learn differently. We need to think about how we can build new interpretations, or even better understandings, of the connections between relations of power, and between differences as they are lived and embedded in different spaces and places. Rather than merely alluding to the differences amongst women, we also want to ask how those differences may become the productive basis for different forms of activism. Critiques of universalism have been implicit in much feminism, especially Black and post-colonial feminism (Mohanty 1991), as well as 'postmodern' feminism (Hekman 1990). However, we would also contend that a politics of difference invites a critique of cultural relativism or liberal forms of atomism through which we can only describe 'the local', only speak for ourselves, or live in a 'now' without reference to the past and the future. Understanding the multifold histories in which differences become mechanisms for the regulation of identities allows us to understand the contingent relationship between different differences.

Our task of thinking *through* feminism – of questioning how feminism operates in different times and places – is also one of thinking *with* feminism, of asking troubling questions made possible by the multiple histories of feminist activism and thought. In order to think through and with feminism, and about transformation in this volume, we have organised the text into four sections: The Rhetorical Affects of Feminism; Boundaries and Connections; Knowledges and Disciplines; and Subject Matters. The sections were constructed by us as editors after the editing of the contributions (all of which began as spoken presentations at the conference – see Sneja Gunew's reflection on the critical implications of this process of rewriting). Each section has an introduction which provides background to the critical debates that inform that section, since each section represents a key area for debate in contemporary feminism. However, the chapters connect in different ways that do not respect the division into sections, since these divisions inevitably involve arbitrary and provisional closure. This introduction has been an attempt to think through some of these connections by posing the question of transformation more generally. It has been informed by the work of many feminists whose voices can be heard in these pages. We would also like to acknowledge our debt to all contributors, and to participants in the Transformations conference, who have helped us to think about transformation in the context of the production of this volume, as well as more generally. Of course, we take responsibility for our failures, but hope that any such failures may occasion further critical debate. It is our hope that the volume itself may become part of the very transformations that it seeks to address.

Notes

1   These represent two ways of conceptualising the relationship between feminism and difference. On the one hand, we can add an *s* to feminism to indicate that there are different feminisms; on the other, we could use feminism in the singular and point to the differences within (through argument). We would argue that the impulse to add an *s* in every instance of using the word 'feminism' is potentially problematic insofar as it presupposes that 'feminism' when used in the singular is untroubled by difference. As editors, we have used the term feminism in the singular, while paying attention to those differences that cannot simply be reduced to differences *between* feminists. We are also quite resistant to the assumption that to add an *s* to a term, particularly one which is so difficult to pin down (and yet so powerful in its effects), is necessarily to make a substantive commitment to analyse differences. Adding the *s* whenever one uses the term 'feminism' can easily become a rather tired and liberal gesture, which declares plurality at the level of naming, but which does not then argue the case for differences that cannot be reconciled into this pluralism.

2   See the journal *differences* (1997), 9: 3.

3   The conference was 'Transformations: Thinking Through Feminism', held at the Institute for Women's Studies, Lancaster University, UK, 17–19 July 1997.

4   We inherited the beginnings of the space from the stalwart efforts of the many women at Lancaster who had been involved in setting up the first feminist courses. Although there is no published history of the development of Women's Studies at Lancaster, Cosslett *et al.* (1996) outline the development of a first-year course; Skeggs (1995a) provides a sense of the MA; and Skeggs (1995b) places Lancaster within the national debates about the institutional conditions for Women's Studies. The July 1998 edition of the UK Women's Studies Newsletter outlines the specific conditions experienced by the co-directors, Celia Lury and Beverley Skeggs, between 1994 and 1997.

5   Of course the idea of a utopia is an impossible one, insofar as it imagines the possibility of overcoming the present, although it is thought or conceptualised in the present.

6   The term essentialism has certainly become an 'accusation' within feminism. See Teresa de Lauretis's critique of feminist work that involves this accusation against radical feminism in order to define itself as postmodern (1990: 255–277). While we share a concern with some essentialist models of the subject, or of the category of

'women' (Spelman 1990; Riley 1982), we also want to question the assumption that essentialism is inherently conservative. See Fuss 1990: 2–16.

7   It is important here not to confuse the performative with performance:

> Performativity must not be understood as a singular 'act' but rather, as the reiterative and citational practice by which discourse produces the effects that it names … [so, for example] the regulatory norms of 'sex' work in a perfomative fashion to constitute the materiality of bodies and, more specifically, to materialise the body's sex, to materialise sexual difference in the service of the consolidation of the heterosexual imperative.
>
> (Butler 1993: 2)

References

Ahmed, S. (1998) *Differences that Matter: Feminist Theory and Postmodernism*, Cambridge: Cambridge University Press.

Bar On, B-A. (1993) 'Marginality and Epistemic Privilege', in L. Alcoff and E. Potter (eds) *Feminist Epistemologies*, London: Routledge.

Berlant, L. (1998) 'Intimacy: Introduction to Intimacy', *Critical Inquiry*, Special Issue, Winter, 281–288.

Brewer, R.M. (1993) 'Theorising Race, Class and Gender: The New Scholarship of Black Feminist Intellectuals and Black Women's Labour', in S.M. James and Abena P.A. Busia (eds) *Theorising Black Feminisms: The Visionary Pragmatism of Black Women*, London: Routledge.

Brown, W. (1995) *States of Injury: Power and Freedom in Late Modernity*, Princetown, N.J.: Princetown University Press.

—— (1997) 'The Impossibility of Women's Studies', *differences: A Journal of Feminist Cultural Studies* 9, 3: 79–101.

Butler, J. (1993) *Bodies that Matter: On the Discursive Limits of 'Sex'*, New York: Routledge.

—— (1996) 'Contingent Foundations: Feminism and the Question of Postmodernism', in J. Butler and J. Scott (eds) *Feminists Theorize the Political*, New York: Routledge.

Campioni, M. and Gross, E. (1983) 'Love's Labour Lost: Marxism and Feminism', in J. Allen and P. Patton (eds) *Beyond Marxism? Interventions after Marxism*, Sydney, NSW: Intervention Publications.

Cornell, D. (1993) *Transformations: Recollective Imagination and Sexual Difference*, New York and London: Routledge.

Cosslett, T., Easton, A. and Summerfield, P. (1996) (eds) *Women, Power and Resistance: An Introduction to Women's Studies*, Milton Keynes, England: Open University Press.

Crosby, C. (1992) 'Dealing with Difference', in J. Butler and J. Scott (eds) *Feminists Theorize the Political*, New York: Routledge.

de Groot, J. and Maynard, M. (eds) (1993) *Women's Studies in the 1990's: Doing It Differently?*, London: Macmillan.

de Lauretis, T. (1990) 'Upping the Anti [*sic*] in Feminist Theory', in M. Hirsch and E. Fox Keller (eds) *Conflicts in Feminism*, New York: Routledge.

Elam, D. (1994) *Feminism and Deconstruction. Ms. en Abyme*, London: Routledge.

Evans, M. (1982) 'In Praise of Theory: The Case for Women's Studies', *Feminist Review* 10: 61–75.

Flax, J. (1990) *Thinking Fragments: Psychoanalysis, Feminism and Postmodernism in the Contemporary West*, Berkeley: University of California Press.

Fraser, M. (1999) 'Classing Queer: Politics in Competition', *Theory, Culture and Society* 16, 2: 107–131.

Fraser, N. (1989) *Unruly Practices: Power, Discourse and Gender in Contemporary Social Theory*, Cambridge: Polity Press.

—— (1995) 'From Redistribution to Recognition? Dilemmas of Justice in a 'Post-Socialist' Age', *New Left Review* 212: 68–94.

Fuss, D. (1990) *Essentially Speaking: Feminism, Nature and Difference*, New York: Routledge.

Gallop, J. (1982) *Feminism and Psychoanalysis: The Daughter's Seduction*, London: Macmillan.

Gatens, M. (1982) 'Feminism, Philosophy and Riddles Without Answers', in S. Gunew (ed.) *A Reader in Feminist Knowledge*, London: Routledge.

Griffin, C. (1989) '"I'm not a Women's Libber, but …": Feminism, Consciousness and Identity', in S. Skevington and D. Baker (eds) *The Social Identity of Women*, London: Sage.

Hall, C. (1992) *White, Male and Middle Class: Explorations in Feminism and History*, Cambridge: Polity Press.

Haraway, D. (1991) *Simians, Cyborgs, and Women: The Reinvention of Nature*, London: Free Association Books.

Harding, S. (1986) *The Science Question in Feminism*, Ithaca, N.Y.: Cornell University Press.

Hekman, S.J. (1990) *Gender and Knowledge: Elements of a Postmodern Feminism*, Cambridge: Polity Press.

Holland, N. J. (1990) *Is Women's Philosophy Possible?* Savage, Md.: Rowman and Littlefield.

hooks, b. (1989) *Talking Back: Thinking Feminist, Thinking Black*, London: Sheba Feminist Publishers.

Levin, D.M. (1989) *The Listening Self: Personal Growth, Social Change and The Closure of Metaphysics*, London: Routledge.

Levy, B. (1999) Conference Report in *Australian Feminist Studies* 14, 29: 219–222.

Lorde, A. (1984) *Sister Outsider: Essays and Speeches*, Freedom, Calif.: Crossing Press.

Lury, C. (1998) *Prosthetic Culture: Photography, Memory and Identity*, London: Routledge.

Lyotard, J.-F. (1989) *The Postmodern Condition: A Report on Knowledge*, trans. G. Bennington and B. Massumi, Manchester: Manchester University Press.

McClintock, A. (1995) *Imperial Leather: Race, Gender and Sexuality in the Colonial Context*, New York: Routledge.

McNeil, M. (1992) 'Pedagogical Praxis and Problems: Reflections on Teaching about Gender Relations', in H. Hinds, A. Phoenix and J. Stacey (eds) *Working Out: New Directions for Women's Studies*, London: Falmer Press.

Martin, B. (1998) 'Success and Its Failures', *differences: A Journal of Feminist Cultural Studies* 9, 3: 102–131.

Mitchell, J. (1974) *Psychoanalysis and Feminism*, London: Allen Lane.

Mohanty, C. (1991) 'Under Western Eyes: Feminist Scholarship and Colonial Discourses', in C.T. Mohanty, A. Russo and L. Torres (eds) *Third World Women and the Politics of Feminism*, Bloomington: Indiana University Press.

Morris, M. (1988) *The Pirate's Fiancée: Feminism, Reading, Postmodernism*, London and New York: Verso.

Nicholson, L. (1990) (ed.) *Feminism/Postmodernism*, London: Routledge.

Nye, A. (1988) *Feminist Theory and the Philosophies of Man*, London: Croom Helm.

O'Sullivan, S. (1982) 'Passionate Beginnings: Ideological Politics', *Feminist Review* 11: 70–88.

Pettman, J. (1992) *Living in the Margins: Racism, Sexism and Feminism in Australia*, St Leonards, NSW: Allen and Unwin.

Riley, D. (1982) *Am I That Name? Feminism and the Category of 'Women' in History*, Basingstoke, England: Macmillan Press.

Rose, J. (1988) *Sexuality in the Field of Vision*, London: Verso.

Scott, J.W. (1988) *Gender and the Politics of History*, New York: Columbia University Press.

Showalter, E. (1989) 'Feminist Criticism in the Wilderness', in E. Showalter (ed.) *The New Feminist Criticism: Essays on Women, Literature and Theory*, London: Virago Press.

Skeggs, B. (1995a) *Feminist Cultural Theory: Process and Production*, Manchester: Manchester University Press.

—— (1995b) 'Entitlement Cultures and Institutional Constraints: Women's Studies in the UK in the 1990s', *Women's Studies International Forum* 18, 4: 475–485.

—— (1997) *Formations of Class and Gender: Becoming Respectable*, London: Sage.

Smith, D.E. (1987) 'Women's Perspective as A Radical Critique of Sociology', in S. Harding (ed.) *Feminism and Methodology*, Bloomington: Indiana University Press.

—— (1988) *The Everyday World as Problematic: A Feminist Sociology*, Milton Keynes: Open University Press.

Spelman, E.V. (1990) *Inessential Woman: Problems of Exclusion in Feminist Thought*, London: Women's Press.

Spender, D. (1981) *Men's Studies Modified: The Impact of Feminism on the Academic Disciplines*, New York: Pergamon.

Taylor, C. (1994) 'The Politics of Recognition', in D.T. Goldberg (ed.) *Multiculturalism: A Critical Reader*, Oxford: Blackwell.

Weedon, C. (1987) *Feminist Practice and Poststructuralist Theory*, 2nd edition, Oxford: Blackwell.

Wollstonecraft, M. (1983 [1792]) *A Vindication of the Rights of Woman*, London: Penguin.

Young, I.M. (1990) *Justice and the Politics of Difference*, Princetown, N.J.: Princetown University Press.

Part I

The rhetorical affects of feminism

Introduction

Beverley Skeggs

In this section the basic tenets of feminism which are sometimes taken for granted – about justice, the personal, activism and morality – are being questioned. Simultaneously attempts are made to formulate new versions of affectivity and to think about how feminist subjects are being produced. All the authors in this section explore how the grammar for contemporary political claims-making is being forged. Particular attention is paid to how feminist subjects are being produced through different rhetorical strategies. Whilst Lauren Berlant and Elspeth Probyn look at the rhetorical calls made and framed by the state in an attempt to interpellate the subject, Vikki Bell, Karyn Sandlos and Penelope Deutscher interrogate how the feminist subjects make their responses. Each chapter in this section shows how different rhetorical strategies are being deployed to generate a 'politics of recognition'. This is a politics, which Fraser (1995) argues may not be helpful for feminism. She documents a shift from the politics of redistribution which predominated in the 1980s to a politics of recognition in the 1990s, in which political claims-making is forged through identity claims, rather than through the exposure of structural inequalities. These identity claims are based, she argues, on a desire to be recognised as someone (a particular category of person). This political claims-making is usually based on singular categorisations (that is, identity claims are usually linked to identity position). They are also invariably tied into a neo-liberal discourse of rights and assimilation.

The chapters in this section address, in their different ways, the limits to this contemporary political formation. But, they also show, because of the intimate link between recognition and concepts of personhood and identity, how difficult it is to escape from the neo-liberal conceptual framework. The challenge of this section is to envisage ways in which politics may involve thinking beyond and outside of bodies, intimacy and selves, beyond that which can be recognised, beyond appearances. Such politics, they argue, will have to including questioning motivation, investment, responsibility and desire and, in a sense, thinking beyond who we are, to where we should be, how and with whom. Thinking beyond the present is inherently difficult and this section attempts to rupture the paradigm of identity which dominates much current political thought and strategy.

The Western national public is now saturated with the personal (for example the explosion of emotions after the death of Princess Diana or the revelations of Clinton's sexual activities). What does this mean for feminism? Has the personal become political in the way that feminists advocated? The rhetorical strategy of the 'personal is political' in early second-wave feminism was used to force an awareness of entitlement; it drew attention to the patterns of occupation of 'the public'. It called into account the evaluation process by which women came to be associated with the irrational, the illegitimate, the insignificant and the private. Pateman (1988), for instance, showed how the social contract in the West was premised on the displacement of women from the public. Many feminists have shown citizenship to be a woman-excluding discourse. The various contributors to this section ask: what value does this rhetorical division between private and public hold? The chapters ask: How can we know what is personal? What designates personal space? What is a 'public space'? Is it the bourgeois public sphere as described by Habermas (1996) and taken up by some feminists? Is it the space of appearances identified by Arendt (Landes 1998)? Is it a space to which only some have access, through, for example, the regulation of citizenship? Is it the state? Recognition claims fragment calls for citizenship into different variants (sexual, intimate, dead, diva: Berlant 1997). Nevertheless, still only some groups can be/go public, whilst others (for instance, gay men) are legislated as always public. Privacy has been associated with some groups of women. Yet, some groups of women are forced to come under public scrutiny (via reproduction, mothering practices and even sleeping arrangement – monitored in the UK by the Department of Social Security), whilst others can claim their practices as inscrutable, intimate and private. These differences in the scripting of intimacy problematise the universal promotion of the revelation of intimacy which has recently now been used to make political claims in the West/North.

The first three contributors to this section, Berlant, Probyn and Bell, explore how 'the wounded attachment' identified by Brown (1995) and developed from Nietzsche's notion of *ressentiment*, energises a particular feminist politics which focuses on itself and celebrates misery. The concept of wounded attachment draws attention to the belief that the experience of pain, hurt and oppression provides greater epistemological authority. Berlant shows how *ressentiment* has enabled the development of identity politics which generates 'a literacy program in the alphabet of that pain'. Showing how concepts of privacy and national attachment have been forged from a limited understanding of (specifically heterosexual) women's pain, she argues that this has enabled the development of a particular national formation in which the currency of distress, hurt and pain are the means by which groups make claims for recognition. This produces a political terrain which is increasingly figured through moralism. The emphasis on wounding and pain as a sign of injustice provides an unreliable basis for justice claims. This is because only some groups can articulate their identities with reference to wounds and pain (and only some would want to do so). This also leads to a relativist collapse within the alphabet of pain through which major forms of distress and death, such as the Holocaust, are equated to narratives of individual personal trauma. The connections that are made across pain can deny and evade issues of power. We thus need a way of discriminating amongst different claims. Even more importantly, we need to understand how particular forms of citizenship, of public participation and of personal understanding are being forged through claims about wounds and pain, thereby limiting understandings of how everyday suffering is actually lived. The currency of distress has led to a displacement whereby awareness of everyday structural adversity on a daily basis is eclipsed by the accounts of exceptional, personal, traumatic pain. Media companies have not been slow to capitalise on this trend (for example Oprah Winfrey, Jerry Springer and Ricky Lake).

Gaining recognition through wound claims has become a compelling cultural strategy, so that telling and testifying become the modes through which national allegiance is forged. There are echoes of this process in the Australian attempts at reconciliation. Stories which were previously hidden, such as the accounts of forced adoption of Aboriginal children, of forced slave labour and of the effective genocidal eradication of substantial numbers of Aboriginal peoples, have led to state calls for reconciliation. In an outline of the public and personal responses to reconciliation, Probyn shows how the Australian national media attempted to produce a form of national sentimentality. She shows how this has made it difficult for feminists to respond. Probyn is uneasy about the unacknowledged disjuncture between an identity politics (feminism) which has been, to some extent, forged out of 'speaking' pain (for example, consciousness raising was predicated on the possibility of speaking about shared experiences of oppression), and the systematic eradication of whole groups of people by the state. Probyn asks: how can a politics forged out of relative privilege contend with such violence? She suggests that feminist thinking may not be up to the task of addressing such disjunctures. Yet Probyn makes us think through how we can use the limited tools that are available to us. This she argues, may not involve making a connection but is, rather, about recognising the limits of connection and thinking through disconnections. Assuming that connections can always be made, she argues, is a form of epistemological arrogance: it assumes that equivalence can be generated. She warns that: differences will not disappear if feminists do not pay attention to them (class and 'race' differences being her examples here).

Probyn (like Berlant) shows that relativising pain, as Berlant critiques, is clearly problematic. The experience of shame, she contends, may be a form of recognising the limits of our responses. It may entail an affective recognition of the lack of commonality produced as a bodily affect. Probyn's chapter is an acknowledgement of the struggles and difficulties involved in knowledge production, which urges caution and circumspection. Telling stories of pain has been very important to the forging of a feminist politics but the limitations of such practices must also be recognised. Probyn calls for forms of politics forged through struggle, not around identity.

Vikki Bell also takes up the theme of *ressentiment* as the impulse to feminist politics. She argues that feminism does move beyond and outside of the bound-aries marked by *ressentiment*. She shows how alliances and disconnections can be formed within this. In considering the relationship between Simone de Beauvoir and Richard Wright, she distinguishes between the rhetorical calls made by femi-nism through *ressentiment* – 'the telling of pain' and the empirical impossibility of making connections. She shows how de Beauvoir invokes parallels to race rela-tions in thinking through the figure of woman. Her connections are made through particular rhetorical and heuristic devices. Bell notes the constructing of all the women as white and of all the men as black .

Taking a rather different tack, Karyn Sandlos asks how feminists 'brand' political struggles in order to generate identifications and commitment. She explores the struggle over visual images, in which they are seen to hold the 'grammar of indisputable knowledge'. She shows how the visual image of Gerri Santoro (a woman whose body was found after an illegal and fatal abortion in the USA in the 1970s) was deployed in political claims-making. She also asks who owns, circulates and has rights over the images used in political struggle. Outlining the battles over the visual representation of dead women and dead foetuses, she shows how forms of citizenship and personhood are generated. Acknowledging that personal outrage is necessary for mobilisation, she shows how central time is to the consolidation and condensing of moral positions. Drawing on focus-group discussions Sandlos draws attention to the significant differences between the visually rhetorical and the empirical. Women activists have very different relationships to this particular image, and these differences, she argues, represent generational changes in feminism. Sandlos points to the need for continual struggle, for careful use of the visual, and for recognition of the limits and the often unforeseen consequences of mobilisation.

Recent feminist research has shown how struggles for entitlement within the law can produce pathology and readability as the law encompasses new forms into its vocabulary (Bower 1997). So, for example, the foetus has become in many Western countries a body, a person, a citizen, through the process of making visible and legal. While the sedimentation and ossification of certain categories has been necessary to feminist mobilisation around rights, this has not always had positive consequences. For this reason, many feminists have become wary of mobilising around rights claims.

Despite this feminist circumspection, Luce Irigaray has not been hesitant in making such claims. In this section, Penelope Deutscher explores how Irigaray questions the basis for a politics of recognition (which has been the focus of much feminist struggle). Related to this, Irigaray argues that sexual difference cannot be recognised in such claims. Deutscher shows how Irigaray sets up a paradoxical call for sexuate rights in order to make us recognise what we want to displace. Irigaray's call involves a particular form of ethics that makes us recog-nise that which cannot be recognised. Two strategies are central to this manoeuvre. The first is the use of rhetorical play through the re-metaphorising of sexual difference; the second is the use of the performative to create such a rhetorical move. The first shows us how all institutional recognition retroactively constitutes the conditions of its own possibility, showing us that rights can never be legitimated. It makes us question the authority of the legitimating agency (for example the constitution). (Of course, this does presuppose that the country in question actually has a constitution.) The second shows that the claim for sexuate rights (for example virginity as a right) works as a form of illocutionary performativity in which the claim has already accomplished an act regardless of its consequences. Irigaray's rhetorical—performative gesture draws attention to the paradoxical nature of the ethics of recognition and to the constrained nature of speech. Deutscher labels this strategy 'post-deconstructive ethics', an ethics that constantly problematises the present and questions performative claims. In this way, Deutscher advocates a movement from a politics of recognition to a politics of performative rights. There is, of course, the further question about whether the call to performative rights is also framed by the ability to authorise performative speech so that it can be heard. In this sense, performativity always involves power, authority and legitimation.

All of the chapters in this section engage with political claims and consider how they can be made and heard. They show how the state frames the terms of many of the debates, through the interpretation of feelings, the incorporation of challenges, and the articulation of legal claims in the construction of citizenship. The contributors also demonstrate the power of the neo-liberal framework of advanced capitalism to shape political discourses. As Bourdieu (1985) argues, theory produces the effects it names. These authors demonstrate how justice may be realised or blocked through performative acts, through the zoning of social spaces and through the limits of recognition. They illustrate the deployment of rhetorical techniques, exploring the consequences of and necessity for different moves. The contributors to this section are, in many respects, sensitive to the different rhetorical ploys which link the subjective to the social in contemporary feminist politics. Hence, generally they advocate forms of political caution and constraint which recognise limits, differences, power and, in some cases, the impossibility of making connections. This is rather different from the universal optimism which characterised much early second-wave feminism, which rhetorically deployed 'sisterhood' and worked rather straightforwardly on building alliances. These authors are aware that each recognition claim may precipitate a counter-claim. They also acknowledge that there are groups who, through processes of disidentification, become excluded from political consideration (Skeggs 1997; Fraser, M. 1999).

Attention to rhetorical strategies may expose gestures made for the sake of alliance which pretend to include, whilst excluding. Differences are frequently invoked in rhetorical forms (often as a mantra) whilst racism and class inequality not only remain intact, but are reproduced through lack of attention. So, for example, through the rhetorical signs of 'lone mother', 'smoker', 'unhealthy school', many Western states create divisions between the worthy and the unworthy. Cultivation of personal responsibility privatises inequality and makes it a matter of personal volition. Understanding this and other positionings and consequent resource allocation is important for how we understand the place and use of rhetorical ploys.

This section represents a collection of reflections on strategy and forms of address. The contributors are trying to envisage situated responses, as well as how these responses are evoked. Overall they suggest that much of what we do in the name of feminism cannot be known in advance. The concept of performativity implies that speech acts (including the rhetorical plays outlined in these chapters), are always somewhat outside of the speaker's control. Hence, our claims, calls and demands may already have realised consequences outside of our control, which we can never envisage. When we frame feminist claims in terms of identity politics, with hopes for recognition: what do we exclude? What possibilities do we close down? What forms of reproduction do we engender? What dis/connections and antagonisms do we put into effect? In raising such questions these authors are investigating forms of politics which move between epistemological questions of what can be known and ontological questions of who can we be, without losing sight of the power relations in which both questions are embedded.

These chapters are, in this sense, highly sophisticated. But sophistication may entail its own problems. For example, Litvak (1997) advocates caution in the use of the term 'sophistication' to describe theories. Discursively, he argues, 'sophistication' conforms strikingly to patrician hauteur. Hence, there is also a need for wariness about such sophistication in the symbolic struggles in which feminists are engaged. Such struggles may unwittingly produce forms of symbolic violence if attention is not paid to how we invoke interest and power. In whose interest does feminism work? is still a central question to be asked and one in which we are always/already implicated.

References

Berlant, L. (1997) *The Queen of America Goes to Washington City: Essays on Sex and Citizenship*, Durham, N.C.: Duke University Press.

Bourdieu, P. (1985) *The Social Space and the Genesis of Groups*, Theory and Society 14: 723–744.

Bower, L. (1997) 'Queer Problems/Straight Solutions: The Limits of a Politics of "Official Recognition"', in S. Phelan (ed.) *Playing with Fire: Queer Politics, Queer Theories*, London: Routledge.

Brown, W. (1995) 'Wounded Attachments: Late Modern Oppositional Political Formations', in J. Rajchman (ed.) *The Identity in Question*, New York: Routledge.

Fraser, M. (1999) 'Classing Queer: Politics in Competition', *Theory, Culture and Society* 16, 2: 107–131.

Fraser, N. (1995) 'From Redistribution to Recognition? Dilemmas of Justice in a "Post-Socialist" Age', *New Left Review* 212: 68–94.

Habermas, J. (1996) *The Habermas Reader*, ed. W. Outhwaite, Cambridge: Polity Press.

Landes, J. (1998) 'The Public and the Private Sphere: A Feminist Reconsideration', in J. Landes (ed.) *Feminism: The Public and the Private*, Oxford: Oxford University Press.

Litvak, J. (1997) *Strange Gourmets: Sophistication, Theory and the Novel*, New York: Routledge.

Pateman, C. (1988) *The Sexual Contract*, Cambridge: Polity Press.

Skeggs, B. (1997) *Formations of Class and Gender: Becoming Respectable*, London: Sage.

1   The subject of true feeling
Pain, privacy, and politics

Lauren Berlant

Liberty finds no refuge in a jurisprudence of doubt.[1]

An abortive abstract

Who gave anyone expertise over the meaning of feelings of injustice? I was sympathetic to the cultural politics of pain in the United States until I felt the violence of its sentimentality: presented as a collective refusal to bear any longer a population's collective suffering, public sentimentality is too often a defensive response by people who identify with privilege, yet fear they will be exposed as immoral by their tacit sanction of a particular structural violence that benefits them. I was a wholly sympathetic participant in practices of subaltern testimony and complaint, until I saw that the stories of trauma that were deemed to exemplify a population's subordination not only tended to confirm the state and its law as the core sites of personhood, but also provided opportunities to divide further dominated populations by inciting competitions over whose lives have been more excluded from the 'happiness' that is constitutionally promised by national life. Meanwhile, the recognition by the dominant culture of certain sites of publicized subaltern suffering is frequently (mis)taken as a big step toward the amelioration of that suffering. It is a baby step, if that. I suggest, in contrast, that the pain and suffering of subordinated subjects is an ordinary and ongoing thing that is underdescribed by the traumatic identity form and its circulation in the state and the law. If identity politics is a literacy program in the alphabet of that pain, then its subjects must also assume that the signs of subordination they feel also tell a story that they do not feel yet, or know, about how to construct the narrative to come.

Pain

The central concern of this chapter is to address the place of painful feeling in the making of political worlds. In this, I affiliate with Wendy Brown's (1995a) concern about the overvaluation of the wound in the rhetoric of contemporary U.S. identity politics (see also Brown 1995b). Brown argues that the identification of minority identity with a wound – a conventional story about the particular and particularizing injuries caused by domination – must lead to the wound becoming fetishized as evidence of identity, which thereby awards monumentality and value to the very negativity that would also be overcome. As a result, minority struggle can get stuck in a groove of self-repetition and habituated resentment, while from the outside it would appear vulnerable to the charge of 'victim politics.' In my view, however, what Brown locates in minority discourse generally has a longer, more specific, and far more privileged genealogy than she suggests. In particular, I would like to connect it to something I call national sentimentality, that is, a liberal rhetoric of promise historically entitled in the United States, which avows that a nation can best be built across fields of social difference through channels of affective identification and empathy.

A current of feeling that circulates in and shapes a political world, national sentimentality transects a longstanding incongruity between two models of U.S. citizenship. In one, the classic Constitutional model, each citizen's value is secured by an equation between abstractness and freedom: an individual cell of national identity provides juridically protected personhood for citizens regardless of anything specific about them. Here, national subjectivity tends to be imagined first as an identification with the law and then with the nation that protects and administers it. In the second model, which emerged from the labor, feminist, and abolitionist struggles of the U.S. in the nineteenth century, a very different version of the nation is imagined as the index of collective life. In this version, the nation is said to be peopled by suffering citizens and non-citizens whose structural exclusion from the utopian-American dreamscape exposes the State's claim of virtuous universality to an acid wash of truth-telling that dissolves its capacity to disavow the comfort of its violence.

Feminism, in particular, participated in establishing the trumping power of suffering stories in the U.S. since abolition and suffrage worked to establish the enslaved Other as someone with subjectivity, defined not as someone who thinks or works, but as someone who has endured violence intimately. Women's traditional identification with suffering on behalf of virtue in the family, and feminism's extension of that structure into the rights talk of national and international public spheres, both enabled the political consensus that situates narratives of trauma on the ethical high ground above interest politics and established the precedent for exaggerating the value of transformations that happen primarily within individual consciences. I do not mean to be saying here that testimonial discourse derived from subordination is invariably a shallow or cynical contribution toward building political worlds. Sometimes it helps to produce genuine social and political transformation and sometimes not. In the liberal tradition of the United States, in any case, it is not simply a mode of particularizing and puncturing self-description by minorities, but *a rhetoric of universality* located, not in abstract categories, but in what was thought to be, simultaneously, particular and universal experience.

Indeed, it would not be exaggerating to say that sentimentality has long been a popular rhetorical means by which pain is advanced, in the United States, as the true core of personhood and citizenship. By citizenship, I refer both to the legal sense in which persons are juridically subject to the law's privileges and protections by virtue of national identity, and to the more experiential, vernacular context in which people customarily understand their relation to state power and social membership. National sentimentality operates when relatively privileged citizens are exposed to the suffering of their intimate Others, so that to be virtuous requires feeling the pain of flawed or denied citizenship as their own pain. Theoretically, those with power will do whatever is necessary to eradicate the misery they now feel vicariously, returning the nation once more to its legitimately utopian odor. In the discourse of national sentimentality, identification with pain, a universal true feeling, would thereby lead to structural social change. In exchange, populations emancipated from the pain of failed democracy would then reauthorize universalist notions of citizenship in the national utopia, which involves believing in a redemptive notion of law as the guardian of public good. The object of the nation-state in this light is to eradicate systemic social pain, the absence of which becomes the definition of freedom.

What does it mean for the struggle to shape collective life when a politics of true feeling organizes so much analysis, discussion, fantasy, and policy? What intrepretation can we offer when feeling, the most subjective thing, the thing that makes persons public and marks their location, takes the temperature of power, mediates personhood, experience, and history, and takes over the space of ethics and truth, or when the shock of pain is said only to produce *clarity* despite the fact that shock can be said to produce as powerfully panic, misrecognition, the shakiness of perception's ground? Finally, what happens to questions of managing alterity or difference or resources in collective life when feeling *bad* becomes evidence for a structural condition of injustice? What does it mean for the theory and practice of social transformation when feeling *good* becomes evidence of justice's triumph? As many historians and theorists of 'rights talk' have shown, the beautiful and simple categories of legitimation in liberal society can bestow on proper personhood the status of normative value, which is expressed in feeling terms as 'comfort'; meanwhile, political arguments that challenge the claim of painful feeling's analytic clarity are frequently characterized as causing further violence to already-damaged persons and the world of their desires.[2]

This chapter will raise uncomfortable questions about what the evidence of trauma is: for in the sentimental national contract, antagonists mirror each other in their conviction about the *self-evidence* and *objectivity* of painful feeling, and about the nation's duty to eradicate it (see Berlant 1997). I am not trying to posit feeling as the bad opposite of something good called thinking: as we will see, in the cases, to follow politicized feeling is a kind of thinking that too often assumes the obviousness of the thought it has, which stymies the production of the thought it might become. My larger aim is to return to the question of the centrality of 'the subject' who so powerfully animates much feminist, anti-racist, and queer work, but whose recent critical life has tacitly imaged society as a space that should be void of struggle and ambivalence.

In particular, our cases will derive from the field of sexuality, a zone of practice, fantasy, and ideology whose standing in the law constantly partakes of claims about the universality or transparency of feeling, a universality juridically known as 'privacy.' I begin by addressing the work of feeling in Supreme Court decisions around sexuality and privacy. But the tendency to assume the non-ideological and unmediated status of feeling is shared by opponents to privacy as well, with consequences that must equally, though differently, give pause: the following section interrogates the anti-privacy revolution legal radicals have wrought via the redefinition of harm and traumatized personhood. The paradoxes revealed therein will not be easily solved by ignoring or condescending to the evidence of injustice provided by the publicized pain of subordinated populations: but it will provide a way to consider what it would mean, and what kinds of changes it would bring, to delaminate the subject from the law that marks her, inducing a break with trauma's seduction of politics in the domains of U.S. citizenship.

Privacy

It would not be too strong to say that where regulating sexuality is concerned, the law has a special sentimental relation to banality. No better example of this can be found than in the foggy fantasy of happiness pronounced in the Constitutional concept of privacy, whose emergence in sexuality law during the 1960s brought heterosexual intimacy explicitly into the antagonistic field of U.S. citizenship. Based on a notion of safe space, a hybrid space of home and law in which people will act legally and lovingly toward each other free from the determinations of history or the coercions of pain, the Constitutional theorization of sexual privacy is drawn from a lexicon of romantic sentiment, a place whose constitution in law would be so powerful that desire would meet moral discipline there, making real the dreamy rule.[3] In this dream the zone of privacy is a national space too, where freedom and desire meet up in their full *suprapolitical* expression, a site of embodiment that nonetheless leaves unchallenged fundamental dicta about the universality or abstractness of the modal citizen.

Much has been written on the general status of privacy doctrine in Constitutional history, a 'broad and ambiguous concept which can easily be shrunken in meaning but which can also, on the other hand, easily be interpreted as a constitutional ban against many things other than searches and seizures.'[4] Sexual privacy was first conceived as a constitutionally mandated but unenumerated right of sexual citizenship in *Griswold v. Connecticut* [381 U.S. 479 (1965)]. The case is about the use of birth control in marriage: a nineteenth-century Connecticut law made it illegal for married couples to use contraceptives for birth control (Guitton and Irons 1995: 7); they were only allowed prophylaxis to prevent disease. To challenge this law, Esther Griswold, director of Planned Parenthood in Connecticut, and Lee Buxton, the chief physician there, were arrested, by arrangement with the District Attorney, for giving 'information, instruction, and medical advice to *married persons* as to the means of preventing conception.'[5]

Griswold stresses the Due Process clause of the Fourteenth Amendment because denying the sale of contraceptives 'constitutes a deprivation of right against invasion of privacy.'[6] This kind of privacy is allotted only to married couples: Justice Goldberg quotes approvingly a previous opinion of Justice Harlan (*Poe v. Ullman* [367 U.S. 497, at 533]), which states that

> Adultery, homosexuality, and the like are sexual intimacy which the State forbids ... but the intimacy of husband and wife is necessarily an essential and accepted feature of the institution of marriage, an institution which the State not only must allow, but which always and in every age it has fostered and protected.[7]

We can see in Harlan's phrasing and Goldberg's citation of it an exemplum of the sentimental complexities of Constitutional law about sexual practice. The logic of equivalence between adultery and homosexuality in the previous passage locates these vastly different sexual events/identities in an unprotected public space that allows and even compels *zoning* in the form of continual State discipline (for example *laws*). In contrast, marital privacy is drawn up here in a zone elsewhere to the law and takes its authority from tradition, which means that the law simultaneously protects it and chastely turns away its disciplinary gaze.[8]

The banality of intimacy's sentimental standing in and above the law is most beautifully and enduringly articulated in the majority opinion in *Griswold*, written by Justice William O. Douglas. Douglas argues that a combination of precedents derived from the First, Fourth, Fifth, Ninth, and Fourteenth Amendments supports his designation of a heretofore unenumerated Constitutional right for married persons to inhabit a zone of privacy,[9] a zone free from police access or the 'pure [State] power' for which Connecticut was arguing as the doctrinal foundation of its right to discipline immorality in its citizens (Guitton and Irons 1995: 7). The language Douglas uses, both to make this space visible and to enunciate the law's relation to it, shuttles between the application of *stare decisis* (the rule of common law that binds judicial authority to judicial precedent) and the traditional conventionalities of heteronormative Hallmark-style sentiment:

> The present case, then, concerns a relationship lying within the zone of privacy created by several fundamental constitutional guarantees. And it concerns a law which, in forbidding the use of contraceptives rather than regulating their manufacture or sale, seeks to achieve its goals by means having a maximum destructive impact upon that relationship. Such a law cannot stand in light of the familiar principle, so often applied by this Court, that a 'governmental purpose to control or prevent activities constitutionally subject to state regulation may not be achieved by means which sweep unnecessarily broadly and thereby invade the area of protected freedoms' (*NAACP v. Alabama* [377 U.S. 288, 307]). Would we allow the police to search the sacred precincts of marital bedrooms for telltale signs of the use of contraceptives? The very idea is repulsive to the notions of privacy

surrounding the marriage relationship. We deal with a right of privacy older than the Bill of Rights – older than our political parties, older than our school system. Marriage is a coming together for better or for worse, hopefully enduring, and intimate to the degree of being sacred. It is an association that promotes a way of life, not causes; a harmony in living, not political faiths; a bilateral loyalty, not commercial or social projects. Yet it is an association for as noble a purpose as any involved in our prior decisions.[10]

Justice Hugo Black's dissent in *Griswold* blasts the majority Justices for the emotionality of what he calls the 'natural law due process formula [used] to strike down all state laws which [the Justices] think are unwise, dangerous, or irrational.' He feels that it introduces into Constitutional jurisprudence justifications for measuring

constitutionality by our belief that legislation is arbitrary, capricious or unreasonable, or accomplishes no justifiable purpose, or is offensive to our own notions of civilized standards of conduct. Such an appraisal of the wisdom of legislation is an attribute of the power to make laws, not of the power to interpret them.[11]

He finds precedent in this critique in a Learned Hand essay on the Bill of Rights that reviles judges' tendencies to

wrap up their veto in a protective veil of adjectives such as 'arbitrary,' 'artificial,' 'normal,' 'reasonable,' 'inherent,' 'fundamental,' or 'essential' whose office usually, though quite innocently, is to disguise what they are doing and impute to it a derivation far more impressive than their personal preferences, which are all that in fact lie behind the decision.[12]

In this view, whenever judges enter the zone of Constitutional penumbra, they manufacture euphemisms that disguise the relation between proper law and personal inclination. Patricia Williams suggests that this charge is at the heart of the fiction of *stare decisis*, which produces *post facto* justifications from judicial or social tradition for judges who inevitably impose their will on problems of law but who must, for legitimacy's sake, disavow admission of the uninevitability of their claim. Legal judgment veils its articulation at the place where interpretive will and desire mix up to produce someone's image of a right/just/proper world (Williams 1991: 7–8, 134–135).

After sexual privacy was donated to the U.S. heterosexual couple in *Griswold* by way of the sentimental reason the Court adopted, a judicial and political nightmare over the property of sexual privacy ensued, whose mad struggle between state privilege and private liberty is too long to enumerate here. We can conclude that the romantic banality that sanctions certain forms of intimacy as nationally privileged remains hardwired into the practice of sex privacy law in the United States. But twenty years later, *Planned Parenthood v. Casey* [112 Sup. Ct.

2791 (1992)] supplants *entirely* the utopia of heterosexual intimacy on which sexual privacy law was based in the first place, putting *women's pain* in heterosexual culture at the center of the story of privacy and legal protections. In this sense, the legitimating force of deep juridical feelings about the sacred pleasures of marital intimacy are inverted and displaced onto the woman, whose sexual and political trauma now constitutes the meaning and value of her privacy and her citizenship.

Planned Parenthood v. Casey was widely seen as an opportunity for a new set of Justices to overturn *Roe v. Wade* [410 U.S. 113 (1973)]. The Pennsylvania Abortion Control Act of 1982 (amended in 1988–89) did not abolish abortion in the state but proliferated the discursive contexts in which it happened, seeking to create around abortion a State-sanctioned, morally pedagogical *zone of publicity*. The new requirements included a 24-hour waiting period; a minor's notification of her parents; a wife's notification of her husband; and expanded standards of 'informed consent' (including a State-authored brochure condemning abortion). The majority opinion has two explicit aims: to affirm the fundamental holdings of *Roe* concerning the sovereignty of women's citizenship, the unity of national culture, and the status of the Court's authority; and to enumerate what it felt was underdeveloped in *Roe*, the conditions of the state's sovereignty over the contexts of reproduction. In other words, as Justice Scalia's dissent argues, the Court's majority opinion seeks to affirm *Roe* while also significantly dismantling it. Its technical mechanism for achieving this impossible feat is the substitution of an 'undue burden' rule for a whole set of other protections *Roe* provides: especially by dismantling the trimester framework that determined the woman's sovereignty over reproduction in a pregnancy's first six months, and substituting for it a rule that favors the State's right to place restrictions on the woman's reproductive practice (restrictions that can then be weighed by courts that will determine whether a given law mounts 'undue burdens' to the woman's exercise of her constitutional right to abortion).

Scalia claims that the majority pulls off this impossible feat (in its claim to refuse a 'jurisprudence of doubt' while making equivocal legal judgments) by disguising its own muddy impulses in a sentimental and 'empty' rhetoric of intimacy:

> the best that the Court can do to explain how it is that the word 'liberty' *must* be thought to include the right to destroy human fetuses is to rattle off a collection of adjectives that simply decorate a value judgment and conceal political choice. The right to abort, we are told, inheres in 'liberty' because it is among 'a person's most basic decisions,' *ante*, at 2806; it involves a 'most intimate and personal choic[e],' *ante*, at 2807; it is 'central to personal dignity and autonomy,' *ibid.*; it 'originate[s] within the zone of conscience and belief,' *ibid.*; it is 'too intimate and personal' for state interference, *ante*, at 2807; it reflects 'intimate views' of a 'deep, personal character,' *ante*, at 2808; it involves 'intimate relationships,' and 'notions of personal autonomy and bodily integrity,' *ante*, at 2810 ...[13]

Correctly, Scalia goes on to point out that these very same qualities meant nothing to the Justices when they heard *Bowers v. Hardwick* [478 U.S. 186 (1986)], 'because, like abortion, they are forms of conduct that have long been criminalized in American society. Those adjectives might be applied, for example, to homosexual sodomy, polygamy, adult incest, and suicide, all of which are equally intimate.'[14]

But Scalia's critique is trivial, in the sense that the majority opinion does not seek to rethink sexual privacy or intimacy in any serious way. The rhetoric of intimacy in the case partly extends from the Justices' need to derive their decisions from precedent.[15] But the majority Justices' most ingenious originality is located in their representation of the specificity, what they call the 'uniqueness,' of the material conditions of citizenship for women in the United States. Because the right to sexual privacy has been individuated by *Roe*, privacy no longer takes place in a concrete zone, but in a 'zone of conscience.' The Justices refer to women's 'anxieties,' 'physical constraints,' and 'sacrifices [that] have since the beginning of the human race been endured by woman with a pride that ennobles her': they contend that a woman's 'suffering is too intimate and personal for the State to insist ... upon its own vision of the woman's role.'[16] Therefore abortion definitively grounds and sustains women's political legitimacy, and their 'ability to participate equally in the economic and social life of the Nation has been facilitated by their ability to control their reproductive lives.'[17]

The Justices here cede that heterosexual femininity in the United States is itself an undue burden, however ennobling it might also be. The de-utopianization of sexual privacy established in *Griswold* and the installation of female citizenship at the juncture of law and suffering is further reinforced by the one part of the Pennsylvania law that the majority finds unconstitutional: the clause that commands women to notify their husbands of their intention to abort. The segment in which this happens exposes women's suffering in the zone of privacy where, it turns out, men beat their wives. They cite evidence, supported by the American Medical Association, that men are raping their wives, terrorizing them (especially when pregnant), *forcing* them to inhabit a zone of privacy that keeps secret men's abuse of women. In short, the 'gruesome and torturous' conditions of marital domesticity in battering households requires the Court *not to protect privacy* for the couple, but to keep the couple from becoming the unit of modal citizenship where privacy law is concerned.[18]

Politics

In the twenty years between *Roe* and *Planned Parenthood v. Casey* the general scene of public citizenship in the U.S. has become suffused with a practice of making pain count politically. The law of sexual privacy has followed this change, registering with symptomatic incoherence a more general struggle to maintain the contradictory rights and privileges of women, heterosexuality, the family, the state, and patriarchalized sexual privilege. This jumble of categories should say something about the cramped space of analysis and praxis which the rhetoric and jurisprudence of sexual privacy has brought us to.

Central to the legal emergence of the politics of trauma against the scene of liberal-patriotic disavowal has been a group of activists from within (mainly academic) legal studies who speak from feminist, gay and lesbian, anti-racist, and anti-exploitation movements. They take their different but generally painful experiences of social hierarchy in the U.S. to require a radical reconfiguration of legal scholarship around 'subjectivity of perspective,' refusing traditional liberal notions that locate the social optimism of law around relatively unimpeded individuality, privacy, property, and conventional values.[19]

In this sense, critical legal praxis opposes national sentimentality, which pursues collective cohesion by circulating a universalist currency of distress within a field presumed to be populated by abstract individuals. At the same time, if subaltern pain is not considered *universal* (the privileged do not experience it, do not live expecting that at any moment their ordinarily loose selves might be forcibly congealed into a single humiliated atom of subpersonhood), subaltern pain is deemed in this context universally *intelligible*, constituting objective evidence of trauma reparable by the law and the law's more privileged subjects. In other words, the universal value is here no longer a property of political personhood, but a property of a rhetoric that claims to represent not the universal but the true self marred by an unfair barring of itself from the universal.

In this political model of identity, trauma stands as truth. Take, for example, an original and impassioned work like Robin West's (1993) *Narrative, Authority, and Law*,[20] which sees as its task the production of moral criticism and transformation of the law from the point of view of a society's victims. West wields narratives throughout the book that reveal the law's fundamental immorality (and therefore its fundamentally immoralizing effect on the subjects who are educated to its standards) where women's lives are concerned, and her powerful feminist arguments for the need to deprivatize women's structurally induced pain testify to the radical changes in the law and other institutions of intimacy that would have to take place if women were to attain legitimacy as social subjects. But West assumes that women's pain is already available as knowledge. To think otherwise is to be either misogynist or guilty of shallow and over-academic postmodernism. Empathy is an ethical rule: 'We must be able to say, to quote my two-year-old, "don't do that – you're hurting me," and we must be able to hear that utterance as an ethical mandate to change course' (West 1993: 19–20).[21]

Not all radical legal theorists simplify pain so as to make the emblem of true wisdom about injustice and its eradication something as sentimental and fictive (to adults) as a child's consciousness: yet the desire for an unambiguous world in West's vision of justice's clarity is not all that idiosyncratic.[22] It is as though the child could build a just world from the knowledge s/he gleans from her hurt because ideology has not yet confused her. Would the child have what it takes to think beyond the immediacy of trauma, to make a context for it? It seems hard for this group of legal theorists to imagine the value of such a question, for a few reasons. One may be due to the centrality of 'pain and suffering' to tort law, which endorses a construction of the true subject as a feeling subject whose suffering disables a person's ability to live at her/his full capacities, as s/he has been doing, and thus requires reparations from the agents who wielded the force. New enumerations of this area are burgeoning – for example, feminist anti-pornography and anti-racist hate speech litigation borrow many arguments from its archive (see Finley 1989; also MacKinnon 1993; Matsuda *et al.* 1993; West 1993; Williams 1991, 1995). Their tactic is to challenge local purveyors of struc-tural violence in order to make racism and misogyny *less profitable*, even symbolically, and meanwhile to use the law to debanalize violence by making illegal that which has been ordinary practice, on the model, say, of sexual harass-ment law.

Kendall Thomas has made an even more extreme argument recently, using the Constitutional model of 'cruel and unusual punishment' to revoke legitima-tion from social relations of violence traditionally authorized by the state and the law (Thomas 1995: 277–293). His essay on privacy after *Bowers* takes up Elaine Scarry's model of torture as a vehicle for the legitimating fiction of state power, claiming that the Cruel and Unusual Punishment clause of the Eighth Amendment should be applied to state discrimination against gays and lesbians (Scarry 1985). The strength and clarity of his vision brings us to the second reason it seems hard for theorists who equate subjectivity in general with legal subjectivity to work beyond the rule of traumatic pain in imagining the condi-tions for progressive social change. Is the 'cruel and unusual punishment' tactic meant to be merely a reversal *in extremis* that points to the sublime banality of state cruelty, or is it a policy aspiration seeking a specific reparation for the specific violation/creation of gay and lesbian identities? Thomas's model only works if the agent of violence is the state or the law; it works only if the domain of law is deemed interchangeable with the entire field of injury and reparation; and if the subject of law is fully described by the taxonomies law recognizes. This position would look awkward if it were rephrased: subjects are always citi-zens. But the fact is that the notion of reparation for identity-based subordination assumes that the law describes what a person is, and that social violence can be located the way physical injury can be traced.

It is not only that lawyers see law as a mirror of the real. The desire to use trauma as the model for the pain of subordination that gets congealed into iden-tities suppresses the difference between trauma and adversity: trauma takes you out of your life shockingly, and places you into another one, whereas structural subordination is not a surprise to the subjects who experience it, and the pain of subordination *is* ordinary life. To say that the traumatized self is the true self is to say that a particular facet of subjective experience is where the truth of history lies: it is to suggest that the clarity of pain marks a political map for achieving the good life, if only we would read it. It is also to imply that in the good life there will be no pain.

Wendy Brown suggests that a replacement of traumatic identity ('I am') with a subjectivity organized by the agency of imagined demand ('I want') will take from pain the energy for social transformation beyond the field of its sensual experience (Brown 1995a: 220–221). For this to happen, however, *psychic pain experienced by subordinated populations must be treated as ideology*, not as prelapsarian knowledge or a condensed comprehensive social theory. It is more like a capital letter at the beginning of an old bad sentence that needs rewriting. To think otherwise is to assert that pain is merely banal, a story always already told. It is to think that the moment of its gestation is, indeed, life itself.

Coda: the personal is also impersonal

Too often, and almost always in the work of legal radicals, the nation-form remains sanctified as a political 'zone of privacy' in *Griswold*'s sense: it holds out a promise that the law can relieve specific individuals of the pain of their speci-ficity, even as the very project of liberal nation-formation virtually requires the public exposure of those who do not structurally assimilate to the national norm (so, if population *x* is relieved of the obstacles to its full citizenship, a given popu-lation *y* will almost inevitably come to bear the burden of surrogacy that expresses citizenship's status as *privilege*). Fighting against these normative strate-gies in legal terms is crucial, a tactic of necessity. If it means telling half-truths (that an experience of painful identity shocks a minoritized subject) in order to change the norms attached to that kind of subject, it still must be a good thing. But thinking that the good life will be achieved when there is no more pain but only (your) happiness does nothing to alter the structures of sympathetic norma-tivity whose articulation with the diminished conditions for liberty in national life I have sketched out in this chapter. The reparation of pain does not bring into being a just life.

Usually this point is made in studies of testimony and the Holocaust, the unspeakable national violence which generates horrific evidence that will always fail to represent the brutal totality of its referent, and which can never be repaired, remunerated (see Felman and Laub 1992; Lyotard 1988). The situa-tions (heterosexual couplehood, marriage, sex acts and reproduction) addressed in this chapter, in contrast, are ever so common, cruel but not unusual, an ordi-nary part of everyday citizenship for subordinate populations in the United States. Such a difference advises replacing the model of trauma I have been describing critically as inadequate material for world- or nation-building with a model, say, of *suffering*, whose etymological articulation of pain and patience draws its subject less as an effect of an act of violence, and more as an effect of a general atmosphere of it. Thus the question of suffering's *differend* might be drawn differently without resulting in the analytic diffusion of any population's subordination into a fuzzy equivalence with that of any other. (But even 'suffering' can sound too dramatic: imagine a word that describes a constantly destabilized existence that monitors, with a roving third eye, every moment as a potentially bad event in which a stereotyped someone might become food for someone else's hunger for superiority, and connect that to a term that considers the subjective effects of structural inequalities that are deemed inevitable under national and transnational conditions. 'Suffering' stands in for that compound word.)

The binary trauma/reparation would not satisfy the conditions of genuine hardship that women in the U.S. endure. Their issues are not as (dis)located in time as trauma is, because these issues are a part of what they are taught to aspire to and value: a world where they are responsible for sustaining all kinds of intimacy and sexual desire; where they are made radiant by having more symbolic than social value; where their much commented-upon agitation at the proximity of intimacy and ambivalence is considered evidence of triviality, greed and/or lack of self-knowledge. This case reminds us that the heavily symbolized are always supposed to take whatever value is accorded them and find a way of being within it; and to spin negative value into the gold of an always deferred future, meanwhile coping, if they can, in the everyday.

Sentimental culture takes its strength from this configuration of contradictions and, in this case, by framing normative femininity and reproduction as the hard-wired work of expressive femaleness, gender praxis becomes established as a ground of solidarity. But because this labor is so mixed up with intimacy, and therefore with the grounds of heterofeminine optimism, political responses threaten the very domain of pleasure that has come to represent fantasies of the good life: contemporary capitalism makes a bargain with 'the personal,' after all, which is that people can have dignity in its domains only insofar as they comply with the inevitability of insecurity in the capitalist world and take on as their own image of agency snatching what they can of assurance, insurance, amelioration. The liberal—radical solution to such positioning has recently been to deploy an ethics of storytelling about trauma against the normative world of the law, to change the conditions of what counts as reliable evidence and argument, and thereby to make something concrete happen in response, something that pays for the past that is ongoing. But the *particularity* of suffering, its overdetermined historicity, suggests the limitation of this trend in witnessing, with all of its presumptions that pain is the only knowledge there is, more eloquent than and superior to the law.

It is in this sense that trauma transcodes heterosexuality in the genealogy of taken-for-granted 'universal' norms that hinge the political with the fantasy of spaces beyond politics in the U.S. political imaginary. As Jacques Derrida has recently argued, the dialectic between situated expression that challenges universalist norms and the categorical universalism of law itself constitutes an incommensurateness already within the law that cannot be overcome by law (Derrida 1992: 61–63). This is why the reparative use of the law on behalf of subordinated identities is sentimental. The subject of sentiment is the 'I' who suffers in a way that seems to surmount these differences (see Zizek 1994: 17).

Political optimism requires a future, any future that might not be more drowning in the present. More than anything, this is the lure of the sentimental contract, the mechanism by which consent is secured to a variety of long term subordinations. But the cost of the contract is the muffling of an analytically powerful and political rage, an equivocation of demand and radical critique, and a concession to short-term coalition building of a politics of the long haul. To interfere with the contract leads to the humiliation by charges of 'irrelevance' to policy and to 'common sense' in an era of transnational capitalist triumphalism, class-bound racism, and sentimental misogyny. Meanwhile, the real is located in the seeming rationality of diminished expectations. This is why it is imperative to place at risk the sense of belonging that national sentimentality promises – not because the bonds of sympathy that secure the ideal nation-state are false or socially harmful, but because they so frequently make ethical a refusal to counter the customary and structural violences of social life, which are deemed somehow extraneous in the face of pain's claims. The everyday of citizenship is a ground that must be fought for: but the struggle must be expanded to include non-sensual experience and knowledge as a part of any 'personal' story, aspects of experience one does not encounter concretely, but which shape one's conditions of possibility nonetheless.

This is what was meant by 'the personal is the political,' a sentence virtually impossible to understand at the present moment. It did not mean that there is only the personal, only a zone of intimate politics, and no such thing as the political. It meant to say that the feelings we acknowledge having are unreliable measures of justice and fairness, not the most reliable ones; and that linked critical vocabularies of pleasure, recognition *and* equity must be developed and debated. I would add to this that the everyday of struggle is a ground on which unpredicted change can be lived and mapped – but the new maps will not reveal a world without struggle, or a world that looks like the opposite of the presently painful one.

Notes

1 *Planned Parenthood of Southeastern Pennsylvania v. Casey*, 112 Sup. Ct. 2791 (1992), at 2803.
2 On rights talk and normativity generally see Sarat and Kearns (1995).
3 Throughout her career Catharine MacKinnon has expressed the standard and, for its time, persuasive feminist critique of privacy law, which deems it a tool of patriarchal supremacy: but her arguments – which purport to be about 'women' and 'men,' but which to my ear are more profoundly about heterosexuality – derive from Court practice through the late 1980s, and do not consider the work jurists like O'Connor have done to deprivatize privacy. See, for example, MacKinnon (1993).
4 Justice Hugo Black, concurring, *Griswold v. Connecticut* 381 U.S. 479 (1965), at 509.
5 Justice William O. Douglas, Opinion of the Court, *Griswold v. Connecticut*, at 480.
6 *Ibid.*
7 Justice Arthur Goldberg, concurring, *Griswold v. Connecticut*, at 499.
8 On zoning and its relation to the production of normative sexuality see Berlant and Warner (1998).
9 Douglas writes:

> Various guarantees create zones of privacy. The right of association contained in the penumbra of the First Amendment is one, as we have seen. The Third Amendment in its prohibition against the quartering of soldiers 'in any house' in time of peace without the consent of the owner is another facet of that privacy. The Fourth Amendment explicitly affirms the 'right of the people to be secure in their persons, houses, papers, and effects, against unreasonable searches and seizures.' The Fifth Amendment in its Self-Incrimination Clause enables the citizen to create a zone of privacy which government may not force him to surrender to his detriment. The Ninth Amendment provides: 'The enumeration

in the Constitution, of certain rights, shall not be construed to deny or disparage others retained by the people.'

(*Griswold v. Connecticut*, at 484)

Justice Goldberg's concurring opinion, which focuses on the Founders' relation to unenumerated rights, adds the Due Process clause of the Fourteenth Amendment to this Constitutional congeries (*ibid.*, at 488).

10 Justice William O. Douglas, Opinion of the Court, *Griswold v. Connecticut*, at 485, 486.

11 *Ibid.*, at 517, fn. 10.

12 *Ibid.*

13 Justice Scalia, dissent, *Planned Parenthood v. Casey*, 112 Sup. Ct. 2791 (1992), at 2876–2877.

14 *Ibid.* Scalia also blasts Justice Blackmun (fn. 2, at 2876) for using a constitutionally meaningless rhetoric of intimacy.

15 A passionate and artful argument about what cases constitute precedent for *Roe* takes place between Justices O'Connor, Kennedy, Souter (*ibid.*, at 2808–2816), and Scalia, at 2860–2867.

16 Justices Sandra Day O'Connor, Anthony M. Kennedy, David H. Souter, Opinion of the Court, *Planned Parenthood v. Casey*, at 2807.

17 *Ibid.*, at 2906.

18 *Ibid.*, at 2827.

19 Critical legal studies, critical race theory, radical feminist legal theory, and an emergent body of work in gay and lesbian culture, power, and the law, encompasses a huge bibliography. Rather than dump a stupidly big omnibus footnote here, let me metonymically signal the archive via a few recent helpful anthologies or extended works: Becker, Bowman and Torrey (1994); Crenshaw *et al.* (1995); Danielsen and Engle (1995); Delgado (1995); Duggan and Hunter (1995); Matsuda *et al.* (1993: 1–15); Smith (1993); West (1993); Williams (1991, 1995).

20 See note 19.

21 Much the same kind of respect and critique can be given to MacKinnon's promotion of juridical reparation on behalf of women's pain under patriarchy. In her work, the inner little girl of every woman stands as the true abused self who is denied full citizenship in the United States. For a more elaborate analysis of the little-girl form in the anti-pornography movement's struggle over women's citizenship, see Berlant (1997: 55–81).

22 Another instance in which a generic child's non-ideological relation to justice is held as the proper index of adult aspiration is to be found in Williams (1991). This work represents the multiple contexts in which (Williams') legal subjectivity inherits, inhabits, and reproduces the law's most insidious violence: the text's syncretic modes of storytelling about these conjunctures leave open some questions about the relation between what she depicts as the madness of inhabiting legal contradictions/allegories of the self in everyday life, and certain scenes of clarity in which children know the true scale of justice and the true measure of pain (in contrast to adults, with their brains twisted by liberal ideologies of property and contract – pp. 12, 27, for example). Perhaps she uses this index because 'Contract law reduces life to fairy tale' (224).

References

Becker, M., Bowman, C.G. and Torrey, M. (1994) *Cases and Materials on Feminist Jurisprudence: Taking Women Seriously*, St Paul, Minn.: West Publishing.

Berlant, L. (1997) *The Queen of America Goes to Washington City: Essays on Sex and Citizenship*, Durham, N.C.: Duke University Press.

Berlant, L. and Warner, M. (1998) 'Sex in Public' *Critical Inquiry* 24 (Winter): 547–566.

Brown, W. (1995a) 'Wounded Attachments: Late Modern Oppositional Political Formations,' in J. Rajchman (ed.) *The Identity in Question*, New York: Routledge.
—— (1995b) 'Rights and Identity in Late Modernity: Revisiting the "Jewish Question"',
   in Sarat, A. and Kearns, T.R. (eds) *Identities, Politics, and Rights*, Ann Arbor: University
   of Michigan Press.
Crenshaw, K., Gotanda, N., Peller, G. and Thomas, K. (1995) *Critical Race Theory: The Key
   Writings that Formed the Movement*, New York: New Press.
Danielsen D. and Engle, K. (eds) (1995) *After Identity: A Reader in Law and Culture*, New York:
   Routledge.
Delgado, R. (1995) *Critical Race Theory: The Cutting Edge*, Philadelphia, P.A.: Temple
   University Press.
Derrida, J. (1992) 'Force of Law: The "Mystical Foundations of Authority"', in D. Cornell,
   M. Rosenfeld and D. Grey Carlson (eds) *Deconstruction and the Possibility of Justice*, New
   York: Routledge.
Duggan L. and Hunter, N.D. (1995) *Sex Wars: Sexual Dissent and Political Culture*, New York:
   Routledge.
Felman, S. and Laub, D. (1992) *Testimony: Crises of Witnessing in Literature, Psychoanalysis, and
   History*, New York: Routledge.
Finley, L.M. (1989) 'A Break in the Silence: Including Women's Issues in a Torts Course,'
   Yale Journal of Law and Feminism 1: 41–73.
Guitton, S. and Irons, P. (eds) (1995) *May It Please the Court: Arguments on Abortion*, New York:
   New Press.
Lyotard, J.-F. (1988) *The Differend: Phrases in Dispute*, Minneapolis: University of Minnesota
   Press.
MacKinnon, C. (1993) 'Reflections on Law in the Everyday Life of Women,' in A. Sarat
   and T.R. Kearns (eds) *Law in Everyday Life*, Ann Arbor: University of Michigan Press.
Matsuda, M.J., Lawrence III, C.L., Delgado, R. and Crenshaw, K.W. (1993),*Words That
   Wound: Critical Race Theory, Assaultive Speech, and the First Amendment*, Boulder, Colo.: West-
   view Press.
Sarat, A. and Kearns, T.R. (eds) (1995) *Identities, Politics, and Rights*, Ann Arbor: University
   of Michigan Press.
Scarry, E. (1985) *The Body in Pain: The Making and Unmaking of the World*, New York: Oxford
   University Press.
Smith, P. (ed.) (1993) *Feminist Jurisprudence*, New York: Oxford University Press.
Thomas, K. (1995) 'A Compulsion to Privacy,' in D. Danielsen and K. Engle (eds) *After
   Identity: A Reader in Law and Culture*, New York: Routledge.
West, R. (1993) *Narrative, Authority, and Law*, Ann Arbor: University of Michigan Press.
Williams, P.J. (1991) *The Alchemy of Race and Rights*, Cambridge, Mass.: Harvard University
   Press.
—— (1995) *The Rooster's Egg*, Cambridge, Mass.: Harvard University Press.
Zizek, S (1994) 'The Spectre of Ideology,' in S. Zizek (ed.) *Mapping Ideology*, New York:
   Routledge.

2 Shaming theory, thinking dis-connections

Feminism and Reconciliation[1]

Elspeth Probyn

Of late I seemed to have misplaced an assurance about the self-evident nature of feminism's connection to political and social injustice. This is probably due to a range of factors, but the splintering of feminism and the nature of the insiderist arguments about its direction are undoubtedly germane. To generalise, this has produced a welter of books and articles aimed at criticising and redressing feminism's direction, and a climate akin to Stuart Hall's description of current postcolonial theory: 'a certain nostalgia run[ning] through some of these arguments for a return to a clear-cut politics of binary oppositions ... between goodies and baddies' (1996: 243). As feminism becomes consolidated in university departments of women's studies, or gender studies, increasingly those of us located within these institutions are called upon as professional feminists or queers, presumed to be qualified as commentators on a wide range of questions. In turn, this raises the vexing question of what it means to reply 'as a feminist'. Of course, the problem of who speaks for whom, and the injunction not to represent all women in the name of an implicitly white feminism, has now been on the agenda for quite some time. But it may also be that 'responses' to this challenge have produced hesitancy, timidity and sometimes solipsism as individuals learn only to speak in their own name. There is also the question of what constitutes something that needs to be responded to. The speed with which 'local' events are now broadcast worldwide has been amply commented on in the name of postmodernist celebration or nihilism. There is then an overwhelming array of events to which one could respond.

If my topic here is the question of how to make feminist theory meet up with the present, it is obviously connected with the issue of how feminists respond to events. My use of 'event' needs some clarification. There is of course the straightforward sense of an event as something noteworthy. But even this common-sense understanding raises questions about what, and to whom, an event might be constituted as important. In turn, this catches at the more elaborate sense that Gilles Deleuze gives to events as a mode of designating the relations of past, present and future. We might say that he thus rescues 'event' from being thought of as monumental, of history as composed of a narration that connects cairn-like structures of the past. In his discussion of a rhizomatic analytics, Deleuze describes 'lived events' as multiplicities of 'historical determinations, concepts, individuals, groups, social formations', all of which coexist 'on a single page, the same sheet' (1993: 32). 'Event' in this way therefore compels us to think about the conjugation of forces: individuals, concepts and theories that at any time enfold the past within the present, constraining or enabling action.

While there is a long history behind the term, I want to think about Reconciliation as an event in order to capture how it was mobilised in 1997. 'Reconciliation' is an initiative first raised by the Hawke Labor government in Australia and actively continued by Paul Keating only to be considerably stonewalled by the present Prime Minister, John Howard, and his Coalition government. Perhaps most crucially, analysing Reconciliation as event breaks with the idea that there would be/can be an inevitable progress in terms of racialised relations between white and black Australians: that the injuries to Aboriginals were part of a 'history' that we were all finished with. With the election of a conservative government, it became clear that such a teleology was not possible. Moreover, as an event, the reappearance of Reconciliation profoundly disturbed the past and present, as well as the identity of actors involved. Indeed, the reproduction of Reconciliation as an event reminds us that all individuals are actors within the interplay of history, racism, concepts and ideas. It also enjoins ideas, theories and bodies in quite visceral ways: for instance, my own individual paralysis was fed by a feeling that the theories that I deal in were not up to the occasion. The question of 'how to respond' was fused at the level of the individual. What could I as a feminist do? What could I as a new Australian possibly say in regard to the question of racism and resentment that was shaking the 'tolerant' and 'lucky' country? As many may know from experience, such questions are guaranteed to make the self and others squirm – at best they evince defeatism, at worst, a paranoid delusion of individual control in the face of systemic inequities.

Thankfully I was jolted out of this morass by attending the Australian Reconciliation Convention. This was a gathering of thousands of white and black Australians held in late May 1997 in Melbourne, in order to set the grounds for further local and national action in terms of furthering Reconciliation. As an important drawing in of the past, its timing coincided with the thirtieth anniversary of the referendum that was to 'bring about basic human rights for Australia's indigenous peoples' (*Convention Program*). Organised by the Aboriginal Reconciliation Council headed by Patrick Dodson, this was an event in commonsensical terms. But beyond being merely noteworthy, it also rearranged assumptions about the past and about what was possible in the present. As part of a wider process, the Reconciliation Convention was a nodal point that brought together nearly two thousand whites and blacks, leaders and ordinary individuals. From the space of many painful and some proud memories, the Convention was to galvanise the delegates and the rest of Australia into further and future action. It took place, however, at a time when the Australian nation was, as it continues to be, fractured by competing accounts of the past and where there was little political vision of the future.[2] It marked the present as a moment of vastly diverging lines. A moment of conflict when a previously unspeakable level of racism is tolerated and fanned by the inaction of the government, when many of the achievements of reconciliation are being ripped apart as the government moves to close down the legal openings and the affective optimism in regard to Aboriginal land rights brought about by the Mabo and Wik rulings.[3] In brief, these rulings finally recognised native entitlement to land based on indigenous inhabitation of country before white invasion. The Convention also coincided with the completion of *Bringing Them Home* (1997), the report of the National Inquiry into the Separation of Aboriginal and Torres Strait Islander Children from Their Families. This inquiry took evidence from 535 Indigenous people about their experiences of the government policies that forcibly removed thousands of indigenous children from their families. Commonly called the Stolen Generations, in the careful words of the inquiry, the laws, practices and policies that continued into the 1970s were dedicated to the removal and the genocidal eradication of the indigenous people of Australia. The Stolen Generations is part of and now most spectacularly represents a long history of both governmental policy and white academic actions (especially on the part of anthropology) that the noted Aboriginal scholar Marcia Langton has summed as: 'imagine an Australia in which no "full-bloods" survived because they [anthropologists] observed the "miscegenation" on the last frontiers and projected its effects into the future' (1993: 198).

More than anything, the forced removal of children who then suffered emotional, economic, physical and sexual abuse by their white 'guardians' has complicated white Australians' relation to the past. This past is structured by the founding colonial and legal myth of *terra nullius*, the conceit of an empty land awaiting the explorer. There is a specific structure of knowledge and ignorance that is the uninhabited ground, the *terra nullius*, of racism and with which reconciliation for whites must first and foremost contend. In speaking about reconciliation I am addressing the singularity of the Australian situation although there may be links to other sites. For instance, the phenomenon of nations apologising is emerging elsewhere: the Canadian government to the peoples of the First Nations, Japan to the 'comfort women', the UK to the Irish about the famine, maybe even the US to its African-American citizens for slavery, and, of course, the vital processes ongoing in South Africa. While these events are inspiring, I will dwell here on the specificities of Australian Reconciliation, both because Australia is where I now live and because I think that generalised models wreak considerable epistemological and political damage. If I argue strongly that feminist engagements must be specific, I would also state that my immigration to Australia entails a responsibility to engage with the structures of white privilege that enabled my relatively easy move.

In simplistic terms, and enabled by the particular spatial myth of the empty land, Australian history could be told as a straight line leading from point zero through to civilisation. But as the evidence accumulates about the shameful nature of the past, the only ones to have a clear line are those who subscribe to a denial of what Prime Minister Howard calls 'the black arm band' version of history. This infamous phrase of Howard's was directed at any critical rethinking of white Australia's past. While the relationship of those in the present to past actions is a complicated one, as Carlos Ginzburg succinctly puts it, if none of our actions can alter the past, we must remember that, 'human actions can deeply affect the *memory* of the past by distorting its traces, by putting them into oblivion, by utterly destroying them' (1994: 118). A recent editorial cartoon in the *Sydney Morning Herald* by Leunig succinctly summarises what happens when the traces of history are destroyed. In an eerily deserted landscape that recalls the image of *terra nullius*, he has depicted the Independent MP Pauline Hanson's racist party, 'One Nation', as an empty ark being filled with bundles of different affects: fear, anger, impotence, paranoia, resentment, in short all the affective baggage of *ressentiment*.[4]

If, as Anne McClintock has argued (1992), the linearity of the concept of post-colonialism is a liability in theoretical terms, in real terms it is also far from straightforward as the present twists hopes for the future. In the Deleuzian sense of the present as event, it 'is what gives a new and unexpected direction to a continuous line' (Boundas 1997: 24). While we may 'know' the past, and project knowledge onto the future, in important ways we cannot know the present. For Deleuze, events 'deterritorialize the present and point towards a different future' (Patton 1996: 14). The question of direction also poses formidable challenges to critical thought. This is a moment when the present rises up, taps you on the shoulder, and says, 'well, what can your theories make of this?' In response to the present, I want to consider a feminist and queer engagement with Reconciliation and the expressions of shame that have heralded its public reception amongst many whites. I do so because, while the exigency of Reconciliation is clear, the links between feminists, queers and Reconciliation may be somewhat hazy even given good intentions on the part of individuals. One of the many lessons I learned at the Reconciliation Convention is that the near-automatic response on the part of feminists to analyse the gender- and sex-related elements of any social situation may need to be reconsidered. Or at least, the type of reaction on the part of some feminists to critique 'patriarchal' relations, or that of some gays and lesbians to focus on the lack of queer visibility, in this context seems rather small minded. Another thing I learned was that white theorists will need to put aside the type of ego attachment that comes with developing 'clever' solutions to present problems. The fact that there is no one solution to Reconciliation, that the present is ongoing, meets up with Stuart Hall's argument that being 'driven by a Promethean desire for the theoretically correct position – a desire to out-theorise everyone else' is not only wrong headed politically and morally, but is also bad theory (1996: 249). If, that is, we want our theories to be up to the demands of the present.

Taking from Wendy Brown's question of whether we can 'develop a feminist politics without *ressentiment*? ... Could we learn to contest domination with the strength of an alternative vision of collective life, rather than through moral reproach?' (1995: 47), I want to map some of the elements that might inform this engagement with Reconciliation. While, as I stated at the outset, the present produces a sense that one must *do something* as opposed to *doing theory*, I emphasise that this is a response from the point of contemporary theory. Yet I hope to show that yoking theory to Reconciliation is not to get me off the hook, rather it is to sink the hook deeply within my thinking.

Against a tendency to generalise about feminism, I should specify that my point of departure is a theoretical position at the intersection of feminism and queer. This intersection has been dominated by attention to the body and to sexual practices, and arguments about the performative aspect of all identity categories. These are theories that are informed by queer experiences, and I want to build on and question the particular queer relation to shame. I want to wager that theories of bodily affect – including foremost that of shame – may be of some use as whites of the Australian nation respond in emotional terms to the fact that they/we have to come to terms with the full historical and present reality of sharing the land with its original custodians.

Elsewhere, and along with others, I have argued that as theorists we are imbricated in what we seek to study. In trying to reroute a tendency towards a solipsist attention to the self, I have also argued that 'the body' or 'desire' are not ends in themselves but rather should be put to work as hyphens connecting practices and ideas (Probyn 1996). The model I took was informed by the work of Foucault and Deleuze, in particular their argument about the relation between theoretical work and politics, figured in the image of a relay race: 'Practice is an ensemble of relays from one theoretical point to another, and theory, a relay between one practice and another' (Foucault 1977: 206). This prefigures yet coincides with the arguments of several feminists who critically integrate the relations of race and gender. In many ways what people like Vron Ware (1996) and Catherine Hall (1996) and others are attempting is a lot tougher than what Foucault and Deleuze were doing in that 1972 interview. For a start, Foucault and Deleuze did not overtly, at least, deal with the concept of difference and the facts of ethnic and sexual inequalities. Nor did they have to contend with the ways in which, as Ware says, 'in recent years the concept of difference [has been] used almost ritualistically to evoke discourses of "race" (and sometimes gender)'. As she puts it, this evocation often occludes actual discussion of racism, and she suggests that 'examination of the way whiteness ("race") intersects with gender and sexuality can shift what can sometimes amount to an obsession with difference toward the less fashionable concept of radical connectedness' (1996: 144–145). In a similar move, Hall critiques white feminist historians for being slow to respond to the black feminist critique which has insisted on the interconnections between the power relations of 'race' and gender' and calls for a model of analysis that can grasp 'the raced and gendered ways in which inter-connections and inter-dependencies have been played out' (1996: 70, 76).

Whilst I am in full agreement with the substance of these critiques, I believe that we need to pay attention to the dis-connections as well as to the connections; or rather that thinking in terms of connection requires consideration of conceptual and material limits that serve as moments of disconnection. In general terms, this necessitates uncoupling feminist and queer theories from gender, the body and sexuality as their privileged objects of study. This is to move away from forms of analysis directed at 'the body' or at 'sexuality', towards those that, while they may be moved by the body and sexual desire, end up at different places. For me, this follows from Deleuze's comment that 'as soon as a theory is enmeshed in a particular point, we realise that it will never possess the slightest practical importance unless it can erupt in a totally different area' (Foucault 1980: 208.). In simple terms, the challenge I take from this is one of redirecting queer and feminist theories so that they erupt within the arena of reconciliation. This is not the disparate application of queer; rather it implies a reconfiguration of the field in which the arguments emerge or erupt – like a potato plant rhizomatically breaking up the ground in which it finds itself. This cannot be some sort of superficial queering predicated on insiderist know-ingness; it means confronting deep ignorance about what reconciliation can be, ignorance of the grounds that may allow for eventual connection and coexis-tence between black and white. Reconciliation is therefore placed at that intersection of ignorance and knowingness that has marked white relations with the indigenous people, laid onto a map of national identity that for much of its official 209 years of occupation was based on an abyss of ignorance: the empty land waiting to be filled with white knowledge, the 'knowingness' on the part of whites about Aboriginal people and culture fuelled by ignorance, the emergent 'clever country'. The point is, as Eve Sedgwick argues, 'to pluralize and specify' that ignorance: to acknowledge a 'plethora of ignorances, and ... begin to ask questions about the labor, erotics, and economics of their human production and distribution' (1993: 25).

At another level, this also means derailing the feminist impulse to connect up 'ritualistically' or automatically the questions of race, gender, sexuality, class, etc. Perhaps ironically, the move to reconciliation must first contend with the recon-naissance (which in the French connotes a grateful recognition) of difference and singularity: the pause of silence heard in *dis-connection*. This entails an argument against the types of connections that routinely and automatically link together quite disparate groups on the basis of what we think we know in the name of Otherness. This is to think about connections and dis-connections made without a ground of *ressentiment*, without the positing of a knowing ground of common suffering, exclusion and oppression.

A sense of that temptation to connect queers and indigenous people can be heard in a poem by Paula Gunn Allen called 'Some like Indians Endure' (1988), parts of which I will now quote.

    i have it in mind that
    dykes are indians
    ...
    indian is an idea
    some people have
    of themselves

dyke is an idea some women
have of themselves
the place where we live now
is idea
because whiteman took
all the rest
...
so dykes
are like indians
because everyone is related
to everyone
in pain
in terror
in guilt
in blood
in shame
in disappearance
that never quite manages
to be disappeared
we never go away
even if we're always
leaving

(1988: 9–13)

In the face of the shame, guilt and remorse that white lesbians may individually feel in regard to the treatment of the indigenous people of Australia as well as those of the Americas and elsewhere, this poem allows for a sense of connection and 'knowingness' that I want to argue is premature. That is, and with the crucial caveat, if it is a white dyke reading and listening to it. That Paula Gunn Allen, a Laguna Pueblo/Sioux and a professor of Native American studies, proffers this connection between Indians and dykes is one thing, and is a testimony to her intellectual and political generosity. It would, however, be a travesty of that generosity if white queers were to take advantage of it to celebrate connections instead of responding to it as a challenge to build and interrogate the grounds for possible connections. Against the plundering of knowledge that takes place under the rubric of cultural appropriation displayed in both commercial ventures but also in a type of white feminist lesbian assimilation of a generalised indigenous spirituality in the name of 'the goddess', Reconciliation must be for whites a challenge to *learn*, and not to *know*. It will be the site of connection only when whites have fully realised the extent of the violent historical and material limits that render impossible any easy cohabitation under the label of 'Other'. At the present moment, shame marks that impossibility.

All this is a rather long lead in to the image of shame that motivates this chapter. As most of the indigenous Australians and some of the whites stood courageously and honourably with their backs to Howard at the Reconciliation

Convention in Melbourne,[5] I sat with my head in my hands in shame. Whilst my shame was in part caused by the spectacle of the white politicians at the Convention, it was also informed by the immediacy of my ignorance, at being unable to place historic figures, incapable of pronouncing Aboriginal names and nations. I was also ashamed at the jabs of knowledge that intruded, imported into this situation: questions like whether there was room for me as a recent white migrant, for those who identify neither as black nor white; I wondered whether a 'People's Movement' based on the civil rights models of the 1960s was possible in these postmodern times. In turn, these questions caused my ears to burn, ashamed at the pettiness.

In the subsequent coverage in the predominantly white press, shame is every-where. Pronouncements of shame on the part of 'ordinary Australians' can be heard in letters to the editor, call-in shows, and literally on the street, as well as from extraordinary ones like the 'lipstick queen', Poppy King, who would not now accept her 1995 Australian of the Year award because she is 'ashamed to say today that I am Australian' (*Courier Mail* 28 June 1997), and the ex-pat Germaine Greer who told an audience in London that 'she would not return to Australia until Aboriginal sovereignty was recognised' (which to many in Australia came as a bit of a relief) (*Sun Herald* 8 June 1997). While it may be heartening that shame seems to be displacing guilt, nonetheless this shame seems to mark the uneasiness of the shifting line between ignorance and knowledge. We experience shame at now knowing the past atrocities, shame at the carefully constructed and preserved edifice of ignorance. Or is it shame at the 'open secret' of Australia's past? At being caught out? Is it the blurring of inside/outside, public/private as this 'new' knowledge based in ignorance is screened in the international scene, prompting the Minster of Aboriginal Affairs, John Herron, to squirm: 'I hate Australians going overseas and dumping on our country' (*Sun-Herald* 8 June 1997).

If this has all the markings of a painful coming-out scene as interlocutors stammer and blush at the telling of the 'open secret', it also marks the difficulty that many white Australians have in coming to terms with the gap between knowledge and ignorance. This often plays out in rather tortuous attempts to find the right analogy. In response to the report on the Stolen Generations even respected writers like Bob Ellis twist and turn trying to find ways to link up white and black realities which are posed as worlds apart. With analogies to the lynch-ings in the American South of the 1930s, to white 'victims of pederastic abuse', and to 'losing a pet dog and never seeing it again', Ellis tries to get his readership to *imagine* the wrongs done to Aboriginals. He ends his column with these lines: 'And I am, today, ashamed to be Australian. How about you?' (*Sydney Morning Herald* 30 May 1997).

While the reasons for shame are clear, and the reports in the media on the Stolen Generations have been crucial in lifting Howard's gag-order on the past, it is still unclear what confessions of shame are going to produce in the present. Like the shame engendered in straights confronted by the gayness of an acquain-tance, the structure here is of oscillation between knowing and ignorance: a type of 'you're kidding?/well I knew all along'. Between knowing and ignorance, what I am afraid of is that we are seeing a generalised model of shame emerging, that the shame of *now* knowing precludes investigation of wide areas of ignorance that remain. As we might attest, being ashamed is painful, and an easy way out is to disengage from the affect, to distance oneself from the object of shame, to fall back on established knowledge now shifted to another site. In this case, one way out of the present shameful conundrum is to construct Reconciliation as about two massive and knowable blocks: whites and blacks, and worse, that the whites are doing something for blacks. Here shame either obscures relations of power, or as a free-floating sentiment can all too easily dissipate the presumably sincere feelings of its speakers.

But what exactly is shame? A dictionary defines it as: distress or humiliation caused by consciousness of one's guilt, dishonour or folly; the capacity for feeling this; the state of disgrace or discredit. It is interesting to note that the train of thought here maps out what may be happening to shame within the Australian public sphere. Thus following the particular events of the Reconciliation Convention and the report on the Stolen Generations, what we have are statements attesting to distress, and/or to the feelings of distress caused by distress at the knowledge of horrific actions. Performances of this were exemplified in the display of emotion in Parliament by the Leader of the Opposition, Kim Beasley, when he spoke about the report on the Stolen Generations, and in the subsequent reactions to it, many of which intimated that Beasley should be ashamed of his demonstration of shame. Beasley is a large man ('big Kim'), prompting one letter writer to the *Sydney Morning Herald* to state, 'That a man of his proportions could stand there and choke on his words was appalling' (4 June 1997), to which another replied more in anger at the 'fat-ist' nature of the remark than at the issue of the Stolen Generations.

If this type of exchange shows up some of the unproductive connections inaugurated by shame, it also displays the dynamics of knowing and ignorance. Faced with shame, the choice is made to ignore the import of its cause in favour of a knowing attack on Beasley's person. As the work of Silvan Tomkins (1995) on affect and shame makes clear, shame is a bodily affect, and moreover it is profoundly interpersonal, or produced within proximity to others. Tomkins defines shame as an 'affect of indignity, of defeat, of transgression, and of alienation' (1995: 133). These are all terms that attest to that feeling when one blunders in and across lines of demarcation, of knowledge, that blushing sense of being caught out on a lie. It is also crucial to note, as Jennifer Biddle (1997) does in her important article, that the cultural structure of shame varies widely, and that Tomkins is writing out of and about a white European attitude. For Tomkins shame is to be seen in the simple acts of hanging one's head, lowering one's eyes. These acts must take place within physical proximity to others: they are both an indication of interest foiled and at the limits of possible communication. While there must be a prior interest and knowledge of the person in order for shame to occur, shame is 'a specific inhibitor of continuing interest and enjoyment'. An example he uses is the moment when 'one started to smile but found one was smiling at a stranger' (1995: 134). And here we might think about that particular feeling of shame when you've misread signals of interest from a woman who turns out to be fatally straight. In fact, the increasingly popular performance of queer codes by those who would never actually have sex with the same sex is a rich area for the production of shame – again the specific modalities are played along lines of knowing (the codes) and ignorance and disavowal ('you didn't really think that I was?').

While Tomkins details a myriad of small acts that result in and from shame, what is more telling is his remark that any philosophy or psychology which does not 'confront the problem of human suffering is seriously incomplete', and that 'the nature of the experience of shame guarantees a perpetual sensitivity to any violation of the dignity of man' (1995: 136). The trick then is how to direct the intensity of shame towards constructing conditions for dignity. As Sedgwick writes, the 'psychological operations of shame, denial, projection around "ignorance" produce pulsations of wild energies' (1993: 25). With Adam Frank, she argues that shame can also open the way to rethinking the connections that are and are not possible amongst different people and groups. They hazard that 'perhaps … [shame] can be a switch point for the individuation of imaging systems, of consciousness, of bodies, of theories, of selves, an individuation that decides not necessarily an identity but a figuration, distinction, or mark of punctuation' (Sedgwick and Frank 1995: 22). Thinking about shame as a local and embodied expression whose meanings are many but are also always finite, limited by its specific manifestation, they argue, may enable 'a political vision of difference that might resist both binary homogenization and infinitizing trivialization' (15).

I want to end by returning to the event/present of Reconciliation. Against a model of ritualistic connection, one point of departure may be in rethinking shame in its differently inhabited, corporeal and historical manifestations. What white gays, lesbians, feminists and queers might bring to this project is precisely a detailed examination of how shame works at a bodily level to open and close lines of connection: shame as a switching point re-routing the dynamics of knowing and ignorance. Unlike empathy, shame does not permit any automatic sharing of commonality: it is that which poses deep limits to communication. Shame can be made to insist on the specific nature of the acts that caused it; it can be made to mark the awesome materiality of its own condition of possibility. It stakes out the moments of possible reconciliation without losing sight of the conditions which have produced their specific feeling and modality. The possibilities of connection are many, but they are also always circumscribed by the finite materiality that shame marks. And it is this marking that is constitutive of localised action, of reconciliation performed in local realities that brings the past into the present. Shame thus can be used to initiate what Sedgwick calls 'a fight not against originary ignorance, nor for originary ignorance, but against the killing pretence that a culture does not know what it does' (1993: 51).

To return briefly to the question of feminists responding to the present, in the image of the relay race, a queer and feminist theory and practice of Reconciliation is to be found in the marking out of the possible connections, as well as respect for the moments of dis-connection. Shame here marks the point when the lines of knowing and ignorance become scrambled and self-consciously entwined. Inspired by a philosophy of coexistence, this is to enrich the idea of a relay of ideas and practices, to see our actions and ideas as coexisting without colonising. It is, I think, of tantamount importance that those whites who have been and are bodily moved by the affect of shame now turn our attentions to the present. In such a way, it may be possible to redirect the flow of shame on the part of the Australian public before it becomes stagnant, strangled in guilt, or squashed by the baggage of *ressentiment* that Leunig depicts as boarding the grim ark of 'One Nation', marooned in an empty land. We need to remember that looking downwards is also a traditional Aboriginal sign of respect for the land.[6] The bodily gesture of shame expressed by whites in the hanging of the head may yet be retrained as an attitude of respect for the indigenous people of Australia, a starting point in Reconciliation.

Notes

1   This chapter constitutes a very initial response to a situation that is deeply historical, and more complex than I am able to adequately convey. For a history of white involvement in promoting progressive politics in regard to Aboriginal issues, see Reynolds (1998). I want to thank the students of the Department of Women's Studies who organised an initial Reconciliation meeting, and the members of the Koori Centre and the Indigenous Studies Unit at the University of Sydney for responding so generously. My thanks in particular to Wendy Brady and Janet Mooney, and to the organisers of the *Transformations* conference, for their comments on earlier drafts of this chapter, I thank Gretchen Poiner, Rosemary Pringle and the *Transformations* collective.

2   This is not to belittle the many efforts both theoretical and practical that are ongoing in rethinking the past, present and future of Australia. Aboriginal scholars and historians have been instrumental in forging new relations and conceptions of the past and the present (Goodall 1996). In terms of bringing history to the present, the collaboration of Marcia Langton and Henry Reynolds on the ABC television series *Frontier*, was crucial (see Reynolds 1996). In terms of responding to the present in more strictly academic terms, Australian philosophers have endeavoured to rework the reach of certain concepts. See, for instance, Paul Patton's (1997) use of Deleuze as a way of offering new lines of thinking in regard to the ramifications of the Mabo and Wik decisions. In terms of grass roots movements, the recently formed group Australians for Native Title is instrumental in bringing national and international attention to land rights, and in other areas, groups like the Anti Violence Project in conjunction with Aboriginal groups formulated a powerful anti-homophobia and violence campaign called 'Black + White + 'Pink'.

3   For a very interesting rethinking of what follows from the Mabo and Wik rulings, see the special issue of *Law, Text, Culture* entitled 'In the Wake of Terra Nullius' (1998).

4   Hanson was expelled from the Liberal party for her racist comments during the 1995 election campaign. She consequently won the seat of Ipswich in Queensland as an independent MP. She is a notable case of seething white *ressentiment* against the so-called advantages of a number of very different groups: Asians, Aboriginals, multinational corporations, and queers. This very diverse grouping both confirms and complicates Nancy Fraser's recent argument that an 'approach aimed at redressing injustices of distribution can end up creating injustices of recognition'

(1997: 25). For an interesting discussion about whether sexual discrimination can be seen in the same terms as racial or gendered injustice, see the exchange between Fraser and Judith Butler (Fraser1998; Butler 1998).

5   Within many Aboriginal communities this is a recognised sign of not wishing to continue the conversation; it is of course a visceral way of marking dis-connection with the speaker.

6   With thanks to Anthony McKnight's contribution to the Reconciliation meeting at the Koori Centre, which raised the central differences between white and Aboriginal physical attitudes to the land.

References

Aboriginal Reconciliation Council (1997) *Convention Program*, Melbourne.

Allen, P.G. (1988) 'Some Like Indians Endure', in W. Roscoe (ed.) *Living the Spirit: A Gay American Indian Anthology*, New York: St Martin's Press.

Biddle, J. (1997) 'Shame', *Australian Feminist Studies* 12, 26: 227–239.

Boundas, C. (1997) 'Deleuze on Time and Memory', *Antithesis* 2, 2:11–29.

Bringing Them Home (1997) Report of the National Inquiry into the Separation of Aboriginal and Torres Strait Islander Children from Their Families, Canberra: Human Rights and Equal Opportunity Commission, Commonwealth of Australia.

Brown, W. (1995) *States of Injury: Power and Freedom in Late Modernity*, Princeton, N.J.: Princeton University Press.

Butler, J. (1998) 'Merely Cultural', *New Left Review* 277: 33–44.

Deleuze, G. (1993) 'Rhizomes Versus Trees', in C. Boundas (ed.) *The Deleuze Reader*, New York: Columbia University Press.

Foucault, M. and Deleuze, G. (1980) 'Entretien: les intellectuels et le pouvoir', *L'Arc* 49: 3–10.

Foucault, M. (with G. Deleuze) (1997) 'Intellectuals and Power', in D.F. Bouchard (ed.) *Language, Counter-memory, Practice*, trans. D.F. Bouchard and S. Simon, Ithaca, N.Y.: Cornell University Press.

Fraser, N. (1997) *Justice Interruptus: Critical Reflections on the 'Postsocialist' Condition*, London and New York: Routledge.

—— (1998) 'Heterosexism, Misrecognition and Capitalism: A Response to Judith Butler', *New Left Review* 228: 140–150.

Ginzburg, C. (1994) 'Killing a Chinese Mandarin: The Moral Implications of Distance', *New Left Review* 208: 107–120.

Goodall, H. (1996) *Invasion to Embassy: Land in Aboriginal Politics in New South Wales, 1770–1972*, Sydney: Allen and Unwin, in association with Black Books.

Hall, C. (1996) 'Histories, Empires and the Post-Colonial Moment', in I. Chambers and L. Curti (eds) *The Post-Colonial Question: Common Skies, Divided Horizons*, New York and London: Routledge.

Hall, S. (1996) 'When Was "The Post-Colonial"? Thinking at the Limit', in I. Chambers and L. Curti (eds.) *The Post-Colonial Question: Common Skies, Divided Horizons*, New York and London: Routledge.

Langton, M. (1993) 'Rum, Seduction and Death: "Aboriginality" and Alcohol', *Oceania* 63: 195–206.

Law, Text, Culture (1998) 'In the Wake of Terra Nullius', 4, 1 (special issue).

McClintock, Anne. (1992) 'The Myth of Progress: Pitfalls of the Term Post-Colonialism', *Social Text* 31: 32.

Patton, P. (1996) 'Introduction', in P. Patton (ed.) *Deleuze: A Critical Reader*, Oxford: Blackwell.

—— (1997) 'Justice and Difference: The Mabo Case', in P. Patton and D. Austin-Brooks (eds) *Transformations in Australian Society*, University of Syndey: Research Institute for Humanities and Social Sciences Publications.

Probyn, E. (1996) *Outside Belongings*, New York and London: Routledge.

Reynolds, H. (1996) *Frontier: Aborigines, Settlers and Land*, Sydney: Allen and Unwin.

—— (1998) *This Whispering in Our Hearts*, Sydney: Allen and Unwin.

Sedgwick, E. Kosofsky (1993) *Tendencies*, Durham, N.C.: Duke University Press.

—— and Frank, A. (1995) 'Shame in the Cybernetic Fold: Reading Silvan Tomkins', in E. Sedgwick and A. Frank (eds) *Shame and Its Sisters: A Silvan Tomkins Reader*, Durham, N.C.: Duke University Press.

Tomkins, S. (1995) 'Shame–Humiliation and Contempt–Disgust', in E. Sedgwick and A. Frank (eds) *Shame and Its Sisters: A Silvan Tomkins Reader*, Durham, N.C.: Duke University Press.

Ware, V. (1996) 'Defining Forces: "Race", Gender and Memories of Empire' in I. Chambers and L. Curti (eds) *The Post-Colonial Question: Common Skies, Divided Horizons*, New York and London: Routledge.

3 Owned suffering

Thinking the feminist political imagination with Simone de Beauvoir and Richard Wright

Vikki Bell

In this chapter, I want to question how we understand the impulse to politics through an examination of the ways in which feminist argument is made, and made to 'work'. In particular, I want to explore the sense in which feminism, as a form of 'identity politics', might be a candidate for the accusation that its politics is fuelled by a form of *ressentiment*.[1] An attachment to a political identity as *the* driving force of political argument might be thought in terms of what Wendy Brown has called a 'wounded attachment'. Such an attachment, rather than enriching the political field, replays a form of class resentment that 'like all resentments ... retains the real or imagined holdings of its reviled subject as objects of desire' (1995: 60). *Ressentiment*, as Nietzsche (1967) understood it, relies upon a negative stance that only says 'no'; its only creative deed is to refuse. *Ressentiment* sets up a figure which rhetorically positions the speaker. That figure is a privileged figure – such as 'the bourgeois white man' – whose positionality is evoked as simultaneously coveted and despised. Moreover, the political vision becomes dominated by an image of suffering that relies upon a particular and *owned* suffering. There is a 'logics of pain' here which depends upon the evidencing of these particular sufferings that work to confer and confirm a politicised identity. Thus my question is: Does feminist argument work in this way, that is, by measuring the sufferings of women against a (necessarily imagined) figure who 'has' that which women are denied? I want to suggest that interrogating feminism as a mode of political argument cannot begin simply with a rejection of the notion of *ressentiment* – since such a rejection itself would be an affirmation of the question in hand; rather, an *argument* has to be advanced that feminism is not simply a politics fuelled by a sense of injustice and privation that is only and 'merely' reactive.

As an initial starting point, it is safe to say that there is, as a hallmark of identity politics, a rhetorical tendency to *ressentiment* as Brown suggests. However, there are times when such a reading of feminist texts cannot be sustained, especially now that, with the various recent rewritings of feminism's histories, there is a questioning of the assumption that feminism can be reduced to such a movement, one based on *ressentiment*. Recent feminist work enables a reconsideration of the political imagination of feminism, and these reflexive rewritings of feminism's histories address, *inter alia*, the sense in which 'feminism' emerges and speaks womanhood. In this chapter, I wish to draw attention to the crafting of the feminist political imagination through a consideration of the way the boundaries of feminism can become blurred, those moments in which feminism surrenders the privileged position accorded female suffering, making identifications that shift the subject of feminism outside the bounds of the particularity of that 'wounded attachment'. I do so in order to argue that, at these points, the notion that feminism is based on *ressentiment* becomes questionable, and different rhetorical and political possibilities emerge.

I set about this task of exploring the boundaries of feminist argumentation through a focus on a particular connection and alliance of Simone de Beauvoir's, possibly the most canonised of feminist writers. In particular, the chapter focuses on the relationship between elements of her work and one of her key contemporaries, the black American writer Richard Wright. The chapter reads the work of de Beauvoir and Wright intertextually with a view to understanding the rhetorical figures that operate within the political positions that are drawn there, and the manoeuvres and conflicts that arise through these figures.

The friendship between de Beauvoir and Wright is one that has rarely been commented upon. Yet, during her stay in the United States, de Beauvoir describes Wright as 'the only person I'm really fond of here, and whom I see with warm pleasure' (1991: 420). And she understood the time spent with the Wrights as a time establishing what she imagined as a quasi-familial relationship with them all (see de Beauvoir, 1991: 430). Wright showed her New York, especially the music scene in the city, took her to Harlem, and no doubt focused her on the question of 'race relations' in the United States. This was an interest that was also encouraged by her relationship with Nelson Algren, who had, according to de Beauvoir's biographer Deidre Bair, 'first suggested she conduct her study of women in the light of the experience of black Americans in a prejudicial society' (1990: 388). She wrote of Wright to Sartre:

> Wright – whom I've come to love with all my heart – came to fetch me and took me to the big Abyssinian church in Harlem, the biggest Gospel Church in the world. We heard the singing and the sermon, and saw how people reacted – they were middle class and pretty restrained, but very impassioned all the same.
>
> (1991: 426)[2]

Wright, for his part, was delighted to have the companionship of de Beauvoir on both sides of the Atlantic, and Ellen Wright became de Beauvoir's editor in Paris. Richard Wright had extended conversations with de Beauvoir and Sartre when he first visited Paris, frequently focusing on the concept of freedom and the responsibilities that thereby befell the individual (Gayle 1980: 201). These conversations clearly had a great impact on Wright's thinking. He wrote, for example:

Sartre is quite of my opinion regarding the possibility of human action today, that it is up to the individual to do what he can to uphold the concept of what it means to be human. The great danger, I told him, in the world today is the very feeling and conception of what is a human might well be lost. He agreed. I feel very close to Sartre and De Beauvoir.

(Journal entry, September 1947, quoted in Fabre 1985: 162)[3]

Clearly the main point of connection between these two writers is the broad sweep of existentialist thinking, with de Beauvoir's engagement and borrowings, and with Wright's less sustained, but sympathetic, forays into that philosophical and ethical realm of thought. My interest, however, is more in the shared political dynamic which is concerned with the theorising and politicising that follows once one has declared that the identity of 'object' is an achievement of the imagination.[4]

While neither writer pushed their explorations very far into the terrain of the other, there are suggestions enough that this project was not far from their thoughts. De Beauvoir is enraged when implored never to write about 'the Negro problem', whilst she was visiting the United States, enjoying as she did the jazz music and clubs, watching 'the marvellous Negro women dance', wandering in the cities and enjoying the racial mix (1991: 414). She tells Sartre that she had read a book by John Dollard (1937):

an excellent book, from which we absolutely must publish huge extracts in *T.M.* It's called *Class and Caste in the South*, by an American sociologist – and the method's as interesting as the content. It's a kind of counterpart to your *Portrait of the Anti-Semite* but on the Blacks – and also scholarly in character.

(1991: 431)

Thus, it appears that the issue of race and racism was a point of reflection for de Beauvoir, as was the position of women for Wright.

The misogyny of Wright's ouevre has been critiqued (see, for example, Decosta-Willis 1986). While I do not intend to defend Wright against the charges made by these critiques, I would suggest that there are more sympathetic readings of his characterisations (see, for example, Gilroy 1993, 1996). Considering the processes involved in writing *Native Son*, Wright suggests that the position of women arose as something that would require extended exploration:

With what I've learned in the writing of this book, with all its blemishes, imperfections, and with all its unrealized potentialities, I am launching out upon another novel, this time about *the status of women in American modern society*. This book, too, goes back to my childhood just as Biggar went, for, while I was storing away impressions of Biggar, I was storing away impressions of many other things that made me think and wonder.

(1987: 38)

This statement serves as evidence for shared, if unexplored, concerns, and alongside the friendship, allows one to hear certain resonances and to pursue certain lines of questioning that can be harnessed for the debate I wish to conduct here.[5]

Recently there has been a closer attention to de Beauvoir as a theoretical writer (see, in particular, Chanter 1995; Lundgren-Gothlin 1996; Moi 1994) drawing attention in particular to her classic work *The Second Sex* (1949) as an ambitious theory of gender development that is produced through an account that draws on a variety of theoretical and philosophical positions. There is, however, another strain to the influences that are registered in her text that are concerned with the issue of 'race', and it is to these that I want to turn in order to prise open the ways in which identity politics operates in de Beauvoir's theoretical writings.[6] As I have argued elsewhere (Bell 1995), there is a sense in which a dynamic between 'race' and gender operates in de Beauvoir's work that offers itself, on the one hand, as evidence of her line of argument, or as a mode of enhancing that argument, whilst, on the other, as a threat to her main thesis, the very notion of *gendered* suffering. Figures of racialised suffering occur at several points in *The Second Sex*, albeit fleetingly, as do direct references to Richard Wright's novels. Tracing these as moments at which de Beauvoir draws parallels and makes comparisons between gender and 'race' enables a consideration of the ways in which her argument illuminates some of the difficulties of fixing certain concepts central to feminist argument as peculiar to the condition of womanhood.

We can explore the issue of equivalence across gendered and racialised modalities of alterity through focusing on de Beauvoir's use of racialised figures. How does she employ these figures in *The Second Sex*? Is she suggesting an equivalence between 'race' and gender? In what sense?

In her introduction to *The Second Sex* de Beauvoir states:

> no group ever sets itself up as the One without setting up the Other over and against itself … In small town eyes all persons not belonging to the village are 'strangers' and suspect; to the native of a country all who inhabit other countries are 'foreigners'; Jews are 'different' for the Anti-Semite, Negros are 'inferior' for American racists, aboriginies are 'natives' for colonists, proletarians are the 'lower class' for the privileged.
>
> (1993 [1949]: xl–xli)

In extending the concept of alterity away from the situation of women, de Beauvoir makes the case that there are some senses in which the alterity ascribed to women is not a position uniquely suffered by them. It is this giving up of the unique position of women as an experience of alterity that intrigues me; what does it mean to suggest that these different forms of racism illuminate sexual oppression?

One might suggest that de Beauvoir's purpose is to enhance her argument about sexual discrimination through the prism of the racial, that it is a form of rhetoric that is an argument by association. I want to argue that, as an initial position, this is undoubtedly the case. Her rhetorical position, moreover, read in this vein, is one that does indeed proceed to a feminist politics that could be characterised by *ressentiment*. Let me make this case more fully before I contend, further, that one might also read these arguments rather differently.

In the passage in which de Beauvoir makes explicit reference to Wright's *Native Son*, the sense in which she regards racial oppression as parallel to gender oppression is made clear. *Apropos* the young girl's development into the dilemma of objectified subject, the subject who must make herself object in order to take up her normalised place in the world, she writes, that:

> it is a strange experience for whoever regards himself as the One to be revealed to himself as otherness, alterity. This is what happens to the little girl when, doing her apprenticeship for life in the world, she grasps what it means to be a woman therein … high as she may raise herself, far as she may venture, there will always be a ceiling over her head … the little girl lives amongst gods in human guise.
>
> (1993: 313)

It is at this point that de Beauvoir draws the analogy, suggesting that:

> This situation is not unique. The American Negroes know it, being partially integrated in a civilization that nevertheless regards them as constituting an inferior caste; what Bigger Thomas, in Richard Wright's *Native Son*, feels with bitterness at the dawn of his life is this inferiority, this accursed alterity, which is written in the colour of his skin: he sees airplanes flying by and he knows that because he is black the sky is forbidden to him. Because she is a woman, the little girl knows that she is forbidden the sea and the polar regions, a thousand adventures, a thousand joys: she was born on the wrong side of the line.
>
> (1993: 313)

De Beauvoir is explicitly employing the notion of a line that separates girls from things she can witness but not enjoy as a participant. Here then is the coveted figure of the man, free to explore regions forbidden to woman. In this passage, this same figure is watched by Bigger Thomas, and is given a racial identity, as white. De Beauvoir's use of Wright is heuristic not sociological, rhetorical not empirical, and it is in this sense that the argument functions to strengthen de Beauvoir's point through association. The scene from *Native Son* which she refers to occurs near the beginning of the novel, as Bigger and his friend Gus contemplate the passing world. Bigger is meditative, watching the plane high in the sky:

> 'Them white boys sure can fly,' Gus said.
> 'Yeah,' said Bigger wistfully. 'They get a chance at everything.'

'I could fly one of those things if I had a chance,' Bigger mumbled reflectively, as though talking to himself.

(1991 [1940]: 460)

This passage sets up a dynamic that is much like one based in *ressentiment*, since Bigger and Gus articulate their dissatisfaction directed at those they can imitate, but cannot *be*. Bigger and Gus can 'play white', imitating the 'ways and manners of white folks', and laugh at themselves and 'at the vast white world that sprawled and towered in the sun before them' (1991: 461). The mimicry however, does not compensate nor does it enable; Bigger positions himself explicitly on one side of a fence, using a perception of relations of privilege as drawn across that fence, as had de Beauvoir and as was (and is) common to much discourse on power:

'Goddammit, look! We live here and they live there. We black and they white. They got things and we ain't. They do things and we can't. It's just like living in jail. Half the time I feel like I'm on the outside of the world peeping in through a knot-hole in the fence …'

(1991: 463)

De Beauvoir's interest was in the social psychology of living as an objectified subject. 'Woman' is obliged to operate in the sexist world in bad faith, for the cultural attempt to make women into objects is one that is doomed to failure. In contrast to Gus and Bigger's play-acting as a way to laugh at those on the 'other side' of the fence, or the 'colour line', for women, play-acting *characterises* feminine subjectivity. As much as 'Man' may imagine her alterity, no existent can really be Other. Thus femininity is an inauthentic state. It is a fantasy, de Beauvoir suggests, of patriarchy; and in order to comply, women present as other, but can never 'be' other. Thus men demand an inauthentic 'play-acting' and women's existence is sublimated:

He wants her to be the Other; but all existents remain subjects, try as they will to deny themselves. Man wants woman to be object: she makes herself object; at the very moment when she does that she is exercising a free activity. Therein is her original treason.

(1993: 295)

De Beauvoir's argument, therefore, is that the complexities of submission and activity in assuming the position of 'other' involve women in inauthenticity. However, she suggests, by contrast, that the relationship that black men have to their 'accursed alterity' is *authentic*, and can therefore become the basis of reaction and rejection of an imposed status as other. The difference is drawn at the level of psychology:

There is this great difference: the Negroes submit with a feeling of revolt, no

privileges compensating for their hard lot, whereas woman is offered induce-
ments to complicity … along with the authentic demand of the subject who
wants sovereign freedom, there is in the existent an inauthentic longing for
resignation and escape; the delights of passivity are made to seem desirable
to the young girl.

(1993: 313)

Having drawn an image of power as operating across a line and between two
groups, therefore, de Beauvoir suggests that there is a difference in the way that
two subordinate groups respond to being on the 'wrong side'. In contrast to the
clear-sightedness of 'the American Negro', women are made to desire femininity,
and therefore to desire their subordination. Her argument implies that women
themselves, and the men around them, comply with gendered regimes, such that
men are 'duped' into a sense of security that these regimes uphold, whilst
women act in bad faith, embracing femininity as an adaption to a situation in
which their embodiment places them. Women desire *both* sovereign freedom and
resignation. Woman's relationship to her position as 'object' provides no easy
route through to political consciousness, since she is faced with a forked road. As
de Beauvoir puts it: '[S]he does not accept the destiny assigned to her by nature
and by society; and yet she does not repudiate it completely; she is too much
divided against herself to join battle with the world' (1993: 370).

A peculiar aporia opens in de Beauvoir's argument insofar as the parallel
between 'race' and gender has become abstracted away from embodied experiences: all the women are white and all the men are black, again. Such a mode of
argumentation has been critiqued before now for its abstractions, historical
complicities and sociological compartmentalisations (see, for example, Bell 1995;
Caraway 1991; Fuss 1989; Spelman 1988; Stepan 1990). My interest in it here is
to pursue the question: given its 'inaccuracies' what is the significance of this
mode of argumentation for thinking the feminist political imagination? Why
does it appear and reappear in de Beauvoir's argument? Is it to be thought as
simply negative – as a mistake or a sloppy mode of argumentation?

Clearly, de Beauvoir's use of the racialised analogy is an attempt to elaborate
her argument through association, a rhetorical strategy that does not convince
empirically, and it is a mode of argumentation which is extremely problematic,
veering close to a psychological essentialism that allows no nuances of gendered
and racialised subjectivities, and which, in its abstraction, makes the position of
black womanhood an impossible one. Does she submit like a black man, with
revolt, or like a woman, with the temptation of complicity? But I want to push
the argument beyond a critique on this level, to suggest that the appearance of
the figure of a black man within a feminist argument is one that has implications
for the way in which the boundaries of the feminist political imagination are
being sculpted.

To return to *ressentiment*, it seems as if de Beauvoir's use of the figure of Bigger
Thomas at this point would characterise her feminist political imagination as one
in which and by which women realise their situation and their duplicity *in order to*

become revolutionary in the same manner as the 'American Negro'. Her choice to present her argument through the character of Bigger Thomas implies a political imagination which is indeed one of *ressentiment*, for Bigger has much about him which would justify describing his spirit thus. Wright purposely made Bigger a difficult character with whom to empathise, unlike his autobiographical figure in *Black Boy* (1945). Wright made Bigger an uncompromising character whose arrogant masculinism bounces off the page. He is a victim of a racist society, certainly, but a young man whose fear leads him to manslaughter; when trying to avoid discovery in the bedroom of a young white woman, Mary Dalton, he smothers her in a clumsy effort to silence her alcohol-induced mumblings. His crime gives him a peculiar confidence:

> He had murdered and created a new life for himself … it was the first time in his life that he had had anything that others could not take from him … Though he had killed by accident, not once did he feel the need to tell himself that it had been an accident. He was black and he had been alone in a room where a white girl had been killed; therefore he had killed her. That was what everybody would say … And in a certain sense he knew that the girl's death had not been accidental. He had killed many times before, only on those other times there had been no handy victim or circumstance to make visible or dramatic his will to kill … There was within him a kind of terrified pride in feeling and thinking that some day he would be able to say publicly that he had done it.
>
> (1991: 542)

If we take the anger of a character such as Bigger Thomas as metonymic of the political impulse behind oppositional movements, then we are thinking in terms of a situation of *ressentiment*. The white men who could fly, the white women who could afford to patronise with their communist politics, the folk who lived in other words 'across the line', produced in Bigger Thomas a loathing that was a mixture of hatred and desire, a need to revile but also to *be* the reviled. Nietzsche spoke of an imaginary revenge, a slave morality that begins with a *ressentiment* that is reactive, that 'says no' to what is 'outside' and different from 'it-self':

> and this No is its creative deed. This inversion of the value-positing eye – this need to direct one's view outward instead of back to oneself – is of the essence of *ressentiment*: in order to exist, slave morality always first needs a hostile external environment; it needs, physiologically speaking, external stimuli in order to act at all – its action is fundamentally reaction.
>
> (1989: 36–37)

The man of *ressentiment* conceives his enemy as evil, and from this basic concept he evolves 'as an after thought and pendant' a '"good one" – himself!' (1989: 39). The spirit of *ressentiment*, therefore, is one that seeks out enemies and evils in order to consider itself of higher morality; it is a negative reactive spirit that ties its sense of self-morality to its reaction to 'sinners'.

Bigger Thomas makes sense of his manslaughter of Mary in terms of his social relation to the Daltons and their associates. He had now acted, and recreated himself as a being of 'new born strength':

> The shame and fear and hate which Mary and Jan and Mr. Dalton and that huge rich house had made rise so hard and hot in him had now cooled and softened … No matter how they laughed at him for his being black and clownlike, he could look them in the eyes and not feel angry.
>
> (1991: 584)

I am not sure that I would be willing to characterise de Beauvoir's 'politics' *in toto* through the character of Bigger Thomas that she invokes. Moreover, Bigger Thomas's sense of facing the 'mountain of white hate' (1991: 712) does show some signs of complexity toward the end of the novel, where the spirit of *ressentiment*, in its simplicity, is not sustained. At this point, all I wish to contend is that de Beauvoir's use of the unlikely figure of Bigger Thomas serves us particularly poorly as an image of shared modalities of suffering and equally badly as an image of oppositional politics. She uses Bigger Thomas as a way of suggesting that the suffering experienced by women, the position of being objectified while remaining necessarily a subject, is one that has been fictionalised by Richard Wright in a different context. But her effort to make this rhetorical move becomes highly problematic, and tends toward both a form of essentialist psycho-logic, positing women and black people as separate, but parallel, modes of subjectivity, identifying sexism and racism as comparable modes of oppression; and, perhaps more importantly, suggesting an *ought* which has feminism based on revolt in the manner of Bigger Thomas. This is, indeed, tantamount to a model of ressentiment, with power figured as a dividing line, and identity politics figured as requiring a strive toward authenticity, with the latter modelled, still, upon a figure of a white masculinity. This is not to argue that the feminist polit-ical imagination never involves, and should never involve, *ressentiment*,[7] but to sound a serious note of caution if the impulse to politics is one that means that feminism becomes bound to an image of ourselves as only ever sufferers.

Beyond *ressentiment*: modes of connectivity

I want to suggest a different way to read the coming together of racialised figures with gendered ones in de Beauvoir's text, and to elaborate this second reading with reference to Wright's work. This involves tracing a different line of argu-ment, one that posits de Beauvoir's use of racialised figures less as a mistake or poor argument, but rather as indicative of a blurring of the boundaries of femi-nism, a blurring which gives up the spirit of *ressentiment* precisely because the connection is made. That is, there is a giving up of a purely gendered suffering, and of a politics based on the exclusivity of women's blocked access to power.

The social experience of oppression, of being socially designated by discrimination, is what enables – and obliges – de Beauvoir to 'give up' the notion that women's suffering is unique, as she herself argues. Her comments imply a shared alterity in terms of a 'condemned passivity' (1993: 348) – between women and, for example, the 'Negroes' of the American South. I want to suggest that, in the moments in which suffering is posited as a shared condition, or that empathy is allowed to pass across the lines of identity, there is less a *ressentiment* and more the shared hunger that is weary, not of man – it is not nihilistic – but of the categories that so bind us to declaring absolute specificities of our positionalities. In this section, therefore, I am suggesting that, despite the coherence of the arguments of the previous section, de Beauvoir's use of racialised figures can be pushed sympathetically. This yields a discussion that moves away from *ressentiment* and parallel arguments, to explore instead modes of connectivity, a way of reading the evocation of 'race' in de Beauvoir as an opening, one that can be pursued, moreover, through other aspects of Wright's work.

That it was at the site of music that de Beauvoir interacted with black people in the United States is significant, to the extent that Wright was also intrigued by the moment of commonality that music appeared to proffer. In *Twelve Million Black Voices* (1978a [1941]), Wright mused upon the possibility that it was the city that created a *common* experience or sentiment: 'Why is our music so contagious? Why is it that those who deny us are willing to sing our songs? Perhaps it is because so many of those who live in cities feel deep down just as we do' (1978: 227). Thus, whilst 'our music makes the feet of the whole world dance' (229), it is an exclusion that forms the sentiments expressed there. Wright's understanding of this exclusion is, moreover, one that he extends *beyond* the experience of black peoples, suggesting that 'we play in this manner because "all excluded folk" play' (228). Wright's understanding of this exclusion is one he sees mirrored in the position of the Irish in relation to the English: 'The English say of the Irish, just as Americans say of us, that only the Irish can play, that they laugh through their tears' (228).

The connection that Wright makes here between the Irish and the black people of US cities suggests the sense in which he is understanding the social nature of the psychology of oppression.[8] This sense of connection that is not based on racial oppression alone is what could lead Wright to the extraordinary argument – extraordinary given Bigger Thomas's position – that Bigger was not only black. On moving to Chicago, Wright wrote:

> *I made the discovery that Bigger Thomas was not black all the time; he was white too*, and there were literally millions of him, everywhere … I became conscious, at first dimly, and then later on with increasing clarity and conviction, of a vast, muddied pool of human life in America. It was as though I had put on a pair of spectacles whose power was that of an x-ray enabling me to see deeper into the lives of men … I sensed too that the Southern scheme of oppression was but an appendage of a … more ruthless and impersonal commodity-profit machine.
>
> (1991: 860–861; emphasis added)

Wright's connection with sociological thought is not surprising in this context. The Chicago School of sociology, with its emphasis on the conditions of the social and its resulting cartography of discrimination, appealed to Wright – and his writing in turn to them. They had a shared interest in what such a 'pair of spectacles' did to one's vision of society, and, especially, to one's vision of the urban environment (see Bone 1986).

Wright's explorations of black lives in the city clearly drew upon his own experience as a migrant, and his broadly Marxist perspective gave him some form of analytic through which to view his own and others' experiences. Nevertheless, in writing *Twelve Million Black Voices* he also utilised the files of his friend, the sociologist Horace Cayton on the black migrant in Chicago. The spirit of this sociology was documentary: its purpose was to see how an impartial mapping of city life would shed light on the standards of living and ways of life found there. Wright's prose tells us of the conditions of life for black migrants, especially in terms of their housing: 'The kitchenette is our prison, our death sentence … with its filth and foul air, with its one toilet for thirty or more tenants' (1978: 212).

The character of Bigger Thomas in *Native Son* is one that is formed from such an experience of the city. The novel opens with him having to kill a rat in their kitchenette, and with the family having to get dressed all in the one room.[9] The lack of privacy, the poverty and the physical strain of such a way of life was to be fully documented in Drake and Cayton's (1945) sociological study *Black Metropolis*, to which Wright wrote a preface in which he emphasised how the work, 'pictures the environment from which the Bigger Thomases of our nation come' (1945: xviii).

The tone of Wright's preface to *Black Metropolis* was less optimistic than some of the sociological views of the Chicago School, as Wright lingers on the city as a source of fascistic sentiment: 'Do not hold a light attitude toward the slums of Chicago's South Side. Remember Hitler came out of such a slum. Remember that Chicago could be the Vienna of American Fascism!' (1945: xx).

In the essay 'How Bigger was Born', furthermore, Wright recalls:

> I've even heard Negroes say that maybe Hitler and Mussolini are all right; that maybe Stalin is right. They did not say this out of any intellectual comprehension of the forces at work in the world, but because they felt that these men 'did things', a phrase that is charged with more meaning than the mere words imply.
>
> (1987 [1940]: 16)

Wright's purpose is to stress that, just as fascism in the form of Hitler's crimes was based upon an exploitation of the hunger and the longing that was in the hearts of Europe's masses, so urban slums of the USA were places where hope and humiliation were long-time bedfellows. Black people came to live in these conditions because, he contends, they responded to the cultural hopes of their times. However, because the chances of succeeding in the terms of capitalist free enterprise are tenuous and unlikely to be realised, there is an appeal in forms of ideological rejection, be they communism or fascism. Thus, Wright shared and wished to add his agreement with the Chicago School sociologists' position that there was nothing *peculiar* about the people of the urban metropolis, but that the *conditions* of the metropolis could be studied through analysis of its impact upon them. Wright noted:

> In *Black Metropolis*, the authors have presented much more than the anatomy of Negro frustration; they have shown how *any* human beings can become mangled, how *any* personalities can become distorted when men are caught in the psychological trap of being emotionally committed to the living of a life of freedom which is denied them.
>
> (1945: xxvi)

Thus Wright maintained that there is a danger associated with the inequalities found in the industrial cities of USA, one that was tied to 'race' and the history of enslavement, but one which was also to do with the class structures of industrialisation. The danger was a result of the way in which urban life had 'evolved', of the way the metropolis was responding to the movement of the culture within which it grew. The conditions of urban living for black people were such that white America relied upon their hope and optimism. In the preface, Wright is explicitly wondering about the psychological consequences that acceptance of these unacceptable conditions had on the urban black American: 'what peculiar personality formations result when millions of people are forced to live lives of outward submissiveness while trying to keep intact in their hearts a sense of the worth of their humanity?' (1945: xxx).

Thus we return to the question that was also the question as de Beauvoir saw it: how had it become possible to live a submissive life, to manage to live as an objectified subject? In Wright's preface this condition has been raised as a question of political outlook, but the reaction of those who suffer the conditions described by him, and by the authors of the study to which he was writing the preface, was not to be predicted. The relationship between suffering and politics resists easy formulations. Certainly it is clear that Wright was interested in moments of law-breaking, moments of fascism and moments of communist or workers' revolutions as possibilities arising from similar sets of circumstances. Frequently, however, as with the case of music mentioned above, he reasserted that creativity, as much as fearful hatred, can arise from comparable, harsh, situations. In a similar way, for de Beauvoir, as we have seen, the reaction to the situation of being on 'the wrong side of the line' is not predictable: it could be one of mimicry and play-acting, an inauthenticity that was, nevertheless, comprehensible, or else it could be a reaction of revolt, an authentic reaction to structural disadvantage. Women were encouraged to the former, she argued, to a life lived in bad faith.

Both writers are suggesting in their different ways that there cannot be an ownership of oppression, that the similarities that cross different forms of subjectivisation can be read as opening a space for a more radical critique than one based on *ressentiment*. De Beauvoir's few attempts in *The Second Sex* to relate the issues at stake to those of racism, and also to anti-Semitism, are moments in which she enables a reading that sees moments of connectivity, that reach out to patterns of discrimination that she regards as similar to, or reflections upon, gender discrimination. For example, apropos of the frustration that women are obliged to cope with in not being able to register feelings and frustrations, not even through recourse to violence, de Beauvoir expands her vision away from the figure of the woman. As we have already seen, de Beauvoir seems to hold that women regard the order of things as fixed, and lack of physical power combines with this sense to produce her resignation to docility (1993: 348–349). The 'condemned passivity', the 'accursed alterity' has the effect of turning the objectified person inward, and in that submission there is a search for a way of conducting oneself in such a world. But this is another point at which de Beauvoir makes a comparison with the effects of racism in the United States, where, she suggests:

> it is quite impossible for a Negro, in the South, to use violence against the whites; this rule is the key to the mysterious 'black soul'; the way the Negro feels in the white world, the behaviour by which he adjusts himself to it, the compensations he seeks, his whole way of feeling and acting are to be explained on the basis of the passivity to which he is condemned.
>
> (1993: 348)

Her use of Richard Wright's work, if heuristic and rhetorical, is also an explicit attempt to acknowledge sociological similarities. Moreover, she expands her comments on 'race' in the United States to comment, briefly, on the racial politics facing African immigrants to France:

> In *Black Boy* Richard Wright has shown how the ambitions of a young American Negro are blocked from the start and what a struggle he had merely in raising himself to the level where problems begin for the whites. Negroes coming to France from Africa also find difficulties – with themselves as well as those around them – similar to those confronting women.
>
> (1993: 732)

I have indicated above the problematic nature of these comparisons, in terms of the way in which they make certain subject positions impossible, and the model of power that they propose, exactly because they come close to an attempt to spread the umbrella of oppression along the lines of a *ressentiment* politics. Nevertheless, I mean to conclude more positively, suggesting that, however fumbled her effort, de Beauvoir does attempt to make a case for the position of womanhood as a subjectivity that can be connected with other subjectivities, and she sees that the recognition of this might proffer women the possibility of an acknowledgement, a recognition and thereby an *existence* in the world.

Such a reading bases much, too much perhaps, on de Beauvoir's racialised metaphors and parallel arguments, those moments when her text enables us to 'see' connections that, in turn, enable one to argue that she surrenders a particularised gendered suffering. Nevertheless, these moments are there, and they suggest a different path, one that highlights the sense in which de Beauvoir's work is in line with an existentialist notion of 'situation', that in our contemporary vocabulary makes her argument clearly an 'anti-essentialist' one. Hence, the quotation above continues: 'it is through attaining *the same situation as* [men's] that she will find emancipation' (1993: 750; emphasis added).

Similarly, in Wright's work, there are implicit and explicit suggestions that the way to challenge racism need not model itself, indeed, would be inaccurate if it did so, on the exclusivity of black people's sufferings. Both his relationship with the Chicago School of sociology and his Marxism would warn against such a characterisation of Wright's politics. Moreover, despite the charges of misogyny that have been levied against him, there are moments when his portrayals of women are nuanced and signal the further complexity of gendered, racialised positionalities (in for example the moving short story 'Long Black Song', 1978b). Any attempt to recast de Beauvoir and Wright's futural visions might well draw strength from an emphasis on modes of connection as creative and open rather than fixed images that stem from models of power which attempt to reduce those connections.

By way of conclusion, therefore, I would argue that it is possible to read de Beauvoir with Richard Wright in such a way that refuses to characterise their politics as involving a spirit of *ressentiment*. For even at these moments when womanhood and the characterisation of Bigger Thomas are brought into proximity, when the vengeful and covetous are presented as the impulses to revolution or political argument, there is the possibility of reading differently. Such a possibility draws on other routes of intertextuality and enables one to see models of politics that refuse the easy presentation of a bounded group of 'the oppressed' who, according to some very stark and reified division, demand to have the attributes and influences of the oppressor, who express the peculiar desire to be remade in the very image of the oppressor. The notion of connectivity does not refer to a mundane sense of connections between people, but it is about the modes, the different ways – not just in terms of experiencing suffering, powerlessness or economic hardship, but also those possible through music, or through sex – that people's lives extend beyond the clarity often imposed by sociological models of power and subjectivity.

Notes

1   Such an accusation has been floated implicitly in feminist debate, but also explicitly: see Tapper (1993).
2   See also Gayle (1980: 194) for mention of Wright's hospitality to de Beauvoir in the USA.
3   According to her biographer Deirdre Bair, de Beauvoir's feelings toward Richard Wright cooled as his marriage with Ellen broke down; de Beauvoir thought that his

interest in racial problems had become 'limited to his own' and his marriage was 'a wreck' (1990: 389).

4   As Butler presents Sartre's argument in her *Subjects of Desire* (1987: 108).
5   See Gilroy (1993: 186) for the suggestion that there is an intertextuality to be explored.
6   Moi (1994) considers 'race' in de Beauvoir in relation to the work of Frantz Fanon.
7   For another view on this, see Marion Tapper (1993), who makes a straightforward argument that *ressentiment* can be the basis of feminist interventions.
8   See also Wright's reference to Joyce in Kinnamon and Fabre (1993: 81).
9   See McCall (1988) who argues that 'racial misery was indecent exposure'.

References

Bair, D. (1990) *Simone de Beauvoir: A Biography*, London: Vintage.

Bell, V. (1995) 'On Metaphors of Suffering', *Economy and Society* 24, 4: 507–19.

Bone, R. (1986) 'Wright and the Chicago Renaissance', *Calalloo* 9, 3: 446–69.

Brown, W. (1995) *States of Injury: Power and Freedom in Late Modernity*, Princeton, N.J.: Princeton University Press.

Butler, J. (1987) *Subjects of Desire: Hegelian Reflections in Twentieth Century France*, New York: Columbia University Press.

Caraway, N. (1991) *Segregated Sisterhood: Racism and the Politics of American Feminism*, Knoxville: University of Tennessee Press.

Chanter, T. (1995) *Ethics of Eros: Irigaray's Rewriting of the Philosophers*, London: Routledge.

de Beauvoir, S. (1991) *Letters to Sartre*, trans. Q. Hoare, London: Radius.

—— (1993, first published 1949) *The Second Sex*, London: Everyman.

Decosta-Willis, M. (1986) 'Avenging Angels and Mute Mothers: Black Southern Women in Wright's Fictional World', *Calalloo* 9, 3: 540–51.

Drake, St Clair and Cayton, H.R. (1945) *Black Metropolis: A Study of Negro Life in a Northern City*, New York: Harcourt, Brace.

Fabre, M. (1985) *The World of Richard Wright*, Jackson: University Press of Mississipi.

Fuss, D. (1989) *Essentially Speaking: Feminism, Nature and Difference*, New York: Routledge.

Gayle, A. (1980) *Richard Wright: Ordeal of a Native Son*, New York: Anchor Press/Doubleday.

Gilroy, P. (1993) *The Black Atlantic*, London: Verso.

—— (1996) Introduction to R. Wright, *Eight Men*, New York: Harper Perennial.

Kinnamon, K. and Fabre, M. (1993) *Conversations with Richard Wright*, Jackson: University Press of Mississippi.

Lundgren-Gothlin, E. (1996) *Sex and Existence: Simone de Beauvoir's 'The Second Sex'*, London: Athlone Press.

McCall, D. (1988) 'The Bad Nigger', in H. Bloom (ed.) *Modern Critical Interpretations: Native Son*, New York: Chelsea House.

Moi, T. (1994) *Simone de Beauvoir: The Making of an Intellectual Woman*, Oxford: Blackwell.

Nietzsche, F. (1967, first published 1887) *On the Genealogy of Morals*, trans. W. Kaufmann, New York: Vintage.

—— (1989, first published 1887) *Beyond Good and Evil: Prelude to a Philosophy of the Future*, trans. W. Kaufman, New York: Vintage.

Spelman, E. (1988) *Inessential Woman: Problems of Exclusion in Feminist Thought*, Boston, Mass.: Beacon Press.

Stepan, N. (1990) 'Race and Gender: The Role of Analogy in Science' in D. Goldberg (ed.) *The Anatomy of Racism*, Minneapolis: University of Minnesota Press.

Tapper, M. (1993) 'Ressentiment and Power: Reflections on Feminist Practice', in P. Patton (ed.) *Nietzsche, Feminism and Political Theory*, London: Routledge.

Wright, R. (1945, first published 1937) *Black Boy*, introduction by D. Fisher, New York: Harper.

—— (1978a, first published 1941) *Twelve Million Black Voices*, in *The Richard Wright Reader*, New York: Harper and Row.

—— (1978b) 'Long Black Song', in *The Richard Wright Reader*, New York: Harper and Row.

—— (1987, first published 1940) 'Introduction: How Bigger was Born', in *Native Son*, Harmondsworth, England: Penguin.

—— (1991, first published 1940) *Native Son*, New York: Library of America.

4 Unifying forces

Rhetorical reflections on a pro-choice image

Karyn Sandlos

Images brand you, burn the surrounding skin, leave their black mark. Like volcanic ash, they can make the most potent soil. Out of the seared place emerge sharp green shoots …

Ann Michaels, Fugitive Pieces (1996)

For two years I have been haunted by an image of a dead woman and the claim it has made on my politics and my academic work. I encountered this image quite by chance, as a reference from a colleague who knew I was interested in how photographs become emblematic of social change movements. The photograph to which I refer shows a woman's bloodied body in stark black and white tones. The woman was found abandoned on a hotel-room floor after an illegal and subsequently fatal abortion. Her name was Gerri Santoro. Since my initial encounter with this photograph, I have been tracing the controversial history of its 25-year circulation within the discourses and image repertoires of pro-choice and anti-choice movements in Canada and the United States.

Others have been haunted by Gerri Santoro's image, as I have been.[1] This chapter will incorporate excerpts from a focus group I conducted with four pro-choice activists who were interested in talking with me and with one another about how the photograph of Gerri Santoro has shaped their activist work. We treated this photograph as a point of entry into a discussion which would explore our relationships to political images and to larger debates over reproductive politics, paying particular attention to the irresolvable tensions and dichotomies which constitute choice/anti-choice debates and political subjects within them.

This chapter will inquire into the relationship between documentary photographs which are understood, by and large, to represent 'reality,' and the political movements which appropriate these images as symbols for collective struggles. In particular, I am concerned with what it means to take up as symbols, documentary images which allow universalizing claims about a collective 'women's experience' to be made. I proceed by mapping some of the discursive landscapes and visual politics through which four pro-choice activists come to understand and construct themselves in relation to a shared political objective or set of objectives over time. In this chapter, I will begin to theorize

SHE HAD A NAME. SHE HAD A FAMILY.

By Roberta Brandes Gratz

SHE WAS LEONA'S SISTER GERRI.

I n April 1973, a photograph of a naked, bloodied woman on a motel room floor, dead from a botched abortion, illustrated an article I wrote for *Ms.* magazine. I knew nothing about her. She simply represented the potential fate of any woman who did not have access to a safe and legal abortion. Today, I am embarrassed to admit that I didn't even think about who the victim actually was. She was any one of us. At the time, the millions of women who, for millions of different reasons, had had abortions did not dare admit it, even to close friends. Revealing the identity of the woman in the photograph would have been viewed as another kind of crime. So I thought then. Today, everything is different.

The sister of the dead woman entered my life a year ago, turning that interesting and meaningful but long past journalistic experience into a profound and provocative new one. It was not the first time that that gruesome picture had come back to haunt me, but it was the most unsettling.

A call came through Gloria Steinem's office alerting me that Leona Gordon, sister of abortion victim Gerri Santoro, was looking for me. She wanted to find out how I had acquired the 1964 photograph for the 1973 article. I was shaken and instinctively anticipated hostility.

Instead, I encountered a pleasant and talkative New England woman from a large farm family, eager to help piece together her sister's story for a television documentary. Her questioning of me actually took up less of our extended conversation than her long and complicated saga of a typical American family in which several of the women had had abortions. Leona seemed as anxious to impart the full story as to know about the photograph. She reminded me of too many of the tragedies I had covered as a young newspaper reporter, when the bereaved seemed almost grateful for the opportunity to share their grief instead of slamming the door in the face of an inconsiderate reporter. Until she had seen it in *Ms.*, Leona did not know of the picture's existence in the files of the Connecticut coroner.

For years, Leona told me, she was shocked that her sister's picture had been used. She would not look at *Ms.* Then, slowly, as the abortion debate turned uglier and uglier, and women who made the painful choice to have an abortion increasingly became the object of derision and scorn, Leona's feelings changed. The picture had been put to good use, she decided, graphically illustrating what no words could. Leona became a pro-choice activist and joined demonstrations in New England. On one side of her placard she placed the magazine photo and on the other earlier photos of Gerri as a young woman, alive, smiling, fun-loving. "This is my sister," the caption read. Our extended phone conversation continued through the life stories of Leona, Gerri, and Gerri's two daughters. No longer was I ignorant of the story behind the photograph, nor did I wish the world to be. Suddenly, I was realizing how easy it was to find oneself in Gerri Santoro's position 30 years ago. In a new way, she was symbolizing the dilemma of countless women. And, to boot, Gerri Santoro's two daughters and my own daughters are about the same ages.

A talented filmmaker, Jane Gillooly, has now given a different life to the photograph in her documentary *Leona's Sister*

Ms. NOVEMBER/DECEMBER 1995

Figure 4.1   Gerri Santoro

Source: Ms. magazine, vol. 6, no. 3, 1995, p. 72

the interconnections between a pro-choice signifier, feminist politics, documentary rhetoric, and theories of political subjectivity.

My analysis opens with a reflection on my own identifications and investments in images and their relationship to activist and academic labor. I write as one who is deeply invested in the representational strategies deployed by activists. As a graduate student struggling to pay the bills while funding for post-secondary education in Ontario, Canada, is undergoing drastic changes, I frequently find myself involved in strategizing meetings in which the central problem is 'how to get a hearing' and how to mobilize support from those less invested in accessible and affordable post-secondary education. Prior to graduate school, I worked as a counsellor in a women's shelter, and as a sexual harassment advisor at a university. As an educator, my role was to provide workshops for community groups that would promote awareness of the systemic and practical barriers which restrict women's access to self-determination. I would conduct these sessions using photographs, sheets of statistics and videotaped documentaries – the visual 'evidence' that the social problem of violence against women exists. I imagined a causal relationship between making social injustices visible and the development of critical consciousness and social concern. Yet, I felt increasingly uneasy with my own epistemological position when, in the face of seemingly striking evidence, I was continually confronted with disbelief or disinterest in the problem of violence against women. These experiences have fueled my interest in theorizing the discursive dynamics which position political actors to reference and authorize oppression through a rhetoric of 'proof' and 'evidence.'

This chapter focuses on how images frame and organize the discourses of particular political struggles, and how these discourses constitute the possibilities for interpreting images. The work of collective organizing often converges around the central problem of how to mobilize support while strategizing in response to the representational tactics of oppositional parties or groups. Images can serve as educative and strategic interfaces between marginalized groups, government, the law, and a wider public. Loaded with evidentiary status and the grammar of indisputable knowledge,[2] documentary images become particularly potent vehicles for the making and authorizing of politicized claims, which forge identifications and align people with specific political agendas.

The pedagogical and political problems which accompany the referencing of images as visual proof of experience are of central concern to this analysis. As Joan Scott has pointed out, the project of making experience visible risks effacing the discursive mechanics through which subjects are produced and positioned (1992: 22–40). Images become meaningful within larger signifying systems and image repertoires, and these shape the reading practices of viewing subjects. Not only do representational strategies need to bring a wider public onside; they must also incite and sustain the commitment of activists over time. Thus, the symbolic articulations of political groups also work to reconstitute the positionings and investments of political actors *within* particular movements. In asking what images reveal to feminists (and to wider audiences) about the causes around which we organize, we might begin by paying attention to *how* shared political agendas are forged through our own representational practices.

Image-traces

The photograph of Gerri Santoro was mysteriously leaked from a coroner's archives in the early 1970s, and published in three editions of *Ms.* magazine (1973, 1977, 1995). In keeping with the genre of documentary police-file photographs, this is a graphic and violent 'crime scene' image of a woman's dead body, following the illegal abortion which caused her death. In the context of powerful and outrage-eliciting images of dead fetuses emerging from the pro-life movement in the early 1970s, a photograph of a woman dead from an illegal abortion procedure presented a timely and important opportunity for pro-choice activists to make visible the material violence of women's restricted access to reproductive choice. Given the visual politics of the early 1970s in the United States, in which fetal images were receiving unprecedented attention within anti-choice campaigns, it is unsurprising that this image ended up in the pages of a major feminist publication. Once made public, the photograph was plastered on placards and displayed at pro-choice rallies nationwide for over two decades. Several activists I have spoken with in the course of this research still keep the photograph of Gerri Santoro pinned on walls or bulletin boards in the offices where they plan and carry out their activist labor.

At the time of publication, Gerri Santoro's identity was unknown to the editorial staff of *Ms.*, and unknown to a larger readership. This anonymity, coupled with the authority of the documentary image, can begin to account for the political import of this photograph as a signifier of the material effects of women's restricted access to reproductive choice. The 1973 publication of the photograph in *Ms.* sparked a controversy over the ethics of publishing a photograph of a dead woman without the permission of her family, and in the absence of any accompanying information which would situate the woman in her specific circumstances. At the time of publication Roberta Brandes-Gratz, the journalist responsible for the article accompanying Santoro's image, could not account for the origins of the photograph, the location of the crime, or the identity of the woman depicted. After lengthy deliberations, the decision to publish the photograph was justified by the editorial staff of *Ms.* on the basis of Santoro's identity being obscured. In that particular political moment, the photograph of Santoro was strategically taken up as an image of an unknown woman who had met the fate of countless other women with restricted access to safe, affordable, and legal abortions.[3]

The proof of the image

It would be difficult to locate a political struggle in which images have played a more central role than they have in debates over reproductive choice. Feminists have done important work in theorizing how dichotomous positionings of women and fetuses operate discursively through still and moving pictures (Duden 1993; Franklin 1991; Petchesky 1987). Still images of fetuses have been decisive in the construction of the ideological landscape of abortion debates since Lennert Nilsson's pivotal photo essay of fetal development appeared in *LIFE* magazine in 1965.[4] In 1984 the video *The Silent Scream* emerged as the first moving image which attempted to portray a 12-week-old fetus as assuming all the subjective qualities and characteristics of an 8-year-old child in 'real time.' As Peggy Phelan observes:

> Fetal imagery, a persistent and ubiquitous force in the abortion debates, is important because it upsets the psychic terrain which formerly located all reproductive visibility within the body of the pregnant woman. Once that independence is established, fetal imagery itself becomes vulnerable to all the potential manipulations of the signifying system.
>
> (1993: 132)

Fetal images are central to the ideological construction of the fetus as a child with an ontological and biological existence which is independent of the bodies of women. In this symbolic configuration, women are constituted as passive carriers of the fetus, in effect, female/maternal storage facilities or fetal 'environments' (Franklin 1991: 194). Images of fetuses as distinct from women's bodies materialize within anti-choice discourses and political campaigns which hold the 'rights' of the fetus over the right of women to make choices in the face of an unwanted pregnancy. In response, pro-choice political campaigns put forth women's unequivocal right to control our bodies and our reproductive functions.

Advances in reproductive technologies complexify the symbolic function of fetal imagery within abortion discourse. Such advances make possible, for example, Nilsson's recent photo essay in *LIFE*, which 'documents the *embryonic journeys* of a varied group of vertebrates, including pigs, monkeys, chickens and humans ... providing a glimpse of how our earliest ancestors made us what we are today' (1965: 38; emphasis added). Here, fetal subjectivity is narrativized through a visual aura of innocence and indisputable scientific authority.[5]

Photographs such as those depicted in *LIFE* photo essays lend a chilling sense of scientific and documentary authority to claims that fetuses can be unproblematically regarded as persons upon whom societies should bestow freedoms and protections under the law. This has set the terms for thinking about what might constitute an equally powerful visual response on behalf of women's reproductive rights, freedoms and protections for over three decades. The question facing the pro-choice movement in the United States in the early 1970s was how to represent the need for women's safe and affordable access to legal abortions within the visual grammar of the day. I am asking how viewers and political subjects were and continue to be constructed within these very terms.

Beyond the surface of the image

Michael Blain points out that the purpose of an 'effective movement rhetorical discourse' (1994: 808) is twofold. A social change movement discourse must construct a field of knowledge which argues the truth of a problem, including a knowledge of the subjects and objects of struggle, *and* constitute an ethics which argues solutions and elicits moral outrage at the actions of opponents (*ibid.*). As well as reacting to anti-abortion campaigns, pro-choice rhetorical strategies anticipate and respond to legal arguments and discourses. Abortion was illegal in the United States until 1973.[6] This was the same year that Gerri Santoro's image was published in *Ms.* magazine. As I have argued, the problem for pro-choice feminists was how to make visible the material violence of women's restricted access to abortion services. In the video, *Leona's Sister Gerri* (1995), Roberta Brandes-Gratz, author of the 1973 *Ms.* article, recalls:

> one has to remember this was a very early moment in the abortion debate and abortion opponents were just beginning to use the 'fetus in the bottle' images. It was a very effective photographic campaign and we just didn't know how to balance that campaign with anything – you know how, what is, has always been that answer to aborted fetuses is dead women.

> (Gillooly 1995)

Political struggles require symbols and representations which mediate the dissemination of knowledge and call up subjects as political actors. Public demonstrations serve as important modes of interpellation, through the collective incitement which is generated when people assemble and appropriate public spaces for political means. Placards and other forms of visual representation promote individual identifications and investments in a shared commitment to collective action. Sustaining this commitment requires the reiteration *over time* of representations through which moral positions can be organized and taken up by political actors.

While considerable feminist analysis has been devoted to the ways in which fetal iconography discursively reiterates the split between women's bodies and their fetuses, also pertinent is the question of how pro-choice images have figured within this reiteration. Pro-choice *and* anti-choice iconographies call up political actors through the construction of unambiguous moral positions on life and death. Taken up as a pro-choice symbol, an image of a dead woman has been, and will continue to be, read in relation to fetal images and the circulating discourses of fetal personhood these images work to mediate. Yet, images of dead women and dead fetuses, symbolizing opposing sides of abortion debates, structure categorical systems of meaning making within the 'field of knowledge' (Blain 1994: 808) of pro-choice/anti-choice debates. In this way, the complexity of issues facing political actors is reduced to dichotomized and morally loaded questions of life versus murder, women versus fetuses, and right versus wrong.

Fetal iconography produces fetuses as subjects in relation to the bodies and interests of women in the face of unwanted pregnancy, contributing to the construction of the legal and feminist problem of competing claims and competing rights. An image of a dead woman responds to this construction in a striking fashion, by inserting women's bodies back into the image repertoire. Yet as Franklin articulates, 'Fetal citizenship contradicts the citizenship of women' (1991: 201). Visual dichotomies through which life is pitted against death obfuscate the discursive mechanics through which the subjects of struggle are constituted through discourses of life, citizenship, and personhood, as they intersect with the legitimizing discourses of science, technology, and documentary realism. However visually compelling an image of a dead woman may be, an image *repertoire* which reproduces the woman/fetus dichotomy perpetuates the myth of the coherent woman subject and the coherent fetus subject. These 'subjects' are continually reconstituted through policies, legal and scientific discourses, *and* political campaigns.

A reiteration of the fetus/woman dichotomy constructs the coherence and boundedness of competing sides of abortion debates in which both pro-choice and anti-choice subjects are produced through their alignment with clear moral positions on the complicated reproductive issues at play. Political subjectivity is constituted, however, through conflicting discursive systems and the material conditions and circumstances in which people are positioned. As Michele Landsberg noted when the Supreme Court struck down Canada's abortion law in 1988:

> Every one of us who fought for reproductive choice over the years knew of outspoken right-to-life doctors who quietly performed 'D&C's' for their trusted, middle-class patients. Every one of us knew at least one story of some anti-choice legislator or crusader whose wife or daughter or cousin or girlfriend quietly asked around for Dr. Morgentaler's address.[7]
>
> (Landsberg 1988: A2)

The relationship of subjects to visual representations of fetal personhood and questions of early human life is made increasingly complex through reproductive imaging technologies which allow us to see fetal development and assess fetal health at its earliest stages.[8] These imaging technologies are reconfiguring the terrain of pro-choice and anti-choice struggles, and opening up grey areas and ambivalences for pro-choice advocates. Fetal protection issues are currently framing legal discourses in Canada and the United States, and challenging feminists to reconsider how their arguments for women's reproductive rights and freedoms can deal with increasingly complex questions of early human life.[9]

In Canada, feminists have fought and won the battle to legalize abortion. Pro-choice advocates recognize, however, that the struggle to obtain full reproductive freedoms for women is far from over.[10] What is required is a radical and continuous reconsideration of how to proceed. What are the possibilities for a rethinking of a pro-choice feminist position, a position which would question the coherences upon which its own stability rests? How might feminists challenge 'a legal and psychic discourse dedicated to defining separations, distinguishing split subjects, and settling schisms' (Phelan 1993: 169–170)? As Phelan suggests, 'This yawning incoherence … will continue to trouble the political realization of reproductive rights while it remains unmarked' (1993: 169-70.).

Collective looking

Images that get taken up as political symbols construct the subject of particular struggles even as they construct viewers as ethical agents and political actors. Pro-choice advocates must negotiate the shifting and competing discourses and constraints of political and legal circumstances, a lack of time and resources, anti-feminist backlash, and the continuing threat of violence. In my discussion with pro-choice activists,[11] I became interested in how women navigate these constraints in articulating pro-choice positions, and how these articulations are forged through the contradictions, ambivalences, and the differing investments of women who share a collective political agenda.

The focus group did not reveal any singular 'reading' of the photograph of Gerri Santoro. This is unsurprising given that the women who participated in the group have been active in pro-choice organizing collectively for well over two decades – some more recently, and others since the days when back-alley abortions were commonplace. The participants' involvement in pro-choice activism has included both paid and unpaid work in abortion clinics, advocacy work, political lobbying and policy development.[12] Their interpretations of the photograph of Santoro traversed historical and contemporary landscapes of pro-choice political organizing, marking the discursive struggle through which political subjectivity is defined in relation to a collective agenda over a rapidly shifting political terrain.

These negotiations are illuminated through the different ways in which the image of Gerri Santoro is understood to work as a symbol of historical and contemporary pro-choice struggles. The parameters of this chapter permit me to utilize only one small section of a lengthy group interview. I have selected the following section from the transcripts as it lends further insight to the questions I seek to address in this writing: How do activists, working with limited time and resources, conceptualize and anticipate the possibilities for interpreting images within the circulating discourses of political struggles? How are the ethical issues raised by controversial images and their particular mobilization managed? How are political actors and wider audiences constituted as subjects and ethical agents in relation to representations of feminist struggles over time?

For two of the activists, the central issue for pro-choice political organizing is, and has always been, women's access to safe, legal, and affordable abortions. Access to abortion was understood by all present to be located within a broader landscape of accessibility encompassing birth control, sexual health education and services, and economic resources for women. One activist's comments signal how she makes sense of the shifting foundations of pro-choice struggles over time:

I mean let's face it the Choice movement is not what it was. Things have changed a lot from, say the late eighties. We're a lot lower profile, you know, it's not the media attention thing that it used to be. So I think that abortion having been realized and access improving has changed the landscape considerably and the issues are different now, although they are the same at the same time. The practical issues that women are facing aren't dramatically different ...

(Sandlos 1997)

In the following passage, two activists negotiate their positionings in this changing political field in response to the question of how the image of Gerri Santoro represents a contemporary politics of choice:

FIRST SPEAKER: I think it works as a unifying force. Another image that struck me was on the march on Washington, a woman who I think was maybe in her mid-twenties, holding up the picture (of Santoro) and above it was, 'Do You Remember?' I think particularly for women who have always had choice, we can't imagine not having choice. I can't imagine not being able to go and demand a diaphragm, the pill, an abortion. I can't imagine not having that, because that has set the course of my life, you know?

SECOND SPEAKER: And I, although not disagreeing, I don't think it does work anymore, personally for me. I think that there's too ... you know, this may just be a function of the fact that I'm in the deep of it eight hours a day, five days a week, so, I have to take that into account. I think that the issues have changed, I think that the focus has changed, I think that the political landscape has changed too much, I think that feminist politics have changed too much.. I think that it (the photograph) definitely could play an important role, but not as an all-encompassing symbol anymore, as maybe a reminder of what we have to avoid, and what we have to, you know, prevent things from going back to ...

FIRST SPEAKER: But when you look at that (photograph) don't you get just a little bit scared?

SECOND SPEAKER: I mean it is scary, I'm not saying that I don't get scared, but there are also a lot of other more current and bigger things we seem to be up against right now. The women that I'm dealing with every day, I'm not scared that they are going to die, do you know what I mean, I'm scared that they're going to have some sort of suffering, or emotional crisis or that kind of thing. I'm scared that they're not going to be able to get access to a medical service they need, but it doesn't cross my mind ... that that, this is, do you know what I mean ... ?

FIRST SPEAKER: Well, yes, but as of Monday night, Tuesday morning, we now have an anti-choice party[13] as the Official Opposition ...

SECOND SPEAKER: It's true, it's very true ... but ...

FIRST SPEAKER: That scares me ...

SECOND SPEAKER: It does, oh it does … I mean like I, you know I …

FIRST SPEAKER: And we have the solvent case[14] coming before the Supreme Court, in which …

SECOND SPEAKER: Oh absolutely, absolutely …

FIRST SPEAKER: A lot of our traditional supporters who were black and white on *choice* aren't, on this issue …

(Sandlos 1997)

The first speaker's description of a woman in her mid-twenties holding up the image of Gerri Santoro at the (pro-choice) march on Washington with the words 'Do you Remember?' emblazoned across it speaks to activists with long histories of involvement in pro-choice organizing, for they are indeed the ones who can remember the days when abortion procedures were illegal and dangerous. Placards like this position pro-choice activists within a struggle which is both won and yet to be won at the same time. When the placard is held up by a woman who is too young to 'remember,' younger activists who might not identify directly with the image of Santoro itself are called up through a performative and temporal disjuncture. In this manner, the photograph of Gerri Santoro mediates the identifications and moral obligations of younger pro-choice activists who are interpellated into the discourses of pro-choice movement in relation to the freedoms that have been won for them by other pro-choice feminists.

The activists who participated in the focus group stressed their shared concern that many pro-choice events seem to be attended by 'grey heads,' that is, women who have been active in pro-choice organizing since the days when abortions were illegal and contraception was unavailable. One activist in her early twenties described herself as a 'rare sight' at pro-choice gatherings. In the exchange above, this activist struggles to articulate her inability to identify with the image of Gerri Santoro within the context of her front-line work in one of Canada's major cities in 1997. As she goes on to describe it, safe abortion services are available in Canada's major centers, yet they may still be inaccessible to women who do not possess health cards, economic resources, or transportation. Women also continue to face moral judgments from some health-care professionals in hospitals where abortions are provided.

This activist stressed that sexual health education and prevention of unwanted pregnancies are as integral to her front-line practice as are accessible abortion services. For her, then, the image of Gerri Santoro is a pro-choice signifier which is no longer timely or relevant. While the other activists in the focus group shared the same vision for pro-choice service provision, they differed in their continued investment in Santoro's image as a 'unifying force' for the ongoing struggle. In the above exchange, the stakes for activists who are called up differently in relation to a collective political symbol are framed in the context of the recent appointment of an anti-abortion party as the official federal opposition. Santoro's image is emphatically read by one activist as a counterpoint to the threat of anti-abortion legislation.

In the activists' interchange, collective identifications are also constructed in relation to an *internal* threat, when concern is expressed by one activist that many long-standing pro-choice supporters who were once 'black and white' are expressing moral ambivalence in relation to the 'solvent case' – a recent Canadian legal case in which fetal personhood was at issue. The 'solvent case' is one in which a young Aboriginal woman's chemical addiction was deemed harmful to her fetus. The woman was institutionalized in a rehabilitation center against her will. At the time of the focus group, the case was receiving a great deal of media attention, leading to a Supreme Court hearing in which a finding in favor of fetal rights would have instantiated fetal personhood within Canadian law. This was an anxious time for Canadian pro-choice supporters and activists, who were struggling to make a case for women's reproductive autonomy amidst the circulating discourses of fetal vulnerability.[15] In this context, *collective* identifications are forged through the photograph of Gerri Santoro when it is read against the threat of potential anti-choice legislation in the *ambivalence* of the current political climate.

It is in this manner that the younger activist's refusal to identify with the image of Gerri Santoro as an 'unifying force' for pro-choice organizing is discursively negotiated. Gerri Santoro's image is framed by one activist as a symbol of fear which must call up the identifications of any pro-choice activist who is aware of the multiple threats to a contemporary pro-choice agenda. Here, a pro-choice agenda pivots around maintaining gains which have been previously won, and furthering the objectives of pro-choice movement over time. In the exchange between the two activists, Santoro's image is constituted by one activist as a clear and therefore unifying signifier of 'choice' in a political moment when the moral ambivalence of pro-choice supporters threatens the stability of a collective movement. In this moment of negotiation, being a pro-choice activist means aligning oneself unequivocally to a 25-year-old political symbol.

How does the photograph of Gerri Santoro continue to represent a political agenda which pivots around 'choice,' particularly when the meaning of 'choice' fluctuates within the discourses of pro-choice movements? The reiteration of 'choice' as a rallying call for a movement works, for example, through the articulation of one activist who recounted a story of a recent pro-choice public event that she had attended, at which many other 'providers' and activists were present. She recalled,

> I was one of the speakers of the evening and I was one of the very few people who said the word abortion from the podium. I was watching for it and I was listening for it. There were major providers there, major people in the struggle. And I made a point of saying the word out loud, so that we all sort of remembered why we're here. And there was some sort of colorful phrasing used in place of the word abortion. There was a lot of 'women have the right to make choice' and 'women the right to have … ,' and I said 'women the right to have safe abortions.' And so I see that as a different, difference in the struggle …

(Sandlos 1997)

When I questioned how other activists in the focus group understood the absence of the word 'abortion' from that evening's discussion, the responses varied. One participant recalled how the word 'abortion' has historically been a contentious referent for the struggle, in part because it conjures up graphic and violent images like that of Gerri Santoro. Another activist suggested that the absence of the word 'abortion' from the discussion might signify the ways in which the political discourse around reproductive freedom is changing alongside the recognition of abortion rights as located within a larger framework of women's reproductive health. Clearly, the mobilization of the term 'abortion' as a unifying moment at the pro-choice gathering signals an important tension for pro-choice feminists.

How do activists organize and sustain a commitment to a changing movement over time? The activist who used the term 'abortion' at the pro-choice event sought to 'remind us of why we are all here' – in effect, to call up the collective identifications and investments of other activists in a sustained commitment to pro-choice organizing. Yet the excerpt from the focus group which I have provided suggests that pro-choice feminists identify differently with long-standing icons and terms which may fail to signify the complexity of issues facing contemporary pro-choice organizers. These differences are rhetorically negotiated through the strategic mobilization of words and symbols within pro-choice movement discourses.

Conclusions

Can one image reflect the discursive struggle to define and redefine a movement's objectives and the conditions of political subjectivity over time? This question inevitably points to additional questions about *how the image is read* in particular contexts and political moments.[16] Images which seem to offer us the evidence of women's collective experience, a 'truth' upon which political claims can be made, do important work in mediating the construction of the subjects of feminist struggle. The history of Gerri Santoro's image as a symbol for pro-choice organizing raises ethical, pedagogical, and political questions which might be of use to feminists seeking to excavate various histories of feminist activism with a view toward present and future political projects.

In continuing this work, I want to look beyond the surface of images which are understood as symbols for collective struggles with presumably shared political agendas over time. As excerpts from my conversation with pro-choice activists suggest, shared agendas are forged through contradictions and shifting foundations. I see the unstable territory where political symbols exist as the very territory where we might demand of ourselves an accountability to questions of collective representation. As Liz McQuiston has commented, 'Every battle needs identifiable heralds and uniforms; every propaganda campaign needs its visual aids and modes of dissemination' (1997: 9).

How, then, to mark the ways in which Gerri Santoro's image 'brands us,' to make way for the 'sharp green shoots' of which Ann Michaels writes (1996:

218)? My aim has been to trouble the 'taken-for-granteds' which accompany an understanding of politicized images as representative of a singular, fixed, or transparent meaning. I want to insist that the contradictions, tensions, and ethical dilemmas which accompany the political mobilization of contentious images be aired and not-too-easily resolved or laid to rest as relics of history. In this way, it feels important to me that the image of Gerri Santoro remain 'in motion' within feminist visual landscapes, for it is this motion which makes the possibilities for a relationship between viewer and image into a project which is perpetually under construction (Probyn 1995: 9). Images and words, understood to interact with viewers in generating multiple meanings, make for fascinating texts around which feminists might gather in the name of continually regenerating feminist *movement*. If we are, as Lauren Berlant has suggested, to engage in a 'politics of the long haul' which questions the terms of its referent (see Chapter 1 in this volume), how we question the rhetoric of our own images and symbols seems a 'potent' place to begin.

Notes

1 In talking with friends, colleagues, and pro-choice activists, I have found that the photograph of Gerri Santoro is both widely known and profoundly etched in the memory of many feminists, and women not directly involved in feminist pursuits. Some pro-choice activists trace their entry into feminist struggles back to this photograph.

2 Since the mid to late nineteenth century, documentary images have been used as 'evidence' by the media, in police archives, in courts of law, in public health campaigns and by anthropologists seeking to represent the 'other.' Abigail Solomon-Godeau accounts for the 'truth-status' of the image when she writes, 'In part, this derives from the fact that photography, like all camera-made images such as film and video, effaces that mark of its making (and maker) at the click of a shutter' (1991: 180).

3 When the photograph of Gerri Santoro was published in *Ms.* in 1977, Santoro's sister Leona Gordon approached Roberta Brandes-Gratz, the author of the three articles in which the image appeared. Once provided with background information on the 'anonymous' woman in the photograph, Brandes-Gratz began to reconsider the politics and ethics of publishing the image under the guise of anonymity (Brandes-Gratz 1995: 72–74). After Santoro's family came forward, a video was produced entitled *Leona's Sister Gerri* (Gillooly 1995). The video explores the impact of the publication on Santoro's family and community, as well as on pro-choice organizing in the early 1970s in the United States. In the video, members of the editorial staff of *Ms.* weigh the ethics of publishing the photograph against the timely and strategic opportunity it presented for pro-choice visual campaigns.

4 For a discussion of the uses of Nilsson's images in anti-abortion campaigns see Franklin (1991: 195–196).

5 In her discussion of the construction of fetal personhood, Franklin provides examples of the various versions of fetal subjectivity which include

> the construction of the fetus as a patriarchal citizen, the construction of the fetus as the object of patriarchal science, the gendered construction of the fetal self as masculine, and the narration of the fetus in terms of masculine heroism and adventure.
>
> (Franklin 1991: 201)

6 For a detailed historical treatment of the *Roe v. Wade* decision see Petchesky 1990.

7 On 28 January 1988, the Supreme Court of Canada struck down a law that required Canadian women seeking legal abortions to obtain the permission of a 'therapeutic abortion committee.' Under the old law, abortions were provided only in hospitals which were authorized by such a committee to perform the procedure. Dr. Henry Morgentaler appealed a criminal conviction of 'performing an illegal abortion' to the Supreme Court, where it was determined that the abortion law violated women's right to security of the person under the Canadian Charter of Rights and Freedoms. Throughout his career, Dr. Henry Morgentaler has been harassed, threatened, and repeatedly jailed for his advocacy work on behalf of women's right to access a legal medical health service. Dr. Morgentaler pioneered the safest abortion techniques used in Canadian hospitals and abortion clinics today (Landsberg 1988: A2).

8 For an analysis of the politics of pinpointing fetal gender and assessing fetal health through medical imaging technologies see Cartwright 1995: 218–235.

9 For a discussion of the politics of abortion and questions of early human life amongst pro-choice advocates see Gillespie 1997.

10 In 1998, one of Toronto's major abortion service providing hospitals has been shut down because of provincial funding cuts to health care.

11 The women who participated in the focus group are all current or past members of a Canadian pro-choice lobbying organization. The group itself cannot be identified because of my commitment to maintaining the confidentiality of the focus group participants. The women elected to take part in the focus group because they were familiar with the photograph of Gerri Santoro, and wanted to discuss their feelings of connection and disconnection to it.

12 I contacted several pro-choice organizations in Toronto in search of activists who would be willing to devote time to this research. I wanted to keep the number of women in the group small, as the research was in its preliminary stages. While I did not ask the activists to locate themselves in relation to race, sexuality, and class, the group was primarily, although not exclusively, composed of white middle-class heterosexual activists, ranging in age from mid-twenties to mid-sixties. One activist questioned how the identifications of white pro-choice feminists are forged in relation to a photograph of a dead woman who is clearly white. She questioned further whether an image of a non-white woman would have been taken up as a pro-choice symbol the way Santoro's image has been. In future groups I would want to think further about questions of race, class, and sexual orientation in relation to viewing the image of Gerri Santoro, and how this might inform the selection of focus group participants.

13 The speaker is referring to the Canadian Federal Reform Party lead by Preston Manning.

14 In 1997, a Canadian woman who was addicted to solvents was detained in a rehabilitation center in the best interests of her fetus.

15 The 'Ms. G' case was heard before the Supreme Court of Canada in June of 1997. The case was brought forward by Winnipeg's Child and Family Services agency, after the Manitoba court of appeal overturned the court order which forced 'Ms. G' into a hospital. In September of 1997 the Supreme Court ruled in favor of the mother.

16 The three pages from *Ms.* magazine on which the photograph of Gerri Santoro is displayed span twenty-two years of pro-choice organizing. Reading *across* these pages shows how the photograph has been differently framed in the context of pro-choice movement discourses over time. In particular, the captions 'Never Again' (1973), 'Never Again! Never Again?' (1977), and 'She Had a Name, She Had a Family, She Was Leona's Sister Gerri' (1995) signal the ethical, political, and moral questions for pro-choice movement that the photograph has worked to mediate and punctuate.

References

Blain, M. (1994) 'Power, War and Melodrama in the Discourses of Political Movements,' *Theory and Society* 23: 805–837.

Brandes-Gratz, R. (1973) 'Never Again,' *Ms.* 1, 10 (April): 44–49.

—— (1977) 'Never Again! Never Again?,' *Ms.* July: 54–55.

—— (1995) 'She Had a Name, She Had a Family, She Was Leona's Sister Gerri,' *Ms.* 6, 3 (November/December): 72–74.

Cartwright, L. (1995) 'Gender Artifacts: Technologies of Bodily Display in Medical Culture,' in L. Cooke and P. Wollen, (eds) *Visual Display: Culture Beyond Appearances*, Seattle, Wash.: Bay Press.

Duden, B. (1993) *Disembodying Women: Perspectives on Pregnancy and the Unborn*, Cambridge, Mass.: Harvard University Press.

Franklin, S. (1991) Foetal Fascinations: New Dimensions to the Medical-Scientific Construction of Foetal Personhood,' in S. Franklin, C. Lury, and J. Stacey (eds) *Off-Centre: Feminism and Cultural Studies*, London: Harper Collins.

Gillespie, M.A. (ed.) (1997) 'Speaking Frankly,' *Ms.* 11, 6 (May/June): 64–71 .

Gillooly, J. (1995) *Leona's Sister Gerri*, Ho-Ho-Kus, N.J.: New Day Films.

Landsberg, M. (1988) 'Jubilation: The Shabby Abortion Law Has Been Struck Down,' *Globe and Mail* 30 January 1998: A2.

McQuiston, L. (1997) *Suffragettes to She-Devils: Women's Liberation and Beyond*, London: Phaidon Press.

Michaels, A. (1996) *Fugitive Pieces*, Toronto: McClelland and Stewart.

Nilsson, L. (1965) 'The Drama of Life Before Birth,' *LIFE* (April): 54–72A.

Petchesky, R.P. (1987) 'Fetal Images: The Power of Visual Culture in the Politics of Reproduction,' *Feminist Studies* 13, 2: 263–92.

—— (1990) *Abortion and Woman's Choice: The State, Sexuality and Reproductive Freedom*, Boston, Mass.: Northeastern University Press.

Phelan, P. (1993) *Unmarked: The Politics of Performance*, New York: Routledge.

Probyn, E. (1995) 'Queer Belongings: The Politics of Departure,' in E. Grosz and E. Probyn (eds) *Sexy Bodies: The Strange Carnalities of Feminism*, New York: Routledge.

Sandlos, K. (1997) 'Notes from Focus Group with Pro-Choice Activists,' unpublished transcript, OISE/University of Toronto.

Scott, J.W. (1992) 'Experience,' in J. Butler and J.W. Scott (eds) *Feminists Theorize the Political*, New York: Routledge.

Solomon-Godeau, A. (1991) *Photography at the Dock: Essays on Photographic History, Institutions and Practices*, Minneapolis: University of Minnesota Press.

The Silent Scream (1984) American Portrait Films.

5 Luce Irigaray's sexuate rights and the politics of performativity

Penelope Deutscher

In her more recent work, French feminist Luce Irigaray has turned her attention to the domain of civil rights and legal reform. She argues that equal rights need to be reformulated in a conceptual language of sexual difference at a legal and institutional level. In *Je, tu nous* (1993) and *Thinking the Difference* (1994) she proposes a 'bill of sexuate rights' which would constitute an amendment to the French civil code.

Many feminists have analysed the limitations of equal rights strategies, arguing that women have specific needs and entitlements not adequately comprehended in the language of equality. What, then, is the status of concepts of sexual difference in such arguments? When it is argued that sexual difference is not adequately recognised at law, it is usually posited as a fact to which the law is blind. When the issue is taken to be one of recognition, sexual difference is posited as preceding its recognition in law.[1] By contrast, Irigaray's diagnosis of contemporary culture is that it has excluded the possibility of sexual difference. She cannot call for a simple politics of recognition, since sexual difference does not have for Irigaray the status of a pre-existing given subsisting in its integrity irrespective of its failure to be recognised and represented.

Feminist theorists disturbed by the limitations – both philosophical and practical – of equal rights discourse have been interested in Irigaray's attempt to reformulate a politics of sexuate rights in a language of sexual difference. In the words of Drucilla Cornell, 'Luce Irigaray writes that as living, sexuate beings, our identities cannot be constructed without conditions of respect for difference and equality of rights to bring out such differences' (1995: 246n.). But what marks Irigaray's work in this area, as Cornell also acknowledges, is her view that the law, in remetaphorising femininity, would, in fact, be 'instituting' rather than 'recognising' a culture of sexual difference.[2] Cornell also suggests that respect for difference as a conceptual basis for legal rights refers to 'feminine sexual difference, as continually reimagined' (1992a: 281). While many feminist commentators have converted Irigarayan sexual difference into a more simplistic politics of recognition, this chapter discusses those who have dealt more seriously with the circular structure of Irigarayan rights. We can ask from this perspective: How appropriate is Irigarayan sexual difference as a basis for thinking legal reform? What political and conceptual difficulties arise from a circular structure which would simultaneously 'recognise' and 'effect' sexual difference?

Sexuate rights as a basis for legal reform

How does Irigaray mark her ideal of a legal remetaphorisation of sexual difference in formulating proposals for legal reform? Many of the reforms Irigaray proposes are banal, calling for fair treatment of women in the areas of family allowances, media, advertising, taxation laws, and so on. But under the heading of the 'right to human identity' we also find a startling affirmation of women's virginity as a legal right and as a crucial element of feminine identity (Irigaray 1994: 60; 1993: 86–87). In *Je, tu, nous*, she conceives of women as cultivating a kind of 'becoming-virgin': 'There's no doubt we are born virgins. But we also have to become virgins, to relieve our bodies and souls of cultural and familial fetters. For me, becoming a virgin is synonymous with a woman's conquest of the spiritual' (1993: 117). Or, in place of virginity, we could consider substituting Cornell's use of the concept of bodily integrity, or inviolability (Cornell 1995), since Irigaray reconceptualises the term virginity to signify psychological and moral ideas of inviolability. Irigaray's argument is not exactly that women are radically different from men in body and mind. Rather, her position is that the given social is not able to accommodate such a conception and is premised on such a sexual 'indifference'.

Irigaray therefore tries to evoke a conception which she criticises the social for rendering impossible. In other words, her concept of sexual difference is grounded in deliberate paradox. Sexual difference has been excluded, but since this exclusion lies at the heart of phallocentric culture sexual difference is both exterior and interior, both excluded from and enveloped within culture. Irigaray argues that sexual difference both is and is not excluded. She calls for a recognition of sexual difference which she also designates as incoherent within given culture. Her work suggests that concepts of sexuate rights are too weak unless they are able to accommodate an articulation of the paradoxical status of sexual difference. The specificity of Irigarayan sexuate rights is that they are not grounded in a concept of difference which precedes its recognition at law, and this is the point often missed by those who turn to Irigaray for a feminist critique of equal rights.

It is for this reason that Cornell, and also Nicola Lacey, have emphasised the importance of distinguishing between some recent feminist affirmations of sexual difference which attempt to describe women, and a writing of sexual difference which attempts to remetaphorise the feminine (Lacey 1996: 139–140, Cornell 1991: 199–205). Admittedly, the reappropriation of the term 'virginity' and its reconceptualisation is one of the more extreme aspects of Irigaray's 'bill of sexuate rights'. But it does serve at least one important rhetorical function, which is to highlight that these rights are intended to break with a politics of recognition, and to rely instead on the founding politics of remetaphorisation.

In this regard, the Irigarayan project for sexuate rights attributes a particular status to law and the French civil code as founding institutions. The Irigarayan rights could be seen as illegitimate insofar as they would 'recognise' a sexual difference which is (according to Irigaray's own argument) excluded from the social given. But because of the idea of retroactive action grounding her imperative of a legal recognition of sexual difference, she is arguing that the law should 'recognise' sexual identities it, in fact, thereby institutes.[3] The rights 'recognise' a state of sexual difference which cannot be recognised as such. Their justification is that the possibility of such a recognition has been excluded. Their operative logic is that their institutional recognition would retroactively constitute their own conditions of possibility.

Is it appropriate for Irigaray to assert that legal reform should operate outside of the politics of recognition? Also, one can ask, what does legitimate Irigarayan sexuate rights if not the politics of recognition? What can justify the idea that legal reform should found, rather than reflect, sexuate identity? The issue of legal reform operating outside of the politics of recognition has been extensively discussed in relation to Jacques Derrida's analysis of the legitimacy of the Declaration of Independence of the USA. In looking at this material, I will ask how it relates to the Irigarayan demand that sexual difference be given legal institutionalisation.

Performative rights

Derrida asks, '*Who signs, and with what so-called proper name, the declarative act which founds an institution*' (1986: 8)? As I have suggested in relation to the potential status of the 'founding' of the Irigarayan rights, Derrida argues that such a founding act has a peculiar status of 'recognition'. At first, Derrida's discussion provisionally attributes the curiosity to the act's performative operation. Here, we would say that the act effectively accomplishes or enacts that which it 'describes', 'recognises' or 'refers' to. In its intention, the Bill of Rights of the USA institutes the rights of the American people which it invokes. The problem, however, lies in what legitimates the constitution – the people 'signing' it – whose legitimacy to do so is effected only by the speech act:

> Here then is the 'good people' who engage themselves and engage only themselves in signing, in having their own declaration signed. The 'we' of the declaration speaks 'in the name of the people'.

> But this people does not exist. They do *not* exist as an entity, it does *not* exist *before* this declaration, not *as such*. If it gives birth to itself, as free and independent subject, as possible signer, this can hold only in the act of the signature. The signature invents the signer. This signer can only authorise him- or herself to sign once he or she has come to the end [*parvenu au bout*], if one can say this, of his or her signature, and in a sort of fabulous retroactivity. That first signature authorizes him or her to sign

...

> In signing, the people say ... henceforth, I have the right to sign, in truth I
> will already have had it since I was able to give it to myself.
>
> (Derrida 1986: 10)

> The question remains. How is a State made or founded, how does a State make
> or found itself? And an independence? And the autonomy of one which both
> gives itself, and signs, its own law? Who signs all these authorisations to sign?
>
> (Derrida 1986: 13)

Derrida's formulations suggest one possibility for reconsidering the 'impossibility'
grounding an Irigarayan bill of sexuate rights. Her formulation of these rights
results from her argument concerning the extreme degree of structural, symbolic
and institutionalised mediation necessary to the generation of new sexuate identities. But on the other hand, the rights seem to be incoherent because they
'recognise' what does not exist. But, in the light of Derrida's comments, one
could ask whether a conventional bill of rights, recognising the equality of
subjects, is grounded with any greater original legitimacy? Like the conventional
bill, the institutionalisation of an Irigarayan bill of rights recognising sexual
difference would be grounded in a structure of impossibility, insofar as it would
be authorised by its recognition of a referent which does not precede that
moment of recognition. As in the Declaration of Independence, in Irigaray's
imaginary bill of rights the status of the subjects who authorise the bill would be
brought into effect only by the institution of the bill itself. Neither in the
Declaration of Independence, nor in the bill of sexuate rights, do the subjects
entitled to the declared rights precede their legal 'recognition'.

Justifying sexuate rights

Informing the work of both Cornell and Irigaray is the view that the law could
play a significant role in remetaphorising sexual difference. We have seen one
possible argument that sexuate rights need not be considered 'less legitimate' in
their original formulation than 'equal rights'. But this position still leaves room
for considerable debate about what would legitimise the legal institutionalisation
of sexual difference. A second suggestion can be gleaned from Cornell's discussion of sexuate rights. Relying on an interpretation of Derrida's work on justice,
Cornell proposes that legitimation would come only 'after the fact', only with the
eventual cultural possibility of sexual difference.

What can be drawn from Derrida's analysis of justice is not (as some have
worried) an inability to *criticise* the law, Cornell argues. Rather, an account is
offered of the 'justificatory language of *revolutionary* violence'. This depends on
'what has yet to be established, and of course, as a result, might yet come into
being. If it did not depend on what was yet to come, it would not be *revolutionary*
violence' (1992b: 168). She continues by citing Derrida's comments in 'Force of
Law' that 'a "successful" revolution ... will produce *après* coup what it was

destined in advance to produce' and that it may be a matter of generations before it is known 'if the performative of the violent founding of the State is "felicitous" or not' (1992b: 168, see also Derrida 1992: 36). Again, we are asked to reconsider the obvious invalidity of the sexuate rights. Perhaps their validity is not yet something we can assess; perhaps this will be conferred by the future, not the present.

Cornell's implicit suggestion here is that the same deconstructive analysis which destabilises conservative law by demonstrating how it generates the effect of its self-authorisation can be used to formulate the conditions of possibility of revolutionary change. If it is possible to make this parallel, the first point to be noted is that the 'impossibility' *relied* upon in Irigaray's utopian project, and *exposed* by Derrida in 'Declaration', are related in status. If Cornell thinks one can gain a critical lever on the law in its function as a conservative force by emphasising its mystical foundations, then how could the same notion of the mystical foundations of any institutionalisation of sexual difference be used to affirm the Irigarayan project?

With this question open, I turn to the questions directed by David Farrell Krell towards Cornell in the debate which was provoked by Derrida's 'Force of Law' essay:

> Is it not the case that ethics, metaphysics and ontology alike are structured with a view to the Good – to the ultimate, infinite, and universal form of the capital G Good, the capital G that summons and that punishes capitally? Does not an ethics of the Good, precisely in its infinitely good intentions, reproduce the worst violence of the tradition of which it is not only a piece but the keystone? … Is it impossible that the guardian of the machine should be a woman? Or perhaps more neutrally put: What is the possibility of *justice* we call *woman*?
>
> (Krell 1990: 1723–1724)

Krell asks if sexual difference is being elevated to the status of the Good. What is the legitimation for this, particularly insofar as figures such as Cornell and Irigaray are operating outside of the politics of recognition? Have they left themselves trapped in the abyss Balkin describes?

> What can deconstruction possibly tell us about our choice of values if all texts are deconstructible? … What is the source of moral authority to deconstruct in one way rather than another? … Deconstruction … has nothing particular to tell us about justice, or ethics, or any questions of value.
>
> (1990: 1626)[4]

True, one might argue that sexuate rights are 'no less legitimate', and one might argue that sexuate rights will be legitimated 'only after the fact'. But what gives sexual difference and sexuate rights some special entitlement to be justified in this fashion, rather than any other rights? Would not any rights one cared to devise have exactly the same status? Though the deconstructibility of law seems to open the possibility of such a position, an argument can be given for why Irigaray's sexuate rights are, at least in one respect, 'more legitimate'.

Justifying sexuate rights?

From one perspective, and despite the very utopian nature of the Irigarayan bill of rights, the latter could be thought of as 'not less legitimate' than the Declaration of Independence of the USA discussed in this debate. Both are grounded in a paradox of recognition. But Irigaray's emphasis on the status of her sexuate rights as 'impossible' could suggest that they are somewhat more legitimate than such an established and august bill of rights. For conventional law disavows its own mystical foundations. We see this in Derrida's comments concerning the USA's Bill of Rights, which invoke and defer to entities such as God in order to claim a transcendent ground for authority. In the context of that claim to authority, it is a destabilising and critical gesture to indicate, as do Derrida and Cornell, these mystical foundations. Thus, conventional law is grounded in 'impossibility', but an impossibility which cannot be avowed. By contrast, Irigaray's strategy is to insist on the impossibility of her utopian bill of rights. The status of the foundations grounding her bill of rights is, in fact, different from that of a conventional bill of rights. However, the difference is not that the one is less 'impossibly' grounded than the other. Rather the difference occurs at the level of avowal.

Whereas conventional law obscures its grounding in a paradoxical impossibility of recognition, Irigaray *highlights* the impossibility of 'recognition' by sexuate rights of the (sexually different) subject.[5] This is one of the most important aspects of her formulation of these rights. The underlining of impossibility clarifies her understanding of their ethical status. The Irigarayan rights can be read as avowedly 'unjustified'. It can be argued that the strength, and not the weakness, of Irigaray's work on legal reform is precisely her avowal of an 'impossible status'. The Declaration of Independence contains a reference to its legitimisation by divine authority. A deferral occurs here to a legitimating divine point projected as external, transcendent, original. To the extent that Irigaray does not justify her sexuate rights by reference to a blunt fact of sexual difference which the law should recognise, she avoids projecting sexual difference as external, transcendent, or original.

From the perspective of those who consider that deconstruction tells us nothing about our choice of values, the best one could say of Irigarayan sexuate rights is that the paradox of recognition in their imagined institution leaves them 'not less legitimate' than the constitutive time of any bill of rights. But what does arise from this discussion is at least one set of criteria for legitimacy for the rights, and one form of post-deconstructive ethics. Ethics becomes a matter of being prepared to avow, negotiate and work with founding aporia, although this is an extremely difficult position to occupy. A position which does not rely on reference to mythical foundations or stable justification may well be more ethical because less duplicitous, and more prepared to recognise the difficulty of its own politics and the impossibility of an ultimate legitimacy.[6] So, while one suggestion arising from the debate around deconstruction and law is that Irigaray's sexuate rights are not less legitimate than other rights in their original moment, and a second is that they could only be legitimated after the fact, a third is that they could never be legitimated, that this is their point, and that their strength is their greater preparedness to acknowledge this than is seen in some other political philosophy.

Minimally, the suggestion would be that their 'future anterior' or 'retrospective' status does not undermine but rather can be read as sustaining the legitimacy of the sexuate rights, *insofar as it is avowed*. However, the idea that sexuate rights are grounded in a logic Irigaray might understand as performative rather than denotative has recently provoked further discussion. That some feminist positions might be grounded in what is identified as a politics of performativity has led to considerable interrogation about political responsibility in concepts of performativity. This has already been seen in the preceding discussion. The point of Irigaray's concept of sexuate reform may well be to exchange the politics of recognition for a politics of performative rights. But if so, what makes the rights she would see instituted politically responsible? In some discussion, the issue of referentiality (what is the referent for the sexual difference recognised by sexuate rights?) slides into one of 'making things so'. Is it appropriate, is it justified and is it possible, that Irigarayan sexuate rights would make sexual difference 'so'? In addressing this issue, I want first to return to the most well-known philosophical articulation of the concept of performativity.

Words doing things

In John Austin's *How to Do Things with Words* (1962), we are told in many ways about the infelicitous or unsuccessful speech act. I proclaim the words: 'I hereby take you for my legally wedded husband' But if I am not before a legally authorised marriage celebrant, the speech act is unsuccessful. Or I say the words as an actor on a stage – again, no marriage takes place. But imagine that the celebrant is authorised to perform legal marriages and we are in the right conditions (not currently married to other partners, for example). Imagine that we are also in the right context. We are not speaking the words of a marriage ceremony in the context of a play or a joke. Then, when I pronounce the words, the speech act may be described as performative.

In the performative mode of language, the words are said to do the marriage, to constitute it. The speech act brings into effect, with its own enunciation, the 'thing' to which it apparently refers. Austin writes:

> In these examples it seems clear that to utter the sentence (in, of course, the appropriate circumstances) is not to *describe* my doing of what I should be said in so uttering to be doing or to state that I am doing it: it is to do it.
>
> (1962: 6)

He adds that this kind of utterance is neither true nor false. For, '[w]hen I say, before the registrar or altar, etc., "I do", I am not reporting on a marriage: I am indulging in it' (1962: 6).

For Austin, the legitimacy of the words uttered does not inhere in their referring accurately to a situation, to which the words correctly point. The words can be neither true nor false. Instead, through pronouncing the words ('in, of course the appropriate circumstances') one brings into effect what one says. So, there are at least two issues here: an issue of referentiality, and an issue of whether one can make things happen with words, or in Austin's words, an issue of 'can saying make it so?' (1962: 7). These two issues – referentiality and 'making things so' – have been key in the many discussions of performativity in relation to feminism and Irigaray's work which have recently appeared.

(Is this a question of) can saying make it so?

Irigaray has little access to the institutional domains of legal reform and public policy in France. So her words of legal reform are pronounced, but are not pronounced in felicitous circumstances, and not by a speaker authorised to effect legal reform. Saying the words of sexuate rights does not make the thing happen to which they refer: the constitution of sexuate rights. Irigaray would be like the celebrant who performs marriage ceremonies without being legally authorised to do so, or like the actor who says the words on the stage. There may be a performance of the words, but because the words fail to perform the act, they could be described as infelicitous. If this seems clear, what can be made of the fact that theorists have wanted to emphasise the idea of performativity in thinking about these sexuate rights?

A good example of the concern expressed by some about Irigarayan sexuate rights is seen in Lacey's otherwise fairly sympathetic response to them: 'the question of whether particular rhetorics *can* move us forward is a relevant question … [can] rhetorical strategies … dislodge the dominant conception once they move from argument to legal institutionalisation' (1998: 247). For Lacey, the concern about Irigaray's work is exactly its striking naivety with regard to the conditions necessary for legal reform. Irigaray's turn to the formulation of sexuate rights could be seen as a reversion to the language and optimism of institutional reform: 'Irigaray borrows (unusually within her work) the language of …. institutional reform. In doing so, she espouses a curiously naive and apparently instrumental optimism about legal reform' (1998: 245). Here, the rights are read as if Irigaray hopes that performativity is, in the words of Judith Butler, 'the power … of an originating will' (Butler 1997: 51) whose declaration creates the sexual difference it declares.

Lacey does not suppose that Irigaray's position is that her simple declaration of the rights in her published works will make them happen. But she does suppose that, according to Irigaray, the legal institutionalisation of the rights, if they could be effected, would generate the conditions for a culture of sexual difference. It is this which she takes to be a naive instrumental optimism. Lacey supposes that the sexuate rights reflect excessive confidence in the adequacy of legal reform for provoking change. But if one does read Irigaray's material in terms of Austin's material on performativity, it is not clear that they are best interpreted as reflecting optimism in a cause–effect relationship between the institution of rights and a potentially resulting culture of sexual difference.

A return to Austin's material may be useful in this regard. Consider his famously startling example, in which we imagine that someone says to me 'shoot her', and I do (Austin 1962: 101). This is an example of how words can make things happen. Indeed, he qualifies, there are hardly any words that could not be said to make things happen. But, from the outset of *How to Do Things with Words*, this is not Austin's concern. Instead, he reflects on linguistic formulations which *are* simultaneously the deed they seem to 'refer to', such as: 'I declare'; 'I hereby name'; 'I promise'; 'I denounce'. In such cases, as he formulates this, 'the issuing of an utterance is the performing of an action' (Austin 1962: 6). In these sorts of examples, questions about naive optimism would be inappropriate. Would one say, in the case of the classic Austin performative, 'why should we think that because I enounce a promise, the promise will take place'? Certainly, someone might wonder whether I can be relied on to keep my promise. But the speech act which has 'happened' through the event of the speech is the promise itself: this is the point of the concept of performativity in such instances. The concept of performativity revolves not around whether things 'will happen' because of my words, but around what kind of event my words have already constituted. Of course, various effects may also result from my namings, declarations and denunciations, but this is a different issue. To establish the difference, Austin distinguishes between 'illocutionary' and 'perlocutionary' speech acts. Speech acts may be thought of as perlocutionary insofar as they may subsequently lead to things happening. The speech act 'shoot her' is perlocutionary insofar as it may cause a gun to be fired. It is a different matter to assess a speech act insofar as it is 'illocutionary'. It is illocutionary speech which has already accomplished an act regardless of what consequences it may lead to. A promise has been made, for example, or a boat christened, or an order given, or a declaration made, in the moment of the very enunciation of these speech acts.[7]

In light of the way in which Irigaray's material has recently been interpreted in terms of performativity, I propose some rethinking of how this concept might be most usefully brought to bear on her work. I want to read Irigarayan sexuate rights not in terms of perlocutionary performativity (in terms of consequences which might or might not result from their enunciation, or formal institutionalisation) but in terms of their illocutionary performativity, their status as an act of declaration. The question would not then be: would the consequences be all that Irigaray seems to anticipate? The question would be: what kind of act is this already?

Those who question the naivety, or the apparent instrumentalism, of Irigaray's bill of sexuate rights would suggest that it is not appropriate to theorise Irigarayan sexual difference as the basis for legal reform. I agree that Irigaray's bill of sexuate rights is not best understood as an appropriate basis for proposed legal reform in this sense (in consequentialist terms, as if their legal institutionalisation is proposed as a sure way of leading to a culture of sexual difference).

But perhaps the concept of performativity, given that it recurs in several discussions of this material, could be useful in clarifying what we think Irigaray's 'declaration' of sexuate rights is actually supposed to accomplish. Thought of as a utopian program, the discussion does become consequentialist. Is it the case, readers ask, that the legal institutionalisation of sexuate rights would produce the result of installing a culture of sexual difference? The question arises precisely because the rights are interpreted in the context of a politics of performativity, understood consequentially.[8] What is noticeable here is a slide over whether the performativity in question is taken to pertain to a utopia in which sexuate rights are installed (here the idea would be that the founding words are supposed to have an 'effect', that of instituting a culture of sexual difference, and the question becomes, would they really have that effect); or whether the performativity pertains not to a utopian legal declaration of sexuate rights, but to Irigaray's own declaration of these rights in works such as *Thinking the Difference* and *Je, tu, nous*. Either way, certainly the prime question for commentators has been a consequentialist one. Does 'rhetoric' – do the new metaphors for identity which could be offered in the wording of legal reform – have the power to achieve cultural change?

I suggest that Irigaray does not think that the institution of laws recognising sexual difference would alone produce a culture of sexual difference.[9] But, in this imaginary performativity, *if it 'did'*, what does matter is that the rights would not recognise a prior existing truth of sexual difference but would effect what they seem to recognise. They would do, rather than referring to. However, it is certainly not the case that sexuate rights are conceived as capable of instituting a culture of sexual difference in an instrumental sense. Instead, we are asked only to *imagine* such a performative institution.

One strategy, then, is to see Irigaray's rights as performing an imaginary performativity. The rights declare: imagine a context in which it were true that these rights contributed to the institution of what they seemingly 'recognised' in a 'fabulous retroactivity'. And they declare: these rights are not illegitimate, though they do not recognise some here and now 'truth' of men and women. And they are not less legitimate than existing rights, about which we can similarly interrogate the authorization of their original founding.

If we think of the sexuate rights as a declaration of a new bill of rights, does the question of their felicity turn on a social recognition of the authority of the declaration? What if we think of them as a declaration of a radical political perspective? Could they not be thought of as succeeding in this act, an act of declaration? Lacking the authority, Irigaray declares that she too can declare new sexuate rights. Perhaps what is being performed is not the founding of sexuate rights, but the founding of a critical perspective.

In fact, thinking of the movement between the concepts of performativity and performance which occurs in Judith Butler's earlier work, perhaps the sexuate rights could even be thought of as a drag performance, Irigaray saying:

'I can do law, I can do founding authority'. We cut to the founding authority of law, and suddenly, to paraphrase Peggy Phelan, in fact this law appears to be *more* 'unreal' than the sexuate rights because it remains unaware of the artifice that the sexuate rights has made hyper-visible (see Phelan 1993: 103).

Of course, a whole debate has circulated about whether parody is really subversive or not.[10] Didn't the walkers in *Paris Is Burning* both reinforce and reconsolidate the norms they emulated? Does Irigaray reconsolidate the norm she emulates? Perhaps yes, insofar as she appeals to the authority of law. Perhaps no, insofar as she exposes the illusion of founding authority. Repeatedly, we have seen theorists associated with a feminist politics of performativity accused of naivety. How naive to think that these gestures – of parody, or of exposing dehiscence at the heart of law, or gender – will bring down anything. But perhaps Irigaray can be thought of as focusing on the small moments of unease at the heart of the reproduction of systems of law and gender: exposing the fact that law must be reproduced by its recognition, that it is grounded in a fabulous retroactivity. A declaration of sexuate rights does make more visible this artifice. Irigaray may not be subverting institutionalised law, but she may be subverting the assumption of legimate foundations of equal rights discourse in law. If she does not successfully perform legal rights reform, she does perform the 'why not' function in response to the legal rights reform to which she speaks. Irigaray's sexuate rights can be interpreted as performative, not because of what they might 'make happen', but in terms of the act they constitute – an act of declaration: I Irigaray declare sexuate rights. I declare they are not less legitimate.

Judith Butler and the declaration of sexuate rights

I have suggested that, from the perspective of Austin's concept of performativity, it is not clear that Irigaray's sexuate rights should be taxed for the kind of optimism critics such as Lacey are thinking of. In a cause–effect assessment, one questions, as Lacey does, whether the recognition of sexual difference would ensue from legal reform alone. In an assessment of their imagined felicity, one asks whether the declaration of sexuate rights alone would suffice for the institution of sexual difference. Lacey's response is – surely not. Similarly, in an assessment of their actual felicity, the same approach would ask whether Irigaray's attempt to institute sexuate rights succeeds. The response would be no, because Irigaray is not authorised to perform it; because the declaration of sexuate rights is not socially or legally recognised, it has no 'force'. Both responses suppose that the appropriate issue, as we have seen, is the perlocutionary performativity of the rights. Both suggest that Irigaray's declaration of sexuate rights patently lacks the necessary force. In the here and now, Irigaray does not have the force to make her declaration of sexuate rights legally valid. And, even in an imagined legal institution of the rights, such rights would still not (such is Lacey's suggestion) have the force to institute a culture of sexual difference.

In discussing felicitous performatives, Judith Butler interrogates the same issue of when one can be said to have the force to make one's sayings 'so'. It seems, she writes, that 'performativity requires a power to effect or enact what one names' (1997: 49). But when one takes this position, one presupposes that:

> the subject who utters the performative is positioned on a map of social power in a fairly fixed way, and this performative will or will not work depending on whether the subject who performs the utterance is already authorised to make it work by the position of social power she or he occupies.
>
> (1997: 156)

For Austin, we saw that questions of optimism (will my saying make it so?) would be inappropriate in relation to illocutionary speech acts, because their logic is not that of the cause–effect. The speech act simply is the very deed to which it refers; the promise is effected as it is said, as is the declaration, the confession, the order, and so on. This seems to suggest, in the case of the felicitous speech act, what one might describe as an airtight oneness between the word and the deed. But Derrida and Butler, in reflecting on performatives, have demonstrated the illusory nature of this apparent 'airtight oneness' between the speaker's performance of a felicitous performative and its 'success'. This apparent instantaneity covers over the fact that performatives are only felicitous through context, citation and repetition of norms, the appeal to and recognition of conventions. The best example of this is Austin's own examples of the way in which performativity is context dependent: if I have no authority to marry you, no marriage legally takes place. The context must therefore be folded within the event of the words for the 'self-presence' or 'instantaneity' of the word-act to seemingly be rendered. Notice, also, how the judge who installs a situation seems to install immediately with her or his very words, but in so doing s/he implicitly *cites* the law that s/he applies, and speaks in the name of a certain authority.

Crucially, Butler does not emphasise this in order to demonstrate the powerlessness of unauthorised speakers to effect felicitous performatives. Recalling that the performative is always a citation, a repetition or an invocation of conventions, Butler reverses the issue. The point is not how I can be assured that the authority of my speech act is recognised. The point is to realise that this very lack of assurance also opens up the possibility of failure.

When Irigaray is charged with naivety, the supposition is that she has no authority to effect sexuate rights, nor any reason to assume that rhetoric, even legal reform alone, could move us forward. But by the same logic, Judith Butler has suggested that established, conventional law has no ability to ensure that it will stay still.[11] Because of its dependency on citation, context, recognition, speech and speech acts are always somewhat out of the speaker's control, and it is this very fact which can be seen as politically enabling, not disempowering. It is precisely, argues Butler,

> the *expropriability* of the dominant, 'authorised' discourse that constitutes one potential site of its subversive resignification. What happens, for instance,

when those who have been denied the social power to claim 'freedom' or 'democracy' appropriate those terms from the dominant discourse and rework or resignify those highly cathected terms to rally a political movement? If the performative must compel collective recognition in order to work, must it compel only those kinds of recognition that are *already* institutionalized?

(1997: 157–158)

As Butler notes, there can be no assurance of this. It can 'also compel a critical perspective on existing institutions'. Butler's response suggests, first, that we need to reconsider the supposition that, *even thought of in perlocutionary terms*, Irigaray's declaration of sexuate rights is (both from an actual and an imaginary perspective) doomed to infelicity. As she argues, if a performative must compel collective recognition in order to work, there can be no guarantee that it will compel 'only those kinds of recognition that are *already* institutionalized'. Context, recognition and convention dependent, there can be no assurance of exactly how equal rights discourse is recognised, nor any assurance of how the language of rights can resignify once 're-territorialized' by the disenfranchised (Butler 1997: 158). Certainly, Irigaray has no means of controlling the consequences which may arise from declarations of sexuate rights, whether legal, authorised, recognised, or not. But their very declaration may be thought of as the kind of unexpected result which can arise from conventional equal rights discourse, and the way in which that discourse is reappropriated in unpredictable ways. Lacey's response focuses on the lack of power of language to move us forward. However, Butler would ask us to focus on the way in which sites of apparent power such as institutionalised equal rights discourse are open to unexpected forms of response which can move us forward. This is the risk to which all speech acts are open. A good instance can be seen in Irigaray's declaration of sexuate rights. There is some degree of unpredictability in the way in which these may travel, and be read, in different contexts, but politically one should affirm the way in which institutionalised law is open to this degree of unpredictability, however small.

This said, what fascinates in Butler's response is its ability to simultaneously reconsider the illocutionary infelicity of the bill of sexuate rights. Butler's concept of the *expropriability* of the dominant, 'authorised discourse' is not just that, in a perlocutionary sense it has the power to provoke unexpected consequences, that some may come to rework or resignify terms such as rights to rally a political movement, for example. Butler's concept questions even the apparent instantaneity of speech acts thought of as illocutionary. Again, that instantaneity relies on convention and citation of norms. The marriage and the order work only because they cite conventions of ceremonies and orders which we recognise. If we do not recognise these conventions and ceremonies, or not in the same way, they act differently for us. It is true, then, that there is no guarantee of how Irigaray's sexuate rights can work even in their instantaneity as a declaration of radical political perspective. For some, the act may act as such, for others, it *may* act as naivety or poetry. But again, one could argue, we need this level of unpredictability, because it is this unpredictability which allows for the possibility that equal rights law, so institutionalised, acts for Irigaray not as that which we recognise as authorised, but as that tradition which we recognise *as* what we want to displace. As Butler writes in response to Catharine MacKinnon and Rae Langton:

> That the utterance can be turned, untethered from its origin, is one way to shift the locus of authority in relation to the utterance. And though we might lament that others have this power with our language, consider the perils of not having that power of interruption and redirection with respect to others.
>
> (Butler 1997: 93)

In this chapter, I have interpreted Irigaray's bill of sexuate rights in terms of the concept of performativity in several ways. First, I asked how Irigaray's bill of sexuate rights is justified, and argued that Irigaray may have an ethics, but not a justifiable ethics.[12] Her emphasis that hers is an 'impossible politics' underlines this. The concept of performativity helps in the first instance to emphasise the fact that the rights are theorised as having a circular logic, justified only by the sexual difference they would institute. This is not, of course, to say that the legal institution of sexuate rights would necessarily institute a culture of sexuate difference, nor that their current, literary declaration leads to the increased material possibility of the Irigarayan rights. The Irigarayan rights may be 'no less illegitimate' insofar as they would recognise that which does not precede the act of recognition, but this does not make them legal, nor necessarily effective in other reliable ways. Instead, in the first instance I suggested that their imagined performativity simply highlights that Irigaray's sexuate rights are not justified by a prior state of sexual difference. Irigaray does not argue that as a cause–effect relation, the rights would produce sexual difference, but takes the position that the advent of a culture of sexual difference would justify the rights. One can agree with those who have argued that nothing currently justifies these rights, but it is not clear that this is a point made against Irigaray's work.

Is Irigaray able to justify the position that sexual difference is a good? No, and while there are many weaknesses and inconsistencies in her work, I am arguing that this is not one of them. Instead, I am suggesting that it is when Irigaray is at her best that she does not 'make justice a woman'. No politics can be ultimately grounded, ultimately legitimate. A good politics is one which recognises this, however difficult the recognition, rather than appealing to ideals of 'recognition', 'justice as self-evident', the 'actual' or the 'good'. To some extent sexual difference is sometimes depicted by Irigaray as a fact to be recognised. But her work reflects the most difficult and rigorous politics to the extent that it is prepared to bear with its own paradox that it is a politics 'of the impossible' which tries to recognise that which cannot be recognised.

For some commentators, unjustified politics are irresponsible, and feminist politics of performativity constitute an example of just such a politics.[13] For others, the politics may be irresponsible because of the uncertainty of what they would produce.[14] Butler's argument is particularly useful: we need the uncertainty of how speech acts operate and signify, both from a perlocutionary and from an illocutionary perspective, for there to be the possibility that existing discourse can signify differently. And while Irigaray's own politics must themselves be subject to that uncertainty, it is only because of that same degree of uncertainty in relation to existing discourse that the possibility of her politics opens up at all.

Notes

1   In the words of Christine Littleton, for example, equality analysis is phallocentric because it is inapplicable once it encounters 'real' differences (Littleton 1991: 44). In 'Polity and Group Difference', Iris Marion Young criticises politics of equality which define citizens in terms of what they have in common, as opposed to how they differ, and where universality in a legal context means 'laws and rules that say the same for all and apply to all in the same way; laws and rules that are blind to individual and group differences' (1990: 114). Lacey (1996) offers an excellent overview of feminist criticism of the language of equal rights, and discussion of the need for recognition of sexual difference. The best summary of Irigaray's work on legal reform is to be found in Schwab 1996.

2   I think this position can be maintained despite formulations from Irigaray which do evoke the need for 'recognition' of sexual difference. Such formulations need to be read in the context of her position that our culture has excluded sexual difference, and the position, discussed later in this chapter, that hers is a 'politics of the impossible'.

3   Irigaray's proposals for legal reform interconnect with her proposals for reforms at the level of language, religion, intersubjective ethics, media, and economic exchange. A culture of sexual difference would require reform at all these levels, and not at the level of law reform alone. This is a point overlooked by arguments that legal reform alone is not a reliable means of achieving social change. It can be argued that Irigaray's position is not that this is the means by which to achieve a culture of sexual difference, but instead, that a culture of sexual difference could not be achieved unless there was change at all these levels. From this perspective, her philosophy need not be seen as reflecting naive or instrumental optimism.

4   Many have resisted this interpretation of deconstruction, finding that its value is precisely in its complication of politics, its questioning of the desire for political certainty. For a particularly helpful discussion of these different figurings of the politics of deconstruction, see Grosz 1997.

5   Where Cornell insists on Derrida's analysis of law as 'feigning presence' (Cornell 1992b: 157), I am arguing here that Irigaray sometimes formulates her sexuate rights so as not to 'feign presence'. This is the difference between an argument which *exposes* law as grounded in mystical foundations, and one which *affirms* Irigarayan rights as similarly grounded.

6   On this issue, see Grosz 1997.

7   For a discussion of the difference between performatives thought of as illoctionary and as perlocutionary, see Butler 1997, and also Langton 1993, discussed by Butler.

8   For example, Lacey points out:

> What is distinctive about projects such as those of Irigaray and Cornell is that they operate first and foremost at an imaginative and rhetorical level ... these

kinds of projects are primarily interested in the shape and dynamics of the institution of language.

(1996: 140)

And then:

> rhetorical strategies … presuppose an understanding of how discursive and material practices and changes interact, of how power flows through the social body [and] … depend upon the development of institutionally oriented social theoretic insights. Without this, … they [cannot] attain any understanding of what their effects may be.

(143)

9 As stated above, her position is very clear that a culture of sexual difference would require reform at all institutional, symbolic, social and interpersonal levels, including reform to religion, language, the economy, the relationship to technology, nature, love and friendship, in addition to legal reform.
10 See in particular hooks 1992.
11 In *Excitable Speech* (1997), Butler is not discussing Irigarayan sexuate rights but more generally the issue of performativity and revolutionary change.
12 Huffer criticises feminist theorists of performativity, particularly Judith Butler, for their 'disregard for ethical questions'. She contrasts this material with the work of Luce Irigaray: 'Unlike Butler, Irigaray places ethical questions at the center of her consideration of epistemological problems of identity and truth' (Huffer 1995: 21). Others (for example Krell), discussed above, have suggested that the problem with this kind of politics is precisely that it presupposes a capital G Good, which presupposes its own justification. What justifies a politics of sexual difference? I disagree with Huffer's pitting of Irigaray against Butler, in terms of their commitment to ethics. In this chapter, I suggest that Butler's analysis of the politics of performativity can be helpful in thinking about the status of Irigaray's sexuate rights, precisely because it helps to displace a reading of them as simply justified by the truth of sexual difference.
13 'While the intended liberatory aims of feminist and queer performativity are laudable, performative theory tends to be flawed by its disregard for ethical questions' (Huffer 1995: 21).
14 'A politics which denies the relevance of its own effects may fairly be accused of some degree of irresponsibility' (Lacey 1996: 143).

References

Austin, J. (1962) *How to Do Things with Words*, ed. J O. Urmson, Oxford: Clarendon Press.
Balkin, J.M. (1990) 'Tradition, Betrayal and the Politics of Deconstruction', *Cardozo Law Review* 11, 5–6 (Special Issue: 'Deconstruction and the Possibility of Justice'): 1613–1630.
Butler, J. (1997) *Excitable Speech: A Politics of the Performative*, New York and London: Routledge.
Cornell, D. (1991) *Beyond Accommodation: Ethical Feminism, Deconstruction and the Law*, New York and London: Routledge.
—— (1992a) 'Gender, Sex and Equivalent Rights', in J. Butler and J.W. Scott (eds) *Feminists Theorize the Political*, New York and London: Routledge.
—— (1992b) *The Philosophy of the Limit*, New York and London: Routledge.

—— (1995) *The Imaginary Domain: Abortion, Pornography and Sexual Harrassment*, New York and London: Routledge.

Derrida, J. (1986) 'Declarations of Independence', *New Political Science* 15 (Summer): 7–15.

—— (1992) 'Force of Law: The "Mystical Foundation" of Authority', in D. Cornell, M. Rosenfeld and D.G. Carlson (eds) *Deconstruction and the Possibility of Justice*, New York and London: Routledge.

Grosz, E. (1997) 'Ontology and Equivocation: Derrida's Politics of Sexual Difference', in N.J. Holland (ed.) *Feminist Interpretations of Jacques Derrida*, University Park, Penn.: Pennsylvania State University Press.

hooks, b. (1992) 'Is Gender Burning?', in b. hooks, *Black Looks: Race and Representation*, Boston, Mass.: South End Press.

Huffer, L. (1995) 'Luce *et veritas*: Toward an Ethics of Performance', *Yale French Studies* 87 ('Another Look, Another Woman'): 20–39.

Irigaray, L. (1993) *Je, tu, nous: Toward a Culture of Difference*, trans. A. Martin, New York and London: Routledge.

—— (1994) *Thinking the Difference: For a Peaceful Revolution*, trans. K. Montin, London: Athlone Press.

Krell, D.F. (1990) 'Response to the Panel on Deconstruction, Ethics and the Law', *Cardozo Law Review* 11, 5 and 6: 1723–1726.

Lacey, N. (1996) 'Normative Reconstruction in Socio-Legal Theory', *Social and Legal Studies* 5, 2: 131–157.

—— (1998) *Unspeakable Subjects: Feminist Essays in Legal and Social Theory*, Oxford: Hart.

Langton, R. (1993) 'Speech Acts and Unspeakable Acts', *Philosophy and Public Affairs* 22, 4: 293–330.

Littleton, C. (1991) 'Reconstructing Sexual Equality', in R. Kennedy and K. Bartlett (eds) *Feminist Legal Theory*, Boulder, Colo.: Westview Press.

Phelan, P. (1993) *Unmarked: The Politics of Performance*, New York and London: Routledge.

Schwab, G. (1996) 'Women and the Law in Irigarayan Theory', *Metaphilosophy* 27, 1 and 2: 146–177.

Young, I.M. (1990) *Throwing Like a Girl and Other Essays in Feminist Philosophy and Social Policy*, Bloomington and Indianapolis: Indiana University Press.

Part II

Boundaries and connections

Introduction

Sara Ahmed

The emergence of Black and post-colonial feminism has posed a critical challenge to some of the organising premises of white and Western feminist thought. While a starting point has been a recognition of the ethnocentric and colonialist basis of much feminist work (Carby 1992; Mohanty 1991), Black and post-colonial feminists have also provided a positive rethinking of how feminism can be put to work in a way which does justice, not only to the existence of differences between women, but to the historical fact that the international and gendered division of labour positions women in relationships of antagonism. By drawing attention to the antagonistic relationship between women, Black and post-colonial feminists have provided us with different ways of thinking about feminist research and the production of knowledge, feminist activism and the 'making' of connections, the processes of identity formation and identification, and the relationship between gender and other forms of social differentiation. Indeed, the recognition that gender is a relational category, and that colonialism and racism are themselves gendered processes, has allowed Black and post-colonial feminists to offer analyses which are sensitive to the nuances and complexities of power relations as they are lived, constructed and contested in different times and places.

In the first instance, Black feminists, working in different locations, have made a powerful critique of how white feminists have produced understandings of gender relations that have assumed whiteness as a norm. Such forms of understanding involve the othering of Black women within feminist discourse. Audre Lorde makes this point powerfully: 'as white women ignore built-in privilege of whiteness and define *woman* in terms of their own experience alone, then women of Color become "other", the outsider whose experience and tradition is too "alien" to comprehend' (1980: 117). Through recognising the othering of Black women within feminist discourse, Black feminists have complicated the very category of 'woman'. Elizabeth Spelman suggests that the notion of a generic 'woman' functions in feminist theory in a similar way to how the notion of a generic 'man' has functioned in Western philosophy – it works to exclude an analysis of the heterogeneity that inflects the category, and so cuts off an 'examination of the significance of such heterogeneity for feminist theory and political activity' (1990: ix). The violence of such othering demonstrates *what is at stake* in the assumption that woman has an essential and stable meaning. Such an assumption conceals the borders that define the very meaning of woman (whereby woman comes to stand for 'the white woman'). The stability of woman is hence an effect of power relations: that is, it is an effect of those who have the power to define or authorise the criteria for what or who is 'woman'.

Furthermore, Black feminists have also suggested that we need analyses of power which presuppose the relational nature of forms of social differentiation. That is, an individual is not identified as gendered in one instance, and then racialised in another. These forms of identification work *simultaneously* to produce specific subject positions. It has been suggested that an analysis of how race and gender collide in the production of subject positions is essential if we are to understand the specific experiences of Black women.[1] Such a relational model also requires that we refuse to understand forms of difference as additive: that is, as 'adding' together to produce an accumulative identity (Brewer 1993). Rather, differences intersect with each other, suggesting that the experience of difference is one of contradiction and instability. Black feminists have hence pointed to the processes of *identification* which produce contradictory and unstable subject positions, where subjects are addressed or 'hailed' in many different ways (Ahmed 1997; Boyce Davies 1994; hooks 1989). The critique offered of racism, as a relationship of dominance and subordination, also means that Black feminism emphasises that differences operate at the level of group formation rather than 'the individual' (or, rather, the individual is differentiated by being identified as a member of a social group), and that differences therefore function as markers of power.

But it is difficult to talk of Black women, or even Black feminism, in the singular. This difficulty is compounded by the fact that the category 'Black' is very much contested, both within feminism and more generally. There are significant national differences here. In the United States, for example, the category of 'Black' tends to be used to refer to women of African descent, while in the UK Black has been used more generally as a political category for those groups who have been made other through the normalisation of whiteness (see Mirza 1997). But while it remains impossible to talk about Black women as if they were a unified group, or of Black feminism as if it was a consistent set of ideas, it nevertheless remains politically important for Black feminists to contest the dominant narratives of white feminism for the way in which they other 'Black women'.

Certainly, the questioning of what it might mean to identify as Black women has produced some engaging political and intellectual work, which recognises the instability of the categories of 'Black' as well as 'women', as well as the complexity of their intersections. The attention to the intersection between race and gender has allowed feminists to investigate the historical legacies of colonialism and the way in which they have also been informed by class and sexuality (McClintock 1995). This understanding of colonialism as gendered, sexualised and classed has led to the emergence of what has been called post-colonial feminism. Post-colonial is another tricky term[2] which, when it is interpreted as 'after' colonialism, can have some deeply conservative implications, and if used to describe 'where we are now' can work to flatten out some significant differences in the relationship between particular nations and regions and the legacies of European colonialism (Ahmad 1993; McClintock 1994). However, post-colonialism can also be understood as a body of work that attempts to understand how colonialism has persisted after so-called *de-colonization*, given the fact that colonialism did not just involve formal (geo-political and military) and administrative structures of control. Post-colonial theory, in the work of scholars such as Edward Said (1978), Frantz Fanon (1975) and Homi Bhabha (1994), has provided models of how colonialism operated as a form of knowledge, codification and subjectification. Colonialism involved not only the production of knowledges about 'the others' or 'the colonised', but also the production of the very category of 'the other' or 'the colonised' in order to secure and legitimate the identity of the colonisers (the West, the Occident, England, and so on). Given this, colonialism is deeply embedded in psychic, linguistic and social domains, as well as in political and economic structures. As a result, the formal dismantling of empire does not signal the end or 'posting' of colonialism. The 'post' in this version of post-colonialism does not suggest 'after colonialism', but announces the recognition of the persistence of colonialism in everyday life as well as institutional formations, at the same time as it announces an attempt (not always successful) to produce ways of understanding and knowing that question, if not resist, these colonial relations of othering, in part by pointing to how these relationships themselves fail to fix the colonised in a subordinate position.

Feminists such as Gayatri Spivak (1993), Jenny Sharpe (1993), Rajeswari Sunder Rajan (1993) and Anne McClintock (1995) have worked with post-colonial theory, and sometimes against it, by demonstrating how the relations of othering that produced the category of the coloniser (by defining the categories of 'the native', 'the orient', or 'the subaltern') are gendered and sexualised. For example, Gayatri Spivak has examined the category 'subaltern woman' and the contradictory attempts to speak for her within both British imperial discourse and Indian national discourses (1988). Looking at the various writings on the practice of sati (widow burning), which either condemned the practice as primitive (imperialist discourse) or celebrated it as traditional (nationalist discourse), Spivak examines how the subaltern woman is always spoken for. This silencing is not a result of her lack of agency, but of the failure to hear her, precisely because she, within these discursive and institutional limits, had become a symbol of either the survival of the empire/hu-man-ity, or the survival of the nation.

Certainly, there has been much concern in post-colonial feminism with the politics of representation and the political question of who speaks for whom. Partly, this involves also a critique of this connection between imperialism and Western feminism. That is, post-colonial feminists have paid attention to the way in which Western feminism has also spoken for subaltern women, for example in the form of nineteenth-century missionary discourse, or within contemporary international politics (Mohanty 1991). However, the question is not just a discursive or rhetorical one about who is speaking or not speaking. Also at issue here is the material relationships of production which position 'third world women' as a cheap labour source. Although the complexity of power relations within nations needs to be properly investigated (not all women in 'first world' nations are positioned in the same way, given racial and class stratification, as well as the division between citizens and immigrant workers), the gendering of the international division of labour is clear. The relation between first world consumption and third world production suggests that women are not only positioned differently from each other, but that they are also positioned in relationships of *antagonism*. Hence, Black and post-colonial feminists have complicated the political representation – who speaks for whom – as an instance of a material relationship of production, consumption and exchange.

As a result, there has been much concern recently with thinking through the changing nature of the international landscape from a Black or post-colonial feminist perspective. How does 'globalisation' affect Black and third world women? What is the impact of the transnational flow of people, objects and images on gender and racial identities? Certainly, if we were to introduce Black or subaltern women, in all their differences, to the scene of international politics, we could make some provocative and disturbing reflections. We could see the dangers of a politics which celebrates movement and the transgression of borders given that the majority of the world's refugees are Black women. Or we might understand how the very language of globalisation fails to account for how the imaginary global village involves forms of domination rather than inclusion, or even how the construction of 'the global' as the emancipation of space takes place through the use, regulation and control of the bodies of Black or third world women. Or we could examine the impact of migration on the everyday world and local communities which women inhabit through examining the gendering of diasporic space (Brah 1996). The task here is to question the way in which the West has constructed 'the global', and the crossing or transgression of the borders of nation-states, and to consider local differences and sites of struggle.

Throughout, the history of questioning and critique has been directed towards white and Western feminists for their complicity with the legacies of colonialism. But despite this, the work of many Black and post-colonial feminists has not simply involved the critique of universalism in white and Western feminist theory, but also an attempt to think how we can make alliances between women who are positioned in relationships of antagonism. For example, although Chandra Mohanty provides a powerful critique of the way in which Western feminism has used universal categories to understand gender relations (1991: 53), she has also called for a politics of coalition and alliance. According to Mohanty, feminists need to make connections through a process of dialogue and exchange while also paying attention to the differences and antagonisms that make some connections difficult, if not impossible, to make.

In a later book, Chandra Mohanty and M. Jacqui Alexander suggest that feminist activism does not occupy the space of the local or the general, but is about bringing local struggles together to form collective struggles:

To talk about feminist praxis in global contexts would involve shifting the unit of analysis from local, regional and national culture to relations and processes across cultures. Grounding analysis in particular, local feminist praxis is necessary, but we need to understand the local in relation to larger, cross-national processes.

(1997: xix)

Here, the project is to produce knowledges which explain the relationships between the local and the general in order to generate connections between local and collective political struggles. Mohanty and Alexander open out the possibility of a feminism which is transnational, and which moves across national borders and boundaries, given that those boundaries are already unstable, but in a way that does not simply repeat the history of colonialism. Hence, the history of Black and post-colonial feminist thinking has pointed to the centrality of boundaries (who draws them? can they be drawn differently? who moves across them? can it be done differently?) and connections (how are they made? how can we make them differently?) to feminist research and activism.

Hence, in this section, the authors consider how feminism can move across borders and boundaries, that is, across these key spatial markers of social difference and antagonism. They also consider how feminism inevitably does cross such boundaries, given the economy of difference which connects the 'local' with the 'global'. Here, the agenda is not simply about celebrating or reaffirming the value of difference. Rather, the authors assume that differences cannot be separated from relationships of power and thus from the construction and enforcement of the borders that allow us to imagine and inhabit the local, the national and the transnational. A concern with difference can be thought of in terms of a concern with the borders and boundaries which both allow and disallow the movement and flow of peoples, objects and images.

Throughout this section, there is hence a reflection on the relationship between feminist politics and the processes of globalisation. In the first chapter, Gayatri Chakravorty Spivak offers an analysis of the way in which globalisation and the production of global knowledge can have problematic consequences for subaltern women. In particular, she questions the assumption that giving subaltern women access to telecommunications is necessarily emancipatory. With a cautious study of the rhetoric of the event 'Global Knowledge '97' (Toronto) and accompanying images, Spivak suggests that telecommunications can serve to transform the heterogeneity of indigenous knowledges (impossible to grasp in the present) into property or capital: here, the 'subaltern woman' is, quite literally, up for sale. Such a reading of the production of global knowledge in the 'international civil society' involves a questioning of how feminism itself can become implicated in the transformation of indigenous knowledge into property. Unless feminism can itself learn 'to learn from below', some of its positions – for example the call for the emancipation for women through access to information technologies – will be complicit with the 'gendered will for globalisation'. Spivak does not ask 'metropolitan solidarity to stop'. But she does suggest it should 'take more trouble'.

In the following chapter, Ngai-Ling Sum also questions how feminism has operated as a form of metropolitan solidarity in the use of the liberal rhetoric of universal rights. She examines the limitations of some of the discursive construction of 'women' and 'women's rights' in the Fourth World Conference on Women held in Beijing in September 1995, looking in particular at the narrative of sameness and difference in Hillary Clinton's keynote speech. Sum asks how feminism can work, or be put to work, differently, and guides the reader through some recent debates about the role of difference and hybridity within 'transversal politics'. However, she suggests that feminism can take more trouble, not by simply emphasising difference and the crossing of borders in dialogue, but by considering the hybrid nature of *governance*. That is, she suggests that feminism needs to investigate interpersonal and interorganisational levels of activity, in order to deal with how differences can be 'managed' at an institutional level. Here, the critique of universalist Western feminism leads to a concern with the practical questions of how differences and antagonisms can be dealt with more justly in the very (trans)formations of international politics.

The critique of how liberal feminism can operate to overlook differences and antagonism, or how feminism can be complicit in the 'gendered will for globalisation' by making claims on behalf of subaltern women, is here not just negative, but affirmative. Through offering such critiques, the authors are, at the same time, suggesting other ways of thinking about feminism, and other ways of understanding its role in constituting as well as crossing borders. This move to affirm through critique is also clearly evident in Sneja Gunew's chapter. Gunew also begins with the 'pitfalls' of identity politics. In particular, she examines the relationship between identity and the domain of the visual. She suggests that, through the constant imperative to visualise difference, racism can move beyond the biological, to 'find' difference on or in the body of culture. Her reading suggests that identity politics can become complicit in cultural racism: by calling for visibility, that is, for differences to be recognised within the public domain, such a politics could also serve to fetishise those differences in the assumption that *being seen* is the proper goal of an emancipatory politics. However, the bulk of Gunew's argument is focused not on the critique of the visual coding of differences in identity politics, but on thinking about how such politics could work beyond the domain of the visual. Here, she examines another key sense, that of sound or aurality. Gunew offers a reading of the work of Evelyn Lau, a Chinese Canadian writer, in order to consider what happens when the visual body fails to be identified given a gap between sound and image. Gunew's critique of the role of the visual in identity formation hence allows her to demonstrate how a politics of desire can affirm the place of the other by moving beyond the coding of differences.

Certainly, in this section, the question of how feminism can operate otherwise, given that the contexts in which women come to identity or act as feminists are profoundly overdetermined by racism and colonialism, is central. Partly, this involves a concern with how women in different places are already connected in some way through the international and gendered division of labour. Such connections are ones of profound social antagonism. If this is the case, then how can solidarity between women be transnational? Such a question suggests that feminism is a politics of *making connections* by understanding the limits of connections. Solidarity must be struggled towards, rather than assumed. The concern with how feminism can make connections is clearly evident in the final chapter in this section, by Gail Ching-Liang Low. She examines how contemporary discourses of identity impact on our understanding and teaching of texts to do with migration and multiculturalism, such as V.S. Naipaul's *The Enigma of Arrival* and Farhana Sheikh's *The Red Box*. In her reading of these texts, and her account of the difficulties of teaching them, Low examines the problem of making identifications across cultural boundaries. She suggests that collective identifications always *fail* to find a referent, but that this failure is the very basis for the mobilisation of collectivity. That is, by 'not fitting' a given political label or identity, subjects can identify across social or cultural boundaries, and can make connections elsewhere. Her chapter allows us to rethink how can we make connections with others without assuming we inhabit the same place: these are connections which are also moments of disconnection.

Throughout, this section suggests that connections between different sites of power must be made rather than assumed. Making connections is not about overcoming relationships of antagonism, but working with and through those relationships. We can make connections only insofar as we recognise that we do *not* inhabit the same place. Making connections is also a way of rethinking the importance of boundaries in feminist politics. In all the chapters, the concern with transnational, post-colonial and Black feminisms is about building alliances and recognising the complexity and contingency of configurations of power in a globalised economy of difference. The authors suggest ways of transforming feminism in order that feminism can deal with transformations in this globalised world, and in order that feminism can become a transformative politics.

Notes

1   Gloria T. Hull, Patricia Bell-Scott and Barbara Smith address this issue in terms of the twin inadequacy of 'Women's Studies' and 'Black Studies'. They write:

> Women's Studies courses ... focused almost exclusively upon the lives of white women. Black studies, which was much too often male-dominated, also ignored black women ... Because of white women's racism and black men's sexism, there was no room in either area for the consideration of lives of Black women.
>
> (1982: xx–xxi)

2   The tricky nature of the terms used to describe issues of racial, cultural or national difference reflects that the very language to describe such differences is a legacy of empire (this relates to racial categories such as 'black' and 'coloured' and to spatial and geo-political categories such as 'third world' and 'developing countries'). It is difficult, of course, to find another language. We need to employ these terms differently, to reflect on their limits, and to work with them in order to work against them.

All terms are open to new meanings as they are employed in different contexts. However, despite the potential embedded in the iterability of all terms (Butler 1997), we need to remember 'who' has enunciative authority, that is, who has the authority to stabilise some meanings over others.

References

Ahmad, A. (1993) *In Theory: Classes, Nations, Literature*, London: Verso.

Ahmed, S. (1997) '"Or is it just a sun tan?": Auto-biography as an Identificatory Practice', in H. Mirza (ed.) *Black British Feminism*, London: Routledge.

Alexander, M.J. and Mohanty, C.T. (eds) (1997) *Feminist Genealogies, Colonial Legacies, Democratic Futures*, London: Routledge.

Bhabha, H. (1994) *The Location of Culture*, London: Routledge.

Boyce Davies, C. (1994) *Black Women, Writing and Identity*, London: Routledge.

Brah, A. (1996) *Cartographies of Diaspora: Contesting Identities*, London: Routledge.

Brewer, R.M. (1993) 'Theorizing Race, Class and Gender: The New Scholarship of Black Feminist Intellectuals and Black Women's Labour', in S.M. James and A.P.A. Busia (eds) *Theorizing Black Feminisms: The Visionary Pragmatism of Black Women*, London: Routledge.

Butler, J. (1997) *Excitable Speech: A Politics of the Performative*, London: Routledge.

Carby, H. (1992) 'White Women Listen: Black Feminism and the Boundaries of Sisterhood', in Centre for Cultural Studies, University of Birmingham (eds) *The Empire Strikes Back: Race and Racism in 1970s Britain*, London: Hutchinson.

Fanon, F. (1975) *Black Skin, White Masks*, London: Paladin.

hooks, b. (1989) *Talking Back: Thinking Feminist, Thinking Black*, London: Sheba Feminist Publishers.

Hull, G.T., Bell-Scott, P. and Smith, B. (eds) (1982) *All the Women Are White, All the Blacks Are Men*, New York: Feminist Press.

Lorde, A. (1980) *Sister Outsider*, Freedom, Calif.: The Crossing Press.

McClintock, A. (1994) 'The Angel of Progress: Pitfalls of the Term "Post-Colonialism"', in F. Barker, P.Hulme and M. Iverson (eds) *Colonial Discourse/Postcolonial Theory*, Manchester: Manchester University Press.

—— (1995) *Imperial Leather: Race, Gender and Sexuality in the Imperial Context*, London: Routledge.

Mirza, H. (1997) *Black British Feminism: A Reader*, London: Routledge.

Mohanty, C.T. (1991) 'Under Western Eyes: Feminist Scholarship and Colonial Discourses', in C.T. Mohanty, A. Russo and L.Torres (eds), *Third World Women and the Politics of Feminism*, Bloomington: Indiana University Press.

Rajan, R.S. (1993) *Real and Imagined Women: Gender, Culture and Post-Colonialism*, London: Routledge.

Said, E. (1978) *Orientalism*, Harmondsworth, England: Penguin.

Sharpe, J. (1993) *Allegories of Empire: The Figure of Woman in the Colonial Text*, Minneapolis: University of Minnesota Press.

Spelman, E.V. (1990) *Inessential Woman: Problems of Exclusion in Feminist Thought*, London: The Women's Press.

Spivak, G.C. (1988) 'Can the Subaltern Speak?', in C. Nelson and L. Grossberg (eds) *Marxism and the Interpretation of Culture*, Urbana: University of Illinois Press.

—— (1993) *Outside in the Teaching Machine*, London: Routledge.

6   Claiming transformation

Travel notes with pictures

Gayatri Chakravorty Spivak

In February 1997, there was a show at the Guggenheim called *Rrose is a Rrose is a Rrose: Gender Performance in Photography*. Guggenheim's in-house magazine (1997) makes the following comment on the catalogue for the show:

> There's a limit, however, to how seriously one can take these images, and the editors are fond of contrasting deliberately shocking or titillating pictures with those that supply an ironic poke to the ribs. Witness the book's final pages, where a blue-filtered Sorrenti photo of a model attempting to push her fist down her throat sits opposite the figure of a tattooed Cindy Sherman coyly pantomiming putting a gun to her head. She could be saying, 'Gee, look what I've done.' It is a compelling statement.

I was thinking of this piece when I proposed my title. I did not then realise that I would glimpse some limits – that compelling and coy pantomime suicide – in a place rather remote from the terrain of the exhibition.

In late June 1997, a conference took place in Toronto called 'Global Knowledge '97' with approximately 1,500 participants from 124 different countries.[1] Women were extravagantly foregrounded.[2] Nowhere was this foregrounding more evident than in the breakfast hosted by the Independent Committee on Women and Global Knowledge, 'to honor women's contributions to information and communication technologies (ICTs)'. This event was sponsored by 'the Knowledge Based Industries of the Royal Bank of Canada'. We can consider the speech of the co-founder, Kathryn White, who is also the President of the Canadian Committee for UNIFEM. White's speech certainly claims 'Gee, look what we've done', as it also claims the white person's burden: 'authentic development carries an implied weight of trust which we must all be ready to accept'. Perhaps I should say half the white person's burden, for White goes on to suggest that in 'the reality of a new century and a new technology … the soul of the new machine, the soul of creativity is in the primordial partnership of men and women'.

For some years now, some of us have been calling for strategy-driven, rather than unacknowledged or disavowed, negotiations with the powers held by phallocentrism, however unpleasant the task. We could not have foreseen this absurdity. White's demands, as I perused them moving through rural Bangladesh, devastated by pharmaceutical dumping on land and women, seem frivolous. They seem frivolous enough to match the mood of Pierre Molinier's *Grande mêlée* (1960) – though nowhere near as radical in its power. I rename it 'Wolfensohn among the Girls' (Figure 6.1). **Transformation no. 1**

Joseph Stiglitz, senior vice-president and chief economist of the World Bank further emphasised that, in 1996 alone, 'US $240 billion of private foreign capital flowed into developing countries, a testimony both to the improved policies in developing countries and advanced information technologies...' (1997: 23). Stiglitz does not mention gender. It is left for Kathryn White to 'extend' on Stiglitz as follows: 'Markets and competition drive access issues. The driver of development ... is women and the families and communities they care for.'[3] The word 'driver' carries the superficial irony mentioned in the article on the Guggenheim catalogue (1997), rather more cruelly than an ordinary 'poke in the ribs'. (The analogy is thickened if we include the implications of the word 'driver' in software technology. Before long we will think of the connection between 'natural' and 'artificial' intelligence.) White reduces resistance to global exploitation to a demand for more woman-friendly language on software: 'in learning girls and women are likely to blame themselves for mistakes – boys and men blame the tool. So why, software developers, do you give me "error messages"? Why not "hints for getting the confounded thing running again?"'

When cross-dressing is no longer empirically available in the visual field, then

Figure 6.1   'Wolfensohn among the Girls'

Source: Blessing *et al.* 1997

it is time to cry 'error'. Many years ago, I wrote a post-affluent formula which gained a certain popularity: 'We must unlearn our privilege as loss.' As time passed, and I became aware of the sheer narcissism of the practical politics of unlearning one's privilege, I quietly changed it to 'learning to learn from below', but nobody paid much attention. Today I want to change another old phrase of mine – 'sanctioned ignorance' – about which I get regular queries in the mail from all over the world. I want to mock this 'sanctioned ignorance', which inhabits much metropolitan cultural work, with a rather more strongly worded error message. **Transformation no. 2**.

Walking into her perilous partnership, White does not seem to know that, when the poorest are opened to 'free' telecommunication, they are actually being positioned to offer up information that can be marketed. The quick establishment of the World Trade Organisation to consolidate and transform the 1995 General Agreement on Tariffs and Trade (GATT) meant precisely this opening of the rural poor and the indigenous to super-exploitation through Trade Related Intellectual Properties or TRIPs:

> As GATT, the institution had no autonomous power or independent leverage or financial sanction. As WTO, it is evolving into an all-powerful supra-national government with more muscle than the UN. The largely Northern lobby used the claim of 'discriminatory trade practices' to justify WTO ... Under the ... WTO, Intellectual Property Rights are interpreted in the broadest possible terms – as 'trade related Intellectual Properties.' ... this has unwarranted implications because it at once includes what is not original but has always existed in nature.[4] ... Henceforth the South will have to pay between $50 to 100 billion annually in royalties for patents. – Because WTO now interprets the absence of patent protection as an illegal trade barrier.[5]
>
> (Sadeque 1996: 28–30)

I must cry 'error' because I am not sure that White's speech can be understood merely in terms of sanctioned ignorance. On the text of her speech, which was made available at the conference, the words 'It helps if I understand my own motives' are crossed out and substituted by 'Interpret what they know [and] what we know together'. Her unease. How long will it last? Can this be read as a variation of pantomime suicide? We must have the energy and the resources to follow through with the autopsy – another name for the kind of activism that Sadeque is calling for.

Sometime in the 1870s, Marx wrote of the transportation industry as an enterprise whose commodity was movement (1978: 135). His prescience was reflected in Saskia Sassen's recent remark that the reterritorialisation of New York's Times Square was one of *de*territorialisation (unpublished communication). Times Square was the nexus of many strands of global telecommunication. Consumerism, immediately available in the empirical field, was not the major issue. Sassen's point was not picked up by the assembled architects, theorists and social activists. Global Knowledge '97 exploits this species of knowledge failure in the name of woman. It sells telecommunication as its own justification. In project statement after project statement, access to telecommunication is coded as women's empowerment as such.

I suggest that the real can influence the virtual through the requirement, in any offer of 'free' telecommunication, that information from the South – what used to be called the Third World when First and Second were possible – be up for sale. In examining this, we must necessarily focus as much on the rural as on the visible phenomenon of urbanism, for it is precisely the rural that is targeted by the global today. Old-style urban focus was always metaleptic, and is even more so today.

I think it may now be appropriate to redo the old radical style of speaking about the rural, always in the context of what is still called by some the 'new' social movements. The last time I went to the Socialist Scholars' conference in New York I remarked that the usual suspects on New Social Movement panels were Luddite stories from India and tales of left US participation in Latin America, the Third World next door. Africa is generally not heard from under that heading, the big plenaries are on US or European socialism, plus sensationalist panels on military spectaculars. In contrast, the African woman looms large in the current micro-enterprise-cum-telecommunication brand of global feminism.

Reflecting on such representations allows me to register the significance of a conversation I had at a cultural project of the Council in Foreign Relations in New York. A woman from a prominent US-based Foundation was commenting on the avidity with which Chinese artists had fallen upon examples of Euro–US modernist art at an exhibition sponsored by the Foundation. I remarked upon the absence of an unmarked historiography of modernity in large areas which can only be described as the non Euro–US world.[6] The word historiography was neither noticed nor understood. I was immediately assured that the Ford Foundation was 'helping' various African nations to establish *histories* of their artistic traditions. **Transformation no. 3**. I have no doubt that this involves the establishment of databases and can thus provide a nice alibi for global telematics. Just as the tone of the infomercial on the Inuit school covers for the bold capital logic of the entries discussing business incentives in the conference papers for Global Knowledge '97.

Speaking of the Alaskin Inuit – just as one distinguished in the old days between British imperial policy in Africa and India, French imperial policy in Algeria and in Viet Nam, and just as I have offered a cryptic contrast between the imaging of Japan and Africa, so too we must distinguish between multiculturalist patronising of the indigenous in the metropolis and biopiracy and human DNA-patenting among indigenous communities in the global periphery.

With such a distinction in mind, I do of course still honour the impulse to undo the opposition between anthropologist and Aboriginal, especially when it is a feminist oral history that leads to a testimonial. In earlier days, all we needed to ask was the question of the subject of representation: can the desire of the person behind the work be represented so transparently or be so unproblematically assigned? But in a contemporary context, we must learn to acknowledge that the subject–object relationship is itself woven in the textile of the history of the present. Correspondingly, we cannot only insist on what is unusual enough, heaven knows: the phenomenal diversity of aboriginal gazes is never an uncoded field that can be presented as such. In addition, in globalisation, we must be prepared to acknowledge knowledgeably that the transformation of indigenous knowledges into intellectual property deliberately bypasses the question of the subject.

I used to call the ability to make such distinctions 'transnational literacy'. Transnational literacy defines literacy in terms of whether one has a rudimentary idea of the particular national-state as being on the dynamic grid of geopolitics and global capital, rather than from the national-origin fantasies of eloquent metropolitan migrants. As with most of my exhortations, the phrase was picked up with alacrity in some quarters, but no real effort to follow it up was made. Today that effort is on the other side – it is the stuff of globalising decisions. Talk of 'economic literacy' and 'legal literacy' for women is rampant in the globalised discourse of telecommunications. What is being blocked is precisely the broader perception of *transnational* literacy that would allow 'error messages' to flash through.

If the colonial subject was largely a class subject, and if the subject of post-coloniality was variously racialised, then the subject of globalisation is gendered. It is well known that, for globalisation, or the establishment of the same system of exchange all over the world, state structures must be undermined. Deregulation and privatisation are hence recurrent themes of Global Knowledge '97. If the economic arms of globalisation are the World Bank, the International Monetary Fund and the World Trade Organisation, then the political arm is, increasingly, the United Nations. The UN and the powerfully collaborative Non-Governmental Organisations (NGOs) form what is increasingly called an 'international civil society' – to distinguish it from states. 'International civil society' was a phrase much used in Global Knowledge '97. The target of this international civil society is Woman. Here, one group – women of the Northern hemisphere, especially of the diasporic professional classes – are helping to exploit another, quite as the old colonial subject used to do the dirty work of the coloniser (or my grandfather the work of the local landowners while they practised the sitar in Calcutta).

The declared goal of the World Conference of the International Women's Year, held in Mexico City (1975), is the incorporation of women as 'an integral part of the global project for the establishment of a new world order' (United Nations 1995: 178). This document shares the disingenuousness of all such documents without offering any realistic plans for infrastructural change. If one takes into account the fact that the subjects of public declarations are routinely constituted by rusing a performative into a constative, then many UN declarations and resolutions make fascinating study.[7] An important step in the constitution of 'woman' as subject of development-in-globalism, if not fully fledged globalisation, is the six-point Platform of Action of the Fourth World Women's Conference in Beijing. If the woman constituted as 'Woman' is to be acted upon, her 'situation' must also be epistemologised and available, and the affective coding of 'value' must be agreed upon and in place. Since most of my field contacts are in Bangladesh, I have examined most carefully the Global Platform of the UN and its translation into Bangladeshi 'reality'. In the process, Bangladeshi women's reality acquires an original other than itself against which to measure and know itself. I cannot draw out the implications of this here, but they may be obvious.[8]

It is within this epistemological undertaking that a general gendered will for globalisation is being constituted. This is the female client of micro-credit: the grass-roots rural woman who receives weekly credit from a local or global NGO, to be repaid weekly, at a rate lower than the money lender's, but higher than the rate of commercial credit. These loans are supposedly for setting up micro-enterprises. But in fact it is well known that the contemporary frenzy for micro-credit involves no infrastructural reform or training other than infiltration into the culture of gendering itself. But the *Ecologist* is wrong to describe the phenomenon in the following way:

> In the current global climate, micro-credit, by itself, as a poverty alleviation tool is analogous to giving someone a fishing pole, and telling them to go and fish – in the wake of the giant trawler whose net spans the horizons.
>
> (Singh and Wyshamn 1997: 42–43)

The analogy would apply only if the fishing poles contributed to the activity of the net.

When a pregnant officer of Women's World Banking, who repeatedly spoke of the male foetus in her womb, invokes Chandra Behn, a member of the celebrated Self Employed Women's Association (SEWA) as her endorsement, who was the primordial male? The WWB officer spoke of opening 'the huge untapped market of poor Southern women to the international commercial sector'. When SEWA was founded in the early 1960s, Ella Bhatt, the founder, had no such ambition. And then, when Jean C. Monty, the CEO of Northern Telecom, 'urg[es] developing countries to review their development plans to ensure that sufficient priority is given to investment in telecommunications as well as deregulation', it becomes hard to distinguish between capital and female: 'The World Bank's [Consultative Group to Assist the Poorest] ... appears to be narrowly focused on microlending as an end in itself. And the means to that end, critics charge, may do more damage to "empowerment leaders" than good' (Singh and Wyshamn 1997: 42)[9]. **Transformation no. 4**.

Thus women's micro-enterprise, the undertaking most recommended at the Beijing Conference (1995), alongside access to telecommunications, become the two 'targets' of global feminism. Letters to Least Developed Countries (LCDs) have already been sent out in the wake of the Toronto conference. Africa is as prominent on the client list as it is on any list of 'emerging markets'.

Another important figure in this gallery is the female purveyor of 'culture' as subject of 'culture'. The conference on Global Knowledge opened with a charismatic First Nation Canadian who, in a pathetic triumphalist parody of the colonial encounter, gave the 'talking stick' to the Governor. Of the five injunctions tied to the stick, there was only time for two. The very first – 'do not show anger' – would disqualify resistance right from the outset. The next image (Figure 6.2) is just such a female subject of 'culture'.

The woman in this image is an international model, divorced from an Anglo-Saxon husband, who has come home to her native Bangladesh to start up an export business. I certainly wish her as much success as The Body Shop or *Comme des garçons*, also run by women. I am concerned about her patent transfers to Europe: her relationship to 'the Weavers of Bangladesh' is the cultural equivalent of DNA patenting, but I see no reason to single her out for censure. I find her interesting because of her self-staging as cultural icon – no micro-credit cellular phone for her.

UN-style telecommunicative feminism insistently crosses the aporia between electronic monoculture and the irreducible idiomaticity of whatever can be called 'culture'.[10] Noticeably, the woman on the calendar is not a feminist. She is

Figure 6.2   A Bangladeshi model and cultural icon turned entrepreneur

Source: Personal Collection

caught in the more general aporia of cultural staging as such. Common sense might tell us that anything that can be called 'culture' is in differance with the being-ness from and out of which it is recognised and formalised, in some interest. Culturalism and multiculturalism are always interested. Of course, this irreducible difference and *Nachträglichkeit* – this differance – *is* not simply there to be imaged. But a simulation of it, a miming, is caught on video in my possession. It is the kind of context-dependent fleeting instant that would not show well on the page. I am obliged instead to describe it.

In that layered videographic moment the double bind is painful. There is our female entrepreneur and her urban middle-class cultural troupe, pretending to be rural Bangladeshis. **Transformation no. 5**. Here and there are the actual rural Bangladeshis, looking on with bemusement. Here is an urban underclass drummer, not part of her troupe, dressed in some ruralish costume, doing her drumming as she has always done it. The videographer rushes the embarrassing de-authenticating moment.

Within this problematic, it is interesting that the woman has taken as her motto the phrase *ekla chalo re* – walk alone. It is the refrain of a song written by Tagor, established in the popular imagination, and written in support of Gandhi's idiosyncratic heroism in the cause of national liberation. It is as if the poet had said to the nationalist, if no one responds to your call, walk alone. The entrepreneur cuts off the vatic conditional and reduces it to a version of self-regarding individualism. Gandhi too had staged himself as the cultural subaltern. The British-trained barrister had taken off his suit and put on a loin-cloth. An entire discourse of the displacement of culturalism from nationalism and transnationalism waits for us here. Tragedy to farce.

Somewhere in the middle is postcoloniality, there and here. A rare glimpse of nationalism into postcoloniality (**Transformation no. 6**?) in rural India is given in Mahasweta Devi's 'Murti'.[11] The critique of this transformation is embodied in a woman there, pared down to nothing but hunger and wisdom.

I have no time to read with you this exquisite story. Rather, I end with an image from the sort of locale in rural India that Devi's story inhabits. I am not a cultural conservative, nor a religious fanatic. Yet I would like permission to mourn the disappearance of a cultural idiom, as we, in globalisation, transform.

Figure 6.3 is a photograph by Kalo Baran Laha. Laha is a hotel owner in the country town of Purulia in West Bengal. He takes photographs for his own plea-sure, establishing a record of the life mostly of Aboriginals living in the region. This photograph, of a boy looking up obliquely at the clay and wattle frame of the image of Durga and her family, worshipped annually, is a little off Laha's usual beat.

A small-town boy or a rural boy, one cannot know. The photographer seems to have caught the subject unawares. The boy gazes at the image. The eyes in the absent, spectral head return his gaze. The image returns habitually every year, a return that directs his gaze: as habit, the image will be destroyed, plunged in the river with great pomp and circumstance and mostly male enthusiasm, at the end of the five days. It is the polytheist habit institutionalised – to see in the

Figure 6.3   A West Bengali boy contemplating an image of the goddess Durga and her
family

Source: Personal collection

obviously transient and ephemeral the possibility of alterity – that conjures up
the goddess's absent yet gazing, living head for the boy. It bears repetition: it is
not just that the image is not yet ready, but that even when fully assembled and
gorgeous, it will carry its imminent death. The day of triumph – *bijoya* – is also
the day of renouncing the simulacrum – *protima bisharjon* – of floating – *bhashan* –
all words in grass-roots vocabulary. And yet the gazes lock. In fact, if the image
had been fully formed, the picture would have signified differently, for the
goddess's fixed and stylised gaze (which I, like the boy, can imagine), would be
angled at the other corner of photographic space. The boy's expression does not
lend itself to quick characterological analysis; in my reading, there can be none.
The polytheist gaze is not phenomenal.

If we read the photograph through Sigmund Freud's essay in 'Fetishism', we
would expect a fascinated gaze, and we would expect a doubled anxiety of
castration and decapitation (1961–76: 152–157). But this is another 'culture',
and I do not mean that word in some silly multiculturalist way. I mean it with
fear, for entry into that culture – however museumised – is our only means for
transformation. This is the message of the perfunctory feminism that enters the
Southern woman's house with loan in hand, teaching her to fight an enemy not
necessarily constituted along the same lines. If, for example, the boy in the
photograph had looked between this humble, unfinished, great goddess's legs, as
Freud's boy in 'Fetishism' would, then he would 'see' the absent gaze from the
not-yet-assembled human head of the defeated buffalo, in a representation of
the incarnating-moment caught in the icon. Is this why polytheism (not a good

word, but we will let it pass) is scary, because of such powerful females, improbably limbed? What does it 'mean' that this representation, of this boy at least (we must beware of making a singular presentation exemplary, although Freud sometimes forgot this lesson), will not prove the case for subject-constitution on an error about genitals? To pose this question is to make Freud 'real'.[12]

I will not open my usual Kleinian argument here, since that will divert this line of thought too far.[13] I will simply repeat that the 'polytheist' is not phenomenal, that in every act of Hindu worship or presentification, alterity must be instituted in the material – *pranpratistha* – and then let go at the end, and that the relative permanence of built space (which organises so much Hindu violence today) is irrelevant. There is a non-passage between (above? below? beyond? beside? what I am calling the polytheist gaze forever trembles on that brink) the boy's actively 'polytheist' gaze.[14] All feminist transformations of global scope will have remained negotiated within his 'cultural' (not necessarily deliberate) participation: that gaze, locked perhaps in the spectral gaze of the great goddess, will have fallen short of our benevolence.

No psychoanalytical culturalism will help me formalise this cultural moment which, in the general sense, formalises whatever 'I' might 'be'. I want to stand in my helplessness, with you, for a moment, as we inevitably proceed towards convenient and efficient solutions. As we must.

Notes

1   I am grateful to Farida Akhter for access to conference papers. The opinions expressed are my own. This chapter was originally written as a conference paper about another conference. For my feelings about the culture of conferences see Spivak (1996).
2   Two points should be mentioned here. First, there was extensive criticism of the conference in North America that was disseminated on the Internet. Such criticism did not, however, foreground the issue of global exploitation. And second, the foregrounding of women was apparently in response to an objection made by women about the fact that there were no women in the conference as it was originally planned. This was explained to me at a conference on Gender and Globalisation at Berkeley, California, in March 1998, by a member of the audience who did not identify herself beyond mentioning that she had been part of the Toronto conference. Let us call this *transformation degree zero* – the dire effects of a feminism still understood as a body count. My interlocutor at Berkeley was offended by my criticism. But this is the schizophrenia that one inhabits if, in the Asian (and no doubt African, Australian, Latin American) context, one's activities go below the power lines of metropolitan solidarity. I am not asking metropolitan solidarity to stop. I am asking it to take more trouble.
3   'Access issues' is hand-corrected to 'issues around ICT development'.
4   Generations of my students have misunderstood how a thing can be a value without being a use-value, which is slightly different from 'commons' – communally held land. The latter is also of great importance, of course, but is a historically distinct mode or production, rather than a theoretically distinct form of value. See Spivak (forthcoming (a)).
5   My only objection to this otherwise brilliant pamphlet by Najma Sadeque is that it does not emphasise the production of the colonial subject in imperialism and thus cannot emphasise our complicity, which we must acknowledge in order to act.

6 For a spirited account of such an alternative historiography in the case of China, see Dirlik (1995).

7 In 'Declarations of Independence' and 'For Nelson Mandela', Jacques Derrida has respectively explained the phenomenon and distinguished between repressive and emancipatory constitutions, that both share this originary differance (1986: 7–15).

8 This epistemologisation culminates in the UNESCO-supported *Encyclopaedia of Life Support Systems*, which redefines ecology as one of the 'four main categories of threats to security, namely: *military, economic, social* and *ecological threats*', and associates the 'timescale of the *far past* … with *inactive* approaches where there is no concern for environmental degradation and sustainability' (UNESCO 1997: 13; emphasis mine). An entire network is being created here. Different people will have constructed this source, and history will have been rewritten.

9 Resistance to this is already afoot. For a news items reporting peoples' retaliation upon a micro-lending World Bank supported NGO (Proshika) after the death of three women and an infant, see the *Daily Star* (1997) and *Inkilab* (1997).

10 The distinction between genome and race – the latter an elusive phenomenal item coding positions with identity – is part of this. There is a limit that is not accessible to the being's phenomenality. In Marx, it is abstract average labour; in Freud, the metapsychological; in Heidegger, the ontico-ontological difference; and in Derrida, the originary differance. We cannot conjure transformative agency at this limit.

11 In Gayatri Spivak (trans.), *Old Women* (1999).

12 Both the earlier Sudhir Kakar (1981: especially 154–211) and the earlier V.S. Naipaul (1978) had concluded, coming from quite different politics but applying a 'real' Freudian standard, that Indian man has not passed Narcissus. They changed their minds through varieties of cultural conservatism from which approaches such as mine are to be distinguished.

13 Lacan's geometrics of the gaze pre-comprehends Oedipus and cannot be significantly helpful here.

14 A much broader argument about the *dvaita* rather than the 'polytheist' structure of feeling is advanced in Spivak, 'Moving Devi' (forthcoming (b)). There is a more extensive discussion of the photograph in this article.

References

Blessing, J. (1997) *Rrose is a Rrose is a Rrose: Gender Performance in Photography*, New York: Guggenheim.

Daily Star (1997), July 6.

Derrida, J.(1986) 'Declarations of Independence', *New Political Science* 15: 7–15.

Devi, M. (1999) 'Murti', in Gayatri Spivak (trans.) *Old Women*, Calcutta: Seagull Books.

Dirlik, A. (1995) 'Confucius in the Borderlands: Global Capitalism and the Reinvention of Confucianism', *boundary 2*, 22, 3: 229–273.

Freud, S. (1961–76) *The Standard Edition of the Complete Psychological Works, Vol. 21*, New York: Norton.

Inkilab (1997), July 6.

Kakar, S. (1981) *The Inner World: A Psycho-Analytic Study of Childhood and Society in India*, New York: Oxford University Press.

Marx, K. (1978) *Capital: A Critique of Political Economy*, Vol.2, New York: Vintage.

Naipaul, V.S. (1978) *India: A Wounded Civilization*, New York: Vintage Books.

Sadeque, N. (1996) *How 'They' Run the World*, Lahore: Shirkat Gah.

Sassen, Saskia, unpublished communication, Columbia University, 1996.

Singh, K. and Wysham, D. (1997) 'Micro-Credit: Band-Aid or Wound', *Ecologist*, 27, 2: 42–43.

Spivak, G. (1996) 'Setting to Work (Transnational Cultural Studies)', in P. Osborne (ed.) *A Critical Sense: Interviews with Intellectuals*, New York: Routledge.

—— (forthcoming (a)) 'From Haverstock Hill Flat to US Classroom: What's Left of Theory', in J. Butler and K. Thomas (eds) *What's Left of Theory*, New York: Routledge.

—— (forthcoming (b)) 'Moving Devi', *Cultural Critique*.

Stiglitz, J. (1997) 'Harvesting the Benefits of Knowledge', *Financial Post*, June 14.

UNESCO (1997) *Conceptual Frameworks: Encyclopedia of Life Support Systems*, Whitstable, England: Oyster Press.

United Nations (1995) *The United Nations and Advancement of Women (1945–1995)* New York: United Nations.

7 From politics of identity to politics of complexity

A possible research agenda for feminist politics/movements across time and space

Ngai-Ling Sum

The Fourth World Conference on Women was held in Beijing between 4 and 15 September 1995. As in several other recent United Nations Conferences, alongside an official event, an NGO (Non-Governmental Organizations) forum was organized.[1] On this occasion, feminists from the West/North met colleagues from the East/South to exchange accounts of their experiences. In some quarters, the Beijing Conference has been hailed as marking a new North–South alliance as well as exemplifying the sort of global/transnational forum in which a transformative feminist politics may be discussed. However, since such a 'united sisterhood' is less evident concretely, one can also examine the Beijing event to discover the difficulties and limits of a transformative politics. Indeed, from its re-emergence in the 1970s, feminism has shown few signs of unity. Feminist scholars still disagree strongly about the nature of (the) 'female subject(s)' and activists continue to debate strategic issues. In both respects, the scope of the discussion has been widened as the hegemony of familiar Western disputes (such as those among liberal, socialist, radical, and cultural feminisms) has been challenged by black, third-world, ethnic-minority, and post-colonial feminisms, each with their own strategic dimensions.

This chapter seeks to highlight some of these divergences by locating Hillary Clinton's conference remarks in the Enlightenment 'time–space envelope'. The concept of 'time–space envelope' refers to the configuration of historically changing, practically produced, structurally inscribed and strategically oriented nexi of social (and, hence, power) relations which together give a more or less coherent form and spatio-temporal identity to a social space (Massey 1994; Sum 1996).[2] In this regard the often criticized Enlightenment 'meta-narrative' can be understood materially as well as discursively as a hegemonic, encompassing time–space envelope which is variously articulated with other time–space envelopes. Clinton's construction of a 'rights-based female subject' at the Fourth World Conference is located within the Enlightenment time–space envelope (see the first section below). Such a framework has been challenged, even in the USA, by some critical feminists and it is even more alien to women located in other times and spaces (see the section 'Multiple feminisms', on China). This challenge has particular purchase for those who regard gender relations as strongly embedded in, and overdetermined by, relations of culture, race, ethnicity, and nation.

Conceptualising identities as embedded in time–space envelopes enriches the understanding of their great diversity and heterogeneity. The rediscovery of such multiplicities is at the heart of questions of 'difference' in feminist debates. Debates around this question are closely tied to concepts such as subjectivities, essentialism, strategy, and even 'borderlands'. Instead of offering a comprehensive assessment, this chapter can only examine particular theoretical strategies discussed in the scholarly work of Gayatri Spivak, Donna Haraway, Chandra Mohanty, Aiwha Ong, and Nira Yuval-Davis. My aim is to go beyond this subjectivity-centred debate and to examine feminist politics across time and space as a complex interactive social field. With regard to the latter, I attempt to synthesize two bodies of literature, namely Bakhtinian-inspired work on 'dialogism' and recent work on 'governance' as the complex art of steering multiple agencies, institutions, and systems. This chapter ends with a possible research agenda on the structured complexity of this kind of politics. Let us start with Clinton's liberal female subject.

Liberal female subjects and the enlightenment time–space envelope

The Fourth World Conference on Women has been hailed as marking a new North–South alliance. Coordinated by transnational fora and networks, this alliance is supposed to launch opportunities for feminists to exchange accounts of their experiences and to explore strategies for linking women's movements across time and space. One particular expectation of such an alliance is that it will link women in and through human rights. This perspective on the alliance was reinforced by Hillary Clinton's speech at the Conference. In constructing an imaginary 'sisterhood', Clinton's speech[3] invoked a gendered version of human rights designed to unify the 'rights-based' female subjects located in diverse functional and geographical terrains. The construction of the subject is premised on 'modified rights' and seeks to transcend androcentric views of human rights by rediscovering women.

Conceptually as well as historically, mainstream human rights discourse tends to ignore the question of how its norms/practices apply to women. This marginalization of women's issues is closely linked to the domination of malestream notions of human rights. NGOs have recently begun to enter into the human rights field by putting women's rights on the agendas (Hom 1992: 280–281; Romany 1994: 90). This modification of the human rights approach occurred in Clinton's speech in so far as she highlighted women's rights to empowerment by emphasizing their participation in public/international space:

> I believe that, on the eve of a new millennium, it is time to break our silence. It is time for us to say here in Beijing, and the world to hear, that it is

no longer acceptable to discuss women's rights as separate from human rights.

(Clinton 1995: 3)

This privileging/essentializing of the female subject in public discourse about 'rights' may involve an attempt to win American hegemony in building a 'united sisterhood'. Negative images and practices concerning 'women as victims' have a key rhetorical role in this regard. Thus, to strengthen her claim for 'feminist empowerment through rights', Clinton referred to baby girls being 'denied food, or drowned, or suffocated'; 'girls (being) sold into the slavery of prostitution'; 'women [being] doused with gasoline, set on fire and burned to death'; and 'women ... subjected to rape as a tactic or prize of war' (Clinton 1995: 3). Invoking a 'victim' identity enabled Clinton to construct a 'united sisterhood' – a tactic reinforced by the use of 'we/us/our' (mentioned thirty-three times), familial symbolism (invoked seventeen times), and references to the domestic bases of female sociality. The following comments illustrate Clinton's 'familial' discourse:

Whether it is while playing with our children in the park, or washing clothes in a river, or taking a break at the office water cooler, we come together and talk about our aspirations and concerns. And time and again, our talk turns to our children and our families.

(Clinton 1995: 1)

What we are learning about the world is that, if women are healthy and educated, their families will flourish. If women are free from violence, their families will flourish. If women have a chance to work and earn as full and equal partners in society, their families will flourish.

(Clinton 1995: 2)

These unified identities, expressed in and through such 'victim' and 'familial' discourses, are nonetheless related to differences among women. But, for Clinton, these are narrated mainly in geographical and functional terms:

I have met new mothers in Jojakarat, Indonesia, who come together regularly in their village to discuss nutrition, family planning, and baby care. ...I have met women in South Africa who helped lead the struggle to end apartheid and are now helping build a new democracy.

(Clinton 1995: 2)

At this very moment, as we sit here, women around the world are giving birth, raising children, cooking meals, washing clothes, cleaning houses, planting crops, working on assembly lines, running companies, and running countries.

(Clinton 1995: 2)

However different we may be, there is far more that unites us than divides us. We share a common future. And we are here to find common ground so that we may help bring new dignity and respect to women and girls all over the world – and in so doing, bring new strength and stability to families as well.

(Clinton 1995: 1)

Our goals for this conference, to strengthen families and societies by empowering women to take greater control over their own destinies, cannot be fully achieved unless all governments – here and around the world – accept their responsibility to protect and promote internationally recognised human rights.

(Clinton 1995: 3)

Such narrations of women's 'differences' highlight how gender relations are shaped by economic and geographical differences, but this is secondary to the basic similarities rooted in 'victimhood' and 'familial' concerns. This is reinforced by Clinton's imaginary 'liberated future' in which women are empowered by stripping human rights of their androcentric bias.

Multiple feminisms and diverse time–space envelopes

Women's movements in the USA in the 1980s rejected the image of a 'united sisterhood' and put more emphasis on the multiplicity of organizations and structures. This can be seen in the emergence of lesbian and heterosexual feminisms, feminisms of colour, and the proliferation of identity politics. From these various movements, some groups responded to specific crises and policy issues relating to women's lives, such as rape, battery, poverty, and health care. Others are more cultural in orientation. In the latter case, some radical cultural feminists have undertaken such projects as founding women's record companies, bookstores, restaurants, art galleries, and publishing houses. In academia, there is also a growth in courses related to women and/or ethnic studies addressing issues of diversity stemming from the intersections of gender, race, culture, and class. This proliferation of approaches indicates the emergence of various post-Enlightenment time–space envelopes in which feminists question the idea of 'unified sisterhood' and its associated universalization of 'the liberal female subject'. Instead, critical feminists foreground the issue of 'difference' and diverse identities (for example Haraway 1988; Ong 1988; Trinh T. 1989; hook 1990; Goetz 1991; Mohanty 1991).

Applying these perspectives, Clinton's speech can be criticized for its essentialization of the 'liberal female subject' – which places all women in Enlightenment time and space. Such a Eurocentric conception of world historical time radically dis-locates and de-temporalizes emerging feminisms by conflating them (or, at least, judging them) through the philosophy and experience of middle-class, white, and Western women. In such models, Western humanism (read progressive/

modern) is constructed as both centre and telos: and non-Western women and the 'East' (read backward/traditional) are constructed as peripheral 'others' destined for eventual assimilation into the European tradition. Such an 'unmodified liberal feminism' leaves questions of cultural/racial/ethnic diversity and the prospects of 'unified sisterhood' un(der)-examined (Mohanty 1991: 6; Lai 1995: 288). Furthermore, the liberal female subject it constructs is not universal: it even lacks resonance within the West,[4] let alone outside of it (Coomaraswamy 1994: 39). It is a weak and limited narrative because it freezes women's identity and subjectivity in the Enlightenment time–space matrix by generalizing and essentializing an idealized account of Western women's experience and conditions across time and space; it disembeds Western and Eastern women from historically contingent power relations, and it ignores and silences the multiple and resistant voices of women located at diverse points in the complex social matrix formed by race, class, culture, nation, and other subject positions. Clinton's speech might have some ideological impact in an Enlightenment context, but it is certainly open to challenge from a post-colonial/post-Enlightenment perspective, let alone from women located in entirely different times and spaces.

We have need to consider women from developing countries with quite different historical, cultural, and economic experiences from those in the West. These experiences include colonialism, a recent history of nation-building, and different forms of insertion into global capitalism. The issues with which such women are concerned are inevitably different from those in the West/North. These differences are apparent in the very use of rights discourse. In the West, rights are constructed as the property of the individual. However, in many developing countries, rights are constructed in relation to the nation-state and development, as well as community and religion (Ong 1996: 119–121). For example, in (post-)Mao China, women's rights are inscribed in a party-state discourse on gender as institutionalized through the All-China Women's Federation (ACWF) (Barlow 1991: 146–147). It forms part of China's state-sponsored rhetoric and there are no equivalent forms in the USA and Western Europe. Official emancipatory rhetoric emphasizes the distinctive contributions of women but subsumes them under the general public agenda coded in terms of 'gender equality'. This official feminism and its imagined liberation are reinforced by reference to strong female party leaders and emancipated daughters (Liu 1991: 23; Lai 1995: 293). These images are constructed and regulated by the Chinese state so as to gain an inroad to the private world of women through a public ideology of gender equality. In contrast to Western struggles for full public acceptance of women's human rights oriented to using them to reconstitute their role in the private sphere, the Party line on 'women's rights' in (post-)socialist China proceeds from a party-dominated public sphere into a politicized private realm. This public discourse might produce a 'politicized female subject' that could be the subject of the movement. Engendered rights in the public sphere are granted according to temporally and spatially contingent redefinitions of the Party's and the nation's needs and are typically subordinated to the collective good as Party cadres define it. In this regard, the Chinese female subject is defined by contingent rights which communicate, through the ACWF, the changing demands of the Party over time (Hom 1992: 281–282).

Parallel to the development of the official female subject has been the emergence of semi-official and spontaneous feminist groups initiated by the ACWF and women intellectuals/professionals since 1986 (Howell 1996: 136–138). Exactly how the official subject may interact with the spontaneous feminist groups in generating a new agenda for women is largely unclear at this point. But it is clear that the spontaneous movements are searching for other female subjectivities and new identities that could combine women's nurturing roles, women's domestic and reproductive roles, and the emerging commercialization and objectification of women in post-socialist China. In this regard, some Chinese feminist scholars argue that 'women's rights-ism' (*nuaquan zhuyi*) may be too political and places too much emphasis on women's relationship with the public sphere.[5] They see the Chinese female subject(s) as locating themselves in 'female-ism' (*nuxing zhuyi*) which seeks psychological and cultural emancipation by deploying women's points of view and standards to remould society with men in it. Thus, their struggle moves beyond an exclusive concern with the public sphere, and addresses other sexual and psychological dimensions of women's emancipation (Zhang 1995: 37–39). Such understandings and their associated search for different female subjects arise in the context of a state-dominated/top-down regime of power, communicated and monitored by the ACWF. In this regard, Chinese female subjects define themselves selectively in relation to an embedded time–space envelope which is marked by post-socialist developmentalism, and party domination, coupled with a nationalism that has been emerging in the 1990s. Even if there are some groups which define their identity in terms of 'rights' discourse, they exist only as a kind of hit-and-run guerrilla feminism which can hardly form a permanent (op)position against the state and its apparatus, for example, the ACWF.

Multiple female subjects and the question of 'difference': from essentialism to boundary/transversal politics

My examination of Clinton's liberal female subject and other time–space envelopes shows the limits of the so-called 'united sisterhood', and the way it names, and then refuses, differences. The awareness of multiple female subjects embedded in different time–space envelopes is at the heart of the question of 'difference'. Thus, the challenge for feminist scholarship is to realize women's multiple voices without losing all of the analytical power of the category of 'women'. The terms subjectivities, essentialism, strategy, and even 'borderlands' have had a key conceptual role in meeting this challenge. The aim is to go beyond positionalities/strategies by examining feminist politics across time and space as a complex interactive social field. To do this I focus on particular theoretical strategies discussed in some recent scholarly work. Let us start by analysing Gayatri Spivak's concept of 'strategic essentialism'.

Some feminists seem reluctant to abandon a core common identity as an important political foundation for empowerment strategies and as a basis for coalition building. One of the most persuasive arguments advocating such an approach has been propounded by Spivak (1988). For her, retaining the concept of 'essentialism' serves as a provisional interventionist strategy. Spivak suggests 'female identity' is produced and regulated in relation to particular contexts and axes of power. This makes it possible to deal with several identities according to the axis of oppression at issue in particular situations, without necessarily tying individuals to a specific all-purpose identity. This approach is akin to Alcoff's (1988) notion of positionality, in that it understands identity, not as an immutable internal property of the person, but as relative to constantly shifting external contexts. Moreover, pointing beyond the theoretical logic of positionality, the notion of 'strategic essentialism' also requires that such notions of identity be employed only for emancipatory and not for oppressive purposes.

This position is useful in that Spivak calls our attention to the structural contexts/social relations that have scripted female subjects and their essentialisms. In this regard, the female subject can be seen as a conceptual migrant whose identity is constituted by external conditions and moves strategically from one form of essentialism to another. This position is useful for three reasons: it can be employed self-consciously to deconstruct categories and identities rather than to reinforce stereotypes and exclusions; it offers oppressed groups some strategic anchorage points to fight back; and it enables subjects to travel from one anchorage point to another as conjuncture and strategic objectives change. Nonetheless, Spivak's recommendation seems to rest on an account of subjectivity that is unitary but serialized. This move invokes both post-structuralism and strategic essentialism and also recognizes the existence of multiple voices. But it is less clear that one can examine this multiplicity in terms of a series of distinct voices, especially given the complex interweaving and continual re-embedding of identities and subjectivities. The latter often involves the tangled, shifting, and highly mediated consciousness and subjectivities (e.g. complex self/other hierarchies) as well as the inter-personal and/or inter-group communications among feminists embedded in diverse time–space envelopes.

Other feminist scholars are less concerned with essentialism and are more willing to depart from some kind of an Archimedean standpoint. These tendencies are especially prominent in the work of Donna Haraway. She rejects the claim to totalizing knowledge and fixed subject position, arguing instead for 'situated knowledges' that rest on the concept of objectivity (Haraway 1988). Defining objectivity as 'critical positioning', she embraces 'situated and embodied knowledges' and rejects relativism as 'a way of being nowhere while claiming to be everywhere' (1988: 586, 583, 584). Given the situatedness of knowledges, 'the knowing self is partial in all its guises, never finished, whole, simply there and original; it is always constructed, situated together imperfectly, and therefore able to join with another, to see together without claiming to be another' (1988: 586). In this regard, Haraway has introduced a politics of engagement in which situated subjects need not rely on 'essence' to act together.

She pursues such an engaged politics through a critique of the concept of objectivity and the assumption that subjectivities are compatible and can merge into a 'collective subject position'. Such a belief reflects a universalizing aspiration that views 'difference' as mediated by objectivity, and, in the final epistemological instance, 'difference' becomes a problem (O'Leary 1997: 58–59).

On the other hand, the question of 'difference' finds distinctive treatment in the work of some post-colonial feminist scholars such as Chandra Mohanty and Gloria Anzaldua. Their work interprets 'difference' as a political site to conduct a war of position. Both of them deploy metaphors such as 'boundary' or 'borderlands' as places to stand and political sites for the construction of critical oppositional knowledges. More specifically, Mohanty (1991) sees the 'boundary' as a site of resistance and she uses the image of the 'diaspora' to launch a war of position against the prevailing hegemonic regime of truth. This kind of boundary subjectivity and resistance politics represents a challenge to interpretations of 'difference' as a problem or mere empirical variation. However, this kind of boundary politics with its foundation in an 'inside–outside' representational paradigm is certainly not without its problems. For the boundary as a site of resistance against the hegemonic regime of truth also becomes a site for reinscribing this regime and reinforcing its (colonial) impact. Similar advancement and tensions can be detected in Anzaldua's work (1990: xv) when she uses the spatial image of 'borderland' to map a 'fertile' ground for developing and enhancing the sort of 'mestiza consciousness' that straddles cultures, drawing on each but belonging to neither. This hybridized conception of 'alien consciousness' does not mark the end of the colonial relationship; on the contrary, it may reinforce it. In short, this border trope underpins a kind of boundary politics that reinscribes the boundary in and through resistance (Jagose 1993: 223).

More interestingly, the work by Aiwha Ong (1995) and Nira Yuval-Davis (1997) advances a transformative kind of boundary politics. They conceptualize boundaries, not as sites of resistance, but as permeable and transversal. Indeed, Ong sees boundaries as conducive to communicating transnational and even translational subjectivities (1995: 366). In line with this approach, Ong envisages a boundary politics that transforms through transgression. Such an emphasis on boundary as sites of transformation is also clear in the work of Yuval-Davis. She develops a model of 'transversal politics', which places a critical importance on 'dialogue' (1996: 125). Drawing from the agenda developed by Italian feminists, Yuval-Davis elaborates this dialogical process by highlighting the ideas of 'rooting', 'shifting', and 'transversalism'. For Yuval-Davis, this means:

> The idea [is] that each participant brings with her the rooting in her own membership and identity but at the same time tries to shift in order to put herself in a situation of exchange with women who have different membership and identity. They call it 'transversalism' – to differentiate from 'universalism' which by assuming a homogeneous point of departure ends up being exclusive instead of inclusive.
>
> (Yuval-Davis 1997: 130)

Yuval-Davis's transversal perspective contains two vital elements related to the process of 'shifting': first, it should not involve self-decentring (that is, giving up one's own roots and set of values), and second, it should not homogenize the 'other' but recognize 'differences'. Such a transversal politics and its complementary communicative practices of 'rooting' and 'shifting' open up the transgressive and dialogic possibilities of identity politics. But it can also be seen as a limited form of 'dialogism' in that it risks being restricted to an invited elite group within the 'epistemological community' which shares some common attitudes towards power and conflict. Furthermore, it works with 'differences' that are negotiable – it is unclear how non-negotiable 'differences' would be managed. A transversal politics also decouples the dialogic process from the question of how the identities of self/other are constructed, and overemphasizes the importance of the message as opposed to the identity of its bearer in determining the boundaries of a dialogue – what matters for Yuval-Davis is that communication occurs, but one cannot overlook the role of those involved in dialogue. The model of transversal politics also ignores the complex internal relations and potential mutual disturbance between 'rooting' and 'shifting' insofar as communications may be rooted in a self-referential logic that cannot be 'shifted' in and through reinterpretation of internal codes or to the extent that the persuasiveness of communications may be so great that interlocutors give up their roots and are rejected by those on whose behalf they are speaking. Finally, it neglects the path-dependency of dialogues in favour of a voluntarist path-shaping perspective – but the outcome of dialogue is never independent of its course or its social embeddedness; and it overlooks other levels of agency and their specific dynamics (for example inter-organizational communication and learning, which may be relevant to such a transversalist process).

From politics of identity to politics of complexity: feminist politics / movements as 'hybridic governance'

Given such complexities and the infinite number of identities that might be involved, feminist politics can no longer be confined within a limited form of dialogism. There is a need to go beyond subjectivities, consciousness, identities, and inter-personal dialogue by taking into account other levels of agency. This chapter proposes a shift of the object of investigation from the politics of identity to the politics of complexity. Whereas the politics of identity may well appear complex (especially to those involved in Yuval-Davis's kind of transversal communication), it typically displays an unstructured complexity and is therefore difficult to 'govern'. Conversely, the 'politics of complexity' refers to the problem of how to introduce order into chaos and/or to derive order from chaos. In discussing this form of politics, I attempt to synthesize two bodies of literature, namely, Bakhtinian-inspired work on 'dialogism' and recent work on 'governance' as the complex art of steering multiple agencies, institutions and systems (Kooiman 1993; Jessop 1998).

In certain ways, Bakhtin's dialogism supplements Yuval-Davis's idea of 'transversal politics'. His concept, which focuses on the social nature of meaning creation, can generate hybrids that are achieved in and through the recursive struggles in adjudicating the self/other relations. Thus, dialogism provides the arena in which identities are articulated and new norms are (re)constructed (Holquist 1990). This concept can supplement Yuval Davis's idea of 'transversal politics' in three ways: it recouples identities with the dialogic process; it focuses on the inter-discursive space and the recursive struggles that are involved in new meaning creation; and it highlights the structurally conditioned and social nature of the dialogic process between self and other.

The supplementation of 'transversal politics' by Bakhtinian 'dialogism' still leaves the structural/social nature of the dialogic process under-examined. This chapter argues that one can complicate the latter by linking it with recent work on 'governance'. Governance can be analysed at inter-personal, inter-organizational, and inter-systemic levels. On an inter-personal level, the social nature of meaning (re)construction can be seen as a kind of 'self-organizing' activity in which self/other meanings are debated and (re)constructed. Both Bakhtin's work and the literature on governance may serve to sensitize us to the social and institutional embeddedness of this inter-discursive space of inter-personal coordination. At this inter-personal level, 'hybridic governance' involves self-reflexively monitoring the art of self–other (re)construction, formalizing inter-personal networking to engender negotiation and hybridization, and using selective memories to reinforce trust. This is obviously governance at its simplest level. Governance can also be considered at other levels of agency, especially the inter-organizational and its interaction with the inter-personal.

Inter-organizational relations may involve negotiation and negotiation systems directed towards realizing normative innovations that may transform culture. Crucial to the success of such arrangements is building inter-organizational capacities that synergetically reinforce those of individual organizational members. This can be seen as the building of a 'negotiated community' that is formed around dialogues that involve both positive and negative coordination. The latter encourages interlocutors to take account of possible adverse repercussions of their own actions on the other and to exercise self-restraint as appropriate. This kind of negative coordination can become the starting point for positive coordination that involves multilateral exploration and concerted strategic action towards a common issue.

When applied to feminist politics across time and space, a shift from a subjectivity-centred politics of identity to a politics of complexity may involve a new research agenda. 'Hybridic governance' are systems that are based on interactive learning amongst a broad range of operationally autonomous and interdependent subsystems across multiple boundaries and social relations (for example patriarchal, capitalist, and religious, nation-building) (Jessop 1998). Rejecting any predetermined universalism/essentialism, the nature of 'difference' must be accepted as the object of study in the politics of complexity. In general, three levels of 'embedded' social organization in feminist politics/movements are relevant to a 'hybridic governance' understanding. They are: inter-personal networking (for example, consciousness-raising groups/conversation circles), inter-organizational negotiation (for example, within and between NGOs), and inter-systemic relations (for example, political, economic, legal, scientific, educational, and medical) and their relation to the lifeworld (for example, the broader set of racial–gender relations) (Habermas 1984).

By way of charting a new and preliminary research agenda, we can try posing some of the following questions at these strategic levels. What kinds of self–other relations are constructed in the inter-personal dialogues among multiple female subjects and how are they hybridized? Do they involve the building of new loosely coupled networks that enable multiple female subjects and groups to communicate? Do they span together individual groups embedded in multiple time and space and cross-cut by diverse social relations? Do these groups act as carriers of different sub-goals and attendant conflicts? Are they entering into dialogues that are yet uncharted by norms and, if so, what are the new identities that are being constructed? Are these networks directed towards some kind of organizational 'intelligence' such as directed negotiation, tolerance, and strategic utilization of ambiguity at the boundary? What are the discursive and extra-discursive practices, if any, that are deployed to reduce noise in inter-systemic communication so as to enhance mutual sensitivity to autonomous logics? What are the discursive and extra-discursive practices, if any, that are deployed for negative coordination, that is, encouraging sub-units to take account of the possible adverse repercussions of their own actions on third parties or other systems and to exercise self-restraint as appropriate in blurring the inside–outside divide? Are these three levels of governance mutually supportive in coping with the governance of complexity in feminist politics/movements?

These questions may cast light on the search for order from chaos in feminist politics across time and space. It is equally valid to pose another set of questions that may be related to the chaotic side of structured complexity. These relate to the dilemmas involved in the dialogic process between multiple female subjects and groups; the coordination problems and constraints that are involved in communication between multiple female subjects; the difficulties in bridging their diverse temporal and spatial horizons; the power relations in these loosely coupled networks that affect their access and coherence; a failure to redefine objectives or search for new identities in face of continual disagreement among individuals and groups; the effectiveness of noise reduction mechanisms in promoting mutual sensitivity to autonomous logics; the impact of the discursive and extra-discursive practices that are deployed for negative coordination in creating 'synergetic differences' (Sum 1998) (for example complex types of (un)equal others); and the disjunctures between the spatialities and temporalities between the three levels of governance. It is through the co-examination of order and chaos that one may gain insights into the structured complexity and evolutionary nature of feminist politics/movements across time and space.

In conclusion, I want to argue that imagined identities such as Clinton's 'united sisterhood' and 'liberal rightism', are constructed within the Enlightenment time–space envelope. Such an orientation has been challenged even in the USA by some feminists and is even more alien to women located in other times and spaces. There is a growing awareness of the culturally and socially embedded nature of feminisms. These 'embedded feminisms' and their multiplicities are at the heart of the question of 'difference'. Debates around this question are closely tied to concepts such as subjectivities, essentialism, strategy, and even 'border-lands'. This chapter seeks to shift the debate from a subjectivity-centred politics of identity to an examination of feminist politics/movements across time and space as a complex interactive social field. With regard to the latter, I attempt to bring together two bodies of literature, namely Bakhtinian-inspired work on 'dialogism' and recent work on 'governance' as the complex art of steering multiple agencies, institutions and systems. In particular I suggest a 'hybridic governance' understanding of the politics of complexity of feminist politics/movements. More specifically, the hybridic governance (dis)order is inhabited by a multiplicity of time–space specific modes of communication at different levels that may/may not be mutually reciprocating.

Notes

1   Over 30,000 participants gathered to exchange ideas and accounts of their experiences and prepare for lobbying the official conference. There were over 4,000 workshops and panels, covering a range of topics including abortion rights, wages for housework and sexuality.
2   This term was first presented, but not well specified, in Massey (1994). I have redefined it in this text.
3   It is unclear from the text whether Hillary Clinton penned her own address or simply spoke the words of an official speechwriter. For my purposes this is not important.
4   For a reworking of the concept of democracy by feminist theorist, see Phillips (1991).
5   This can also be seen from the work of Western scholars outlining the 'inequality' of Chinese work places (Croll 1983) and in their criticism of the Chinese Communist Party's approach to the woman question as creating a 'public patriarchy' (Stacey 1992).

References

Alcoff, L. (1988) 'Cultural Feminism versus Poststructuralism: The Identity Crisis in Feminist Theory', *Signs* 13 (Spring): 405–436.
Anzaldua, G. (ed.) (1990) *Making Faces, Making Soul: Creative and Critical Perspectives by Feminists of Colour*, San Francisco, Calif.: Aunt Lute Books.
Barlow, T.E. (1991) 'Theorizing Woman: Tunu, Guojia, Jiating (Woman, Chinese State, Chinese Family)', *Genders* 10 (Spring): 132–160.
Clinton, H. (1995) 'Remarks for the United Nations: Fourth World Conference on Women', Beijing, China, 5 September (gopher://gopher.undp.org/unconfs/women/gov/950905175635) [accessed 15 February 2000].
Coomaraswamy, R. (1994) 'To Bellow like a Cow: Women, Ethnicity, and the Discourse of Rights', in R.J. Cook (ed.) *Human Rights of Women: National and International Perspectives*, Philadelphia: University of Pennsylvania Press.
Croll, E. (1983) *Chinese Women Since Mao*, London: Zed Press.
Goetz, A.M. (1991) 'Feminism and the Claim to Know: Contradictions in Feminist Approaches to Women', in R. Grant and K. Newland (eds) *Gender and International Relations*, Milton Keynes, England: Open University Press.

Habermas, J. (1984) *Theory of Communicative Action, Vol. 1: Reason and the Rationalization of Society*, Boston, Mass.: Beacon Press.

Haraway, D. (1988) 'Situated Knowledges: The Science Question in Feminism and the Privilege of Partial Perspective', *Feminist Studies* 14: 575–599.

Holquist, M. (1990) *Dialogism: Bakhtin and His World*, London: Routledge.

Hom, S.K. (1992) 'Female Infanticide in China: The Specter of Human Rights and Thoughts towards (An)other Vision', *Columbia Human Rights Law Review* 23, 2: 249–314.

hooks, b. (1990) *Yearnings: Race, Gender and Cultural Politics*, Boston, Mass.: South End Press.

Howell, J. (1996) 'The Struggle for Survival: Prospects for the Women's Federation in Post-Mao China', *World Development* 24, 1: 129–143.

Jagose, A. (1993) 'Slash and Suture: Post/colonialism in Borderlands/La Frontera: The New Mestiza', in S. Gunew and A. Yateman (eds) *Feminism and the Politics of Difference*, St Leonards, N.S.W.: Allen and Unwin, 212–227.

Jessop, B. (1998) 'The Rise of Governance and the Risks of Failure: The Case of Economic Development', *International Social Science Journal* 155: 29–45.

Kooiman, J. (ed.) (1993) *Modern Governance: New Government–Society Interactions*, London: Sage.

Lai, M. (1995) 'Female But Not Woman: Genders in Chinese Socialist Texts', in C. Siegel and A. Kibley (eds) *Forming and Reforming Identity*, Genders 21 (special issue): 287–318.

Liu, L.H. (1991) 'The Female Tradition in Modern Chinese Literature: Negotiating Feminisms Across East/West Boundaries', *Genders* 12: 22–44.

Mohanty, C.T. (1991) 'Under Western Eyes: Feminist Scholarship and Colonial Discourse', in C.T. Mohanty, A. Russo and L. Torres (eds) *Third World Women and Politics of Feminism*, Bloomington: University of Indiana Press.

Massey, D. (1994) *Space, Place and Gender*, Minneapolis: University of Minnesota Press.

O'Leary, C. (1997) 'Counteridentification or Counterhegemony? Transforming Feminist Standpoint Theory', *Women and Politics* 18, 3: 45–72.

Ong, A. (1988) 'Colonialism and Modernity: Feminist and Re-presentations of Women in Non-Western Societies', *Inscriptions* 3, 3/4: 79–93.

—— (1995) 'Women Out of China: Travelling Tales and Travelling Theories in Postcolonial Feminism', in R. Behar and D. Gordon (eds) *Women: Writing Culture*, Berkeley: University of California Press.

—— (1996) 'Strategic Sisterhood or Sisters in Solidarity? Questions of Communitarianism and Citizenship in Asia', *Indiana Journal of Global Legal Studies* 4, 1: 107–136.

Phillips, A. (1991) *Engendering Democracy*, Cambridge: Polity Press.

Romany, C. (1994) 'State Responsibility Goes Private: A Feminist Critique of the Public/Private Distinction in International Human Rights Law', in R.J. Cook (ed.) *Human Rights of Women: National and International Perspectives*, Philadelphia: University of Pennsylvania Press.

Spivak, G.C. (1988) 'Can the Subaltern Speak?', in L. Grossberg and C. Nelson (eds) *Marxism and the Interpretation of Culture*, Urbana and Chicago: University of Illinois Press.

Stacey, J. (1983) *Patriarchy and Socialist Revolution in China*, Berkeley: University of California Press.

Sum, N.-L. (1996) 'The "Hegemonic" Force of Hillary Clinton's "United Sisterhood"', *New Political Economy*, 1 (2): 278–282.

—— (1999) 'Three New Kinds of Orientalism and Global Capitalism', in A. Brah, M. Hickman and M. Mac An Ghaill (eds), *Global Futures: Migration, Environment and Globalization*, London: Macmillan, 99-121.

Trinh, T.M.-h. (1989) *Women, Native Other*, Bloomington: Indiana University Press.

Yuval-Davis, N. (1997) *Gender and Nation*, London: Sage.

Zhang, N., with Wu Xu (1995) 'Discovering the Positive Within the Negative: The Women's Movement in a Changing China', in A. Baus (ed.) *The Challenge of Local Feminisms: Women's Movements in Global Perspective*, Boulder, Colo.: Westview Press.

8 Operatic karaoke and the pitfalls of identity politics

A translated performance

Sneja Gunew

> I wanted to know Helen's body so well I could climb in and zip up her skin around me.
>
> Evelyn Lau, *Other Women*

The register of the visible

The title of the lead article in a relatively recent and controversial issue of the lifestyle magazine *Vancouver* was 'Greetings from Asia Town'; the accompanying visual consisted of a collage of women's faces, both 'Caucasian' and 'Asian', with some dissolving into each other.[1] The accompanying article suggested that Vancouver's population would be half 'Asian' in the next century and that the resultant mix would precipitate either tribalism (with its suggestion of serial conflict) or the kind of 'morphed' assimilation illustrated by the collage (North 1996). Although the latter might be perceived as the more benign alternative, it could also be read as conjuring the spectre of miscegenation, the blurring of differences as the direct result of genealogical contaminations. Indeed, the visibility of 'difference' is itself registered via these markers of normative racialisation. The visible body itself, what the viewer sees in terms of its corporeal inscriptions, supposedly 'explains' these differences which, in turn, evoke both the incommensurabilities of postcolonial theory (the untranslatabilities of cultural difference) and the 'lifestyle incompatibilities' of 'culturalism' or cultural racism. The latter is at the core of what Etienne Balibar has dubbed (rather alarmingly) academic racism:

> theories of academic racism mimic scientific discursivity by basing themselves upon 'visible evidence' (whence the essential importance of the stigmata of race and in particular of bodily stigmata) ... they mimic the way in which scientific discursivity articulates 'visible facts' to 'hidden causes' ... a violent *desire for* immediate *knowledge* of social relations.
>
> (Balibar 1991:19)

Balibar goes on to elaborate this nexus between racism and the visible as leading to a further convergence of racism and the politics of cultural difference:[2]

> Ideologically, current racism, which in France centres upon the immigration complex, fits into a framework of 'racism without races' … It is a racism whose dominant theme is not biological heredity but the insurmountability of cultural differences, a racism which, at first sight, does not postulate the superiority of certain groups or peoples in relation to others but 'only' the harmfulness of abolishing frontiers, the incompatibility of life-styles and traditions; in short … a differentialist racism.
>
> (Balibar 1991: 21)

In an attempt to uncouple the visible from such mechanisms of naturalised racism as described above, I wanted to find a way to take into consideration another of the senses, that of hearing. As noted, the register of the visible permeates much current theory, but the aural dimension, including the category of voice and, for example, accent, has remained somewhat under-theorised. Following this train of thought suggested that classical Western opera might represent a particularly fertile field which was appropriate, for the genre of the conference presentation itself, where these speculations were first aired. In an exploratory effort to investigate these fields, I recently 'staged' a performance piece dealing with the first novel of Canadian poet Evelyn Lau.[3] Clearly the attempt to separate the visual from the aural functions more clumsily in print and is symptomatic as well of the impossibilities of translation at the heart of all cross-cultural and, for that matter, cross-disciplinary work. On the other hand, an alertness to ways in which translation is intrinsic to many of these debates is also signalled by the sometimes awkward transitions between the 'here' of the conference performance and its other temporalities when translated for the conference publication (which traditionally expunges any reference to the original context and delivery). I will therefore try to evoke the interpretive strategy for this endeavour, while at the same time attempting to foreground its limitations. Retaining a first-person narrator in an academic essay is also an attempt to convey the performative aspects of this chapter.

Working against the usual aural expectations set up by a conference delivery, the introductory 'mise-en-scène' (an obligatory exercise when minority or non-canonical writers are being used) deliberately excluded my reading voice when, for the first fifteen minutes, a series of overhead transparencies were projected which began with extracts from Lau's novel (Lau 1995: 184, 189–90), and from one short story (Lau 1993: 50), followed by the cover of her second collection of poems, *Oedipal Dreams* (Lau 1992), with its iconic portrait of the artist. The fourth transparency, which commented on, amongst other things, this cover, was from a piece by the Canadian critic Misao Dean:

> Evelyn Lau's picture on the cover of *Oedipal Dreams* is a stark white mask, heavily marked with eyeliner and lipstick in order to evoke the classic female face of Chinese opera. Sold under the sign of the 'oriental girl', who is stereotypically both the mincing and modest virgin and the mysterious and

sexually skilled courtesan, Lau's books are marketed in a way that evokes both racist and sexist stereotypes.

Lau disclaims responsibility for this public image ... 'I like the fact that the photographs don't look like me as a person, because I wouldn't want to be walking down the street and be instantly recognizable. So there's definitely an element of disguise there too.'

(Dean 1995: 24–25)

The fifth transparency was from an interview with the Canadian journalist Jan Wong:

Evelyn Lau is wearing a baggy oatmeal sweater. So it's not immediately apparent she is one of the few surgically unassisted Chinese women in the world to require a DD-cup bra ... But back to Lau's past. Now, I left my comfortable Montreal home at 19 to voluntarily haul pig manure in China during the Cultural Revolution. But I have trouble understanding why someone so smart would drop out of school and run away from home at 14 and end up as a junkie-whore. Yes, it's hard to be the dutiful daughter of immigrants from China and Hong Kong, the kind who consider friends a frivolity and an 89 per cent exam mark a failure ... But I'm a parent now. Millions of Canadians have overcome such traumas, if that is the word, without self-indulgent melt-downs.

(Wong 1997: A11)

The final transparency was accompanied by the first moment of sound in the presentation and consisted, perversely, of an extract from the soundtrack of the film made of Lau's first text, the autobiographically based *Runaway: Diary of a Street Kid* (Lau 1989). The extract chosen dealt with a heuristic moment in the film when the protagonist experiences an epiphany in the consulting room of her analyst:

EVELYN: It's like all the stuff about how great you are. It gets to me you know, with Larry, with all of them. And when they come it's like I've done something right for once. Right from the beginning I felt that, that I'm good for something, that I belong.

DR. HIGHTOWER: Go on.

EVELYN: In prostitution, I mean, I can fulfill someone. Here, right now! Which I could never do with my parents.

DR. HIGHTOWER: Yes.

EVELYN: I could never ... I could never do with my parents. Does it matter if it's only a john? I mean it's somebody. I mean, at home I could never please them. I could get 95 or do 6 hours of housework and never go out. Always hoping for something, you know. Some sign of love. But nothing was ever good enough. Dad left me and she, she would have a ruler, or her hand, or her mouth. I never had a mouth. She called me

> lazy, fat, ugly, stupid slut … every day. And I swallowed it in. And hated
> myself. O.K., O.K. maybe they do treat me like a piece of meat on the
> street but at least I'm appreciated there.
>   Otherwise I'm nobody.
> DR. HIGHTOWER: You're not nobody Evelyn. That's what they taught you
> but it's not true … No!
> EVELYN: No. I just wish they could have liked me for who I am … Yeah.
> Yes … Thanks.
>
> (*The Diary of Evelyn Lau* 1993)

At this point my own voice was introduced in a series of questions: What
happens when the visual intervenes, in print or the mind's eye of the reader,
when we join the voice to a body, have the voice issue from what has been coded
as a 'visible minority' face? How might one circumvent the 'disguise' of the
stereotype (to echo Lau), the 'orientalist' camouflage Lau's public persona apparently adopts so that her private self won't be recognised in the streets?

One way to arrive at an answer is to consider what we, as readers or audience, desire from the so-called minority writer who becomes constructed as part
of the current quest for 'cultural difference' and who is often covertly racialised
(or sexualised) as 'deviant'. The term 'desire' and its link with 'differential
racism' (as described above) suggests the field of psychoanalysis for, as Ali
Rattansi, following Homi Bhabha, has pointed out, 'The ambivalence of racism
… is particularly open to psychoanalytic interpretation for it is in psychoanalysis
that the notion has its strongest roots … [it] does not reduce all racisms merely to
supposedly eternal and universal psychic mechanisms' (Rattansi 1995:
272–273).[4] The question of desire in psychoanalysis, is posed, for example, by
Slavoj Zizek: 'The original question of desire is not directly "What do I want?"
but "What do others want from me? What do they see in me? What am I for
others?"' (Zizek 1996: 117). How, in other words, can we as readers *not* project
the expectation that Lau should 'inform' us about what would, in Canada, be
termed her 'visible minority status', acknowledge it in some way and, if not, how
do we avoid constructing her in terms of a refusal or denial? These expectations
are the familiar burdens imposed on the minority writer (Gunew 1994).

Canadian poet and short-story writer Evelyn Lau represents an enigma in a
Canadian and North American west coast context where Asian-American and
Asian-Canadian ethnic or diasporic canons are being hastily assembled with a
great deal of relish, given the demographic changes along the west coast over the
past decade (Cheung 1997; Karpinski and Lea 1993; Lee and Wong-Chu 1991;
Lim and Ling 1992; Silvera 1994; Wong 1993). The semi-autobiographical work
which shot her to precocious fame at the age of 18, *Runaway: Diary of a Street Kid*,
dealt with a protagonist preferring a life on the street to the constrictions of
family expectations projected upon her. That the family were Chinese immigrants was almost deliberately incidental, in the written text at least. The
expectations concerning the Chinese as 'model immigrants' in terms of their
abilities to assimilate are succinctly outlined in the extract quoted earlier by jour-

nalist Jan Wong, herself the author of a recent bestseller, *Red China Blues: My Long March from Mao to Now* (1996). In the film made of Lau's book it was another matter, for the demands of the visual medium meant that the ethnic identity of the protagonist and her family inevitably registered a certain kind of coded presence. Following this first text, Lau's poetry and short stories have subsequently explored an overtly heterosexual underworld of sadomasochism, prostitution and drug addiction and have been seen as deliberately avoiding any hint of a racialised perspective, in relation to which she supposedly has an 'insider's' knowledge (Dean 1995; Kamboureli 1997: 534). It may be, however, that an emerging group of Chinese-Canadian critics interpret the insider–outsider dynamics differently. For example, in the words of Elaine K. Chang, 'Throughout *Runaway*, Lau identifies herself as Chinese only when her ethnicity signifies a measure of difference, and not sameness or "belonging"' (Chang 1994: 114). Lien Chao, author of the first full-length study of Chinese-Canadian writing in English, perceives Lau's highly self-conscious individualism as being at odds with the 'collective' impetus of other Chinese-Canadian writers who are at pains to write their community into Canadian culture and history (Chao 1997:156–184). Chao also perceives Lau's subject matter as restrictive and stereotypical. Thus, from many directions, Lau is perceived as flouting or refusing the so-called 'empowering' categories with which critics are eager to provide her, rarely appearing in anthologies of Asian-Canadian writing and, by her own account, refusing to participate in 'multicultural' events (Lau 1994b).

For those of us who, for several decades, have attempted to deconstruct totalising national–cultural narratives and their attendant regulatory institutional regimes in the name of women, of anti-imperialism and critical multiculturalism (Gunew 1994), her apparent refusal precipitates a revisiting of a range of theoretical issues. These include ones around the question of how to situate the authority to speak and write for those designated minority cultural players and how to set up interpretive strategies which move beyond the thematisation of cultural difference. This is crucial because thematisation, in turn, functions to reinforce difference as a mechanism leading to marginalisation, since difference is always posited in relation to an implicit (and invisible) hegemonic norm. The dominant reference points for minoritarian questioning of the hegemonic are a mixture of postcolonial histories with their legacies of scepticism towards totalising theoretical frameworks, invocations of anti-racism (often in opposition to the perceived wimpy liberalism of multiculturalism) and the perceived essentialisms of identity positionings. The slick invocation of terms such as 'tribalism', 'ethnic absolutism' and 'ethnic cleansing' in relation to coverage of the war in the former Yugoslavia in particular (Gunew 1997) are competing with principled attempts to constitute local pedagogies which incorporate an ethics of recognition in relation to minorities. In the necessary tension between global diasporas, with their networks and coalitions, and localised manifestations and negotiations, how might one locate or construct intellectual and pedagogical interventions that avoid the compromised categories of 'ethnic community' and of the general reductionism of identity politics?

The debates around identity politics have a particular resonance within global feminism, although their detailed meanings are often dependent on local contexts. Identity politics itself was seen as arising out of 'consciousness-raising' tactics which are historically associated with the birth of second-wave feminism and led from the articulation of women's differences to the definition of other group differences. But, increasingly, these differences have congealed into imprisoning essentialisms which are often perceived as obscuring more than they illuminate, of occluding intra-group differences and 'intersectional identities' (Crenshaw 1995: 333). Critics such as Nira Yuval-Davis warn that an identity politics which couples women with ethnicity within the political framework of multiculturalism obscures the political (rather than simply cultural) nature of ethnicity and can lead to the kinds of fundamentalism currently on the rise all over the world. Indeed, as she contends, political ethnicity uses 'cultural resources to promote its specific purposes' in the name of the self-enclosed ethnic community in which women rarely are permitted to play a progressive role (Yuval-Davis 1994: 411). Martha Minow argues that identity politics 'may freeze people in pain and also fuel their dependence on their own victim status as a source of meaning' (Minow 1997:54). She goes on to state that, 'Identity politics tends to locate the problem in the identity group rather than the social relations that produce identity groupings' (Minow 1997: 56). In *Solidarity of Strangers: Feminisms after Identity Politics*, Jodi Dean states that 'The articulation of particular identities has led to the rigidification of these very identities. At the legislative level, this rigidification appears as the reinforcement of minority status with its negative connotations of inferiority' (Dean 1996: 5). She suggests that:

> framing the debate as an opposition between solidarity and reflection prevents us from acknowledging the ideals shared by both sides. Supporters of identity politics are united by the ideals of inclusion and community. They struggle against exclusions enacted in the name of universality. They endeavor to establish a space of belonging, a community that strengthens its members ... Similarly, detractors and critics of identity politics also struggle against exclusion, this time that exclusion effected by the very sign of identity ... They want to ensure that those aspects of the self that elude the boundaries established by any identity category will not remain silenced or neglected but will be allowed to appear and develop in all their differences and particularity.
>
> (Dean 1996: 6)

The solution however, as argued by Analouise Keating in the context of the struggle by 'women of colour' to assert their own politics of difference, is 'not to abandon all references to personal experiences but rather to take experientially based knowledge claims even further by redefining identity' (Keating 1998: 36). Keating draws on Chela Sandoval's concept of 'differential consciousness' and, like Rattansi, on Homi Bhabha's notion of 'ambivalent identification' as a way to move to such new definitions of identity.

This is why Lau's case seems such an exemplary and compelling one. Do we see her as a minority writer who refuses the 'ethical responsibility' of representing her community, choosing the deliberate individualism often associated with the subjectivity of late capitalism (Elam 1997)? Or do we use her example as a way to move beyond the constraints of identity categories which figure the 'new racism' described by Rattansi, or the limits identified by the feminist critics cited above? The following discussion comprises some sketchy notes towards a possible interpretive strategy for approaching such texts. Having attempted to 'set the scene' and to explain how a project to establish the anti-universalist focus on cultural difference has been appropriated by a 'new racism' organised around an economy of visibility and, in particular, an emphasis on the visibly-racialised body, I will now link the question of the visible to the acoustic: voice and sound, the aural dimension residing within these questions.

The acoustic register

In marked contradiction to film, one of the cultural domains where there is conventional acceptance of the disjunction between visible bodies and audible voices is opera. Western opera demands a suspension of disbelief not only with respect to the 'fat tenor/soprano' and the nubile characters they are asked to represent, but, also in relation to the gender-crossings and 'color-blind' casting that have always been present in this medium. What the audience 'see' does not get in the way of what they are asked to imagine. Until recently, for example, few of the *non*-European roles in the standard canonical repertoire were actually sung by those from the requisite categories, but there have, however, been flurries of controversy around cases where leading roles were sung by non-European singers.[5] A systematic study of the chequered history of race and opera has still to be written.[6] Generally speaking, opera audiences are accustomed to hearing the voice and imaginatively substituting a very different body from the one which they see on the stage. So how might this affect a reading of Lau's work in relation to the question of desire as posed by Zizek?[7]

In the reviews heralding the reception of *Other Women* critics wondered whether Lau would, or could, ever move beyond a somewhat romantic adolescent rebelliousness suggested by the prevailing obsession with the underworld of sadomasochism and prostitution (Chao 1997; Gunning 1995; Kornreich 1996). My argument is that, in a sense, Lau's work invites a more allegorical reading. Allegory is the supreme modality where what you see is not what you get, and opera, in its splitting of the visible and the audible, helps us recognise this.

Indicative of soap opera rather than opera proper, the novel's title, *Other Women*, suggests that the women referred to are those who disrupt the dyad of the heterosexual couple. Instead, the text is narrated from the point of view of the traditional 'mistress' so that the 'other woman' is actually the 'wife'. Thus the whole text, and much of Lau's prose work, can be interpreted as celebrating a nostalgia for the 'normal' via the concept of symbolic identification. One needs to be reminded that, within psychoanalysis, the operations of identification are not with actual people but with possible 'types' or, more precisely and following Lacan, with positions in language where language constitutes the symbolic order. Slavoj Zizek delineates the following distinction between imaginary and symbolic identification:

> Imaginary identification is identification with the image in which we appear likeable to ourselves, with the image representing 'what we would like to be', and symbolic identification, identification with the very place *from where* we are being observed, *from where* we look at ourselves so that we appear to ourselves likeable, worthy of love.
>
> (Zizek 1989: 105)[8]

This site is the place of 'the Other' (the symbolic order) from whence the gaze and the interrogation proceed and thus is identified with social doxa, the hegemonic codes of the social world. As constituted in Lau's work, it becomes the location of social heteronormativity. The symbolic identification of the adulterous woman is with the position of the wife insofar as she connotes the heterosexual couple. She is/they are in the place from which they observe her and where she wants to be. Consider the following extracts (from the first transparency):

> My fantasies of your wife grew increasingly intimate and violent. I wanted to strip Helen naked, to familiarize myself with her body, her responses; I wanted to put my face against her chest and listen to her heart-beat climb towards orgasm, and then the slowing of her breath and pulse. I wanted to examine between her thighs with the probing interest of a physician, to explore the inches of her skin for marks, moles, wrinkles, to measure the proportion of muscle to fat, the density and porosity of her skeleton.
>
> I wanted to know Helen's body so well I could climb in and zip up her skin around me.
>
> (Lau 1995: 184)

> In the months that followed the end of the affair, I thought I saw you, or your wife, everywhere. Your face reflected back at me from the faces of men passing me on the vibrant street at lunch hour. Their eyes flashed like mica, their faces were similarly shaped, and I thought for the first time that in many respects you must be absolutely ordinary, otherwise how could so many strangers bear your resemblance? Yet none of them survived a second look. And so it went for your wife as well.
>
> (Lau 1995: 189–190)

What are described here are not imaginary identifications with an ideal self but attempts to gesture towards a place from which the 'normality' of these figures may be registered and atomised. These sections from the novel, as well as the supposedly 'heuristic moment' in the film script (when everything is 'explained'), all point to the identification of a referential moralistic voice echoed as well in the extract from Jan Wong's prescriptive evaluation. There are certain societal standards, designated by invisible or spectral scripts, against which the protagonist transgresses – visibly and stereotypically. Paradoxically, the excesses of sexual perversion and addiction serve to confirm such social standards since the norm as measure is always there as a point of nostalgic invocation, as demonstrated by the closing pages of *Other Women* from which these quotations were taken. What is, at one level, a text dealing with obsessive emotional addiction is, at another level, the reconfirmation of the bourgeois heterosexual couple as constitutive norm for sexual–social relations. The fact that the chapters alternate between first-person and third-person intimate functions as a reminder of the mirror-image, the to and fro, mutually constitutive relationship of the adulterous woman and the wife. That is one kind of reading.[9]

But that is not the whole story and there are other excesses at work beyond this. If we return to Western opera, there are moments when the point of the music, or aria, functions to exceed meaning – as signifying the very disruption of meaning. In the words of Wayne Kostenbaum, 'When heterosexuality unveils itself as *sumptuous* and *delusional*, the libretto shatters, and shadow-knowledges speak ... by loving Butterfly's entrance more than her death ... by never outgrowing this entrance phrase, I can speak another Butterfly' (Kostenbaum 1993: 200). And Michel Poizat in *The Angel's Cry*: 'but when Callas sings, when she's going to kill herself, maybe it's idiotic, but I snap ... it's hearing the voice, the music, I fall on my knees' (Poizat 1992: 26). The music leaks beyond the container of meaning provided by the libretto, the narrative, and thus permits multiple identifications, including gay ones (Abel 1996: 32–34). This exhilaration permits precisely the kinds of disruptive and paradoxical identifications which opera, in a sense, personifies by imbuing a visible and living body with the suggestion of ventriloquism. The instability of corporeality indicated by the imaginative possibilities of opera means that it is a genre where, historically at least and unlike film, the tyranny of the visible has been unseated by the precedence of the aural. We are reminded that, in Zizek's formulation, any manifestation of voice is always to some extent ventriloquised and exceeds the explanatory parameters of the body it ostensibly occupies. In a recent piece, aptly titled '"I Hear You with My Eyes": or, The Invisible Master', Zizek traces what he calls the homologous mechanisms of gaze and voice in the following manner:

> it is as if, when we're talking, whatever we say is an answer to a primordial address by the Other – we're always already addressed, but this address is blank, it cannot be pinpointed to a specific agent, but is a kind of empty a priori, the formal 'condition of the possibility' of our speaking ...
>
> (Zizek 1996: 90)

Which brings us to opera and to *Madama Butterfly*,[10] the most obviously orientalist of operas. In the many recent attentions Puccini's opera has received, much has been made of the fact that Cho-Cho San functions as the traditional good woman who sacrifices herself in the name of maternity.[11] She has also notoriously figured as the paradigmatic orientalist fantasy of the ultimate victim and ultimate seductress, both child and *femme fatale*, a combination informing, for example, Misao Dean's essay quoted earlier. David Hwang's play *M. Butterfly* has explored one kind of gloss on the opera, and David Cronenberg's film of the play a slightly different variation. The sustaining fantasy in these two depictions is that 'Butterfly' really wants to be the cad Pinkerton and vice versa, that Gallimard finally realises he wants to *be* Butterfly rather than to possess her. But isn't this constant seesawing or mechanism of vice versa that which has always sustained such binary frameworks for decades, and isn't this why one needs to find a way beyond such a paralysing impasse? Therefore we return to the delirium of the aria and of music in general as documented by Jacques Attali (1989) and now many others in the developing field of sound theory. Zizek comments:

> Voice is that which, in the signifier, resists meaning, it stands for the opaque inertia that cannot be recuperated by meaning … the moment at which the singing voice cuts loose from its anchoring in meaning and accelerates into a consuming self-enjoyment.
>
> (Zizek 1996: 103–104)

On the one hand, we see on stage the stereotype of Butterfly; we see the stereotype of Lau's adulterous woman and invest it with the 'withheld orientalism' of the author (as suggested by the critics' demands for her to inform us about her 'ethnic' knowledge). But perhaps it is possible to break this move by turning from the visual to the acoustic, by situating Lau's text not in the genre of 'dirty realism'[12] (suggested by the prevailing themes in her work) but in the lyrical genre of opera and sound. This move might also be facilitated (were there time and space) by examining her poetry, which has been identified as traditionally lyrical in style, a contrast perhaps with the confrontational themes of her other work (Wah 1997–98). Considering the disembodiment of the female voice, Kaja Silvermann suggests that perhaps it is the mother whom the daughter wishes to seduce ('both to seduce the mother and be seduced by her', Silvermann 1988: 153), rather than the Freudian heterosexual seduction scenario of the father and daughter. If we recall the film-script extract quoted earlier, there is a classic psychoanalytic example of this scenario in the sublimated form of male analyst and female analysand; meanwhile the protagonist recounts her own family saga as one where the father is merely absent, while the mother has a *mouth*. In *Other Women*, the narrator, speaking of herself in the third person, repeatedly states that: 'It seems incredible to her, that at last she is making a sound' (Lau 1995: 13) and 'she could open her mouth, and with just a few words, enter Helen's life' (Lau 1995: 8). The place of symbolic identification reinforces the norm but, by focusing on sound rather than sight and on the *disjuncture* between body and voice, we are also reminded that the heteronormative couple is itself sustained by the fantasy of its perverse double. What is undeniably all powerful in Lau's text is the open and speaking (singing) female voice[13], which appears to exceed the meanings of normativity we have been attaching to it. Where that delirium may lead in terms of finding other meanings in Lau's oeuvre remains to be seen and would necessarily include her poetry.

Arriving finally at karaoke,[14] one could suggest that it functions as a consummate example of mimicry and ventriloquism. The reason for invoking the odd conjunction of operatic karaoke here is that Lau's work is clearly not operatic in the classic sense since its preoccupations, in *Other Women* at least, suggest an accent on accessories and lifestyles associated with soap opera. Operatic karaoke takes bathroom singing to new soap-operatic heights.[15] It is both the ultimate accolade and parody of this Western musical form, though not necessarily from a race-conscious or postcolonial perspective. Western opera has always exceeded and been constituted by its own parodic contradictions (what you hear governs what you imagine). In Lau's work, the reader's imagined ventriloquisms of the authorial body are undone by the delirium of the textual voice which exceeds the very norms it ostensibly functions to sustain. It might be productive, therefore, to learn to listen for voice outside the traditional narratives of race as presently constituted, with their normative privileging of the visibly raced body. These are the possibilities for exceeding the claustrophobic paradigms of identity politics which can be constraining even when benignly situated in the realms of postcolonial and multicultural interrogations. Here might be a way for those 'intersectional identities' (Crenshaw 1995) and 'differential consciousnesses' (Keating 1998) which are part of the new ways for defining identity to be articulated. Questions of desire ('What do others want from me? What do they see in me? What am I for others?') continue to be posed by those designated minority writers to their audiences or readers.[16]

Notes

1   The popular culture term for the manipulated faces would probably be that they were 'morphing' into each other. The resultant composite invokes the science fiction genre with its twin traditions of utopia and dystopia.
2   I am indebted to Mishra (1996) for leading me to Balibar's work. Note here Rattansi's critique that the 'new racism' is perhaps not so new since national and racist discourses have always been linked in the terms used to delineate 'cultural racism' (Rattansi 1995: 255).
3   At the 'Transformations: Thinking Through Feminism' conference held at Lancaster University, UK (July 1997).
4   Rattansi's essay is particularly indebted to the work of Homi Bhabha, who, following the pioneering work of Frantz Fanon, uses psychoanalytic theory as a useful tool for analysing the hidden structures of colonialism and its aftermaths. See Bhabha (1994).
5   Dame Kiri Te Kanawa is a breakthrough case in point although, it is interesting to note how the blonde wig visibly cancels what the name professes to signify in some of her filmed roles.
6   In their recent fascinating study, Linda and Michael Hutcheon (1996) deal with the many permutations of illness and opera (including AIDS) but don't deal extensively with race. Matters of race have been mentioned in, for example, Kostenbaum (1993),

McClary (1991) and the pioneering work of Catherine Clément (1989), but a systematic study does not as yet, to my knowledge, exist.

7   The reason for invoking Zizek's work is that his current popularity is, in part at least, due to the fact that he is managing to bring together those ancient rivals: Marxism and psychoanalysis. To put it another way, he consistently brings to bear psychoanalytic concepts and intrepretive frameworks on questions of the social and the political. The question of desire in its various manifestations is at the heart of his work as well as being at the centre of the increasingly influential research of Renata Salecl. See their recent collaborative text (Salecl and Zizek 1996).

8   The short quotation hardly does justice to this highly complex interaction, and I recommend that interested readers seek out the fuller treatment (especially Zizek 1989). To amplify, without overburdening this short chapter, Zizek uses the example of 'hysterical theatre' in which the hysterical woman identifies with a particular model of the fragile feminine but does so from the vantage point (the place) of the paternal gaze 'to which she wants to appear likeable' (1989: 106). The underlying question echoes the one quoted earlier: Who sees me in this kind of way?

9   Elaine Chang identifies a comparable move in *Runaway* when she observes that 'Lau asserts her longing for the traditional home' (Chang 1994:109).

10 The story of Puccini's *Madama Butterfly* is set during the American occupation of Japan at the turn of the century and concerns the exploits of Lt Pinkerton, who acquires (indeed marries in a Japanese ceremony) a young geisha (Cho-Cho San) as part of a rental package. Cho-Cho San, or Butterfly, makes the mistake of falling in love with Pinkerton, who returns to his ship and country leaving her pregnant. In the latter part of the opera we observe Butterfly's longing for Pinkerton and pride in their son as expressed to her faithful female servant Suzuki. On being confronted with Pinkerton and his 'American' wife who desire to adopt her son, Butterfly kills herself in a ritual seppuko manner, since death with honour is preferable to life without honour.

11 Note that this scenario is repeated even in 'modern' versions of the tale, such as the musical *Miss Saigon*. See Kondo (1997) for a recent analysis of the 'orientalist' variations and significance of this story.

12 The genre of 'dirty realism', as exemplified by the work of contemporary American novelists including Raymond Carver, Richard Ford and David Mamet, appears to be the dominant interpretive framework for the little critical attention Lau's work has received. My thanks to Michael Zeitlin for information on this genre.

13 The all-powerful female mouth is also reminiscent, of course, of the castrating *vagina dentata*.

14 For the colonial history of karaoke as originating in Taiwan see Chen (1996). I am indebted to Rachel Lee for alerting me to this article. Casey Lum's study (1996) gives it a Japanese provenance.

15 Casey Lum's pioneering study of the role of karaoke in identificatory community processes within three American-Chinese communities associates it with Cantonese opera for one of his groups (Lum 1996, especially chapter 3). To my knowledge there is nothing to link Lau with Cantonese opera though there is a tradition within the Vancouver Chinese-Canadian community (Ho 1994). Lau has stated, in an interview I have been unable to track down, that she listened to *Madama Butterfly* while composing *Other Women*. In this regard it is also interesting to note Lau's poem 'My Tragic Opera' (Lau 1994a), which evokes the scenario of an adulterous woman visiting her lover's house while his wife and children are absent. She insinuates herself into the domestic space, particularly the bathroom, as a way of appropriating the heterosexual family and its everyday life. The 'desiring' identificatory moves I have outlined in relation to the novel are clearly visible here as well.

16 At the end of the conference presentation I played the full film extract (starring the incomparable Sandra Oh, who happens to be Korean-Canadian, as Lau) from which

the earlier soundtrack had been taken. The hope was that the audience would now see this 'ethnic' face as more than merely a 'native informant' on ethnicity.

References

Abel, S. (1996) *Opera in the Flesh: Sexuality in Operatic Performance*, Boulder, Colo.: Westview Press.

Attali, J. (1989) *Noise: The Political Economy of Music*, Minneapolis: University of Minnesota Press.

Balibar, E. (1991) 'Is There a "Neo-Racism"?', in E. Balibar and I. Wallerstein (eds) *Race, Nation, Class: Ambiguous Identities*, trans. C. Turner, London: Verso.

Bhabha, H. (1994) *The Location of Culture*, New York: Routledge.

Chang, E. K. (1994) 'Where the "Street Kid" Meets the City', in P. Delany (ed.) *Vancouver: Representing the Postmodern City*, Vancouver: Arsenal Press.

Chao, L. (1997) *Beyond Silence: Chinese Canadian Literature in English*, Toronto: Tsar.

Chen, K-H. (1996) 'Not Yet the Postcolonial Era: The (Super) Nation-State and Transnationalism of Cultural Studies: Response to Ang and Stratton', *Cultural Studies* 10, 1: 37–70.

Cheung, K.-K. (ed.) (1997) *An Interethnic Companion to Asian American Literature*, New York: Cambridge University Press.

Clément, C. (1989) *Opera, or the Undoing of Women*, trans. Betsy Wing, London: Virago.

Crenshaw, K. (1995) 'Mapping the Margins: Intersectionality, Identity Politics, and Violence Against Women of Color', in D. Danielsen and K. Engle (eds) *After Identity: A Reader in Law and Culture*, New York: Routledge.

Dean, J. (1996) *Solidarity of Strangers: Feminism After Identity Politics*, Berkeley: University of California Press.

Dean, M. (1995) 'Reading Evelyn Right: The Literary Layers of Evelyn Lau', *Canadian Forum* March: 22–26.

The Diary of Evelyn Lau (1993) dir. S. Gunnarsson, Canadian Broadcasting Commission.

Elam, D. (1997) 'Sister Are Doing It to Themselves', in D. Looser and E.A. Kaplan (eds) *Generations: Academic Feminists in Dialogue*, Minneapolis: University of Minnesota Press.

Gunew, S. (1994) *Framing Marginality: Multicultural Literary Studies*, Melbourne: Melbourne University Press.

—— (1997) 'Postcolonialism and Multiculturalism: Between Race and Ethnicity', in A. Gurr (ed.) *The Yearbook of English Studies* (Special Issue: The Politics of Postcolonial Criticism), Modern Humanities Research Association (UK), 27: 22–39.

Gunning, M. (1995) 'Jury Still Out on the Talents of Evelyn Lau', *Vancouver Sun* (*Weekend Sun*) 2 September: D13.

Ho, R. (1994) 'Site-seeing Vancouver, Positioning Self', in P. Delany (ed.) *Vancouver: Representing the Postmodern City*, Vancouver: Arsenal Press.

Hutcheon, L. and Hutcheon, M. (1996) *Opera: Desire, Disease, Death*, Lincoln: University of Nebraska Press.

Hwang, D. (1986) *M. Butterfly*, New York: Penguin.

Kamboureli , S. (ed.) (1997) *Making a Difference: Canadian Multicultural Literature*, Toronto: Oxford University Press.

Karpinski, E.C. and Lea, I. (eds) (1993) *Pens of Many Colours: A Canadian Reader*, Toronto: Harcourt Brace Jovanovich Canada.

Keating, A. (1998) '(De)Centering the Margins? Identity Politics and Tactical (Re)Naming', in S. K. Stanley (ed.) *Other Sisterhoods: Literary Theory and U.S. Women of Color*, Urbana and Chicago: University of Illinois Press.

Kondo, D. (1997) *About Face: Performing Race in Fashion and Theater*, New York: Routledge.

Kornreich, J. (1996) 'Selling Her Soul', *Women's Review of Books* 13, 6 (March): 17–18.

Kostenbaum, W. (1993) *The Queen's Throat: Opera, Homosexuality and the Mystery of Desire*, New York: Vintage.

Lau, E. (1989) *Runaway: Diary of a Street Kid*, Toronto: HarperCollins.

—— (1992) *Oedipal Dreams*, Toronto: Coach House.

—— (1993) *Fresh Girls and Other Stories*, Toronto: HarperCollins.

—— (1994a) *In the House of Slaves*, Toronto: Coach House.

—— (1994b) 'Why I Didn't Attend the Writing Thru Race Conference', *Globe & Mail*, Toronto, 9 July: 13.

—— (1995) *Other Women: A Novel*, Toronto: Random House of Canada.

Lee, B. and Wong-Chu, J. (eds) (1991) *Many-Mouthed Birds: Contemporary Writing by Chinese Canadians*, Vancouver/Toronto: Douglas McIntyre.

Lim, S.G.-l. and Ling, A. (eds) (1992) *Reading the Literatures of Asian America*, Philadelphia, Penn.: Temple University Press.

Lum, C.M.K. (1996) *In Search of a Voice: Karaoke and the Construction of Identity in Chinese America*, Mahwah, N.J.: Lawrence Erlbaum Associates.

McClary, S. (1991) *Feminine Endings: Music, Gender, and Sexuality*, Minnesota: University of Minnesota Press.

Minnow, M. (1997) *Not Only for Myself: Identity, Politics, and the Law*, New York: New Press.

Mishra, V. (1996) 'Postmodern Racism', *Meanjin*, 55, 2: 346–357.

North, S. (1996) 'Asia Town: What Will the Future Hold for a 50-percent-Asian Vancouver?' *Vancouver* 29, 7 (November): 46–58.

Poizat, M. (1992) *The Angel's Cry*, Ithaca, N.Y.: Cornell University Press.

Rattansi, A. (1995) 'Just Framing; Ethnicities and Racisms in a 'Postmodern' Framework', in L. Nicholson and Seidman, S. (eds) *Social Postmodernism: Beyond Identity Politics*, New York: Cambridge University Press.

Salecl, R. and Zizek, S. (eds) (1996) *Sic 1: Gaze and Voice as Love Objects*, Durham, N.C.: Duke University Press.

Silvera, M. (ed.) (1994) *The Other Woman: Women of Colour in Contemporary Canadian Literature*, Toronto: Sister Vision Press.

Silvermann, K. (1988) *The Acoustic Mirror: The Female Voice in Psychoanalysis and Cinema*, Bloomington: Indiana University Press.

Wah, F. (1997–98) 'Speak My Language: Racing the Lyric Poetic', *West Coast Line* 24.31.3 (Winter): 72–84.

Wong, C.S-l. (1993) *Reading Asian American Literature: From Necessity to Extravagance*, Princeton, N.J.: Princeton University Press.

Wong, J. (1996) *Red China Blues: My Long March from Mao to Now*, Toronto: Doubleday/Anchor, 1996.

—— (1997) 'Evelyn Lau Gets Perfect Grades in the School of Hard Knocks', *Globe & Mail*, Toronto, 3 April: A11.

Yuval-Davis, N. (1994) 'Identity Politics and Women's Ethnicities', in V. Moghadam (ed.) *Identity Politics and Women: Cultural Reassertions and Feminisms in International Perspective*, Boulder, Colo.: Westview Press.

Zizek, S. (1989) *The Sublime Object of Ideology*, London: Verso.

—— (1996) '"I Hear You with My Eyes": or, The Invisible Master', in R. Salecl and S. Zizek (eds) *Sic 1: Gaze and Voice as Love Objects*, Durham, N.C.: Duke University Press.

9 Crossing boundaries
Rethinking/teaching identity

Gail Ching-Liang Low

This chapter is part of a tentative project on how contemporary discourses of identity impact on our understanding and teaching of texts to do with migration and multiculturalism. One of the issues I am interested in is a way of talking and thinking about the problem of identification across cultural boundaries, and beyond the exclusions of 'ethnic absolutism', where cultures are seen to be hermetically sealed within themselves. The recent theorisations of identity as textual, hybrid, performative, strategic and positional offer a way of addressing these difficulties. Questions I am concerned with at present are to do with how border crossings are negotiated in the formation of political identities *and* political affiliations. Questions such as: How can we represent border crossings in a way that does not simply restate the old liberal trick of tolerance as celebration? This is to avoid the attitude: 'it's OK but not in my back yard'. How do we represent difference in ways that do not simply reinstate more of the 'ethnocentric' same? How do we 'perform' political identities given our diverse locations and experiences? How do we begin to connect our experience of lived identity, to what exceeds consciousness as subjectivity? In its more practical incarnations, such a project is linked to my experience of teaching contemporary literature under the sign of 'Asian', 'Black British' or postcolonial, and to a sense that politically progressive labels do not always coincide with the name my students give to their experiences. The problem that haunts some of my more interesting teaching sessions is what is at stake in these identifications – what kinds of futures can one engender and participate in when inhabiting these terms. In particular, we have been concerned with how to move the question of cultural crossings away from the pathology of cultural clash to narratives of 'transformations'. We can understand 'trans-formative' in the dual sense of the word, in terms of bridging thinking across structures and formations, and in terms of depicting a process of change and development in which identities are acknowledged as diasporic, multiple and heterogeneous. My aim in this chapter is modest: I will explore two writers' representations of the crossing of cultural, gender and class boundaries and consider what we can learn from them. The texts to be considered are: V.S. Naipaul's novel-cum-autobiography, *The Enigma of Arrival* (1987), and Farhana Sheikh's *The Red Box* (1991).

Naipaul's *Arrival* is made up of five sections and traces the life of the narrator–writer from his departure from Trinidad to his take-up of an Oxford scholarship, in essence, his 'arrival' as a writer and 'inhabitant' in England. *Arrival* is set primarily in the Wiltshire English countryside and looks in minute detail, across time, at the landscape and characters that people the English country estate. But the novel also includes the young writer's journey to and arrival in London in the 1950s, and describes his encounters with individuals or sets of individuals. Each section of the novel (autobiography) focuses strategically on a couple of characters who are used as 'alter egos' of the main narrating persona. Each character is located within the broader national and historical sweep of postwar suburban expansion and the changing economies of production in the rural countryside. Postcolonial history is also addressed; in particular, the postwar immigration from Europe and the Colonies that led to the creation of a multicultural and multiracial Britain. The array of characters in *Arrival*, including the narrating persona's younger self, enable the narrator to reflect on his desires, his anxieties and his identity, and also to position his dislocation within a history of social change. However, having said this, *Arrival* does not necessarily foreground its awareness of these changes, and the productive tension between private and public history is sometimes hidden by the grammatically undifferentiated self. One is faced with a number of problems when teaching Naipaul's book, but perhaps the two which have come up most frequently when I have taught this novel are problems of genre and the identity/subjectivity interface. Because of the restrictions of space, I will deal with the former only as it impinges on the concerns of the latter.

The very title of Naipaul's fictional autobiography, *Enigma of Arrival*, is calculated to provoke sections of his readership: What does it mean to arrive? Has this writer 'arrived' in the sense of attaining social and educational mobility and status? From George Lamming's critical assessment in the 1960s (Lamming 1960) to Sivanandan's dismissal in the 1990s (Sivanandan 1990), Naipaul's arrival would seem to be a 'selling out' and indication of his nostalgic identification with English culture. If much of Naipaul's former work has been about personal dislocation and cultural fragmentation as a result of colonial legacies, his writing can lend itself all too easily to an allegorical reading of postcolonial cultural, political and democratic activity as half-made makeshift imitations and repetitions. Naipaul seems to deliberately court such assessments in the half-ironic parallels between the British and Roman Empires; his Roman analogies echo the language of the 'Condition of England' discourses of the late nineteenth century, with their anxiety about degeneration and decay at the very heart of Empire. But the analogy also glamorises by association; in *Arrival*, postwar European and colonial migration to the metropolis is conceived as an indication of deterioration, decadence and a falling away from the high points of civilisation:

> Cities like London were to change. They were to cease being more or less national cities; they were to become cities of the world, modern-day Romes, establishing the pattern of what great cities should be, in the eyes of islanders like myself and people even more remote in language and culture.

They were to be cities visited for learning and elegant goods and manners and freedom by all the barbarians peoples of the globe, people of forest and desert, Arabs, African, Malays.

(Naipaul 1987: 130)

Much like the novel's meditation on the linguistic permutation of refuse/refuge in Wiltshire dialect, the 'flotsam of Europe' and Empire (in the contemporary language of racism – 'economic migrants') find shelter in the very heart of Empire.

In Naipaul, desire and negation have almost always taken the form of what Peggy Nightingale, in her introduction to his body of work, has called a 'personal tension between individual assimilation into the dominant English tradition and his political consciousness of the legacy of imperialism' (Nightingale 1991: 531). The writer acknowledges as much when he talks in *Arrival* about the split between two sides of himself, the man marked by the colonial politics of racial exclusions and the writer who aspired to a detached, elegant, knowing and oddly disembodied sensibility. Elsewhere, I've argued that cultural deracination in Naipaul's writing comes from a chain of metaphoric displacements centring on embodiment and disembodiment: the racial body versus the transcendent disembodied voice, the vulnerable, emotional and nervous comic buffoon versus the controlled, detached and self-effacing narrator (Low 1995). One can see the different functions his first-person narratives are put to; for example the split between the detached observer and the speaking subject who is acted upon. If, at times in *Arrival*, the body appears as a kind of abject and physical materialisation of the lumpen proletariat in all their unknowingness and vulgarity, the body is also used symbolically to address the vulnerability of the formerly colonised: their condition of powerlessness is condensed and cathected to their physique. Hence, Naipaul sets up the dichotomy between writer and racialised man as a mind/body dualism. To be writer is to attempt to transcend the racialised and marked body behind:

> I was travelling to be a writer. It was too frightening to accept the other thing, to face the other thing; it was to be diminished as man and writer. Racial diminution formed no part of the material of the kind of writer I was setting out to be. Thinking of myself as a writer, I was hiding my experience from myself; hiding myself from my experience. And even when I became a writer I was without the means, for many years, to cope with that disturbance. I wrote with my indelible pencil. I noted dialogue. My 'I' was aloof, a man who took notes, and knew.
>
> (Naipaul 1987: 117)

But does his later acknowledgement of such a misleading split, and his realisation of the disavowal of his early days, bring about a dispersal of these fears? More importantly, if by this confession we are meant to realise that the narrator's desire to occupy the place of the urbane writer was a kind of misidentification resulting from the poetics and politics of Empire, does the text of *Arrival* testify to the imperviousness of desire to knowledge? For what we have in *Arrival* is an elegy to the passing of a very English pastoral. If you cannot do anything about what you desire, then our vision of emancipatory politics and ethics must be very pessimistic indeed.

But perhaps this version of the conflict between desire and reason is a paradoxical by-product of the assumption of identity as coherent and volitional; one way out of this bleak reading would be to emphasise the novel's examination of identity – however tentative and contradictory – as the product of performance and sedimentation over time. By this I refer to both Judith Butler (1993) and Stuart Hall's (1989, 1990) attempts to think the interface between identity/ subjectivity as identification. Hall in 'Cultural Identity and Diaspora' (1990) and 'New Ethnicities' (1989) speaks of identity not as a state of being, but as a process cobbled out of memory, fantasy, narrative and myth. He suggests that 'Cultural identities are the points of identification, the unstable points of identification or suture, which are made, within the discourses of history and culture. Not an essence but a positioning' (Hall 1990: 226). In *Bodies That Matter* (1993), Judith Butler argues that identity should be shorn of its grammatical metaphysics and seen as the reiterative effect of phantasmatic identifications performed by regulatory discourses over time. Repetition, reiteration, 'citational accumulation' and sedimentation may consolidate normative demands, but they also produce the possibility of resistance. Identification, Butler argues, has to be thus *repeatedly produced*, and in 'the demand that the identification be *reiterated* persists the possibility, the threat that it will *fail* to repeat' (1993: 102).

Returning to *Arrival* we can see both strands at work. As my students always complain in exasperation, Naipaul's narrative is exceedingly repetitive. There is no real plot development and any changes are framed within a cyclic temporality which gives the impression of repetition. The walks the narrator takes, the description of the landscape surrounding him, his recollection of figures, events and narratives from the past, his description, assessment and comments on the individuals that people the text are introduced, described and returned to again and again. The effect, to some extent, is to produce an intensely fastidiously detailed and mimetic novel. Yet, another result of the novel's repetition is that it draws attention to precisely the reiterability and constructedness introduced by Butler's formulations. The novel's mimetic effects are produced in tension with its colonial education and legacy, where the world of the mother country is encountered as a textual world before it is available as lived experience. Hence the narrator invokes its representative precedents: high culture in the form of Constable, Dickens, Wordsworth, Hardy, Eliot, Conrad, and so on, and low culture as in the banal pictures of Friesian cows on condensed-milk tins. The narrator speaks of his time in Wiltshire as a second childhood, of literally learning to read words in their proper, rather than mutated, contexts. Yet the novel's investment in 'origins' is also precisely what enables an intimate knowledge of its 'production'. The improper contexts of words and absent histories are read back as the conditions of the English pastoral setting, the rise of the

Great House and its novelistic legacies. The endless repetition, which forms the basis of the narrating 'I's' understanding of the world around him, is shown to be a product of a process of sedimentation occurring over time and history; a sedimentation which, at times, hides the marks of change: 'So much that had looked traditional, natural, emanations of the landscape, things that country people did … now turned out not to have been traditional or instinctive after all' (Naipaul 1987: 47). Rural workers like Jack who are initially identified as 'a remnant of old peasantry' (22), and manorial staff like Pitton or the Phillipses who seem to epitomise tradition turn out to be 'impresarios' (191) of sorts, good at cultivating the image of solidity. *Arrival*'s self-conscious excavations hint at the constructedness of signs; their iterability and power as a product of colonial regimes, and their mutability across time. Ironically, it is the narrator's (mis)identification with colonial regimes that produces the knowledge of that mutability.

The novel's repetitive structure leads on to a consideration of *Arrival*'s ironic mimicry of generic antecedents, since his narratives are conducted in tandem with established, canonical and literary frames of reference. A strong case can be made for Naipaul's writing as succeeding more by way of ironic restaging rather than by creating and generating alternative forms of colonial writing. Sara Suleri (1992), for example, is right to emphasise the historical moment of Naipaul's 'ambivalence'. By carefully inhabiting the English book with an awareness of his status as colonial interloper, Naipaul manages to portray an uncanny awareness of the staging of desire. The section 'Ivy', which follows 'The Journey', constitutes an ironic echo of the 'Condition of England' rhetoric that dominated the heyday of new imperialism. The late-nineteenth-century national anxiety about the possible decline of Britain's status was linked with a concern about rural–urban migration, and very much obsessed with a biomedical discourse about health and urban degeneration. Naipaul hijacks this language and its focus. 'Ivy' and 'Rooks' chart the disintegration of the manor and its landlord; they also conduct a subtle ironic rehearsal of the English pastoral ideal that fed into the anxiety about the nation's health. Where the previous discourse extolled the (somewhat fictional) virtues of the English squirearchy, the traditional lifestyle of independent production, small estates, household bound by customary and local ties of kith and kin, Naipaul's animation of the pastoral departs from the organic myth and emphasises the wealth and service obtained elsewhere: 'the manor had been created at the zenith of imperial power and wealth, a period of high, even extravagant, middle-class domestic architecture' (Naipaul 1987: 235). The pastoral fantasy turns out to be precisely a powerful myth.

Arrival seeks to tell the story of colonial history as a kind of fearful symmetry where the history of one world is tied up in the history of the other. That colonial reading of history occurs in the manner in which the text seeks to hold on to different temporal, geographical and narrative frames so they gain meaning in relation to one another. For example, the discourse of decline and degeneration is given a Hindu inflection: 'the drum of creation in the god's right hand, the flame of destruction in his left' (Naipaul 1987: 53). Deliberate echoes of different literary texts also occur. For example, the description of the farmyard's dereliction is similar to that of Marlow's description of mechanical decay in the Congo in Joseph Conrad's *Heart of Darkness*. At times, it seems that the narrator's voice is an eerie echo of Marlow's own words: 'Death not as a tableau or a story ... but death, the end of things, as a gloom that got at a man, sought out his heart, when he was at his weakest, while he slept' (Naipaul 1987: 96).

Sara Suleri has argued that Naipaul should be placed squarely within the first generation of postcolonial writers and migrants to London in the 1950s. She argues that Naipaul's position is a 'localised and singular moment' in the post-colonial narrative; he is part of 'a dying generation, whose linguistic and cultural crises will not be duplicated in the engaged violence of a given "third world" history' (1992: 150). Teaching Naipaul is problematic because of the temptation to read his writing as 'representative' of the conflictual story of postcolonial man. The pull is greater for *Arrival* because of its use of the first-person narrative singular and its status as a kind of autobiography. But this must be resisted; individual and public history are not equivalent just as identity cannot be conflated with subjectivity. What is disconcerting about *Arrival* is that its use of the grammatical 'I' (in its various heroic or anti-heroic guises) invites this all-too-easy conflation; the channelling of history and politics into an almost exclusive preoccupation with the question of writerly identity make it difficult to chart the particular structural and institutional shifts that mark the central character's different positions (for example from unknown Trinidadian–Indian writer to winner of literary prizes). If the novel's use of metropolitan generic and literary antecedents is at times ironic, at other times it also functions to impart a sense of narrative order and aesthetic coherence to the different stages of the writing life that seem to override, if not displace, historical awareness. The absence of a consideration of the gendered identity of the writer and the overdetermined spaces of domesticity and work (and what Rob Nixon has called the 'textual extinction of his wife') renders it more easily read as reproducing an English romantic tradition (Nixon 1992: 163).

The fact that Naipaul was conferred the David Cohen British Literature Prize for a lifetime's effort is sometimes read as a simple confirmation of his assimilation into the cultural mainstream. But this all-too-easy dismissal of Naipaul is one that needs to be resisted if only to see very clearly where one should be apportioning blame. What is also worth acknowledging of Naipaul's status as postcolonial 'whipping boy'[1] is that, despite his politics, Naipaul's complicitous position is a position that some of us share. In its preoccupations with hybridity and its location within metropolitan cultures, Naipaul's position is remarkably similar to that of some of us – migrant intellectuals – teaching and writing within British academies. The narrator's remark in *Arrival* of his landlord has resonance beyond the Trinidadian situation:

> it might be said that an empire lay between us. This empire explained my birth in the New World, the language I used, the vocation and ambition I had; this empire in the end explained my presence there in the valley, in

that cottage, in the grounds of the manor. But we were – *or had started* – at opposite ends of wealth, privilege, and in the hearts of different cultures.

(Naipaul 1987: 174; emphasis added)

If teaching Naipaul's novel raises the ethical and political problem of moving beyond a simplistic identity politics towards the more difficult and complex task of marking the different locations and historical positions from which we speak, Farhana Sheikh's *The Red Box* (1991) is a novel that attempts to do justice to heterogeneous subject positions and multiple locations. This text suggests that from within we may find common ground in the quest for a different future. The novel takes as its subject matter the legitimacy of political identification and affiliations. Sheikh's novel is set in inner-city London and some of its leafier suburbs. There is no pastoral England represented here. Rather the text contests what it means to be British. The novel is an investigation into diasporic British Asian identities through the narratives of three women: Raisa is an educationist who interviews Tahira and Nasreen, two 15-year-old girls, in a large comprehensive school in London. The novel charts the memories, lives and fantasies of these women from meeting to meeting. The novel has no cohesive narrative mode. Sections are written in the first- and third-person voice, and sections are scripted in the form of a dramatic dialogue between three women. In the third-person prose sections there is very little overt intervention by an extra-diegetic narrator to smooth out the sometimes abrupt shifts in focalisation as text shuttles from character to character. A long letter written by Raisa to her young interviewees enables a section of the novel to be written in the first person; contributions by Raisa's family members in this letter provide different viewpoints from those of the author of the letter. Substantial sections of the novel are written in the form of interviews conducted between Raisa and her young friends.

The result is a dialogic novel which is careful to reproduce different viewpoints on events, memories and activities, marked as they are by different personas, histories and locations. These are constantly highlighted in the encounters between women. Raisa's position as a relatively affluent and educated older woman is constantly foregrounded against the working-class lives and worlds of the two young girls, even as all three fall within the cultural sign of 'British Asian woman'. As Tahira puts it:

> We might all be girls and we might all be Pakistanis and all that, but we're different, you know. You're even more different than me and Nasreen. You ain't even lived like us. You've never worried about half the things we worry about. Where you live, the people you meet, it's all different. I bet your mum never had to wear no dupatta or work for no pig. I ain't being rude, but it's true ain't it?
>
> (Sheikh 1991: 189)

But if the novel foregrounds differences, it also offers a chance to see how speaking to someone else allows one to rethink one's position in relation to another; identification can form the basis of common ground which brings about the possibility of emancipatory change. Raisa's desire to be accepted by Tahira and Nasreen, her envy of their youthful feel for politics and sense of responsibility, is matched by their envy of her ability to move beyond the familial and cultural expectations, their desire to escape the cycle of working-class poverty, and their investment in her as a friend, mother/older-sister figure. The exchanges between these women allow each to mark, evaluate and reconsider the varying positions they occupy. Behind the movement to acknowledge diversity and heterogeneity is the question of how collective identities (cultural, political, sexual) are enunciated and forged – both filiative and affiliative identities as Asian women.

For Edward Said (1984), filiation denotes 'organic complicity', 'relationships held together by natural bonds and natural forms of authority' such as kinship and familial ties. In contrast, affiliation is defined by bonds which are 'transpersonal', social and cultural products of history and location. Some examples Said provides are 'guild consciousness, consensus, collegiality, professional respect, class and the hegemony of a dominant culture' (1984: 20). Filiation and affiliation are by no means mutually exclusive. Understanding filiative identities is the start of the process of comprehending the nature of collectivities; Raisa's, Tahira's and Nasreen's identities as Punjabi Muslim come from shared familial and cultural rituals governing behaviour and customs: 'As a Muslim, you should know these things … You can't just ignore accepted codes of behaviour … There's no virtue in making strangers of your own family' says Raisa's father (Sheikh 1991: 4). Criticism of behaviour outside the norm is expressed in the form of forgetting yourselves. But when Nasreen justifies her voiced disapproval of what she sees as sexual promiscuities by saying, 'Whereas in our religion, in our way of life, it's more strict' (22), the novel is careful to avoid such easy reification by juxtaposing Nasreen's sense of her obligations with her daydreams of teenage romance and love. Furthermore, Tahira's fraught relationship with boys and Raisa's own memories of her circle of friends in affluent and cosmopolitan Lahore provide a range of experiences from alternative stories to the stereotypical narrative of the strict Asian household. Class, gender and cultural differences render Nasreen's statement more complex and contradictory than it seems: 'Who, Raisa wondered, was Nasreen including in her use of the word "our" in "our" religion and "our way of life"' (23).

The filiative ethnic identity of 'Asianness' is seen increasingly – though not exclusively – to be a product of living in Britain and encountering racism in everyday life. For example, the novel records the headmaster's expulsion of a young Pakistani boy in the language of new racism where race is seen less as a biological category and more as a cultural and national exclusivity. Here racism is reconstructed as 'national culture' and cultural difference becomes a natural basis for excluding others; the headmaster remarks,

It seems that you don't understand some of our ways in this school … It's a criminal offence, in this country, to carry weapons – you do know that? … Why should you be allowed the privilege of an excellent education when you cannot follow our basic rules.

(Sheikh 1991: 77)

The spectacle of a young Asian boy's ritual humiliation by his fellow students binds his onlookers into a collective sense of self; as the narrator (in one of her rarer moments) intervenes: 'each was suffering the shaming of a brother, and the humiliation of her own self' (11). The I/You coalesces into and is experienced as a collective interpellation as Nasreen comments, 'It's not only you that's being insulted, its … everybody, all Muslim, Pakistani … so it's not just an individual that's being offended or insulted' (14). Tahira's desire to be English is deflected by her awareness of injustice: 'I even said once – I want to be white – yeah, its bad innit? But now when I see the English starting hitting the Asians, I think we should fight back' (16).

But it is the understanding of how filiative shade into affiliative identities, and affiliative become filiative identities, that is the book's most important contribution to my concern with political identifications and the kind of transformation that can be effected by these connections. In a conversation as to why 'PLO' was graffitied onto the walls of the school, Nasreen's reply invokes a shared Muslim culture. When Raisa reminds the girls that Palestinians were Christian and atheists too, Tahira's response shifts the terrain onto political affiliations and a shared culture of resistance:

'Cos they're the same as us. Not just 'cos they're Muslims a lot of them. I mean, Sikhs and Hindus ain't Muslims are they, but they're with us here. I mean … over here, in this country, Hindus and Sikhs are all Pakis ain't they, and you don't say PLO 'cos they're Muslims? You might, but lots of people don't.

(Sheikh 1991: 87)

Oppression is structural and material even when it is inscribed on individuals. The anti-racist demonstration by students becomes one way by which the young Asian students and ex-students contest their rights to belong. Dilip Hiro's book *Black British, White British* (1991), which charts the politicisation of Asian Youth in the 1970s, is a timely reminder that filiative identities *can* be mobilised into affiliative identities given the political will and circumstances. In a more recent study, *Cartographies of Diaspora* (1996), Avtar Brah emphasises the need to see Asian identity as performative and not some kind of primordial essence. She argues that the question of how Asian identities are enunciated and forged is as much one of history, location and politics as one of culture. The formation of a new generation of politicised youth groups attests to a 'fundamental *generational* change' in the concept of Asianness:

The emergence of the youth groups marks the coming of age of a new form ... having grown up in Britain, they articulate a *home-grown British political discourse*. They lay claim to the localities in which they live as their 'home'. And, however much they may be constructed as 'outsiders', they contest these psychologically and geographical spaces from the position of 'insiders'. Even when they describe themselves as 'Asian', this is not reaching back to some 'primordial Asian' identity. What they are speaking of is a modality of 'British Asian-ness'.

(Brah 1996: 47)

Sheikh's novel explores the grey area between affiliation and filiation. Raisa's relation with both Nasreen and Tahira is based, in part, on being Asian. Yet within the framework of the novel, shared culture – 'being one of us' – cannot be assumed or taken for granted. Even where Raisa is greeted with familiarity and pleasure, conversations between women foreground their divergent positions. Raisa's status as an affluent and privileged investigator and intellectual is never glossed over. In response to Tahira's mother's open welcome, 'you've come to my house ... you want to ask me some questions, yes?', Raisa replies with evident discomfort and awareness of her 'acquisitive' motives as a researcher, coming to 'take things from you' (Sheikh 1991: 142). Raisa's desire to belong is palpable, and at times she lies in order to merit the remark 'you're one of us'. Her anxiety for the girls' approval is initially framed within the language of filiation:

How would the girls receive her? As a teacher, or as a fellow Pakistani? Would they approve of her, respect her as an *aapa*, or would they reject her for her European clothes, her hairstyle and make-up? Should she have put on *shalwaar kameez*?

(18)

But I think the novel offers other forms and languages of connections. What Raisa learns is that, whilst there are unmistakable differences between the three women, investment in points of contact – in affiliations – is what would sustain women in their quest for different futures.

For Nasreen and Tahira it is the future that grants them agency; for Raisa, it is coming to terms with aspects of her history which have been repressed and by doing so, rethinking herself. The novel, ostensibly an investigation into the identity of young Asian women in East London, ends with the investigator herself. If identification is vital to kinship relations and to the collective interpellation that make up political affiliations, Raisa's revelation at near the end of the novel encapsulates how filiation can become affiliation. Raisa's revelation comes in the form of the discovery of her mother's red box after her death. Looking through her belongings for (signs of) her absent mother, she stumbles on a red box which contains evidence that her mother had done piece-work as a seamstress in a British clothes factory which employed Asian or West Indian women. Yet Raisa's own background is that of an affluent, secularised and professional family. Raisa's discovery of her mother's hidden past jolts her idea of her mother and herself. She finds that she has taken too much for granted; her mother's motivations, thoughts and feelings are more of a mystery than her daughter had initially thought. Her mother's removal to Britain from Lahore, her husband's attempts to remake her life and aspirations in a more cosmopolitan woman, her desire for independence financially as well as socially, and expectations of her as a Muslim woman, create particular unacknowledged tensions. If her father's world, his education and thinking is more transparent, despite his initial distance, her mother's and grandmother's – for all their proximity – is opaque. The opacity extends to women's lives and histories: 'But what was she thinking … what ideas, hopes, longings, dissatisfactions filled my grandmother's mind? I – her daughter's daughter, blood of her blood, a woman, a Muslim – cannot imagine' (Sheikh 1991: 204).

The stability of Raisa's identity is thrown by the discovery that her mother is part of the impoverished and seedy world she does not define as her own. Her desire not to collude with the way society silences these women is part and parcel of her desire to understand Tahira and Nasreen and her identification with them:

> And when she had come upon her mother's red box – how the memory pained her still! – had she then made connections of the sort that Nasreen and Tahira had made so swiftly? Perhaps not. But that was all part of who she was, and who they were. And there was more.
>
> (88)

In her account of the story of the red box, Raisa reveals the personal nature of her more abstract desire for social justice; but she is also equally certain that the clarity of her vision will not always be sustained in everyday life:

> Perhaps I am being irrational in thinking that I was meant to find those wage slips with their harrowing secrets: they played such a decisive part in organising my loyalties and clarifying my sense of the just and the unjust … But clear understandings are not always lasting, for all kinds of reasons.
>
> (226)

Raisa's affiliation with the two young women she meets turns into a filiation of sorts.

A sceptical reader might argue that this is, perhaps, a sleight of hand – Raisa's discovery of her mother's life explains away her identification with and political affiliation to working-class Asian women as 'not too different from you after all'. One could argue that her mother's past is still only a metaphoric connection rather than a material one; Raisa is, after all, not the working-class woman she desires and identifies with; she does not occupy the same subject position as the homeworker and cannot be the subaltern woman no matter how hard she tries. I do not think we are meant to forget Raisa's class position or her history; but perhaps the ambivalence which surrounds the meaning of the red box catches that ambivalent space where affiliation turns into filiation without erasing the differences between the two. Sisters: more than a friend and less than a relation; political affiliations are never easy and the novel's ending registers that ambivalence. If Nasreen's response to Raisa's gesture of conciliation is positive, Tahira's silence is the opposite: 'Tahira had not contacted her', the narrator informs us, 'and wanting was not enough' (228).

Spivak (1989) exhorts us to 'unlearn privilege as loss' in her interventions on the problem of political representation. This is not a question of simple volition, but a question also of structural positionings; in this respect, the difference between Naipaul's and Sheikh's representation of the identity/subjectivity interface is clear. While one can make a case for Naipaul's interrogation of origins through a notion of performance and ironic reconstitution, I have argued in my teaching that the rift between urbane metropolitan writer and disempowered and impoverished Asian, colonial man is not healed despite the narrator's retrospective assessment. The assertion of kinship is accomplished, in many ways, through the grammatical metaphysics of the first-person singular. Yet the 'I' that arrives is, in some fundamental way, not the 'I' that departs; those structural inequalities cannot be bridged and glossed over even via the most fundamental metaphor of filiation. Teaching Naipaul is easy if one takes the text on its own terms as an aesthetic exploration and close reading of language and identity. Sheikh's novel, on the other hand, speaks of no easy resolution to the ethical and political problem of taking account of the other. But this is necessarily the ethical and political lesson that feminist thinking engenders, the anti-foundationalist reminder that women, black and third world are heterogeneous, negotiated and imaginary identities and have no literal and simple referent. Progressive identities such as 'feminist' or 'Black British' do not always fit the name my students give to their experiences; the collective 'we' that emerges from political affiliations can never be taken for granted but must be fought for at some considerable cost and effort.

And this verdict can only be arrived at when the textuality of literature is not interpreted in the narrow sense of the word. While it is almost commonplace to teach literatures of previous historical periods with an eye for interdisciplinary knowledges, the teaching of contemporary texts often lacks this edge. It is almost as if our inhabiting of the same temporal space as that of the writers we deal with allows us to claim a spurious kinship and knowledge of the terrain of these texts that might be unexamined. This returns me to my initial problem and one with which I am only starting to grapple when teaching contemporary literatures which fall particularly under the sign 'postcolonial'. Spivak's exhortation must move us into interdisciplinarity, for 'unlearning privilege as our loss' is a process of marking out and rendering visible the positions from which we speak, positions enabled by certain institutional networks. In an early essay, unlearning involves coming to terms with the political economy of women, of embracing historical and 'so-called empirical research and serious work on subject-constitution' (Spivak 1989: 226). In another essay, unlearning is a coming to terms with regulative psycho-biographies, 'a textuality of material, ideological, psychosexual production' (Landry and Maclean 1996: 60). The challenge for teachers of literary texts is clear even if institutional histories, departmental and research divisions and funding commitments make these very difficult to achieve. Finally, Said's purpose in drawing the distinction between filiation and affiliation is to remind teachers of literature – my profession – of the critical relationships between the world, the text and the critic. To quote Said,

> affiliation is what enables a text to maintain itself as a text … to study affiliation is to study and to recreate the bonds between texts and the world, bonds that specialisation and the institutions of literature have all but completely effaced. To recreate the affiliative network is therefore to make visible, to give materiality back to, the strands holding the text to society, author and culture.
>
> (Said 1984: 175)

Said's argument for affiliation as the 'principle of critical research and as a aspect of cultural process itself' necessitates the crossing of boundaries that we have set for ourselves and that others have set for us. It is the basis by which teaching finds its place in the wider world.

Note

1   This is Sara Suleri's phrase.

References

Brah, A. (1996) *Cartographies of Desire*, London: Routledge.
Butler, J. (1993) *Bodies that Matter*, London: Routledge.
Hall, S. (1989) 'New Ethnicities', in *Black Film, British Cinema*, ICA Documents 7, London: Institute of Contemporary Arts.
—— (1990) 'Cultural Identity and Diaspora', in J. Rutherford (ed.) *Identity: Community, Culture, Difference*, London: Lawrence and Wishart.
Hiro, D. (1991) *Black British, White British: A History of Race Relations in Britain*, London: Grafton.
Lamming, G. (1960) *The Pleasures of Exile*, London: Michael Joseph.
Landry, D. and MacLean, G. (eds) (1996) *The Spivak Reader*, London: Routledge.
Low, G. (1995) 'The Dis/embodiment of Culture: The Migrant in V.S. Naipaul and Bharati Mukherjee', in T. Hill and W. Hughes (eds), *Contemporary Writing and National Identity*, Bath, England: Sulis Press.
Naipaul, V.S. (1987) *The Enigma of Arrival*, Harmondsworth, England: Penguin.
Nightingale, P. (1991) 'V.S. Naipaul: Finding the Present in the Past', in R Ross, (ed.) *International Literatures in English*, New York and London: Garland Publishing.
Nixon, R. (1992) *London Calling: V.S. Naipaul, Postcolonial Mandarin*, New York and Oxford: Oxford University Press.
Said, E. (1984) *The World, the Text and the Critic*, London: Faber.

Sheikh, F. (1991) *The Red Box*, London: Women's Press.

Spivak, G. (1989) 'The Political Economy of Women as Seen by a Literary Critic', in E. Weed (ed.), *Coming to Terms*, London: Routledge.

Sivanandan, A. (1990) 'The Enigma of the Colonised: Reflections on Naipaul's Arrival', *Race and Class* 32 (1): 33–43.

Suleri, S. (1992) *The Rhetoric of English India*, Chicago, Ill.: University of Chicago Press.

Part III

Knowledges and disciplines

of the nature of feminist transformations in philosophy. Her launch point is similar to the one which propelled Ramazanoglu and Holland, in that she notes that much feminist work in philosophy during the last fifteen years has been 'deconstructive', while she wants to think about 'the "reconstructive" task of feminist philosophy'. Indeed, her chapter is a set of reflections about prospects for extended exploration of metaphors within feminist philosophy. Acknowledging that 'metaphors in philosophy are not of course all masculinist', she is interested in 'new imaginative conceptions of philosophy and new philosophical conceptions'. She offers an optimistic reading of the future of feminist philosophy which has benefited from, but not been restricted to, the modes of critique and deconstruction looking towards 'experimental engagements with metaphors and styles and forms of discourse'.

Joanna Hodge is not put off by what she characterises as the 'overwhelmingly male, masculine, masculinist discipline' of philosophy. In fact, she seeks a positive feminist re-engagement with it, through affirmation of maternal inheritance and matrilineal descent in intellectual work and of feminist genealogy within philosophy. She makes an assertive attempt to relocate women at the centre of the philosophical enterprise, encouraging us all to become 'philosophical feminists', involved in the 'production, the invention of concepts rather than ... the winning of arguments' and in 'the deployment of arguments across disciplines rather than the disputing of control of particular disciplines'. She is optimistic about the prospects for 'differential teleologies, differential genealogies ... differential sexual difference' through working in and against particular traditions within philosophy – in her case, that associated with Emmanuel Levinas, Jacques Derrida, Martin Heidegger and Luce Irigaray.

The first three chapters are thus concerned with feminist engagements with philosophy particularly, but not exclusively, through deconstructionism and post-structuralism. In contrast, in my own chapter I turn my attention to technoscience. My autobiographical narratives (focused on trips to the technoscience sites of the NASA launch pad and Disneyworld's EPCOT Center in Florida), which structure the chapter, highlight the technoscientific nature of daily life in the Western world. In the interstices, I trace broad patterns in the development of feminist technoscience studies. The form and content of this chapter register the importance of acknowledging the impossibility of standing outside of technoscience in the late twentieth century, as I consider how else we can understand feminist 'view points'.

The final contribution to this section of the volume emerges not from an overview of the direction of and prospects for feminist theorising about the military domain, but from a particular historical research project about it. Carol Wolkowitz's chapter, as she puts it starkly, 'analyses some of the writings of white middle-class women who were involved in the making of the first atomic bombs in the United States' . Her investigation of US military communities associated with bomb production during World War II is undertaken through the analysis of memoirs of women who lived in these communities. This brings her up against the feminist construction of women as 'outsiders' to military culture, as she traces the threads of female involvement in the making of the first atomic bombs.

The five contributions to this section are all, in different ways, essays of reappraisal of feminist involvement and responsibility in domains (philosophy, technoscience and the military) which clearly have been identified as masculinist and, even, bastions of male power. In this respect their critical dimension is tempered by assertiveness. Readers are likely to respond differently to the specific reappraisals on offer. Overall, the prospect emerging from this collection of writings is both positive and daunting: a transformative feminism without bounds.

References

Birke, L. (1986) *Women, Feminism and Biology: The Feminist Challenge*, Brighton: Wheatsheaf.

Butler, J. (1990) *Gender Trouble*, New York: Routledge.

Code, L. (1991) *What Can She Know? Feminist Theory and the Construction of Knowledge*, Ithaca, N.Y.: Cornell University Press.

Easlea, B. (1980) *Witch-Hunting, Magic and the New Philosophy*, Brighton: Harvester.

Ehrenreich, B. and D. English (1976a) *Complaints and Disorders: The Sexual Politics of Sickness*, London: Writers and Readers.

—— (1976b) *Witches, Midwives and Nurses: A History of Women Healers*, London: Writers and Readers.

—— (1979) *For Her Own Good: 150 Years of Experts' Advice to Women*, London: Pluto.

—— (1983) *Does Khaki Become You? The Militarisation of Women's Lives*, London: Pluto.

Flax, J. (1993) *Disputed Subjects: Essays in Psychoanalysis, Politics and Philosophy*, New York and London: Routledge.

Garry, A. and Pearsall, M. (eds) (1996) *Women, Knowledge and Reality: Explorations in Feminist Philosophy*, 2nd edition, New York and London: Routledge.

Gray, C.H.(1997) *Postmodern War: The New Politics of Conflict*, London: Routledge.

Greer, G. (1999) *The Whole Woman*, London: Doubleday.

Griffiths, M. and Whitford, M. (eds) (1988) *Feminist Perspectives in Philosophy*, London: Macmillan.

Grimshaw, J. (1986) *Feminist Philosophers: Women's Perspectives on Philosophical Traditions*, Brighton: Wheatsheaf.

Haraway, D. (1989) *Primate Visions: Gender, Race and Nature in the World of Modern Science*, New York: Routledge.

—— (1991) 'A Cyborg Manifesto: Science, Technology and Socialist-Feminism in the Late Twentieth Century' in *Simians, Cyborgs and Women: The Reinvention of Nature*, London: Free Association Books.

—— (1997) *Modest Witness@Second Millenium.FemaleMan Meets OcoMouse:Feminism and Technoscience*, New York and London: Routledge.

Harding, S. (1986) *The Science Question in Feminism*, Ithaca, N.Y.: Cornell University Press.

—— (1991) *Whose Science? Whose Knowledge? Thinking from Women's Lives*, Milton Keynes, England: Open University Press.

Hubbard, R. (1990) *The Politics of Women's Biology*, New Brunswick, N.J.: Rutgers.

Lloyd, G. (1984) *The Man of Reason*, London: Methuen.

Merchant, C. (1980) *The Death of Nature: Women, Ecology, and the Scientific Revolution*, San Francisco, Calif.: Harper and Row.

Noble, D. (1992) *A World without Women: The Christian Clerical Culture of Western Science*, Oxford: Oxford University Press.

Rose, H. (1983) 'Hand, Brain and Heart: Towards a Feminist Epistemology for the Natural Sciences', *Signs: Journal of Women in Culture and Society* 9, 1: 73–96.

—— (1994) *Love, Power and Knowledge: Towards a Feminist Transformation of the Sciences*, Cambridge: Polity Press.

Stabile, C.A. (1994) *Feminism and the Technological Fix*, Manchester: Manchester University Press.

Walby, S. (1997) *Gender Transformations*, London: Routledge.

10 Forays of a philosophical feminist

Sexual difference, genealogy, teleology

Joanna Hodge

Giving thanks and dedicating the work in hand

Recently in the philosophical tradition within which I work, it has become clear that all philosophical work has ethical implications. This line of thinking has been developed by Jacques Derrida and Emmanuel Levinas, in their responses to the challenge posed by, indeed the provocation of, the writings of Martin Heidegger. The claim is that all thinking is a response to and an address to an otherness, to the past, to the present, to the future, as a result of taking the form of a response to a demand or challenge, address or imperative, a provocation, which does not have the same location as that in which the thinking, as response, finds itself. This is the thesis of original alterity, which is thus not a thesis, since it hypothesises the instability of the site at which it is posited. The location of thinking is thus split, with Levinas (1961) thinking this as the effect of an imperative beyond being, and with Derrida (1967) thinking this as an ineliminable instability already detectable within the shifting structure picked out in the term, which is neither a word nor a concept, differance. The self-identity presupposed by the positing of theses is a prosthetic move, necessary but illegitimate in advance of the production of an argument for the validity of argument. All language use is thus both ethical and, indeed, religious, in a sense to be clarified, since language is collective and addresses both known and unknown others; knowable and unknowable others, which traditionally, but not exclusively, are addressed in religious discourses, in terms of the divine. This could put into question unthought-through rejections of religiosity within feminist theory, in the name of an equally unthought-through secularism and emancipation. Feminist transformations are already at work on this unsatisfactory division between the secular and the religious which conceals a shared resistance in both to imaging matrilinear descent and affirming maternal inheritance. The task of this chapter is to identify some of the obstacles to an affirmation in intellectual work of maternal inheritance and matrilinear descent.

The structure of the response to and address to the other is one which reveals that it is impossible to match the claim of the other, since that claim is always in excess of any possible response. The address of the other to which I can respond stands in a metonymical relation to all the possible claims which might be made.

The ethical claim is always in excess of any capacity to perform: there can be no moment of satisfaction at having completed the ethical requirement. With an infinity of possible claims, and, with Levinas, this address of the other constituting a relation between the human and the infinite, between the human and the divine, there is an arbitrary moment of decision in which this claim, not that, is taken up; in this arbitrary way and not in that. There is here also an inheritance from Luce Irigaray's ground-breaking work on the patriarchal nature of the philosophical tradition and on the need to construct a maternal genealogy, in *Speculum of the Other Woman* (1974) and in *Sexes and Genealogies* (1987), which is here taken up more expressly in terms of my own experience, negotiating the transitions from female, to feminist, to philosopher and back. My question is how drastically the meanings of these three terms, female, feminist and philosopher, must be transformed to permit these transitions to take place. Thus, while I give thanks to those who invited me to be included in this discussion and seek to acknowledge those who prompted the thinking here at work, I am responsible both for taking up the invitation and for the manner in which I respond. Neither Levinas nor Irigaray, neither conference organisers nor editors are in any sense responsible for the outcome.

This then is the thesis of an excess of responsibility, which is at a certain level indistinguishable from the thesis of original alterity, and is also not a thesis, since it again presupposes an impossible site of articulation: one already dislocated from itself, either between the finite and the infinite, with Levinas, or between an impossible punctual moment of self-presence and the demonstration of the impossibility of such punctuality, with Derrida. These two theses, which are not theses, concerning alterity and responsibility, with which I locate the thinking of this chapter, are borrowed in their impossibility from the interactive effects at work in the writings of Heidegger, Levinas and Derrida. It is a borrowing which cannot be returned, because it is taken without permission and without acknowledgement. In additon to the conference organisers and editors I should also like to acknowledge the invaluable support which I receive from the graduate students at Manchester Metropolitan University, who have been asking me awkward questions, collectively and severally, ever since I arrived back in the North. Third, after organisers and students, but both last and first, I should like to acknowledge the debt of birth, one which, like all true gifts, cannot be repaid, by giving thanks to my mother, who has been my severest and most indulgent critic all these years: a volatile combination. As it turns out, maternal inheritance, matrilinear descent and maternal genealogies will be important for this chapter. These two impossible theses, as unacknowledgeable borrowings, and the threefold thanks, to editors, to questioning students and to maternity, are not irrelevant for what follows, a contribution, then, to 'Transformations: Thinking Through Feminism', in five sections, with five theses.

Ecce femina: disturbing some philosophical presuppositions

There are five key terms for the argument of this chapter: women, tradition, generation, descent and inheritance. The question is whether these can be thought without accepting in advance a masculine notion of filiation, affiliation and succession; or whether indeed they must be thought in order to undo a powerfully inscribed masculinism in the transmission of culture and authority from generation to generation. I shall advance five theses, concerning women and inheritance and the necessarily multiple goals of enquiry. The problem to which the argument is addressed is the following: if truth, authority and power are inscribed in traditions of thought and enquiry, however defined, and if these traditions descend through patrilinear lines of filiation, then how should a woman, how can women, inherit? If inheritance of tradition is entailed, passing from father to son, or next male relative, how can women insert themselves into this transmission, except trans-sexually? Is it possible to inherit as a woman, as a daughter, as a mother, and to transmit that inheritance on, to women, to daughters, to mothers? Can there be female inheritance? Can there be matrilinear inheritance? Can there be feminist inheritance? Can there be feminine inheritance, in the strong sense of the feminine sustained at the point of indifference between the meanings picked out by the terms female, matrilinear and feminist, a point of indifference which coordinates the various female resistances to masculinism? What is the relation between these various inheritances? Is there inheritance in general, gender-neutral inheritance, or is general inheritance, in fact, masculine inheritance, concealing the workings of sexual difference, and is then maternal inheritance a form of special inheritance, through which general inheritance is also shown to be restricted, a form of special inheritance? Is general economy, then, not general, but a masculine economy, and is the restricted economy the means through which to show that general economy is not after all so very general? Is there only patrilinear succession and masculine genealogy? To inherit is it necessary to bear the father's name? And what relation does his naming have to a relation, to an order set up by law, and to the law of the necessity of order? This series of questions constitutes a critical set of issues for women's studies and for feminist theory today.

I propose to approach this question of inheritance and succession by way of the notions of generation, lineage and descent, as constructed within and on the limit of philosophical enquiry in the thematisations of sexual difference, genealogy and teleology. Teleology is the concept mobilised by Immanuel Kant (1791) to hold together his enquiry into the limits of reason and the possibility of knowledge in empirical science, positing the basis on which it may be supposed that there is an orderly world. Genealogy is the term mobilised by Nietzsche (1887) to chart the arbitrary moves of descent and destiny informing the trajectories of human self-evaluation, its positive and negative effects on human flourishing, as a species, in groups and individually. Sexual difference will be shown to be the theme in the twentieth century through which the gender positioning of human beings is shown to play an as yet unidentified role in the temporary stabilisations of human self-understanding, obtained through the analyses of teleology and of genealogy. Genealogy and teleology must then in turn be rethought from the standpoint of an analysis of gender and more generally of difference, while retaining the question: is a general economy always misguided in presenting itself as all-inclusive, such that there is no general economy, no stance from which an inclusivity of differences might be thought?

From the mid-1970s, and increasingly explicitly in the 1980s, sexual difference was thematised rather differently by Derrida and by Irigaray. Derrida problematised the implicit and explicit homo-eroticism in the philosophical tradition, and looked to a future of unanticipatable change, in which some reconfiguration of these relations might be thought to emerge. Irigaray has thematised both the forces at work in the philosophical tradition to contain female, feminist, matrilinear, maternal affirmations and in her *Ethics of Sexual Difference* (1984) she explores the circumscribing gesture made by figures in the tradition, Aristotle, Spinoza, Merleau-Ponty and Levinas, revealing the enduring structures of the repetitions of these same exclusions rather than the hoped-for disjunction of temporal process in which these other relations might be anticipated and inaugurated. For Derrida, the theme is homo-eroticism and its imaginable displacement, in favour of a multigendered domain, of differential hierarchies. For Irigaray, masculine empowerment remains a continuing theme, with no detectable differentiation between homo-erotic and other forms of exclusivity, all such structures bearing for her the identification of a hommosocial and hommosexual character, recognising only sameness. Derrida's thinking of sexual difference is only one aspect of a wide-ranging disruption of dominant forms and frames of thinking and analysis, whereas for Irigaray sexual difference remains to the fore throughout, for reasons which are not in the least obscure.

The relation between these three, sexual difference, genealogy and teleology, brings women's studies into critical tension with the tradition in philosophy in which I work: Kant, Nietzsche, Husserl, Heidegger, Derrida, and, at last, Irigaray, a woman arrives, controversially, with difficulty, in the canon. It becomes clear that it is not simply a question of women's studies learning from the philosophical tradition, but of the philosophical tradition being displaced by the questioning of gender and of sexual difference as put in motion by feminist politics and women's studies. The questions of tradition and transmission are posed by Heidegger, but not in terms of sexual difference. The questions of lineage, inheritance and generation to which Derrida has addressed himself, for example in *Archive Fever* (1994), are not posed with respect to differential genealogies of women and men, and not in relation to the question of the position of women in these lines of descent. In his recent book *Politics of Friendship* (1994) Derrida remarks on the masculinity and covert homo-eroticism within the theme of friendship in the Western philosophical tradition, and its foundational role in relation to conceptions of the ideal political community. While questioning the aporetic nature of both the ideal of political community and the ideal of friendship, and the connection between them, the implicit masculinity of both friendship and citizenship remain peripheral to his enquiry. Nor are they connected to the feminist critiques in which these issues are made central. Such critiques include a notion of politics as simply coextensive with the public sphere, and are grounded in a recognition of the preemptive nature of the production of an excluding masculinity in advance of a constitutive division between a public and a private domain. Arguments for Derrida being a friend of feminist critique, a fellow traveller, would be more convincing if signs of reading feminist theorists who have not themselves already responded to Derrida's own writings were more in evidence. The questions of genealogy and descent are those of Nietzsche, but not in relation to differential teleologies of enquiry, with the goals of overcoming the human made distinct from the goals of overcoming masculinism. He too is not concerned much with women.

This then is my theme: how should a woman inherit, without loss of self? The inheritance in dispute is power, authority, truth; this inheritance is important. The line of questioning comes to me from a double genealogy, through twenty years of engagement with an overwhelmingly male, masculine, masculinist discipline, philosophy, in which all the authorities are men and the question of gender is scarcely posable. It comes through the patrilinear name, and through a matrilinear lineage of North American impatience with male narcissisms. Such subordination to an archaic, now anachronistic, gender inscription of a discipline in process of transformation is, however, only temporary: I am dead as my Liverpudlian father; I am happily still living as my North American mother. As the return of the New World to the Old, to haunt its monosexual cloisters, there is possible this declaration, a declaration perhaps of the intellectual rights of women: Ecce Femina. This then is my first claim, my first thesis: there are women in philosophy; there are women philosophers. This is a new dawn, a new Nietzsche, awoken from dogmatic slumber, and my first rewriting of Nietzsche: for he says, behold the man, Ecce Homo, and in so doing he dissolves the inheritance of two thousand years of Christianity. The exemplary human being for Nietzsche is no longer Christ, but self: true, not self as it is, but as it might be, but still, in some sense, self, in some trajectory of experiential transformation. This then is highly relevant for this theme of transformation. Transformation for Nietzsche is self-transformation: become what you are. The question becomes: is this an option open to women? If I now say, Ecce Femina, can I dissolve the memory of an even longer history of a 2,500-year exclusion zone? Can a woman inherit the philosophical tradition, and, if not, what are the implications for our engagements in thinking today? Can a woman be exemplary in either a Christian or a Nietzschean sense? In what horizon of enquiry and experience and at what time?

Before going any further this evocation of Nietzsche, not renowned for his philogyny, requires explanation. It is from him that the phrases 'ecce femina', and 'forays of a philosophical feminist', are obliquely taken. The first is from the 'behold the man' of *Ecce Homo* (1888) and the second from the forays of the untimely one, in *Twilight of the Idols* (1888), *Die Streifzuge des Unzeitgemassigen*; more usually translated as 'Expeditions of an Untimely Man', thus over-determining the sex of the agent, probably correctly. These expeditions have a relaxed, restorative feel to them; the corresponding expeditions of an untimely woman are, I suspect, more likely to take the form of militaristic or, at least, polemical exercises. What then is the relation between this untimely one and a philosophical feminist, if not the thought that a philosophical feminist is even more untimely than Nietzsche could ever be, even more posthumous, even more polemically charged, even more the philopolemologist, even more necessarily an enthusiast for conflict? To make it clear that I do not detect a proto-posthumous feminist in Nietzsche's texts, consider the following observation, from *Twilight of the Idols*, reading, as they say, as a woman: 'If a woman possesses manly virtues one should run away from her; and if she does not possess them, she runs away herself.'??? Try as I can, writing as they say as a woman, I cannot work out the directionalities of this running. The puzzle to be explored in this chapter is that, in this epoch of untimeliness, of multi-directionality, there are now philosophical feminists. As I said, Ecce Femina; but in what direction are we to run? Should it be towards or away from the sound of gunfire?

Forays of a philosophical feminist: the ends of feminism, the end of male power

My title, 'Forays of a philosophical feminist: sexual difference, genealogy, teleology', makes the claim that, by reflecting on the relations proposed by these three terms, sexual difference, genealogy, teleology, it is possible to address the well-grounded unease articulated by post-essentialist critiques of sexual difference, such as that offered by Sara Ahmed (1998). The problem is to think a genuinely multiple sexual difference, through the displacement of the sequence, one, many, not one, rather than to think in terms of an inertly bipolar, male/female, masculine/feminine, xy/xx. Nevertheless, such concerns also have their place, and I think no one has yet made the joke about the masculinist transcendental = xx; and the feminist transcendental = xy. The task is to think the difference between a conception of difference generating sameness, and of difference procreating a thinking of further differences. To this end I propose a thinking of difference in terms of genealogy and teleology, asking the questions: with what derivation and to what end? A sense for differential genealogy and teleology not only locates sexual difference in a non-exclusionary space, genuinely situated in terms of other dimensions, thought of and unthought of, of difference. It also makes locatable a crossover between physical and cultural biology at work in notions like genealogy, inheritance, succession, generation, procreation.

My key question: on what terms, if at all, can women inherit, poses the very real difference between inheriting as a human being and inheriting as a female, as a daughter, as a mother, as a feminist and as a feminist theorist. All are inscribed in some space suspended between physical and cultural biology. These require examination to consider what the implications of inheriting in these different ways might be. The distinction between genealogy and teleology in particular suggests a relation between origins and ends towards which a certain kind of lineage or descent might be tending. These questions take me in the direction of a technicised Darwinism, a curious hybrid which I take to be the concern of many working in women's studies and feminist theory today. Heidigger's question of technicity goes beyond the categories of arts and sciences: it is neither technical nor human; but he does not think technicity in relation to the position of women as the originary prosthetic material out of which male fantasy, identity, corporeality emerge. This rethinking would have to be a collectively produced retheorising; we need an institute. What I offer today is clarification of some conceptual obstacles to rethinking the relation between biology and machines, between nature and technology in a way other than one grounded in an unthought-through opposition between efficient mechanical causalities and final causes. Statistical causality and DNA variations have changed all that, but concepts have a habit of dragging on after the event of their definitive displacement. A rethinking of the relation between teleology and genealogy would reveal some aspects of this retardation.

This chapter proceeds by advancing five theses, preceded by an empirically contestable claim: here is a woman, or perhaps better: behold the woman. It may seem strange that I should start with an empirical claim: that there are philosophical feminists. This may seem contrary to the practice of philosophy. Nevertheless, I suspect that philosophising always has proceeded by helping itself to some facts of the matter. The question is: to which facts of the matter has it helped itself and to what effect? It is also possible that the fact of the matter here is more than a little paradoxical. For if Aristotelians define man as the rational animal, where are we to find a lineage for rational women? The move from us, to Irigaray, to Simone de Beauvoir, is sufficiently obstructed to suggest the difficulty. Indeed the matter which is taken for granted at the beginning of all philosophy is, according to Irigaray (1987), an active forgetting of a maternal materiality, empowering a male succession and inheritance. Irigaray allows us to think about how a masculine governance of materiality is set up through the forgetting of the indebtedness to the first, primary embodiment, growing as part of the mother's physiology. Some quite startling logics of parts and wholes could be generated by starting from this point.

This point of departure is going to be looped in towards the end of this chapter by considering the difference between generative and procreative thinking, and their respective relations to the setting out of distinctions between species and genera. This chapter then, in advancing its theses, while presupposing its starting point, addresses itself to this question of self-help and matters of fact. *Zu den Sachen selbst*, to the things themselves, is the great phenomenological battle cry; presuppositionless thought, to which a philosophical feminist, on one of her unending campaigns, is perhaps permitted to help herself, reflecting ironically that, while these lineages of the descent of reason are gendered in this way, there can be no presuppositionless thought.

Thus this chapter inscribes itself between Nietzsche's rewriting of Christianity, his Ecce Homo, wondering what the implications might be for women; and

Edmund Husserl's appeal to return philosophy to describing what there is, the things themselves. Husserl hypothesises that ideas or essences which hold meaning in place as pure structures become embedded in everyday meanings and thus become corrupted. The task of philosophy for Husserl is to retrieve the pure meaning as originally intuited and reveal what there really is. This then is his teleology: retrieve the truth from the false opinions and distortions in which it becomes embedded in customary communication and language use. The retrieval of the essence is the goal of the enquiry, which is set as an infinite, repeating, incompletable task. There is no immediate access to essences; we do not immediately intuit what they are, but find them embedded in distorting presupposition. For Husserl the retrieval of essence is a task to be undertaken in order to dispel false understanding and false opinion; but he gives no guarantee that it can be accomplished. The question for our time concerning sexual difference is: one essence or two, or many, or not even one? Do we even know what essences are? If the matrilinear and the patrilinear lineages diverge as strongly as I suspect, then there must be two sets of idealities holding essences in place, one within each lineage, and perhaps then one holding the relation between the two lineages in place, marking the obscuring of maternal inheritance by patrilinear lineage. What then are the effects of trying to think a split lineage, with masculine paternal lineage always masking and obliterating the maternal inheritance, thus generating two matrilinear lineages, one in which the maternal inheritance is obscured and one in which it is retrieved. It is this feminine beyond the femininity of Freudian complementarity to which Irigaray draws attention in *Speculum of the Other Woman*.

Sexual difference, genealogy, teleology

These then are the two theses so far advanced: there are women; there are different lineages of descent, to be called for the purposes of shorthand, patrilinear, for the men of reason; matrilinear for the ironists of the tribe, the hysterical outcast, the one who insists that she is different. According to the first thesis, there are philosophical feminists; according to the second, there both are and are not philosophical feminists. My five theses then elaborate on my starting point, called, for the purposes of argument, philosophical feminism, and on these three ponderous notions in my title, sexual difference, genealogy and teleology, ending, suitably enough, with a thesis about the non-unifiability of teleology, teleology as the study of ends, of finalities, of goals, of the directedness of activity, of purposiveness without purpose, of meaning without direction, of senses without sense. What difference does it make then to invoke a philosophical feminisim in place of feminist philosophy? What different trajectories and temporalities of enquiry do these two, philosophical feminism and feminist philosophy, set up?

I suggest that feminist philosophy has tended towards seeking to establish a form of questioning and a set of problems to be addressed within philosophy, thus tending to foreclose the goals of enquiry, affirming the position of women in philosophy, disputing the control of men. In contrast, a more oblique route, my preferred route, that of a philosophical feminism, attends to the production, the invention, of concepts rather than to the winning of arguments; to the deployment of arguments across disciplines, rather than the disputing of control of particular disciplines; to the question and questioning of meaning. Setting out this distinction requires further attention. Genealogies of each would reveal differential evaluations of the tasks of enquiry and of the relations between disciplines. Both are needed, but each offers distinct responses to the question of how meaning is formed. To the question: is there a divergence of idealities to be established here, generating a multiplicity of unstable essences, or is there a single essential structure of meaningfulness to be disputed? Philosophical feminism gives one kind of response to this and feminist philosophy another.

Sexual difference is a concept which has been produced in contestation with a certain version of philosophical and psychoanalytical traditions and is held in place somewhere between the thinking of Irigaray and Derrida, borrowed one might say by Derrida from Irigaray, by Irigaray from Derrida, and by each from Lacan and from Freud, and from Nietzsche and from Heidegger, perhaps never to be returned. For when men say sexual difference and when women say sexual difference we do not mean, we cannot intend, the same thing. This is the case even if there were two neat distinct essences of maleness and femaleness to hold sexual difference in place, which I doubt. There is sexual difference as mark of my excludability and there is sexual difference as mark of her excludability. There are then at least two ideal meanings, not one, not even one towards which the term distends itself. The same fate I suggest befalls the notion of genealogy and in counter position to Nietzsche's genealogy of morals, in which he shows how values and moralities promote the interests of certain groups within human communities, to the disadvantage of others. It is important to consider how different genealogies might produce different accounts of advantage, to the advantage of feminist women, which, in this case, means those who seek to inherit, or who dispute the easy inheritance of those who take themselves to be entitled. There are also different evaluations attaching to different notions of teleology.

The aim of course is to show how some elements from the philosophical tradition might be released from patrilinear inertia and the interminable mourning of lost unities, and then might be remobilised, redeployed, set in motion in another series of trajectories to think about the transformations of our title, proposing some deformations of thought through which to unblock the all-too-human problem posed by the philosophical inheritance that man is the rational animal and woman the eternal irony of community. The contemporary insistence on the work of mourning seems to me to be the gesture of ressentiment against birth, against women, and against finitude. This inheritance is to be taken up and transformed by performing the required deformation of reason. A feminist inheritance must be transformative in relation to what it inherits. Here then is a grid of differentiation to be produced in the course of this chapter: the distinct lineages of matrilinear and patrilinear descent; we are dead

as our fathers, alive as our mothers; the distinct genealogies evoked by a philosophical feminism as opposed to a feminist philosophy; and now the distinction
between female and feminist inheritances. One accepts from the past, while the
other transforms and transmits into the future. They meet in the form of contestation in the present only if the relation between past, present and future is not
understood. On each side of this list, lineage, genealogy, inheritance, there lie
the notions of disputed origins and disputed generations, disputed pasts and
disputed futures. An origin, a line of descent, a future which did not erase
maternal materiality, a generation which did not privilege the sons, and rein-
scribe sexual difference, a future friendly to my daughters is, I suggest, scarcely
conceivable. But I take it the title of our volume, *Transformations*, calls us to begin
to identify what the obstacles are to such conception. To hear the problem in the
question: what shall a woman do to inherit the law? For inheritance is the law;
and the law is inheritance. What shall I do to inherit the kingdom of the philosophers? Nietzsche teaches will to power and self-affirmation, self-overcoming and
re-evaluation of all values. Of all values. So might the value of law and of inheritance be re-evaluated, transformed, deformed to allow a female succession, in
the name of the mother?

From generation to procreation and back: on thetic and prosthetic phalluses

My first thesis is that there is always a condition for the advancing of theses.
This, the matter unaddressed, of helping oneself to some fact of the matter, or
other, could be termed the prosthetic condition of possibility for the advancing
of theses. Here: that there are women. My second thesis indicates the paradoxical nature of the claim, and points out the differential lineages of male and
female reason: according to one women can and according to the other we
cannot aspire to philosophical reason. My third thesis concerns the differential
evaluations, hierarchies of value and projects of thinking made available under
the divergent terms, philosophical feminism, feminist philosophy, and indeed by
notions of genealogy and teleology. My fourth thesis concerns the differences
between inheritance, as sexually undetermined, female inheritance, feminist
inheritance, and feminine inheritance through the distinction between generative
and procreative inheritance. Thus sexually undetermined inheritance is not
undetermined at all: like Aristotle, it presumes inheritance through manifestation
of resemblance to the father. It always privileges the relation of male to male, of
father to son. Alongside this generative inheritance, I propose a counter-notion
of procreative inheritance, a generous inheritance which does not preserve
resemblance but is open to transformation, one in which perhaps men and
women could be understood to be equally weighted, equally valued, with an
open question as to the sex of the inheritor. I suggest there is also a third form of
inheritance, the inventive, in which the very structure of inheritance itself
remains to be institutionalised. Here then are three different possible models of
inheritance: that of the generative, the one we have, which is supposedly sexually

neutral, but is in fact masculine; that of the procreative, drawing attention to sexual difference, one in which women also count; and that of the inventive, the institution to come, in which the move from bipolar sexual difference, hypothesising two essences, to sexual differentiation, hypothesising, not one, more than one, not even one, might be accomplished.

The substitution of a notion of generation for that of procreation reinstalls a male control over the alarming fecundity of women's bodies, which must bring forth only male children. This substitution and erasure is then covered over in the gesture of essentialising sexual difference. To the end of disturbing this gesture, I thus advance this thesis about a difference between a female inheritance of generation and a feminist inheritance of procreation. This throws into crisis the hylomorphic framing, of a relation between matter and form, and the very shape of materiality is itself again put in question. Perhaps matter is better thought of as a relation between rational and irrational numbers, between the computable and the non-computable, and not at all as a relation between male and female, masculine and feminine. This would then set out a materialism beyond the tired oppositions of essentialism and existentialism, between empiricism and idealism, matter and category. To explore this set of concerns, it will be necessary for philosophical feminism to roam well beyond the limits of established philosophical practice.

The task here is to locate the notion of differential inheritance, with many, not one, not even one inheritance, in balance between two visions of the future: a progress in democracy and popular sovereignty, a democracy to come, and a coming environmental catastrophe. I suggest that Derrida's thinking of sexual difference starts out in the direction of an inventive post-masculinist thinking but slips back first to a thinking of the procreation of recognisable heirs; then to a thinking about the inheritance of psychoanalysis; and then to a thinking of the inheritance of male heirs, generative thinking. This is why I am not proposing that we should all become Derridean, but it is possible to learn from his disruptions and resinscriptions of the restricting forms and frames of thinking which we inherit and which transmit themselves whether we accept or receive an inheritance or not. What then is the domain within which these theses might be advanced and tested out? Some declare that theses must be located in terms of a horizon of enquiry, a goal of discussion, an origin of reason, a fundamental ontology, a polemics of discussion: each, in turn, competing to be the site for filling out the notion of conditions of possibility. Others declare the aporetics of the possibility of the impossible as the impossibility of the possible. Others accept a certain precariousness and arbitrariness in the point of departure, that we start where we must, a certain fatality. Originary prostheticity is the thesis which declares the unjustifiability of theses, except in terms of carrying the discussion from where it starts to where it ends in a way which lends it sense and significance and which shows the necessarily polemical nature of any determination of meaning and order.

The five theses on the ends of enquiry

My first thesis has a prosthetic moment to it. It is presupposed before it is set out: the thesis is that there are women; that there are philosophical feminists; that enquiry always presupposes an unjustifiable point of departure. My second thesis concerns paradox and asymmetry: it points to the asymmetry between patri-linear and matrilinear lineages and their conflicting lessons: that women both can and cannot aspire to philosophical reason, with essence inscribed in diver-gent incompatible lineages. Sexual difference would mark the moment of fracture preventing the retrieval of any unified originary essence of inheritance. My third thesis insists on the differential genealogies of philosophical feminism and of feminist philosophy, of differential genealogies for sexual difference, for teleology, for genealogy itself. My fourth thesis concerns differential inheritances: not just one, more than one, not even one. It insists on a difference between the deployment of prosthetic and thetic phalluses, and maybe no phallus at all; and on a difference between generative, procreative and inventive inheritances. The question here is: how does meaning and order impose itself with what set of differential evaluations of the forces thus held in play, female and male, maternal and paternal, matrilinear and patrilinear, feminine and masculine? Fifthly, lastly and by way of conclusion, there is a thesis about the ends of enquiry, the ends of man, the ends of woman and the end of humanity. These are distinct and are to be distinguished from each other. Roughly speaking, these different ends can be indicated by the notions of meaning, succession, feminism and catastrophe. In brief and in conclusion: there is no single goal of enquiry, certainly not agree-ment and certainly not consensus. Instead I propose differential teleologies, differential genealogies and, above all, differential sexual difference: not one, not even one, but many.

The one sexual difference which has been that installed as the object and motivation for women's studies traces the implications of the significances attaching in history to the two sex and gender positions which have been supposed to supply exhaustive classifications of human beings. This sexual differ-ence has been subject to the challenge that it obscures and erases the decisive impact of class and race in the constitution of privilege and oppression. There is here a contestation between British Marxist theorists insisting more on the signif-icance of class position in relation to the means of production and the concern more fully articulated in North America with the problems of ethnocentrism in the occlusion of the question of race in the production of cultural value. There has been a move in women's studies beyond the analysis of differential oppres-sion into the affirmative mode of discovering and mobilising the resources released by putting in question the monosexual, monoracial, class-appropriated position from which knowledge is authoritatively produced and constructed. This has shifted attention away from questions of sex and gender oppression and towards the more complex question of differential embodiment, and differential empowerment, thus introducing the further dimensions of sexual orientation and the politics of disability. As a result of this challenge and shift, a more complex account of sexual difference can come into view, one which can be located in Luce Irigaray's enquiries but which was obscured by the debate about whether or not her analyses were in league with an unacceptable essentialism.

This more complex account of sexual difference turns away from the analysis of actual empirically sexed and gendered bodies and towards a questioning of the implications of human beings reproducing sexually and biologically. This reveals three further dimensions of sexual difference, beyond the differences of sex and gender: the differential involvements in procreation; the differences of generational position; and the differences of a theorising of human knowledges which does and one which does not accept that these structures of intergenerational transmission provide the framework within which human beings understand and theorise their world. These further dimensions of sexual difference have come more clearly into view now as result of science fiction and the bio-engineering possibilities of non-sexual, non-biological reproduction. The most obvious level of concern is the fact that women, not men, carry babies to term. The transmission of genetic inheritance and generational relations of dominance and dependency are less obvious levels of enquiry which open out in such cross-generational questions of sexual difference. Here there is no longer the focus on who now is positioned as either female or male or as displaced by the opposition. The question becomes one about the outcomes and condition for that first, most obvious level at which difference makes its mark, shifting difference from a single structure into the registers of differential positioning in relation to parenting and childhood, inheritance and transmission of genetic endowment, lineage and succession. These further dimensions of sexual difference open out once the version of it associated with differences between two sexes has been displaced. The end of enquiry here then is a transformation of a thinking of sexual difference away from a bi-polar essentialism towards a trans-generational thinking of procreation and invention of human relations.

References

Ahmed, S. (1998) *Differences That Matter: Feminist Theory and Postmodernism*, Cambridge: Cambridge University Press.

Derrida J. (1967) *Of Grammatology*, trans G. Spivak (1975), Baltimore, Md.: Johns Hopkins University Press.

—— (1972) 'Differance', in *Margins of Philosophy*, trans., with additional notes, A. Bass, Brighton: Harvester Wheatsheaf.

—— (1973) *Speech and Phenomena: Introduction to the Problem of Signs in Husserl's Phenomenology*, trans. D.B. Alison, Evanston, Ill.: Northwestern University Press.

—— (1994a) *Archive Fever: A Freudian Impression*, trans. E. Prenowitz (1996), Chicago, Ill.: University of Chicago Press.

—— (1994b) *Politics of Friendship*, trans. G. Collins (1997), London: Verso.

Heidegger, M. (1951) *The Question of Technology and Other Essays*, trans. William Lovitt, New York: Harper and Row.

Husserl, E. (1907) *The Idea of Phenomenology: Five Lectures*, ed. W. Biemel, trans. W.P. Alston and G. Nakhnikian (1964), The Hague: Nijhoff.

Irigaray, L. (1974) *Speculum of the Other Woman*, trans. C. Burke and G.C. Gill (1985), Ithaca, N.Y.: Cornell University Press.

—— (1984) *An Ethics of Sexual Difference*, trans. C. Burke and G.C. Gill (1993), Ithaca, N.Y.: Cornell University Press.

—— (1987) *Sexes and Genealogies*, trans. C. Burke and G.C. Gill (1990), Ithaca, N.Y.: Cornell University Press.

Kant, I. (1791) *The Critique of Judgement*, trans. W.S. Pluhar (1994), Indianapolis, Ind.: Hackett.

Levinas, E. (1961) *Totality and Infinity: An Essay on Exteriority*, trans. A. Lingis (1969), Pittsburgh, Penn.: Duquesne University Press.

Nietzsche, F.W. (1887) *On the Genealogy of Morals*, trans. W. Kaufman (1967), New York: Vintage Books, Random House.

—— (1888a) *Ecce Homo: Or How One Becomes What One Is*, trans. R.J. Hollingdale (1979), Harmondsworth, England: Penguin.

—— (1888b) *The Twilight of the Idols: Or How to Philosophise with a Hammer*, trans. R.J. Hollingdale (1990), Harmondsworth, England: Penguin.

11 Philosophy and the feminist imagination

Jean Grimshaw

During the last fifteen years or so, there has been an explosion of publishing in feminist philosophy. Much of this work might be called 'deconstructive', in a broad sense; it has undertaken a critique of the sexism and phallocentrism of much of the Western philosophical tradition. In this chapter, however, I want to think about the 'reconstructive' task of feminist philosophy: the creative and transformative task of rethinking philosophical issues with a feminist orientation, and of asking what conceptions of 'philosophy' might be apt for feminist purposes. More specifically, I want to discuss the role of metaphor and imagination in philosophy.

In *The Philosophical Imaginary*, Michele le Doeuff writes:

> Even when a certain coyness leads some authorities to pretend that they do not know what philosophy is, no agnosticism remains about what philosophy is not. Philosophy is not a story, not a pictorial description, not a work of pure literature. Philosophical discourse is inscribed and declares its status through a break with myth, fable, the poetic, the domain of the image.
>
> (1989: 1)

In so far as the presence of image and metaphor in philosophy has been recognised, it is usually, she suggests, seen as 'inessential', extrinsic to the theory, a mere heuristic or pedagogical device. This is not true of all contemporary philosophers; the conscious deployment of metaphor, for instance, is central to the work of Heidegger. But, as Martha Nussbaum has noted, the predominant tendency in Anglo-American philosophy is to treat style and content as separable. Nussbaum describes the dominant style of philosophy in the 'analytic' tradition as 'a style correct, scientific, abstract, hygienically pallid, a style that seemed to be regarded as a kind of all-purpose solvent in which philosophical issues of any kind at all could be efficiently disentangled, any and all conclusions neatly disengaged' (Nussbaum 1990: 19).

Nussbaum argues that form and content in philosophy are closely related. If, as she believes, the role of philosophy is to articulate views or visions of what 'a good life' for human beings might be, then, she suggests, certain kinds of fiction, involving narrative, metaphor and the 'thick' description of life events and contingencies may be more apt than a 'dry' academic style for conveying certain kinds of philosophical truth or insight.

The texts of Western philosophy are frequently riddled with narrative, story-telling and metaphor. (Plato is a prime example.) But too strong a contrast between a 'literary' and a 'non-literary' type of philosophical style might suggest that some philosophical works are devoid of 'literary' devices. And this is not the case. All philosophical writing has a 'style', a rhetoric which aims to convince, and which is never reducible to any 'content' which might be paraphrased or more abstractly stated. One of the most powerful rhetorical devices in recent philosophy has been precisely that of the 'plain-speaking man', a dry or 'cold' academic style which is nevertheless devoid neither of metaphor, nor of its own rhetorical devices. The effect of this style is to underline the supposed objectivity and authoritativeness of its practitioners, who have been predominantly male.

Le Doeuff suggests that images and metaphors are essential to the philosophical text. The narrow version of the hypothesis that she wants to defend is that interpretation of metaphor and imagery in a philosophical text goes together with a search for points of tension in that text. The broader version is that the imagery employed works both for and against the philosophical system. It functions to sustain something that the system cannot justify (but also needs). Le Doeuff discusses, for example, metaphors of northern and southern isles in Kant's *Analytic*, and a range of metaphors deployed by Descartes, from the foundations of buildings to the branches of trees. A good example of the deployment of metaphor (though not one discussed by Le Doeuff herself) would be the role of metaphor in Plato's *Phaedrus*. In 'Plato's Pharmacy', Jacques Derrida (1981) notes how in this dialogue Plato, in the persona of Socrates, inveighs against writing as a means of conveying the truth, as opposed to the living speech and presence of the philosopher. The paradox, of course, is that Socrates never wrote anything; but Plato writes to convey what Socrates said. To evade this dilemma, Socrates tries to distinguish between 'good' and 'bad' memory of what the teacher said. 'Bad' memory, he suggests, merely relies on written marks, but 'good' memory' resides in the soul. Derrida points out, however, that 'good' memory is metaphorically conceptualised in terms of writing; 'good' memory is a 'writing on the soul'. Writing thus returns, in the form of metaphor, to undermine its own denial.

In 'White Mythology: Metaphor in the Text of Philosophy', Derrida (1982) suggests that it is not just that philosophical texts deploy metaphor. Metaphor, he says, is less in the philosophical text than the philosophical text is in metaphor. The very idea of philosophy has been constructed around metaphors of theory; it is arguable that all theoretical enterprises are premised on a 'founding metaphor' which underpins their articulation and application. Consider, for example, the ways in which some theories of the 'influence' of the media have been premised on what is called a 'hypodermic' model of influence, such that the effects of watching TV are seen as almost literally 'injectable' into the viewer; and consider the implications this view of 'influence' has had for feminist discussions of pornography.[1] In the case of Plato, the founding metaphors for philosophy were those of the sun, the visible, light and illumination. Historically, the metaphors through which the enterprise of philosophy has been thought are legion. Here are just a couple of such metaphors: drawing on the theory of recollection, Plato portrays Socrates at times as a midwife, bringing to birth philosophical ideas which the participants in a Socratic conversation did not know they possessed, or as a gadfly, stinging his interlocutors out of their conventional complacency. Richard Rorty suggests that the metaphor of the 'mirror' has underpinned the centrality of epistemology to modern philosophy, and has been central to the philosophical project of asking whether or how the mind could 'reflect' nature adequately (1980).

Many discussions of metaphor and philosophy have been what I have called 'deconstructive', aiming perhaps, as Derrida does, to explode any pretensions philosophical theories might have to 'truth' or 'presence', or, in the case of many feminist critics, to expose the phallocentrism of many dominant metaphors in philosophical texts, or the 'false universalism' of metaphors of the nature of philosophy. Le Doeuff's enterprise, in *The Philosophical Imaginary* (1989), is also 'deconstructive' in the sense that it explores the ways in which philosophical texts may, via metaphor, 'give themselves away', undermine that which they also intend to assert. But, according to Le Doeuff, metaphor does not *merely* undermine a philosophical text, it also functions to sustain it, as that which it may not be able to 'justify' explicitly or in its own terms, and yet also needs. In *Hipparchia's Choice* (1991), Le Doeuff argues that philosophical theories should give up their pretensions to be seen as wholly 'transparent' or self-justifying; they should be seen as provisional, situated by the perspective of the writers who produce them (though capable of addressing others not in that situation). Part of this 'situatedness' of theory lies in the metaphors it deploys or by which it is articulated. In *The Philosophical Imaginary*, Le Doeuff mostly sees metaphor as the unacknowledged support of theory. But, whilst metaphors themselves can never be wholly 'transparent', and whilst effective ones are not adopted merely through a process of abstract volition and reflection, there seems to be no reason why they should not be acknowledged or reflected upon. This raises the question of how and why some metaphors might come to seem illuminating; what is it, if anything, that they can change; can they be 'timely'; what role might they play in the feminist imagination, or in the 'reconstruction' of philosophy with a feminist orientation? The literature on metaphor is enormous, but here I would like to draw on aspects of the work of two writers in particular, Jean-Jacques Lecercle and George Lakoff and his collaborators, since it seems to me that their views of metaphor intersect in particularly interesting ways with aspects of feminist philosophy.

In *The Violence of Language* (1990) Lecercle is critical of those who see language as a 'system' beyond which there is only nonsense and chaos. The rules of grammar and semantics, he argues, may form a kind of 'frontier', but things which infringe grammatical or semantic rules can often be understood, and the 'frontiers' of language always remain arbitrary and unstable. Language is intrinsically rule-breaking as well as rule-governed. Lecercle uses the term 'the remainder' to characterise the qualities of language which can never be formalised into a system – that there is a 'remainder' is constitutive of language, and its fundamental 'rule' is that you can ignore all rules, if you feel like it. Lecercle borrows the concept of the 'rhizome' from Gilles Deleuze and Félix Guattari. A 'rhizome' is a structureless root which proliferates anarchically in many directions such that a final 'source' can never be found. The rhizomatic nature of language can be seen at its clearest in the kind of word play which involves punning, alliteration, paranomasia, the activation of associations familiar to particular groups of speakers. A 'remainderless' language which could be a wholly transparent means of information and communication is a mere fantasy.

Rather than seeing language as basically rule-governed and conventional and metaphor as a 'breakdown' which allows a certain amount of creativity, Lecercle sees language as basically metaphorical, and rules and conventions merely as *a posteriori* attempts at reducing this profuse inventiveness. Language can 'run wild'. Given a modicum of syntactical coherence, almost anything can be given a meaning. So, whilst a sentence such as 'Colourless green ideas sleep furiously' may seem semantically incoherent, it is not hard at all to imagine ways in which it could be given meaning. Metaphors can open up almost any path in language; this, of course, is seen at its clearest in poetry. And the line between what is and is not *seen* as metaphorical is shifting and unstable.

Lakoff (Lakoff and Johnson 1990) suggests that much of our everyday language, which we might think of as 'literal', is metaphorically structured in the sense that one 'domain' is mapped on to another; one type of thing is conceptualised in terms of another. Here are some examples he discusses: 'Argument is war'; 'Theories are buildings'; 'Love is a journey'; 'Time is money'; 'Ideas are food' (one could add many other examples from the history of philosophy or science, including: 'Nature is a woman'; 'The scientist is a lover (or rapist)'; 'Ideas are children'; and 'The philosopher is a midwife'.

Lakoff sees 'Argument is war', for instance, as a kind of 'root' metaphor which underlies a host of everyday ways of thinking about the processes of discussion and argument; expressions, for example, that use terms such as 'attack', 'winning', 'defeat', 'evasion', 'strategy', 'weak points', and so forth. Some of the concepts associated with war may overlap with those associated with other things, and not all of the concepts associated with war will be applied to the process of argument. What would be recognised as a metaphor or as figurative in ordinary language may often be understood as a process of extending the metaphor 'Argument is war' by drawing into play some aspect of war which is not normally associated with argument.

Whilst many of the everyday expressions associated with 'Argument is war' would not normally be seen as metaphorical, and might well appear as lexical items in dictionaries, since Lakoff sees the basic process of metaphor as 'understanding one kind of thing in terms of another' he argues that they *are* metaphorical. They are, he suggests, 'metaphors we live by'; they provide us with open-ended experiential gestalts which both organise and help to construct our experience.

Criticisms of this view of metaphor, however, have suggested that defining metaphor so broadly does not allow us to give an adequate account of the creative role of metaphor; of the ways in which language we explicitly interpret as metaphorical through the perception of semantic anomaly forces us to wonder, to compare, to rethink, to imagine different possibilities.[2] I would propose instead a 'pragmatic' account of the distinction between the metaphorical and the literal, such that the term 'metaphorical' is reserved for expressions which retain or create the power to generate a sense of semantic anomaly or imaginative extension of meaning. One reason I would propose this is that I think it allows us to give an interesting account of some aspects of the process of doing feminist philosophy.

Consider a new metaphor for the processes of discussion and argument, 'Argument is horticulture', and imagine yourself confronted with statements such as the following:

> We need to water this argument.
> This idea needs pruning.
> We'd be clearer if we repotted these thoughts.
> These ideas need putting into the sunlight.
> This theory won't be ripe until the autumn.
> This book doesn't have deep enough roots.

One could also, of course, produce expressions which provided some overlap with 'Argument is war': attacking diseases or blights; using weedkiller on our thoughts; and so forth. Indeed, some common expressions already seem to draw on notions of horticulture; think of 'having a fruitful period of research leave'. Nevertheless, the metaphor 'Argument is horticulture' offers a different overall kind of gestalt, within which to frame the processes of intellectual discussion; a different model of human activity with which to compare it.

A way of reinterpreting Lakoff, I think, is to say that he invites us to react *as if* the derivatives of 'Argument is war' were metaphors. In ordinary language they are no longer: they have become literal or lexical. They no longer generate the sense of semantic anomaly produced by the idea of watering or repotting one's ideas, or putting them into the sunlight. But by tracing colloquial and familiar statements back to the one which encapsulates them, 'Argument is war' (which is *not* in fact a metaphor we explicitly use), they are defamiliarised. In claiming that we often see argument as war we are invited to retrace the reasons why its derivatives are so familiar, to analyse the practices which they seem to describe, to consider precisely the fact that they have become 'common sense', and that they affect not only the ways in which we think, but the ways in which we behave.

This process might be seen as one of remetaphorising the familiar; coming to see it as somewhat strange, by the analytic defamiliarisation of aspects of our speech and language, by seeing related patterns in our behaviour, and by engaging in debate on how and why we speak and act in these ways. This seems to me to be quite a good characterisation of many of the 'deconstructive' aspects of feminist philosophy. Janice Moulton (1983), for instance, offers an analysis of what she called 'the adversary paradigm' in philosophical discussion, where the sole object of the enterprise is to attack and defeat the position of an interlocutor seen to be an opponent, rather than to cooperate in an exploration of ways in which problems might be solved. Her arguments invite us not merely to recognise the ways in which the metaphor 'Argument is war' may help to structure philosophical practice, but to consider the reasons why that metaphor might be seen as masculine in orientation. Margery Collins and Christine Peirce (1976) explore the metaphors of 'holes' and 'slime' in Sartre's characterisation of the female body in *Being and Nothingness*. They argue not only that Sartre saw the female body itself as that which is sunk in 'immanence' or the 'en-soi', but that this relegation of the female to the realm of immanence constitutes a conception of 'female nature' which contradicts what Sartre himself sees as the founding premises of his own philosophy, namely that there is no such thing as 'human nature'.

This 'deconstructive' kind of analysis of masculinist metaphor in philosophy has been an integral part of feminist philosophical work. But metaphors in philosophy are not of course all masculinist, and, if the deployment of metaphors is something which philosophy cannot do without, that raises the question of how and why we might want to deploy metaphor in new or 'constructive' ways.

Metaphors for (or within) intellectual enterprises cannot just be invented by fiat. As Judith Butler notes in *Excitable Speech*, 'Autonomy in speech, to the extent that it exists, is conditioned by a radical and originary dependency on a language whose historicity exceeds in all directions the history of the speaking subject' (1997: 28). In addition, a metaphor has to 'catch', to be 'seen' or 'grasped', to be felt as apt or appropriate, and the conditions for this cannot be created merely by individual (or group) intention. So what are these conditions?

Lecercle notes that the understanding of metaphor is overdetermined. Its force may sometimes depend on resources that are specific to a particular language, including intertextual resonances. Hence there is notorious difficulty in translating metaphors. But, he argues, historical conjunctures are also linguistic conjunctures which are rooted in common experience and understandings within particular social situations and social groups. The command of a language shared with other speakers on which the understanding of a metaphor depends requires a historical depth. It depends on linguistic 'sedimentation' that reflects the contradictions and struggles that make up the realm of the social. (This is well illustrated by Raymond Williams's (1976) work on 'Keywords'.) Language can never merely be a neutral instrument for naming.

Language should not be thought of simply as an abstract system of signs. The meanings of words can impact directly on bodies. They may injure or wound; they can make my heart pound or my pulse race; they may, in Butler's words, 'enter the limbs, craft the gesture, bend the spine' (Butler 1997: 159). They are endowed with force and, in certain circumstances, they can even kill. Whilst much poetic metaphor may seem like 'play' whose effects on the world around are slight, Lecercle suggests (borrowing terms again from Deleuze and Guattari) that metaphor may reach out towards metamorphosis. Words may not only injure or wound; they may also heal or reconcile. They may work to reinforce dominant or oppressive social structures. But they may also work to destabilise these; at times even an injurious word (such as 'nigger') may not merely be used, but also mentioned or cited in such a way that attention is drawn to its power to injure or harm. Or the 'word that wounds' can itself become an instrument in a redeployment that destroys the prior territory of its use. Feminist writers, for instance, have sometimes reclaimed injurious words such as 'bitch', 'hag' or 'crone' and used them in new and celebratory ways.[3]

To speak is always, in a certain sense, to act. But, as Butler argues, the historicity which enables a speech act to 'work' may also enable it to 'exceed' its moment of enunciation and be transformed in new contexts. Derrida writes of the 'break' as a structural feature of any sign; signs must always break with prior contexts in order to sustain their own iterability as signs. What Derrida fails to ask, however, is how it is that certain utterances can break from prior contexts with more ease than others, why some of them can carry such force, or why some might come to seem apt, empowering, more able to destabilise 'the ordinary' than others.

New conceptions of 'philosophy' emerge through reflection on praxis, and by metaphorical comparison with other forms of praxis. Feminist views of philosophy have mostly found their 'sedimentation' elsewhere than in standard histories or conceptions of philosophy. They involve defamiliarising and 'remetaphorising' taken-for-granted notions of 'what philosophy is', and the imaginative task of finding new metaphors for a sense of what it is we are doing.

The philosopher, for instance, has sometimes been seen as a kind of cartographer, or an explorer, mapping intellectual rather than physical landscapes. Wittgenstein, in his attempt to rethink the nature of philosophy in his later work, from time to time compared philosophy to therapy. Implicitly or explicitly, philosophy has sometimes been compared to engineering or plumbing. A striking example of the latter is a recent essay by Mary Midgley entitled 'Philosophical Plumbing' (1996), in which she suggests that the role of the philosopher is to identify the powerful, intricate and sometimes dangerous patterns that underlie much of our thinking, to see why they cause the problems that they do, and how they might be modified. Foucault at times thought of his work as a toolbox, which might be deployed in differing ways depending on the particular purposes of those who used it. Luce Irigaray (1985) compared the apparatuses of Western philosophical thinking to machinery, and wrote that her own interventions were not designed to produce yet another theory of which woman would be the object, but to jam the theoretical machinery.

It is not a question of trying to find some new and stable definition of 'feminist philosophy', nor is it an attempt to say 'what philosophy really is'. It is more a process of 'seeing-as'; of a retrospective rethinking, in the light of the intuitive or apparent aptness of a metaphor or set of metaphors, of what we have been doing, and an openness to thinking about the suggestiveness of these metaphors for ongoing praxis.

The metaphors through which we might rethink philosophy, the types of human activity to which we could compare it, are potentially many and varied, and it is not the case that only one of them might be apt. One might, at one moment or conjuncture, think of philosophy as one type of activity, but deploy another metaphor at times in response to the limitations of the first. Metaphors need not be exclusive of each other, and they may serve different purposes.

The same is true not merely of overall conceptions of the 'nature' of philosophy, but of philosophical theories themselves. One might, for instance, become aware of the ways in which certain philosophical theories of the self have been premised on metaphors of 'boundaries', of the self as a kind of 'walled city'; or of the ways in which metaphors of vision (including that of a 'perspective') have dominated many theories of knowledge. Such an awareness can lead to an investigation of the points of tension within such theories, where the metaphorical and rhetorical devices within which they are framed may open up the unintended, and reveal not only potentialities which are inconsistent with the theory, but suggest different metaphors. If the self is a walled city, for instance, what lies 'outside' it and why, and how might that exploration lead to a destabilisation of the conception of the self from which one started? At the same time, do metaphors of boundaries also have a certain usefulness for feminist purposes when thinking about the self, at least as a corrective to the kinds of views which have seen women's selves as wholly merged with those of others? Questions like these may lead not so much to the wholesale rejection of metaphors, but rather to their rearticulation, extension or adaptation.

The process of 'seeing-as' involves a recognition that the meanings of new metaphoric conceptions, and the ways in which they may be 'taken up' by differently located audiences, can never be wholly transparent. The rhizomatic and anarchic possibilities opened up by any deployment of language can never be controlled in advance; in a profound sense we do not know and cannot predict what will happen in encounters between feminism and philosophy. What we write can always 'escape' us; it can generate meanings and responses which may surprise us. And it may at times 'speak' to those whose social situation is radically different from our own; the social locatedness of philosophical writing does not mean that it can never speak to those who do not share that social location. We need new and imaginative conceptions of philosophy and new philosophical conceptions, which help us both to recognise their locatedness, and to avoid the traps of unthinking imperialist assumptions that any conception of philosophy or form of philosophical discourse could be apt in the same ways for all readers or audiences. But we also need to recognise the 'open' texture of philosophical discourse; to assume the kind of 'universalism' which is precisely *not* premised on the idea of a homogeneous universal readership, but on the recognition that our words can always escape us, spark off new meanings, or provoke rearticulations generated by new contexts of reception.

Communication does not have to assume transparency; it can often survive lack of understanding, failures of mutuality, large gulfs between intention and reception. It can also, at times, survive the impossibility of always eliminating all forms of inequality in discourse in such a way that no speaker could ever be disadvantaged, or that all speakers might always be on terms of perfect equality. It does, however, require an ongoing sense of the provisionality of philosophical discourse, a consistent reflexivity about what it is we think we are doing, and an openness to the ways in which what we write or say might be contested by others.

The recognition that what we write can always 'escape' us and that meanings are never transparent and can never be finally fixed means that there can be no final consensus about 'what philosophy is', and no viable feminist orthodoxies in philosophy. It is not a question of saying 'Philosophy is … ' or 'Philosophy is really like … ', in essentialist ways that appear to claim that we have finally discovered the 'true' nature of the activity. Nor should philosophical theories be interpreted as making claims about 'what the world is really like'. It is more a question of saying 'Think of philosophy as … or as if … '; or, 'Think of the self as … or as if … '; or 'Think of knowledge as … or as if … '. This process involves metaphor. If it seems problematic to think of philosophy as a 'mirror' of the world, then proposing a new conception of philosophy will involve new metaphors which are likely to find their sedimentation elsewhere than in standard histories of the subject. Or, if metaphors of walled cities seem problematic when thinking about the self, what new metaphors might seem apt and where might they take us? The kinds of questions that arise are these: how useful is the metaphor; how far and under what aspects can one take it; what kinds of illumination might it provide; does it allow us to understand some things better; what moves does it suggest and where might it break down? '"True" or "false"?' does not capture these questions. There might nevertheless be very good reasons, in certain conjunctures, for seeing certain metaphors as more apt or fruitful than others. Recognising the role of metaphor in philosophy can provide a way of ceasing to impale ourselves on the 'objectivist' dilemma whereby that which makes no claim to be seen as 'the truth', *simpliciter*, can only be dismissed as subjectivist whim or as necessarily confined to the precise social location from which it arose.

As Butler writes: 'Language takes on a non-ordinary meaning in order precisely to contest what has become sedimented in and as the ordinary' (1997: 145). Here, she is referring to and defending the need for academic discourse. But the notion of the 'non-ordinary' can equally well apply to metaphor, to language which is not lexical, which may create an effect of semantic anomaly, but which nevertheless can be given a sense which can be explored, and which might provide a new 'gestalt' within which experience can be both framed and constructed. Linguistic agency cannot be thought of as an abstract autonomy; our utterances are produced and sedimented by histories which we do not create, and have effects which we cannot ultimately determine, predict or control, and of which we may be unaware. But *within* this historicity and unwittingness, I believe there is a space also for the conscious and intentional operation of feminist imagination, for experimental engagements with metaphors and styles and forms of discourse. Consider, for instance, the kinds of illumination that might be provided by Irigaray's metaphor of 'the two lips' as a way of contesting phallo-centric metaphors of 'identity' (Irigaray 1985). Consider the need for 'remetaphorising' the kinds of mechanical or industrial metaphors of birth which have become gynaecological 'common sense', and the need to 'reimagine' birth as a subject of feminist philosophical concern. Consider the importance new metaphors of the self might have for exploring notions of 'identity' or of relations and connections between human selves.[4] It is, I think, this kind of imagination which has characterised much feminist philosophy, and which provides the hope of further transformations.

Notes

1   I owe this example to Martin Barker, a colleague of mine at the University of the West of England. For further examples of the use of metaphor within theory, see, for instance, T. Kuhn, 'Metaphor in Science' and D. Schon, 'Generative Metaphor: A Perspective on Problem-Setting in Social Policy', both in Ortony (1993).
2   See, for example, the work of E.R. MacCormac (1985).
3   A notable example of this 'reclamation' of injurious words is the writing of Mary Daly (1979).
4   Emily Martin (1987) discusses the ways in which metaphors of menstruation, birth and menopause are deployed in gyaecological texts. Morwenna Griffiths (1995) deploys a number of metaphors, including those of a 'web' and of 'patchwork' to try to rethink questions about self and identity in a way which adequately recognises fluidity, change and hybridity. She also refers at various points to the work of Lakoff (Griffiths 1995: 171).

References

Butler, J. (1997) *Excitable Speech: A Politics of the Performative*, London: Routledge.
Collin, M. and Peirce, C. (1976) 'Holes and Slime: Sexism in Sartre's Psychoanalysis', in C. Gould and Wartofsky (eds) *Women and Philosophy*, New York: Putnam.
Daly, M. (1979) *Gyn/Ecology*, London: Women's Press.
Derrida, J. (1981) *Dissemination*, Chicago, Ill.: University of Chicago Press.
—— (1982) *Margins of Philosophy*, Brighton: Harvester Press.
Griffiths, M. (1995) *Feminisms and the Self: The Web of Identity*, London: Routledge.
Irigaray, L. (1985) *This Sex Which Is Not One*, Ithaca, N.Y.: Cornell University Press.
Lakoff, G. (1987) *Women, Fire and Dangerous Things*, Chicago, Ill.: University of Chicago Press.
—— (1993) 'The Contemporary Theory of Metaphor', in A. Ortony (ed.) *Metaphor and Thought*, Cambridge: Cambridge University Press.
—— and Johnson, M. (1990) *Metaphors We Live By*, Chicago, Ill.: University of Chicago Press.
—— and Turner, M. 1989) *More than Cool Reason*, Chicago, Ill.: University of Chicago Press.
Lecercle, J.J. (1990) *The Violence of Language*, London: Routledge.
Le Doeuff, M. (1989) *The Philosophical Imaginary*, London: Athlone Press.
—— (1991) *Hipparchia's Choice*, Oxford: Oxford University Press.

MacCormac, E.R. (1985) *A Cognitive Theory of Metaphor*, Cambridge, Mass: Massachusetts Institute of Technology Press.

Martin, E. (1987) *The Woman in the Body*, Milton Keynes, England: Open University Press.

Midgley, M. (1996) 'Philosophical Plumbing', in M. Midgley, *Utopias, Dolphins and Computers: Problems of Philosophical Plumbing*, London: Routledge.

Moulton, J. (1983) 'The Adversary Paradigm', in S. Harding and M. Hintikka (eds) *Discovering Reality*, Dordrecht, Boston and London: D. Reidel.

Nussbaum, M. (1990) *Love's Knowledge*, Oxford: Oxford University Press.

Ortony, A. (ed.) (1993) *Metaphor and Thought*, Cambridge: Cambridge University Press.

Rorty, R. (1980) *Philosophy and the Mirror of Nature*, Princeton, N.J.: Princeton University Press.

Williams, R. (1976) *Keywords: A Vocabulary of Culture and Society*, London: Fontana.

12 Still telling it like it is?

Problems of feminist truth claims

Caroline Ramazanoglu and Janet Holland

Can feminists tell the truth?

The differences between the English-language feminist texts of the 1970s and those of the 1990s are striking. The excitement of wild women telling new truths – confronting patriarchy, naming their existence, making up new words, digging up their history, sharing subordination and empowerment across their differences, disintegrating disciplines, proposing men as a gender rather than the norm, revealing the power relations behind claims of natural difference – are being displaced by volumes telling little about people's lives, but questioning everything about truth and how it can be known: Feminism and Philosophy, Feminism and Deconstruction, Feminism and Postmodernism, Feminism and Epistemology, Methodology, Knowing.

The 1990s academic feminist has to exercise extreme caution in making any claims about what the social world is like, or risk being snubbed as essentialist and foundationalist. But feminists, like others, do have good ideas, relevant experience and political judgements about what the social world is like, and why political transformation of gender relations is still an issue. There is a danger, as Kate Soper points out, that as feminists become more sensitive to the conceptual difficulties of the issues they have raised, they risk losing sight of feminism's 'original goals' (1990: 221).

Effective political strategies for social transformation of gender relations require knowledge of what is to be transformed. Despite current theoretical complexity and challenges to epistemology, feminists can still justify their theories of knowledge, and so can make claims for feminist knowledge of people's lives. The epistemological foundations of feminist knowledge (as of any other knowledge) will remain contested. Feminists cannot know for sure what gender is, or what gendered lives are like, just because they see the social world through feminist theory. However, political expediency demands that as feminists we go on investigating and accounting for people's gendered social existence and explaining how we justify the knowledge we produce (Holland *et al.* 1998).

This chapter is located in the tension between the political necessity (for feminists) of establishing what power relations actually impinge on real people's lives (which requires some project to establish what does and does not happen to women), and the problem that feminists cannot simply tell the truth about women's lives, because both 'women' and 'truth' are socially constituted and so unstable. This obliges feminists to specify what feminist knowledge is for, and how any validity can be claimed for it. When Judith Butler warned feminists not to use taken-for-granted assumptions about the existence of women and the female subject, she usefully noted that deconstructing assumptions about a feminist subject who produces knowledge of the world is not the same as abandoning this subject (1992: 14–15). Butler asks whether feminism should become self-critical about the processes that produce and destablise identity categories, and answers:

> To take the construction of the subject as a political problematic is not the same as doing away with the subject; to deconstruct the subject is not to negate or throw away the concept; on the contrary, deconstruction implies only that we suspend all commitments to that which the term, 'the subject' refers, and that we consider the linguistic functions it serves in the consolidation and concealment of authority. To deconstruct is not to negate or dismiss, but to call into question and, perhaps most importantly, to open up a term, like the subject, to a reusage or redeployment that previously has not been authorized.
>
> (Butler 1992: 15)

Questioning the authority of feminists to speak as subjects with specialist knowledge of gender relations is not the same as invalidating their knowledge. 'Knowing like a feminist', however problematic its assumptions, has produced different knowledge of social life; different from that which ignores or deconstructs gender relations and silences women. Feminist knowledge of people's lives, however, can certainly be challenged; feminism is an area of diversity, debate and struggle, rather than one of the orthodoxy, essentialism and censorious authority often attributed to it.

Not only do feminists have to defend their knowledge of gendered social existence, but 'knowing like a feminist' presupposes both that there is 'one who knows' and something real that can be 'known'.[1] Both these assumptions have come under attack. The most powerful challenges have come from two rather different sources: on the one hand, there are postmodern and poststructural deconstructions of feminist subjects (for example Hekman 1997); on the other there are examinations of the epistemological implications of social divisions between women (for example Collins 1990). Feminism is in trouble if these challenges are ignored, as they do provide grounds for contesting the validity of feminist knowledge. Although feminist theorists have responded to postmodern and poststructuralist challenges, and to social divisions between women, in different ways, the political implications of *just* deconstructing feminist knowledge have been noted (for example Benhabib *et al.* 1995; Braidotti 1991; Elam 1994;). If feminists are to go on 'telling it like it is', they have both to produce knowledge of social existence and to question how knowledge and knowing selves are produced and made authoritative.

Questioning what it means to know like a feminist, however, produces intractable problems: feminists are not authorised to tell general truths about gender simply because they live as women. However sensitively and reflexively feminists try to produce knowledge, and however carefully they qualify and justify their judgements, there are no unproblematic ways of making knowledge claims. Despite these problems, feminists have demonstrated women's everyday experiences of living through real relations of power that are dangerous, unjust and improper. Through these demonstrations, they have also established that other relations of power intersect with those of gender, giving some women considerable power and privilege. Experiencing power relations (such as those of domestic or racial violence) is not the same as producing general knowledge of these relations; theorising such relations is not wholly separable from people's experiences of them. Feminism implies some political commitment to connecting lived experience with knowledge claims in order to effect political transformation.

Two initial problems emerge in trying to produce distinctive feminist theory that works for social transformation. First, 'women' and 'men' are not simply natural categories, and so defining who is a woman is an area of political struggle. This has the potential to undermine claims to knowledge that are distinctively feminist. Second, poststructural, postmodern and deconstructionist critics have contested feminist claims to knowledge of women's lives through debates on how knowledge is produced and made powerful, and how social life is organised through the truth claims that become authorised and legitimated in particular ways of thinking (Benhabib *et al.* 1995; Braidotti 1991; Hekman 1997; Scott 1992). These challenges have been illuminating in many respects and have produced strong arguments that 'woman' or 'women' cannot be taken for granted as a natural category. In accepting this deconstruction of 'woman', however, feminism loses its knowing subject (Butler 1990; Riley 1988). Once 'woman' is viewed as a socially constructed and historically variable subject, feminists have to rethink how their claims to knowledge of gendered social existence can be justified, and how and why specific knowing subjects are constituted.

Are feminists women? ('women'? 'Woman'?)

Judith Butler questions the 'authorising power' that positions certain utterances as authoritative by asking who is it that gets constituted as the feminist theorist who knows (1992: 9–10). She comments: 'No subject is its own point of departure … The critique of the subject is not a negation or repudiation of the subject, but, rather, a way of interrogating its construction as a pregiven or foundationalist premise' (Butler 1992: 9). In Butler's view, 'woman' is neither a ground nor a product, but an accomplishment and a possibility. This is not, she says, to pronounce the death of the subject, but to do away with insidious versions of it, especially since subjects (such as 'woman') are constituted through exclusion (Scott 1992). What may be wrong with assuming a 'knowing feminist', in Butler's view, is the kind of subject she may be constituted as. She questions any feminist claims to speak for women as if 'woman' was a fixed category.

Some of these arguments have been taken up (often without the careful qualifications of their originators) by caricaturing 'feminism' as irrevocably essentialist, foundationalist and humanist (Grant 1993). This can promote the incorporation of politically toothless, abstracted and fragmented feminisms into male-centred thought and largely male-dominated academies (Hawthorne 1996: 487). Academic feminism can become increasingly locked into the agenda of male-centred philosophy and deconstructionism that regulates how we may think about how we think, rather than extending and refining knowledge of material relations of power, and so what feminists may or may not legitimately say about gendered social existence.

Reflections on how feminists know what they know and how they are constituted as 'knowers' can be productive, but cannot *replace* investigation of social life. There are political dangers in producing feminist knowledge as the specialised preserve of relatively privileged, academic women who are incorporated into higher education and scholarship, in conformity to the conventions of professional respectability (see Stanley 1997). Acknowledging that women are not simply women (wherever the apostrophes fly) need not mean abandoning feminist claims to knowledge.

Denise Riley, for example, comments that although instability in the designation 'women' is the lot of feminism: 'it would be wildly perverse to deny that there can be *any* progressive deployments of "women" – all the achievements of emancipation and campaigning would be obliterated in that denial' (1988: 98). Judith Butler has also argued that difficulties in establishing what 'woman' means does not mean the category of 'women' should not be used politically (1992: 15–16). Butler notes the problem that 'women' remains a normative and exclusionary identity, and an area of 'rifts among women over the content of the term' (which implies that there are women who dispute 'women') (1992: 16). Establishing a normative foundation for settling the question of what 'women' means, would, she says, simply call into question who would set such norms (1992: 16). We might argue that feminists cannot rest here, since establishing who counts as 'woman' is not simply a struggle over norms. While anyone can perform femininity only some people are materially female (Holland *et al.* 1994).

The argument that the boundaries between male and female, masculine and feminine, bodies and their meanings, are culturally produced and so variable is a strong one (see for example Butler 1990, 1993; Haraway 1989; Riley 1988), but this does not make women disappear (Ramazanoglu 1995).[2] Confusions about the significance of embodied differences arise because there are normative struggles around what sense is made of organic, reproductive difference. There are not in practice two mutually exclusive, wholly natural sex/gender categories, so the boundaries of 'woman'/'man' are culturally variable, and there is an area of, say, intersexuality, hybridity, normative confusion, social regulation, where differing cultures draw, disrupt and police their gender boundaries differently. Sabina Sawhney comments on the concept of *hijra* as a category of existence that is experienced as 'neither here nor there' since it cannot be encompassed by the dualism of woman/man (1995: 197). Sawhney draws on a sense of intermediate positions between woman/man to make sense of this category in English: 'the *hijra* in common Indian parlance is an umbrella name referring to eunuchs or men who have emasculated themselves, intersexed people, hermaphrodites, persons with indeterminate sexual organs, impotent men, male homosexuals and even effeminate men who are *hijra* imposters' (Sawhney 1995: 198).

The question of who is woman/man/neither-woman-nor-man can (within limits) be answered differently within different ways of knowing. The differences lie mainly in how far there are dualistic categories in the culture, how those who live between male/female have their social existence, and what meanings and value are given to these differences. (The notion of intersexuality is an attempt to produce a more tolerant understanding of how these boundaries are drawn.) Given cultural differences, the question of who is a woman is primarily an empirical one which needs to take political account of how boundaries of gender categories are drawn and with what effects. Defining what (materially, politically, discursively) a woman (or a man) is, requires empirical investigation of what people have in common in terms of both their constitution as gendered subjects and the material conditions of their social existence. A politics of difference has emerged alongside knowledge of both common interests and social divisions between women. The question of who is a woman remains then empirical, but also normative, contingent and contested.

Feminists cannot claim authoritative knowledge of political and sexual identities unless they take these to be fixed or essential truths, but equally feminists cannot afford to abandon the investigation of specific power relations, their intersections and effects on the grounds that these are unknowable. Feminists' personal knowledge of women's lives and social divisions between women makes them reluctant to abandon investigation of the social world as a source of knowledge. Reflection on experience is a critical basis for political work and feminist consciousness (Kelly and McWilliams 1997).

Feminists face practical and political, as well as epistemological, problems in claiming valid knowledge of power relations while accepting powerful intellectual arguments that all knowledge is socially constructed. But Kate Soper comments that there are 'material circumstances' in women's lives that have been 'relatively unaffected by changes at a discursive and "Symbolic" level' (1990: 242–243). She argues that there is a 'sex-specific but universal quality of certain conditions of general experience which justifies and gives meaning to collective gender categories' (1990: 243). For feminists, it is this element of shared material conditions of existence (which have to be established through conceptualisation and investigation), rather than a universality of essence or meanings, which enables them to speak as women. If feminists want to claim knowledge of social existence, and if the authority to speak for women does not come from being women (and presumably a feminist knower could be male, intersexed or other), then feminists do need to justify with what authority they may speak.

Telling it like it is? Justification and validity

The problems of producing knowledge of gender relations are not just intellectual, there are also ethical, political and embodied issues in justifying feminist claims to speak about social reality. If there is no general or agreed way in which people can be recognised as women/men, rather than something else, the validity of feminist knowledge will depend on the power of feminist theory to make sense of people's experience at a level at which it can be acted upon. Feminism is a response to the subordination and abuse of women as well as to the conceptualisation/language of 'subordination', 'abuse' and 'women'.

We can interrogate the creation of any feminist subject who claims authority to produce feminist knowledge, but interrogating the creation of subjects does not produce knowledge of social existence. Interrogations are only as good as the interrogator; deconstructions produce deconstructions. At worst, interrogation can lead to an endless regression of interrogating the interrogation, while feminists are still left with needing to make sense of gender relations and people's lives (Elam 1994).

It is around both the grounding and the authority of feminist knowledge claims that there are serious epistemological differences between disparate feminist visions – stretching from absolute foundationalism to absolute relativism. Close to one pole are those who (while being critical of a naive foundationalism) retain some notion of a knowing subject producing feminist knowledge as potentially scientific and so having to be validated – as in debates on a successor science (Haraway 1991). Near the other pole are those who embrace relativism, instability, diversity and (through the notion of deconstructed subjects constituted through language, practice, iteration or whatever) deny the possibility of general knowledge. Most feminists, including us, adopt more or less contradictory positions between these extremes in which they do value their knowledge and experience of social existence and want some means of validating this knowledge, but also acknowledge that any way of telling the truth is socially constituted, discursively organised and legitimated. Donna Haraway usefully likens this to trying to climb a greased pole while holding on to both ends (1991: 188).[3] Her point seems to be that not only is holding a greasy pole hard, but in order to get any further we need to keep hold of both ends.

If we decide to value and so (however problematically) validate feminist knowledge of social existence, this means taking a stand against relativism on the grounds that there really are material conditions of gendered power. As Kate Soper has commented: 'one does not want to lend oneself to the kind of anti-naturalism and anti-objectivity which removes all grounds for discriminating between what can truly or falsely be said of women. Or at least I do not' (1990: 222).

A relativist focus on deconstructions of language or representations can be productive, but it can also be limited (Hartsock 1997; Smith 1997). If feminism is to have transformative power, we cannot evade the difficulty of justifying what we know by collapsing knowledge either into language, or into instability, uncertainty and diversity. Transformation requires both theories of power that can name real power relations (which are always conceptualised) and judgements (which are always normative) of which power relations are oppressive. There are particular difficulties in justifying how to bring theories, judgements and lived experience together. We need valid knowledge of social life in order to judge which power relations should be transformed; but in knowing what is unjust and should be transformed, we need general criteria of judgement that can only be justified politically and ethically (Ramazanoglu 1998). Feminists can respect differences of judgement about gendered power relations, but not to the point of, for example, accepting domestic violence as good for women. Political pressures to transform real social relations require that we are able to judge between them. In order to judge between them, we need knowledge of what they are like. This is what makes justifying feminist knowledge claims so difficult.

Feminist identification of, and opposition to, rape, for example, comes both from knowledge of what rape is like and from the judgement that there are real power relations affecting people's social existence that are unacceptable. This judgement is clearly political, ethical and potentially universalising. We choose what we want to transform, because we think it *ought* to be transformed into something better. As we produce valid knowledge for effective transformation we are producing appropriate theory; in producing appropriate theory we make claims to knowledge of what is to be transformed. Feminists are never going to agree on everything they know, or judge oppressive, but they should be account-able for both the validity of the knowledge they produce and the judgements they make of their own and other people's social existence.

Producing understandings of rape (including male rape, date rape, marital rape) and judging what will and will not do, for example, are heavy political responsibilities and urgent political tasks. People who have raped or been raped have their own understandings of their experience and do not necessarily agree with each other in their judgements of the morality of what has happened, or with feminist theories of these experiences. Rapists and the judiciary may see rape in terms of natural sexuality; people who have been raped may draw on discourses of gender/sexuality that make them feel in some way responsible; they may be silenced by the violence of the experience, or lack any appropriate language for expressing what has happened to them.

Feminists do not have any moral or other authority to decide for others what their experience of rape is. Cathy Winkler, who had had counselling to help her make sense of what her own traumatic experience of rape meant, tells of how the 'truth' of her rape changed for her. Her rape was initially 'a dark cloud of horror', but on reading an article on rape which included a rapist's account, she suddenly recognised her rape as the price of her own escape from death:

> As I read the rapist Chambers' words, I spontaneously screamed in a death-defying manner and my body evacuated its contents. My body told me that I was now safe to confront that meaning because I was alone, without people to deny my experience.

(1994: 260–261)

Different feminists have constructed knowledge of rape differently, but Vikki Bell points out that there is a 'basic feminist argument about rape: that it is about the social relations between men and women' (1991: 98).

Feminist theories of rape are ways of making sense of the reflections and experiences of those who rape and have been raped. This does not make rape a fixed or essential or even wholly knowable experience, but neither is rape just silence, or social construction, or anecdotes. It is always theorised as rape – otherwise the event has some other meaning (Holland *et al.* 1992) – but people's accounts of rape are not arbitrary impositions of meaning. Mary Hawkesworth comments that violence is not a fiction that admits free play of signification, suggesting that all stories of rape are not equally valid (1989: 555). It is perfectly possible to insist that valid knowledge of rape should be informed by accounts of experience without insisting either that experience simply tells the truth, or that theory dictates what experience is. Yet we can claim feminist theories of rape as political violence to be better than patriarchal theories of women's natural propensity to be raped. Nancy Hartsock suggests: 'I want to privilege some knowledges over others because they seem to me to offer possibilities for envisioning more just social relations' (1997: 373). Knowledge of rape as sited in sexual politics, and knowledge of variations in how it is connected to other power relations, is necessary knowledge for social transformation.

The problems of how feminists can justify their knowledge claims have led to consideration not only of how feminists are socially constituted as knowing selves claiming better knowledge, but also what collectivities they think within and are accountable to. These concerns have led to discussions on how we might think about a 'community' within which feminist knowledge claims are authorised. The notion of a feminist epistemic community is not equivalent to an idealised scientific community in which reasonable chaps question or accept communal assumptions.[4] Rather, feminist discussions have explored how to identify actual epistemic communities within which feminist, or any other knowledge, is generated (Nelson 1993: 123).

Feminism's epistemic communities

Claiming knowledge of our own gendered lives and of the lives of others demands criteria for judging between contested stories of power relations and their effects. We have to specify to whom feminist knowledge is accountable and whom our theory-making serves – particularly when making and authorising knowledge is part of our professional lives (Lugones and Spelman 1995: 504).

Feminists have demonstrated the politically biased and exclusionary basis of foundationalist epistemology through which women were (and to a large extent still are) excluded from the scientific epistemic community (for example Gatens 1991; Harding 1991). Lorraine Code argues that feminists need strategies to challenge this exclusion by claiming their cognitive competence and authority, their knowledgeability and their right to know (1987: 218). She also suggests making explicit the nature of the epistemic communities within which criteria of validation are established, since such strategies have to be mounted in collective social critique and active constructions of meaning. By engaging in critique, feminists can clarify how and why power confers the status of knowledge; that knowledge itself confers and is conferred by power. We can explore both the notion of epistemic community and the constitution and exclusionary practices of actual epistemic communities.[5] Feminists are deconstructing knowledge and the power to know authoritatively, but also establishing possible grounds for validating feminist knowledge (without either reasserting inappropriate foundations, or sliding into relativism – for example losing our grip on one end of Haraway's greased pole (Haraway 1991: 188)).

The point is not to defend the boundaries of a fixed group of those authorised to say what counts as knowledge. (This would raise all the earlier problems, for example, of who decides who is a 'woman'.) Rather, the point is both to investigate and to question how and why validation and authority come about, and how differing processes of validation become authoritative or not (reason versus emotion; science versus superstition; masculinism versus feminism; white theory versus black experience). If feminists are to speak 'truths' (rather than tell stories which others can justifiably disregard as personal, marginal, irrelevant, biased), then feminist epistemologies must identify grounds for feminist knowledge claims that do not altogether abandon criteria of scientific validity (in the sense of some connection to the material world of people and events (Haraway 1991; Smith 1997; Soper 1990)), but are also self-conscious, questioning, reasonable, open and just.

A notion of an epistemic community implies: similarity and difference; the existence of an inside and an outside (with the outside playing a critical role in the constitution of the inside); potential battles over where boundaries fall, who has the power to draw them and what inclusion/exclusion means. Attention to the grounds of epistemic authority can help to clarify how knowing selves are constituted and how practices of inclusion/exclusion operate in the processes of authorisation and in dealing with challenges to authority. Western feminists, white feminists, privileged women have had well-documented problems in claiming validity for general knowledge of women's lives when such knowledge is not well connected to a range of gendered lives, and is not authorised in differently constituted epistemic communities.

Increasingly feminists are clearing this philosophical ground and, in line with a multiplicity of feminisms, are proposing feminist epistemologies and identifying the agents and effects of these epistemologies (Alcoff and Potter 1993; Collins 1990; Lennon and Whitford 1994). Morwenna Griffiths has usefully identified four common threads running across this multiplicity of feminist positions. She argues that they all: assume the self, a subjective position (including 'experience') as a starting point, which contests the possibility of achieving objective knowledge; they take a moral/political stance and, although they may disagree about details of value and power, they take these positions as integral elements of knowing; theory and theorising are taken as fundamental; all recognise that it is not possible to acquire stable, unchanging knowledge, since all knowledge must be subject to critique from other viewpoints and may need fundamental revision in the light of criticisms (1995: 59–61).

These commonalities across feminism's differences create the possibility for more explicit examination of feminist epistemic communities. All knowledge is, in practice, produced within the bounds of a community of knowers who generate and validate what is known. What is distinctive in discussion of feminist epistemic communities is the conception of such communities as agents of epistemology, in opposition to the foundationalist view of the individual, as the agent of knowledge, following rules of method in a scientific community as the validating agent (Assiter 1996; Code 1987; Nelson 1993).

A crucial element in identifying validating collectivities for feminism would be the recognition that we are not collections of independently knowing individuals (Nelson 1993: 124) but members of collectivities needing to interrogate our constitution as collectivities – we only know for some 'we', and this 'we' needs to be established and reflected upon. Lorraine Code argues that: 'The construction of knowledge is an intersubjective process, dependent for its achievement on communal standards of legitimation and implicated in the power and institutional structures of communities and social orders' (Code 1991: 132).

Western feminism is always in danger of appropriating other people's experience by incorporating it into Western theory. We do not have any neutral notion of a universal humanity as an epistemic community, and yet feminists, through commitment to transformation of unjust gender relations, are tied to normative, universalising assumptions implicit in notions of emancipation and transformation. So the boundaries of epistemic communities need to be made explicit and open to negotiation.

In Code's view, epistemic dependence is crucial to the very possibility of being an epistemic agent (1991: 131). Feminists (or anybody else) cannot be independent knowers since, as knowing subjects, we are always already dependent on membership of collectivities. Through critical reflection on the social/political constitution of epistemic membership we begin to understand what is possible and also what is exclusionary in our way of thinking and our intellectual practices (including what is exclusionary in masculinist/relativist deconstructions of foundations and in associated academic careers). We can concur with Hawkesworth that: 'Knowledge, then, is a convention rooted in the practical judgements of a community of fallible inquirers who struggle to resolve theory-dependent problems under specific historical conditions' (1989: 549).

Although feminist social theory has largely abandoned the certainty of scientific, objective knowledge, feminists still want to validate knowledge claims (for example of domestic violence, gendered difference, historical specificity) as the basis for political transformation. Such claims require criteria of validation that are not reducible to the authenticity of personal experience, nor to the rules of scientific method, proof and falsifiability, nor to multiple readings of texts. Feminist politics addresses material realities, social relationships and real injustices that cross every social and cultural boundary, and feminists are not always good at identifying particular power relations that privilege them personally. We cannot embark on effective transformation of gender relations without valid knowledge of the complexity of what is to be transformed.

As epistemically-dependent individuals, we have no authority to offer any general solutions to how feminists may justify their knowledge of power relations. The deconstruction of 'woman'/'man' and interrogations of the constitution of gendered/knowing subjects will remain a useful step in clarifying how feminists make knowledge claims, but will not produce knowledge of gendered lives. Our understanding is always limited, but taking transformation seriously means taking responsibility for our own entanglements in power relations. As we make knowledge claims, our experience is always limited, so the experiences of others can disrupt our own acceptance of invisibly familiar norms as natural or general. Being explicit about how we make our feminist epistemic communities, and making our dependence on them both open and open to question, compels us to clarify and justify what we think we know.

Feminists are not authorised to speak for women simply because they are women, or politically committed to gender equality. Yet producing knowledge of gender relations remains both politically urgent and epistemologically problematic. We have argued for making space to attend to epistemological (and other) challenges to feminist knowledge claims, without losing the moral responsibility of responding to the political urgency of unjust and dangerous social relations of gender, and examination of the interaction of other relations of power with those of gender.

Feminists should continue to investigate gendered lives and power relations, (including women's exercise of power) if we are to be able to grasp what people's lives are like across our differences. We can both make our epistemic communities and our criteria of validity explicit and also show how we are accountable for the knowledge we produce and our judgements between knowledge claims. Feminists need not claim any general position of epistemological privilege in order to argue that some stories of gender relations are better than others.

Notes

1   Thanks to Heather Brunskell for discussion of these problems.
2   Nancy Fraser suggests that while Judith Butler expresses normative commitments against exclusions and for anti-racism, her work (in *Gender Trouble* (Butler 1990) and *Bodies that Matter* (Butler 1993)) does not help feminists 'to map the links among various discrete, discursive regimes and thus to theorize the construction of hegemony' (Fraser 1995:162–163). She argues that Butler overestimates the 'emancipatory potential' of gender-bending performative possibilities in everyday life and underestimates the possibilities for depoliticising them.
3   Haraway comments:

> immortality and omnipotence are not our goals. But we could use some enforceable, reliable accounts of things not reducible to power moves and agonistic, high status games of rhetoric or to scientistic, positivist arrogance. This point applies whether we are talking about genes, social classes, elementary particles, genders, races, or texts; the point applies to the exact, natural, social and human sciences, despite the slippery ambiguities of the words *objectivity* and *science* as we

slide around the discursive terrain. In our efforts to climb the greased pole leading to a usable doctrine of objectivity, I and most other feminists in the objectivity debates have alternatively, or even simultaneously, held on to both ends of the dichotomy, which Harding describes in terms of successor science projects versus postmodernist accounts of difference and I have sketched in this chapter as radical constructivism versus feminist critical empiricism. It is, of course, hard to climb when you are holding on to both ends of a pole, simultaneously or alternately.

(1991: 188)

4   Hammersley and Gomm examine the problem of how we decide what is true/untrue once we can no longer appeal to a neutral notion of 'science' (1997: 5.3, 5.4). This is a problem that has always confronted feminism, but Hammersley and Gomm oppose emancipatory research (of which they take feminism as an example) to 'the pursuit of scientific knowledge'. This enables them to label feminist research as biased in ways that the proper pursuit of truth should not be (1997: 5.4). They argue that, to the extent to which researchers with emancipatory goals

> redefine the goal of enquiry as the promotion of some practical or political cause, we see them as sources of motivated bias and believe that they must be resisted by social researchers. They threaten to destroy the operation of the research communities on which the pursuit of scientific knowledge necessarily depends.
>
> (1997: 5.4)

This 'booming voice of reason' (Temple 1997: 5.1) comes from their attempt to specify an academic epistemic community which can regulate what may or may not be claimed as true accounts of social existence. Feminists need not redefine the pursuit of truth as the promotion of political ends but, by exposing the politics of validation in *any* pursuit of truth, they are helping to make the nature and politics of epistemic communities clearer.

5   Dorothy Smith says:

> The notion of "actual" in my writing is like the arrow on the map of the mall saying "You are here", that points in the text to a beyond-the-text in which the text, its reading, its reader, and its concepts also *are*. It is, so to speak, where we live and where discourse happens and does its constituting of "reality" (1997: 393).

bell hooks has noted actual exclusionary practices in that, while the work of white feminists can be accepted as 'theory', the work of working-class women and women of colour is treated as 'experiential' (McDowell 1995: 106), leading McDowell to question how the privileging of theory contributes to exclusion.

References

Alcoff, L. and Potter, E. (1993) *Feminist Epistemologies*, London: Routledge.

Assiter, A. (1996) *Enlightened Women: Modernist Feminism in a Postmodern Age*, London: Routledge.

Bell, V. (1991) 'Feminism, Foucault and the Desexualisation of Rape', *International Journal of Sociology of Law* 19: 83–100.

Benhabib, S., Butler, J., Cornell, D. and Fraser, N. (1995) *Feminist Contentions: A Philosophical Exchange*, London: Routledge.

Braidotti, R. (1991) *Patterns of Dissonance: A Study of Women in Contemporary Philosophy*, Cambridge: Polity Press.

Butler, J. (1990) *Gender Trouble: Feminism and the Subversion of Identity*, London: Routledge.

—— (1992) 'Contingent Foundations: Feminism and the Question of "Postmodernism"', in J. Butler and J.W. Scott (eds) *Feminists Theorize the Political*, London: Routledge.

—— (1993) *Bodies That Matter: On the Discursive Limits of 'Sex'*, London: Routledge.

Code, L. (1987) *Epistemic Responsibility*, Hanover, N.H.: University Press of New England.

—— (1991) *What Can She Know? Feminist Theory and the Construction of Knowledge*, Ithaca, N.Y.: Cornell University Press.

Collins, P. Hill (1990) *Black Feminist Thought: Knowledge, Consciousness and the Politics of Empowerment*, London: HarperCollins Academic.

Elam, D. (1994) *Feminism and Deconstruction: Ms en Abyme*, London: Routledge.

Fraser, N. (1995) 'Pragmatism, Feminism and the Linguistic Turn' in S. Benhabib, J. Butler, D. Cornell and N. Fraser *Feminist Contentions: A Philosophical Exchange*, London: Routledge.

Gatens, M. (1991) *Feminism and Philosophy: Perspectives on Difference and Equality*, Cambridge: Polity Press.

Grant, J. (1993) *Fundamental Feminism: Testing the Core Concepts of Feminist Theory*, London: Routledge.

Griffiths, M. (1995) *Feminisms and the Self: The Web of Identity*, London: Routledge.

Hammersley, M. and Gomm, R. (1997) 'Bias in Social Research', *Sociological Research Online* 2, 1 (http://www.socresonline.org.uk/socresonline/2/1/2.html)

Haraway, D.J. (1989) *Primate Visions: Gender, Race and Nature in the World of Modern Science*, London: Routledge.

—— (1991) *Simians, Cyborgs and Women: The Reinvention of Nature*, London: Free Association Books.

Harding, S. (1991) *Whose Science? Whose Knowledge?: Thinking From Women's Lives*, Milton Keynes, England: Open University Press.

Hartsock, N.C.M. (1997) 'Comment on Hekman's "Truth and method: feminist standpoint theory revisited": Truth or Justice?', *Signs* 22, 2: 367–374.

Hawkesworth, M. (1989) 'Knowers, Knowing, Known: Feminist Theory and Claims of Truth', *Signs* 14, 3: 533–557.

Hawthorne, S. (1996) 'From Theories of Indifference to a Wild Politics', in D. Bell and R. Klein (eds) *Radically Speaking: Feminism Reclaimed*, London: Zed Books.

Hekman, S. (1997) 'Truth and Method: Feminist Standpoint Theory Revisited', *Signs* 22, 2: 341–365.

Holland, J., Ramazanoglu, C., Sharpe, S. and Thomson, R. (1992) 'Pleasure, Pressure and Power: Some Contradictions of Gendered Sexuality', *Sociological Review* 40, 4: 645–674.

—— (1994) 'Power and Desire: The Embodiment of Female Sexuality', *Feminist Review* 46: 21–38.

—— (1998) *The Male in the Head: Young People, Heterosexuality and Power*, London: Tufnell Press.

Kelly, L. and McWilliams, M. (1997) 'Taking on the Dinosaurs: Liz Kelly Interviews Monica Mcwilliams about Women's Political Involvement in the Northern Ireland Peace Process', *Trouble and Strife* 35: 7–15.

Lennon, K. and Whitford, M. (eds) (1994) *Knowing the Difference: Feminist Perspectives in Epistemology*, London: Routledge.

Lugones, M.C. and Spelman, E.V. (1995) 'Have We Got a Theory for You! Theory, Cultural Imperialism and the Demand for the "Woman's Voice"', in N. Tuana and R. Tong (eds) *Feminism and Philosophy: Essential Readings in Theory, Reinterpretation and Application*, Oxford: Westview Press.

McDowell, D. (1995) 'Transferences: Black Feminist Discourse: The "Practice" of Theory' in D. Elam and R. Weigman (eds) *Feminism Beside Itself*, London: Routledge.

Nelson, L. Hankinson (1993) 'Epistemological Communities', in L. Alcoff and E. Potter (1993) *Feminist Epistemologies*, London: Routledge.

Ramazanoglu, C. (1995) 'Back to Basics: Heterosexuality, Biology and Why Men Stay on Top', in M. Maynard and J. Purvis (eds) *(Hetero)sexual Politics*, London: Taylor and Francis.

—— (1998) 'Saying Goodbye to Emancipation? Where Lyotard Leaves Feminism and Where Feminists Leave Lyotard', in C. Rojek and B. Turner (eds) *The Politics of Jean-François Lyotard*, London: Routledge.

Riley, D. (1988) *'Am I That Name?': Feminism and the Category of 'Women' in History*, London: Macmillan.

Sawhney, S. (1995) 'Authenticity is Such a Drag!', in D. Elam and R. Weigman (eds) *Feminism Beside Itself*, London: Routledge.

Scott, J.W. (1992) 'Experience', in J. Butler and J.W. Scott (eds) *Feminists Theorize the Political*, London: Routledge.

Smith, D.E. (1997) 'Comment on Hekman's "Truth and Method": Feminist Standpoint Theory Revisited', *Signs* 22, 2: 392–398.

Soper, K (1990) *Troubled Pleasures: Writings on Politics, Gender and Hedonism*, London: Verso.

Stanley, L (ed.) (1997) *Knowing Feminisms: On Academic Borders, Territories and Tribes*, London: Sage.

Temple, B. (1997) '"Collegial Accountability" and Bias: The Solution or the Problem?', *Sociological Research Online* 2, 4 (http://www.socresonline.org.uk/socresonline/2/4/8.html).

Winkler, C. (with K.Wininger) (1994) 'Rape Trauma: Contexts of Meaning', in T. Csordas (ed.) *Embodiment and Experience: The Existential Ground of Culture and Self*, Cambridge: Cambridge University Press.

13 Techno-triumphalism, techno-tourism, American dreams and feminism[1]

Maureen McNeil

A tale of two visits

In 1966 I boarded a Greyhound Bus in Toronto for an almost three-day journey. I was bound for Florida to stay with my aunt who was estranged from my Catholic family, in part because she had married a divorced man. In recent years I have joked that this trip was my family's attempt to get rid of me. It does seem extraordinary in this age of increased Western awareness of the dangers facing (certain) children and young women, that my parents would send me off with little money, on a trip which involved stopovers in bus stations in some very rough parts of the USA, to arrive more than two days later, after midnight, at the other end of North America, to meet a relative no family member had seen for about five years! But I was a would-be itinerant worker, going to the gold-rush land and boomtowns around Cape Canaveral for summer work. My parents' endorsement of this adventure perhaps came because of their own background as migrant workers, from working-class families in a chronically economically depressed part of Canada: my mother had travelled from Cape Breton, Nova Scotia, to Boston to be a domestic servant; my father went to Europe in the armed services during World War II; then they both moved to Toronto, seeking employment. For them my trip was not extraordinary.

As it turned out, I got more than I bargained for in Florida, but I did not get a job. My parents' and my own hopes that I would make my fortune, or at least earn my keep for the next year of high school, were thwarted by the lack of public transport, crucial because my aunt and uncle (like so many others in that area) lived in an isolated trailer park. There were, however, other compensations. I walked onto what seemed to be the set of an American soap opera that, to use a 1960s phrase, 'blew my mind'! My aunt had constructed a new, much younger identity for herself, in which I quickly became complicit as I learned not to choke or protest as she referred to her younger sister (my mother) as her older sister. My new-found uncle worked at 'the Cape' (as it was called). A union man, he was handsome, with a macho veneer. Despite the bravado, I thought he was a gentle guy – Jimmy Dean meets Ricky Nelson (an American pop singer of that era), and he had at least one former wife. His sister was what I would now identify as an Imelda Marcos figure: she had a wall full of shoes. But more significantly for this chapter, she was secretary to the deputy director of NASA.[2] The scandal which was the buzz when I arrived revolved around her daughter who was having an affair (this was the first time that I had knowingly met someone who was having one) with one of the foremen at the Cape. Then two trailers down, there was Vicki-the-writer: she was my lifeline, providing me with a steady, if eclectic, stream of reading material. This included detective fiction, *The Complete Works of William Shakespeare*, as well as *The Art of Loving* by Erich Fromm. (My aunt was convinced that Fromm's text was a dirty, that is, pornographic, book.) There was also my uncle's nephew, who looked like a character (albeit a somewhat chubby one) from the popular 1960s American television programme *77 Sunset Strip*. He was well equipped for the part, with his convertible and his slick-back hair. He was the only single man I met that summer and, rather predictably, I fell in love with him. After all, he had been a member of the Green Berets[3] and he was my only reliable source of transport – taking me to mass (the drive-in cinema served as a Catholic church on Sundays mornings) and to drive-in restaurants. He also worked at the Cape.

I spent much of that summer fantasising about my hoped-for romance, deciphering the complexities of my aunt's new family and unpacking her fabrications about her old one, eating chocolate fudge ice-cream, learning how to cook (American style) fried chicken, and devouring Shakespeare, Fromm and other less savoury texts provided by Vicki. The official high-point of my visit came when my aunt's sister-in-law managed to get me a ticket to watch the Gemini II launch[4] from the official viewing stands. I wrote some very bad poetry after that, waxing unlyrical about all things American. It is perhaps not surprising that men and rockets figured prominently in that poetry: but there was no reference to my real American love – chocolate fudge ice-cream.

Almost twenty-four years later, in spring 1990, I returned to visit my aunt and uncle during a year spent as a visiting professor at a small liberal arts college in Pennsylvania. By now my aunt and uncle were integrated into my family, my aunt having finally 'come out' as an older woman. Although this was again a family visit, I would probably have been classified as a tourist – coming, in part, to visit the now well-established tourist sites of the EPCOT Center at Disney World, Orlando, Florida; and NASA's Spaceport, USA, at the John F. Kennedy Space Center. Ironically, although I passed as a tourist, this was also a work trip: I wanted to observe, reflect on and write about these sites of technological tourism.

Although bits of my aunt's neighbourhood were vaguely familiar, this was a very different world from the one I had visited twenty-four years previously. Fortuitously and bizarrely, many of the same characters reappeared: the sister-in-law had retired from her NASA post and was living again with a rich, reactionary former husband. I did not check out her shoe wardrobe, but an estate in New York State and a big house and boat in Florida indicated that her consumption proclivities had continued apace. Her daughter, now installed in what I suspected was a truly boring marriage, made a brief appearance. Only Vicki-the-writer and the would-be-lover nephew were missing. The aura of boomtown and gold rush was gone: my aunt and uncle were ageing and marginal figures, without medical coverage, dependent on family benevolence and living in the shadow of more prosperous days. I saw them now as victims of American capitalism and managing in straitened circumstances, despite the stinginess of the US State and its wealthy citizens. In my returning incarnation, I was a much more suspicious, cynical character. Critical of heterosexuality, I was, nevertheless, still susceptible to its snares: I was recovering from recent episodes of non-romantic heterosexuality with lefty Brits – so-called 'new men' – whose escapades cast ex-members of the Green Berets in a rather positive light. The development of the Cape and the age of NASA and military boom had left its mark on the region but had clearly stopped. The future of NASA was shaky and the subject of considerable public debate: could the fragile US economy afford its extravagance? The focus of development in the region had shifted to another kind of gold-rush site – Orlando and Disney World. This time I did not want to write poetry; I wanted to write critiques of all things American, particularly its science and technology, from a feminist perspective.

For my return visit there was no privileged access to official viewing stands to gaze amazed at American technological achievement and to marvel at the prospect of a technological adventure. I joined the masses and made my trek as something of a 'post-pilgrim' (Urry 1990) to two key shrines to technological achievement. In 1966 bus tours of the Kennedy Space Center were introduced and by 1990, when I returned to this part of Florida, Spaceport USA was a full-blown tourist site, consisting of a museum – the Gallery of Spaceflight – the Galaxy Center with theatres, exhibitions and an IMAX cinema, a Rocket Garden, the requisite gift shop and cafeteria – the Gift Gantry, the Orbit Cafeteria and Lunch Pad – and bus tours of the massive site. I also ventured to the region's new boomtown – Disney World – and I joined the crowds flocking to the EPCOT (Experimental Prototype Community of Tomorrow) Center. The full name is easily and often forgotten, which is just as well, since the acronym refers to the residential community of Walt Disney's dreams and not to the realised EPCOT site (Zukin 1991: 224–225).[5] When it opened in October 1982, EPCOT had two components – *Future World* (the Disney exposition of technolog-ical progress realised through corporate America[6]) and *World Showcase* (a Disney gesture to multiculturalism and global diversity[7]). Disney World, the most popular tourist site in the world, the paean to American middle-class white culture and values thus *incorporates* (literally, given the corporate sponsorship and perspective which sustains it[8]) an exposition of technoscientific progress. The play-off between the two sites is between, on the one hand, technology, progress, and conformity in *Future World* and, on the other hand, the gestures towards representations of diversity and its packaged, tamed exoticisation in the *World Showcase*.

Reflections on two sets of adventures in techno-wonderland, Florida

My narrative thus far has been constructed as a narrative of transformations, some of which were made explicit while others remained implicit: from travel for work to tourism, class mobility, from the Cold War to the New World Order, the transformations wrought by capitalism and consumerism, transformations of identity, technological transformations, and, most important for this volume, the transformations of feminism. This is part of a larger project, but in this chapter I concentrate on the last two axes of transformation – technological transformations and the transformations of feminism.

Nevertheless, it is crucial to note the particular setting of my story. This part of Florida has been, since the 1960s, a major site for the construction and dissemination of certain kinds of 'American dreams'. That is, it has been a site for the articulation of the dreams of certain kinds of Americans – white, middle-class, heterosexual Americans – and the realisation (of their representational form) through technological development and material transformations. This area of Florida has experienced major technological transformations, beginning with the thousands of acres of swamp 'reclaimed' for Disney World. Technological triumphalism, faith in corporate America, investment in the nuclear family, endorsement of heterosexist hegemony, and a racist insistence on the civilising mission of white, middle-class America are the stuff that built this sight. A NASA pamphlet, which I brought back as a souvenir of my original visit, made this clear: 'The area was inhabited by primitive Indians as early as 2000 B.C. … American colonization began about 1821 … During the construction of the Spaceport, Indian burial mounds and numerous relics of these eras were discovered and preserved' (NASA n.d. (a)). This imperialist mission was also apparent in the commentary of Dr Charles Fairbanks of the University of Florida quoted in a booklet on the Spaceport (from about 1966): 'This was one of the areas where Western civilization came to the New World, and now it is the area from which our civilization will go forth to other worlds' (NASA n.d. (b)).

I have to limit my exploration of this rich territory and I shall do this by focusing on the figure of me viewing technoscientific spectacle. After watching the Gemini space launch from the official viewing stands at Cape Canaveral, I wrote poetry which circulated clichés about this wonderful opportunity, about witnessing 'history in the making'. When I returned to that site in 1990, I participated with thousands of others in a much more dispersed collective witnessing of the triumphs of American technoscience. There were at least four differences between these opportunities for homage to technology which I can highlight. First, my 1990 visit to Spaceport USA inserted me into a carefully engineered, 'mass' experience, in contrast to my exclusive observer status (even if I secured my pass by happenstance) in the 1960s. Second, the dimensions of the techno-logical witnessing during my second visit were much more elaborate and extended. Furthermore, my second encounter with technological achievement in this part of Florida required extensive technological intervention to create the spectacle or sense of awe. The IMAX cinema and film and the 'person movers' rides/shows (such as 'Body Wars') at EPCOT were characteristic of these facilitating devices. In 1966, I simply stood on the stands and viewed the spectacle through 'my naked eyes'. Finally, I saw the display of technological triumph differently in my second visit because of my critical feminist perspective. This brings me to two reflective interludes, which I will title 'Women watching I: viewing the spectacle of technoscience' and 'Women watching II: feminist views of technoscience'.

Women watching I: viewing the spectacle of technoscience

This section of this chapter was inspired by Donna Haraway's apposite comment: 'Women lost their security clearances very early in the stories of leading-edge science' (1997: 29). She explains that women have historically been denied the status of legitimised 'witnesses' of science.[9] This generalisation has been fleshed out in a stream of feminist and feminist-influenced scholarship (including Barbara Ehrenreich and Deirdre English's 1970s pamphlets (1973a, 1973b) on witchcraft and midwifery, Caroline Merchant's (1980) and Brian Easlea's (1980) crucial investigations of the foundations of modern science, Margaret Rossiter's two-volume charting of women in science in the USA (1982, 1995) and David Noble's graphically titled *World Without Women* (1992)). Nevertheless, I want to linger on the image of women's *watching* rather than *witnessing* the spectacles which have constituted technoscience. I want to muse on the fact that I *was* given security clearance and on the many women, men, and children who, since 1982, have eagerly bought passes (passports, clearances) into the EPCOT Center.

There has been a preoccupation with vision in much feminist analysis of science and technology – interrogating 'the male gaze' and the ways in which science facilitates and effectively becomes the watching of women (Haraway 1992; Keller 1992; Jordanova 1989; Cartwright 1995). Invoking the instances cited above of me and other women viewing the spectacles of technoscience, I would suggest that this rather different trope could be an interesting field for feminist exploration. Here I shall mention a few moments that illustrate the terrain for such research.

Donna Haraway refers to Elizabeth Potter's reading of Robert Boyle's seventeenth-century text, *New Experiments Physico-Mechanical, touching the Spring of the Air*, which describes experiments with air-pumps and provides an account of a demonstration attended by upper-class women which involved the evacuation of the air in a chamber containing birds that were killed by the process. These women interrupted the experiments, demanding that air be let in to rescue the birds. Boyle reported that in order to facilitate such experiments, the men decided to assemble at night thereby avoiding female disruption (Haraway 1997: 31).

Joseph Wright of Derby's 1767–68 painting *Experiment with a bird in the air-pump* shows women and children observing a male experimenter. There have been diverse interpretations of this painting which I shall not explore at this point. However, the painting does seem to convey both the interest and the unease amongst the female observers.

There is the related apocryphal story of the debate between Bishop Samuel Wilberforce and Thomas Henry Huxley on Darwinian theory, held on 30 June 1860 at the Oxford meeting of the British Association for the Advancement of Science. This is widely regarded as a key moment in the history of science, not least because, as one commentator has noted, 'No encounter between science and religion has been more often described' (Moore 1979: 60). In the midst of this gentlemanly clash, a lady fainted and was carried off.

These are diverse representations of women observing the spectacle of science. Two of these representations are apocryphal narratives about women's excessive bodily reactions to the spectacle of science which resulted in men banishing them from – carrying them off – the stage of science. At least two of these representations exemplify women's disqualification as potential 'modest witnesses' of science. There is much which could be investigated about these representations. It would be interesting to explore *which women* have been permitted such viewing, *in which circumstances* and *which women* do *not* get a 'look in'. So, for example, class privilege was crucial in each of the instances considered above. Related to this, some important research is now being done on heterosexual coupledom and daughterhood in providing entrees into science for some women (Abir-Am and Outram 1989).

In highlighting the figure of women watching science I intend more than a call for new research. Behind my cursory explorations is the claim that these moments are crucial in the making of science and in the making of gender differences. Hence, the figure of the woman viewing technoscientific spectacles must be juxtaposed with that other key figure – 'the modest witness' of science.

This figure has emerged in recent science studies and cultural studies of technoscience, invoked by Steven Shapin and Simon Schaffer in their much lauded-book *Leviathan and the Air-Pump: Hobbes, Boyle, and the Experimental Life* (1985). Shapin and Schaffer contend that the foundations for modern science were established in the seventeenth-century through Robert Boyle's pivotal role within three constitutive technologies:

> a *material technology* embedded in the construction and operation of the air-pump; a *literary technology* by means of which the phenomena produced by the pump were made known by those who were not direct witnesses; and a *social technology* that incorporated the conventions experimental philosophers should use in dealing with each other and considering knowledge claims.
>
> (Shapin and Schaffer 1985: 25)

Experimental philosophy spread through and with these material practices: these were the apparatuses for the production of what could count as scientific knowledge. As Donna Haraway explains, these 'three technologies, metonymically integrated into the air-pump itself, the neutral instrument, factored out human agency from the product' (1997: 25). The gentleman natural philosopher (subsequently, the scientist) emerges as the 'modest witness' in these practices. He (but more specifically, generally, a white, European, upper- or middle-class male) is 'the legitimate and authorized ventriloquist for the object world, adding nothing from his mere opinions, his biasing embodiment' with 'the remarkable power to establish the facts' (Haraway 1997: 24). His is the 'culture of no culture', as Sharon Traweek (1988) has memorably noted. As Haraway contends: 'His narratives have a magical power – they lose all trace of their history as stories, as products of partisan projects, as contestable representations, or as constructed documents in their potent capacity to define the facts' (1997: 24). The 'modest witness' effects a strict division between the technical and the political.

The construction of the genealogy of the 'modest witness' is a valuable contribution to science studies. Shapin and Shaffer have highlighted the politically and socially constructed nature of the Scientific Revolution. They are good at showing its class components, if ineffectual in dealing with its gender dimensions (Haraway 1997: 23–39). But the figures of 'excessive women' viewing the spectacle of technoscience illustrated in my narrative of technological adventures in Florida, and in the apocryphal representations of out-of-control women watching science in the making, must be added to this picture. I am suspicious about the *modesty* of the witnessing and would like to blow open the questions of by whom and where science is made. Moreover, I am deeply sceptical about origin stories – even *progressive* origin stories (as Shapin and Schaffer's appears to be). The modesty of the witnessing has always required another kind of watching and another kind of story that was much less modest – embodied in popular observations of spectacles of technological triumph and in tales of technological wonder. In fact, I would claim that the promise of technological progress lies hidden behind the documentation of the observations and experiments of the modest witness. The modesty of the scientific gentleman in the experimental mode as the 'ventriloquist of nature' can only be sustained by a more popular and far more excessive relationship to technological promise. As Haraway observes: 'Dazzling promise has always been the underside of the deceptively sober pose of scientific rationality and modern progress within the culture of no culture' (1997: 41).

Implicit in my proposed reconstruction is the contention that the *making* of science is a much more dispersed activity than even its more progressive storytellers would have us believe. This contention challenges the exclusivity of those who identify themselves as legitimate (legitimised) makers of science and questions the modesty of their witnessing. Moreover, this involves taking the term *techno*science, which has currency in recent science studies and cultural studies of science, seriously.

Women watching II: feminist views

I want now to switch my attention to another kind of viewing of technoscience – the meta-viewing which has yielded feminist perspectives on technoscience.

While the first part of this chapter proposes the foregrounding of the female viewer, the second part of my project examines the feminist viewer and feminist views of technoscience.

From the 1970s through the 1990s feminism provided me with an alternative vantage point. The transformed 'me' who returned to Florida in 1990 saw the world 'through feminist eyes'. I want to play out the metaphors and explore the experiential, as well as the cognitive dimensions of this apparent transformation. When I returned I was much more distanced and detached. In fact, I toured both EPCOT and Spaceport, USA, on my own, acutely aware of being outside of the nuclear family and the heterosexual couple. Nevertheless, I was mindful that the real outsiders were the ones who did not get through the gates – those marginalised in and by the American dreams generated and mobilised at these sites.[10] But there was a further dimension to my distance: I had deliberately and self-consciously taken a *critical distance* from the technological triumphalism, the celebratory tone, the worship of the corporate sponsored and state-sanctioned American visions of progress which were the preferred messages on offer there.

I will label my vantage point – the platform from which I viewed EPCOT and Spaceport, USA – as 'feminist science critique'. Pursuing the theme of vision, I would say that I felt that my new viewing stand facilitated a *clearer* vision. I was convinced that I was able, through the tools provided by feminism (and other critical frameworks), to see more of the picture of what science and technology really were. But there were other dimensions to that clarity. It required detachment and distance – a kind of standing above.[11] In addition, there was an emotional dimension to it – a kind of standing alone – what Elspeth Probyn (1996) might call an 'outside belongings', that was both pleasurable and painful.

I have been sketching the way in which feminism transformed my view of technoscience. This was a view from outside and it depended on its outsider status: the mode of ideological critique provided an alternative vantage point. I would propose that there were at least three problems around this approach. First, like all forms of ideological critique, feminist critiques of science had an elitist dimension, embodying some version of the claim 'I can see what the masses cannot see.' The political tension about this elitism has haunted much feminist analysis from the 1960s to the 1990s.[12] Second, such a critique involved highly rationalistic politics which ignored emotional investments, identifications, pleasure, etc. Finally, in many respects, it was a rather pessimistic politics.

In global historical terms, the ground was shifting beneath my feet when I made that trip in 1990: my viewing stand was being dismantled. There are many 'world' events that occurred in 1989–90 to which I can refer: the destruction of the Berlin Wall, the transformations in eastern Europe, the release of Nelson Mandela, and so on. More locally (this refers to my daily life, not geographical location), the *mode* of feminist critique of science was itself being reconsidered. Fresh perspectives were informing feminist thinking about science (including, most notably, Donna Haraway's 'Cyborg Manifesto' (1992[1985])) and these were shaking the foundations of feminism's viewing stand. Developments on the international political scene, poststructuralism and postmodernism, changes within feminism, and other developments were blurring the picture, disrupting the clarity of vision. I became far less sure of where I stood.

Since then there have been two predominant feminist strategies for getting things in focus around technoscience which I shall consider briefly: advocacy of a feminist 'successor science' and cyberfeminism.[13] The feminist 'successor science' project, as discussed by Sandra Harding (1991: 295–312) and others involves attempts to reform the practices and principles of the established natural sciences in the wake of feminist critiques. Cyberfeminism, in its 1990s incarnation, revolves around the figure of the cyborg – the hybrid of machine and organism – and is influenced by cybernetic theory. It posits a continuity between animals and machines which can be studied through the overarching framework of systems theory. In Britain, Sadie Plant (1997) has been the predominant exponent of cyberfeminism. In Plant's version of cyberfeminism the symbiosis between a distinctively feminine mode of rationality and changes associated with information technology holds out the promise of the defeat of patriarchy.

The attraction of these two feminist projects has been, I suspect, that they provide new vantage points and positive strategies for feminists in contemporary engagements with technoscience. In contrast to feminist science critiques, the advocates of these approaches are much more up front about the *attractions* of technoscience. In the case of feminist successor sciences, this has been expressed through orientation around the pursuit of objectivity and a reworked version of the Enlightenment project of progress through scientific knowledge (Harding 1991). For cyberfeminism this takes the form of enthusiasm for technological change associated with recent developments in information technology and its spin-offs.

There is much that could be said about the strengths and weaknesses of these particular feminist technologies of revisioning technoscience. Whilst acknowledging their appeal, I am also mindful of the limitations of these strategies. To me, the prospect of a feminist 'successor science' has always seemed a limited and limiting revisioning in its acceptance of various aspects of science-as-it-is. Moreover, given the entrenchment of establishment technoscience, the prospects for the realisation of a feminist successor science – of a science altered in response to feminist criticisms – seem at best, remote.

Despite its widespread appeal, cyberfeminism has come under critical feminist scrutiny (Squires 1996; Adam 1997). Judith Squires is unequivocal in her assessment, describing it as

> the distorted fantasy of those so cynical of traditional political strategies, so bemused by the complexity of social materiality, and so bound up in the rhetoric of space-flows of information technology, that they have forgotten both the exploitative and alienating potential of technology and retreated into the celebration of essential, though disembodied, woman.
>
> (1996: 209–210)

I share many of Squires's reservations about cyberfeminism. It worries me because of its naturalisation of gender differences, its ahistorical, rosy picture of both technology and women and its denial of the need for political struggle. It assumes that technological change – particularly in information technology – will guarantee increased power for women. Holding out the promise of a feminist technological fix, cyberfeminism is messianic in its vision.

Despite my dissatisfactions, rather than dismissing these movements within feminist politics of technoscience I prefer to reflect about their appeal. I regard these new feminist viewing stands as constructions resulting from important reactions to the pessimism of feminist ideological critiques of science and technology. Moreover, they have been fuelled by a democratic impulse to give feminist perspectives on technoscience a much wider appeal.

The feminist fascination with prospects for a 'successor science' and with cyberfeminism also seems to be a reaction to the distancing characteristic of feminist science critiques. But both these solutions are much too neat for me: as I see it, as feminists we are simultaneously both *within* and *outside* of technoscience. As I have tried to evoke in my opening narratives, technoscience permeates our quotidian life-stories. Nevertheless it is very difficult to deal with this tension between critique and enmeshment.

While some feminists have been lured by the attractions of being either outsiders or insiders to technoscience, some of the most effective recent feminist commentators in this field have employed striking visual metaphors to evoke the ambiguity of feminist positionings and to conceptualise technoscience. Donna Haraway's (1992) cyborg is the most popular and widely adopted/adapted figure of this kind.[14] In a related exposition, the feminist anthropologist Emily Martin employs three images, 'the citadel, the rhizome, and the string figure', 'to allow us to picture the discontinuous ways science both permeates and is permeated by cultural life' (1998: 24). Furthermore, in her recent book (1997), Haraway uses the optical metaphor of *diffraction* to designate the yearning for somewhere else, for change, for transformation, whilst living and, as she describes it, often appreciating and admiring technoscience. I would put this somewhat more strongly as yearning for change and transformation, whilst we are implicated in the *making* of technoscience, as it were, as *witnesses* of/to technoscience.

While I welcome these powerful and evocative analyses and images, my concern is about the seduction of the visual: my fear is that we have been much better at playing with the figures than we have been at change in other realms. Perhaps a similar dissatisfaction lies behind Evelyn Fox Keller's reflection that 'feminist theory has helped us to re-vision science as discourse, but not as an agent of change' (1992: 76). Significantly, even in this critical evaluation, the imagery of vision is employed. My reservations can also be illustrated by invoking visual imagery to pose the question: has preoccupation with textual and figurative revisioning allowed us to glaze over the political working through required to transform technoscience? Moreover, there are other questions to be asked, such as: Who shares and can participate in this revisioning? The play with visual imagery comes up against differences in taste and cultural capital, suggesting that there are other stakes involved (e.g. the political strategies of avante-gardism versus other political approaches). Feminists have looked at and conjured 'the male gaze of science', modest (and immodest) witnessing of science, both amazed and critical gazing at technological spectacles, cyborgs, the citadels of technoscience studies, and yearned for diffractions, but there is little indication that technoscience has been politically transformed.

Revisiting and revisioning techno-wonderland, Florida

To return to my title – techno-triumphalism, techno-tourism, American dreams and feminism, this chapter has been about my troubling over and of:

- the relationship between the production (techno-triumphalism) and consumption (techno-tourism) of technoscience and the gendering of this divide
- the attractions and hollowness of '*the* American dream'[15] and American dreams and the relationship between feminist figurations and feminist transformations.

In 1994 I returned to techno-wonderland in Florida. This was during another period spent as a visiting academic – this time in Canada. I had come to Nova Scotia in an identity made possible by feminism, facilitated by the Canadian state education system and financed by the vestiges of this social-democratic, liberal state, as a visiting professor of women's studies from England and, hence, as a very privileged migrant worker. The ironies in this particular transformation were not lost on some members of my Canadian family. Once again I took a trip to Florida, in part, to visit my aunt and uncle. This time, their ageing was noticeable and my uncle had a mouthful of rotten teeth: he had not had any dental coverage or treatment for many years. There was good news on this front, at least, as treatment was imminent, because his rich sister had undertaken to pay for it. I was combining my trip with a holiday with friends. They were coming to Florida for a conference and for the first time in my life I was a tourist of academia as I sat in on their conference. It was a management studies conference and the event disillusioned me about the use and abuse of one piece of technology – overhead projectors. The mode of our subsequent holiday was much more postmodernist than that of my preceding visits: we did 'the nature trip' to the Everglades and we didn't quite cruise in that most postmodernist of locales – Miami Beach. When I go to EPCOT Center I am told that much of the site is to be transformed, with new and more exciting attractions. When I go to Spaceport, USA, I am mindful of new USA–Russia technological collaborations: the space race has been transformed into extra-terrestrial collaboration. The Toronto *Globe and Mail* had described this new phase of space exploration a few weeks before my visit in the following way: 'The U.S. shuttle Discovery blasted off at dawn yesterday with a Russian Cosmonaut aboard, opening a new space age free of Cold War rivalry. It's ... the first time that astronauts and cosmonauts have been launched in the same spaceship' (4 February

1994: 1). How am I to see this new technoscientific panorama? How might we, as feminists, transform it?

Notes

1 I am conscious of the linguistic appropriation of the adjective 'American' involved in its exclusive association with the USA, rather than with the plethora of nations and peoples who could legitimately identify with this label. However, for the purposes of this chapter, I am deliberately invoking the narrow, conventional usage of the term, as referring to all things associated with the USA.
2 The National Aeronautics and Space Agency was established as a civilian agency of the US government on 1 October 1958 'to carry out the peaceful exploration and use of space' (NASA 1992: 2).
3 Green Berets were the markers of the men who fought in the most renowned American regiment during the Vietnam War.
4 The USA manned space flights through the NASA programme were organised into three sequential series of 'missions' from 1958 to 1981: Mercury, Gemini and Apollo. It was Apollo missions which landed men on the moon for the first time in 1969.
5 In fact, the model community that Walt Disney first proposed has now been established on the Orlando site. It is called 'Celebration'.
6 The wording of this phrase is deliberately dualistic in its reference to both the site which was realised 'through corporate America' and to 'the vision of progress' on offer which is constructed as the product of corporate America (Bryman 1995: 106, 130, 145–149).
7 William F. Van Wert describes the World Showcase as 'a world zoo of different cultures' (1995–96: 200).
8 As Van Wert suggests, EPCOT displays

> both the inadequacies of the past and the large corporation that is *already* seeing to our needs in the future … The House of Energy ends in Exxon … The Story of the Land and Harvest comes to us courtesy of Kraft.
>
> (1995–96: 203)

Many of the corporate sponsors of exhibits at Future World (e.g. Bell Telephone, Exxon, General Motors, Eastman Kodak, Kraft Food Products) had been sponsors of pavilions at the 1939 World's Fair at Flushing Meadows, New York (Zukin 1991: 227).
9 Donna Haraway draws here on the terminology of Steven Shapin and Simon Schaffer (1985), who describe the practices of modern science emerging from the practices associated with the experimental spectacle and figure of 'the modest witness' who observes the natural world. See below.
10 Alan Bryman (1995: 92, 129) observes, as I did, that the clientele is overwhelmingly white, middle-class American families.
11 I have noted that many commentators writing about Disney theme parks discuss their relationship to the attractions in terms of 'distancing' themselves (or not) from the 'mass' pleasures on offer at such sites. Michael Billig explicitly frames this in terms of ideology critique:

> Any writer who wishes to criticize the Disney phenomenon has a problem: what sort of tone, and indeed literary form, should be adopted? If writers enter into the fun of things, they risk losing the critical edge: the resulting voice will be that of the contented customer. On the other hand, if critical writers stand back from the masses in their millions, then they risk sounding superior. Their voices may

then resonate with disdain, as their prose looks down on the uncultured, unthinking masses, wallowing like pigs in the troughs of superficial pleasures.
(1994: 151)

12 There has been some acknowledgement of this within feminism, but also related debates about the critic's stance on popular culture have emerged in cultural studies. Theodor Adorno's (1991) dismissal of popular music is a significant touchstone in these controversies. Louis Althusser's account of Ideological State Apparatuses (1970) was also influential in conceptualisations of the pervasiveness of ideology that only a few intellectuals could 'see through'. Interestingly, while Michael Billig writes cogently on the tensions around the position of the critic, he tends to assume that feminists have less problem about this – because they deal with misery rather than pleasure (1994: 152).

13 Judith Squires contrasts the views of three key, but very different, 'cyberfeminists' – Shulamith Firestone, Donna Haraway and Sadie Plant: 'Firestone ends *The Dialectic of Sex* with a section called 'Revolutionary Demands'. Haraway writes her Manifesto to find political direction in the 1980s; Plant, writing in Major's anti-political 1990s, has no sense of political project at all' (1996: 209). In considering here the cyberfeminism of the 1990s, Firestone does not figure in my assessment. Although the feminist cyborg figure originates with Haraway's *Cyborg Manifesto* (1992[1985]), I would contend that her approach to technoscience cannot be reduced to cyberfeminism.

14 Martin draws on Haraway's (1994) exploration of critical science studies through the metaphor of the game of cat's cradle.

15 The phrase 'the American dream' refers to the possibility of self-realisation through meritocracy: the myth that unlimited possibilities of political freedom and economic success are available to all regardless of 'race', ethnicity, class, gender or religion.

References

Abir-Am, P.G. and Outram, D. (eds) (1989) *Uneasy Careers and Intimate Lives: Women in Science*, New Brunswick, N.J. and London: Rutgers University Press.

Adam, A. (1997) 'What Should We Do with Cyberfeminism?', in R. Lander and A. Adam (eds) *Women into Computing: Progress from Where to What?*, Exeter: Intellect.

Adorno, T.W. (1991) *The Culture Industry: Selected Essays on Mass Culture*, edited with introduction by J.M. Bernstein, London: Routledge.

Althusser, L. (1970) 'Ideological State Apparatuses', in *Essays on Lenin and Philosophy*, London: New Left Books.

Billig, M. (1994) 'Sod Baudrillard! Or Ideology Critique in Disney World', in H.W. Simons and M. Billig (eds) *After Postmodernism: Reconstructing Ideology Critique*, London: Sage.

Bryman, A. (1995) *Disney and His Worlds*, New York: Routledge.

Cartwright, L. (1995) *Screening the Body: Tracing Medicine's Visual Culture*, Minneapolis: Minnesota University Press.

Easlea, B. (1980) *Witch-hunting, Magic and the New Philosophy*, Brighton: Harvester.

Ehrenreich, B. and English, D. (1973a) *Complaints and Disorders: The Sexual Politics of Sickness*, Old Westbury, N.Y.: Feminist Press.

—— (1973b) *Witches, Midwives and Nurses: A History of Women Healers*, Old Westbury, N.Y.: Feminist Press.

Fromm, E. (1962) *The Art of Loving*, London: Allen and Unwin.

Haraway, D. (1992[1985]) 'A Cyborg Manifesto: Science, Technology, and Socialist-Feminism in the Late Twentieth Century', in *Simians, Cyborgs, and Women: The Reinvention of Nature*, London: Free Association Books.

—— (1994) 'A Game of Cat's Cradle: Science Studies, Feminist Theory, Cultural Studies', *Configurations* 2, 1: 59–71.

—— (1997) *Modest Witness@Second Millenium.FemaleMan Meets OcoMouse™:Feminsim and Technoscience*, New York and London: Routledge.

Harding, S. (1991) *Whose Science? Whose Knowledge? Thinking from Women's Lives*, Buckingham, England: Open University Press.

Jordanova, L. (1989) *Sexual Visions: Images of Gender in Science and Medicine between the Eighteenth and Twentieth Centuries*, Hemel Hempstead, England: Harvester Wheatsheaf.

Keller, E.F. (1992) *Secrets of Life/Secrets of Death: Essays on Language, Gender and Science*, New York and London: Routledge.

Martin, E. (1998) 'Anthropology and the Cultural Study of Science', *Science, Technology & Human Values*, 23, 1 (Winter): 24–44.

Merchant, C. (1980) *The Death of Nature: Women, Ecology and the Scientific Revolution*, San Francisco, Calif.: Harper and Row.

Moore, J.R. (1979) *The Post-Darwinian Controversies: A Study of the Protestant Struggle to Come to Terms with Darwin in Great Britain and America 1870–1900*, Cambridge: Cambridge University Press.

NASA (n.d. (a)) *John F. Kennedy Space Center: America's Spaceport*.

—— (n.d. (b)) *John F. Kennedy Space Center*.

—— (1992) *NASA Kennedy Space Center's Spaceport USA English Tourbook*.

Noble, D. (1992) *A World without Women: The Christian Clerical Culture of Western Science*, New York: Alfred A. Knopf.

Plant, S. (1997) *Zeros and One: Digital Women and The New Technology*, London: Fourth Estate.

Probyn, E. (1996) *Outside Belongings*, London and New York: Routledge.

Rossiter, M.W. (1982) *Women Scientists in America: Struggles and Strategies to 1940*, Baltimore, Md.: Johns Hopkins University Press.

—— (1995) *Women Scientists in America: Before Affirmative Action 1940–1972*, Baltimore, Md., and London: Johns Hopkins University Press.

Scott, J. (1992) 'Experience', in J. Butler and J.W. Scott (eds) *Feminists Theorize the Political*, New York and London: Routledge.

Shapin, S. and Schaffer, S. (1985) *Leviathan and the Air-Pump: Hobbes, Boyle, and the Experimental Life*, Princeton, N.J.: Princeton University Press.

Squires, J. (1996) 'Fabulous Feminist Futures and the Lure of Cyberculture', in J. Dovey (ed.) *Fractal Dreams: New Media in Social Context*, London: Lawrence and Wishart.

Traweek, S. (1988) *Beamtimes and Lifetimes: The World of High Energy Physics*, Cambridge, Mass.: Harvard University Press.

Urry, J. (1990) *The Tourist Gaze: Leisure and Travel in Contemporary Societies*, London: Sage.

Van Wert, W.F. (1995–6) 'Disney World and Posthistory', *Cultural Critique* Winter: 187–214.

Zukin, S. (1991) *Landscapes of Power: From Detroit to Disney World*, Berkeley and Oxford: University of California Press.

14 Nuclear families

Women's narratives of the making of the atomic bomb

Carol Wolkowitz

This chapter analyses some of the writings of white middle-class women who were involved in the making of the first atomic bombs in the United States during World War II.[1] Addressed mainly to the feminist literature on the relationship between gender, war and science, it will also offer a critical deconstruction of the history of American 'psychic numbing', its longstanding refusal to confront the 'full truth' of Hiroshima and Nagasaki (Lifton and Mitchell 1995: xv; see also Alperovitz 1995; Boyer 1994; Griffin 1994). However, one should not imagine – as these sources tend to imply – that there is a single prevailing version of the story. We need to ask about the range of ways it has been narrativised, and what roles women have played in the telling. In this chapter, I examine how the women's reminiscences serve to document comradeship between women as well as other very positive values, but they rarely try to look at events from outside the perspective of their personal attachments. Consequently, present-day readers may read in them a gender-specific discourse of denial, one shaped partly by the women's own structural relationship to the Manhattan Project. Thus these accounts may say something about impediments to the adoption of a wider, more critical perspective, to our ability to transform or transcend the limitations arising from our own situations.

I have become interested in this story because it is part of my own. During World War II my father, drafted into the American Army, served first as a technician at the University of Chicago, and then in one of the plants in Oak Ridge, Tennessee, where a huge industrial complex was built to separate Uranium-235 from heavier isotopes of U-238. The other sites set up by the army under what became known as the Manhattan Project were the more famous Los Alamos, where the actual bomb mechanisms were fabricated, and Hanford, Washington, where plants for the making of plutonium were established.

All this took place before I was born, but for my parents the mythic quality of their lives in Oak Ridge echoed long after they had left. My mother had put together a family album just after the war, a curious amalgam of photographs of her and my father, their car, their house, the community theatre in which they acted – all the paraphernalia of early married life – combined with newspaper clippings announcing the 'birth' of the bomb and revealing the existence of the three secret installations to the rest of the world: the public framework of their private world. Although I was never able to discuss this document with my mother, who died at a young age, it has always fascinated me. At the time of the women's peace camp at Greenham Common in England, when women attached mementoes of their children and family lives to the barbed wire fence as part of their protest against the siting of nuclear missiles, it came back to me strongly. The message of Greenham Common was to evaluate public events from the standpoint of women's personal attachments, seeking to attack public morality from the point of view of women's maternally based moral reasoning. But this is very problematic indeed, and not only because, as was pointed out at the time, of its valorisation of traditional femininity. Even if my mother had wished to challenge the legitimacy of Oak Ridge's purpose (and I like to think she did, to a certain extent), it would have been difficult to unpick the strands linking what she valued in her marriage and involvement in community institutions to Oak Ridge's role in the manufacture of the bomb.

Since Greenham, feminist theory has debated the different ways in which war defines and reproduces particular constructions of gender, and vice versa. Feminist approaches to war often polarise men's and women's actual relationship to war, for instance by contrasting men's 'missile envy' (Caldicott 1984; Russell 1989) to women's concrete, personal styles of moral reasoning, based in motherwork and other caretaking activities which predispose them to pacifism (Ruddick 1989). However, as Judy Wajcman (1991) and others have argued, the idea of 'caretaking as a model of virtue' (Kaplan 1996: 164) tends to reproduce patriarchal dualisms, and makes it difficult to understand women's roles in maintaining and reproducing 'warist' societies. Rather, we need to deconstruct 'war talk', showing how it eliminates 'the feminine' (Cooke and Woollacott 1993: ix).

The feminist debate over gender and nuclear weapons has followed a similar pattern, sometimes replicating rather than challenging the invisibility of women. The emphasis has been on the masculinity of nuclear weapons, a trend set by Brian Easlea's *Fathering the Unthinkable* (1983), although the focus of later writings shifts attention from the identification of weapons development with biological maleness (toys for the boys, 'nuclear phallacies') to the deconstruction of the sexist jargon, sanitised abstractions and dualisms though which weapons developers defend themselves emotionally and deny the deadly consequences of their work. As Carol Cohn says, expert languages position the speaker as winner rather than victim or 'wimp' (1993, 1989). Although in the wider feminist literature on war women's involvement in munitions production is now well documented, in writing on atomic weapons and warfare women are present only as those who resist them, or as victims.

This chapter focuses on the personal narratives which married, white middle-class women who lived in Oak Ridge or Los Alamos wrote in the years after the end of World War II, in which, behind the jokey anecdotes and personal reminiscences, are hidden the contradictions and uneasiness I feel looking at my own mother's mementoes. I analyse these narratives partly as discursive constructions of the wartime experience, as war stories which incorporate the feminine. They make palpable the way in which personal and relational values were literally inscribed on and within this most violent of wartime projects, by women themselves, in the process of writing themselves into the story. In so far as space allows, and in contrast to most feminist analyses of nuclear weapons as signs of masculine violence, I am also reading these narratives for evidence of the actual social relations within which the making of the atomic bombs was embedded.

Personal narratives and discursive contests

Personal narratives need to be read against and in relation to other versions of their story. Although oppositional personal narratives have been used to challenge US government deceptions (Gallagher 1993; Tredici 1987), personal memory has also been deployed to defuse new, critical interpretations of events, as in the debate over the proposed Smithsonian Institute exhibition in Washington, DC, marking the fiftieth anniversary of Hiroshima (Goldberg 1995). As against archival evidence showing that dropping the atomic bombs had been unnecessary to end the war and had been undertaken for other reasons, the US media chose to present the emotionally charged memories of Army veterans as offering more reliable evidence of the inevitability of the bombings (Alperovitz 1995; Boyer 1994; Freedland 1995; Goldberg 1995).

With the exception of Fermi (1954) and Libby (1979) the main autobiographical accounts I am examining were first drafted in the years immediately after World War II. However, as these women were unable to find publishers, they remained untouched until edited and produced by local history societies and other publishers after 1975. Other material comes from interviews or collections of articles written later, but which have the air of long-rehearsed memories. Although their publishing history makes setting them in historical context difficult, read as 'texts of identity' (Rosenberg 1993) these narratives indicate something of the gendered, racialised and classed nature of subjectivity and agency of a particular group of women in relation to immediate postwar controversies.[2]

Boyer (1994) and Lifton and Mitchell (1995) see the period after August 1945 as one of contestation between competing understandings of the meaning of the atomic bomb. The US government tried to pre-empt debate by preparing in advance an official account of the making of the bombs, the Smyth Report (reproduced in Brown and MacDonald 1977), and by limiting journalists' visits to Hiroshima or Nagasaki. Although by the end of 1949 public opinion in the United States had been almost completely subordinated to what Lifton and Mitchell call the 'official narrative' (1995: xvi), Boyer's and Lifton and Mitchell's analyses of contemporary media suggest that the first reactions had been much more varied, including ethical misgivings, concern for the victims, fears of future attacks on the US, and worries about the lack of control over military decisions. If the main tenor was expressions of jubilation at the end of the war, there was also an admixture of admiration with shock and horror. According to Robert Jungk the scientists were seen as mythical figures, over-lifesize Titans, as 'the gods from hell' (1958: 218). Even some of the scientists began to see themselves as 'brilliant collaborators with death' (Jungk 1958: 231), as a 'league of frightened men' (232). The few eyewitness reports shamed some Americans, as illustrated in an epic poem by a Californian, Hermann Hagedorn, also cited by Boyer (1994):

> When the bomb fell on America it fell on people.
> It didn't dissolve their bodies,
> But it dissolved something vitally important to the greatest of them and the least,
> What it dissolved were their links with the past and with the future ...
>
> (Jungk 1958: 237)

In this context, I think personal reminiscences of the scientists as ordinary human beings, as family men, have a particular resonance. This is not to say that the physicists were not the ordinary men their wives claimed; as Carol Cohn later comments, what she saw in the technostrategic analysts she met was not 'cold-bloodedness' but 'charm, humor, intelligence, concern and decency' (1989: 130). Her liking can be compared to other feminist writing which pictures the inventors of nuclear weapons as monstrous incestuous fathers in 'nuclear families' (Caputi 1996) or which concentrates on their ability to detach themselves from ordinary human emotions. My point is to locate the projection of the scientist as a 'nice man' in self-understandings and public opinion at particular times.[3]

Pioneer communities

We can begin to look at these narratives by focusing on the 'arrival story' which almost all of them contain, one which usually signals the adoption of a new identity, for the duration. According to Laura Fermi (1954), wife of physicist Enrico Fermi, many European refugees to begin with experienced Los Alamos as a stage set in a Western film. People going to Oak Ridge too were conscious of starting a new life. Two comments in a volume combining reminiscences and recipes are typical of most of the entries:

> I was a bride of 18 when I came to Oak Ridge ... Mostly I remember how much rain there was that first year ... We were always walking in a sea of mud.
>
> (*Cooking Behind the Fence* 1992: 1)

> We had a difficult time back in the early days ... just keeping bread on the table. Many women made their own bread, biscuits, corn bread, and rolls to save money and to save time from standing in lines.
>
> (ibid.: 26)

They recall concrete details, the constant mud or dust, depending on the season, the housing – the Cemestos houses, graded in size from A through F, 'demountables', flattops, Victory cottages, hutments and dormitories were rented from the Roane-Anderson Corporation, as well as old vacation resort motels, patched-up barns, former garage buildings, even chicken coops. There were few commercial facilities, people were unable to tell their relatives where they lived or what they did, and the community was set apart from its Appalachian neighbours by cultural and intellectual differences as well as security regulations. Behind the fence, community organisations thrived – amateur orchestras, community theatres, bridge clubs, the multi-faith chapel. For many residents, themselves the children of immigrants, it was an opportunity to experience themselves both as settlers, as pioneers, as they still call themselves, and as the guardians of culture: 'it was something unlike anything before: one culture replacing another, a new people taking the land of the old' (Overholt 1987: xvi).

Joanne Gailar's autobiography, *Oak Ridge and Me*, was published in 1991, but she wrote Part I just after World War II, already aware of their lives as social history. She describes four different places she and her husband lived, including an off-area motel they shared with sixteen other married couples. Although each twosome had their own room, there was only one kitchen. Their communal life was unusual as compared to prewar norms: there was a cleaning rota, with three couples taking responsibility for three weeks at a time. Space in the one refrigerator was rationed – the bottom shelf was reserved for milk and infant feed and each couple limited to nine ice cubes every nine hours. Although each wife cooked her husband an evening meal, which they ate at separate tables, the overall arrangements gave credence to the belief in the wider area that Oak Ridge was an experiment in socialised living, simply because so many people lived in dormitories and ate in communal cafeterias and guest houses. Following a piercing essay on her experience of early widowhood, Gailar, who later became a professional writer closely involved in community affairs, uses womanly metaphors to look back on her experience: 'Oak Ridge is mother and sister; Oak Ridge is home … Oak Ridge is child – belonging to me in that special sense that she belongs to all of us who settled her and made her our own' (1991: 145–146). Because the more prestigious Los Alamos lacked the large-scale industrial production facilities of Oak Ridge or Hanford, more of the residents were theoretical physicists, mathematicians and laboratory technicians. Laura Fermi says that 'Los Alamos was all one big family and all one big accent; everybody in science was there, both from the United States and from almost all the European countries' (1954: 226).

The title of *Standing By and Making Do: Women of Wartime Los Alamos* (1988) evokes the conventions of the warrior's wife keeping the home fires burning. Significantly, it is not Hiroshima or Nagasaki but the Trinity Test which is seen as the climax of the sojourn: 'This is the story of three years of working and marrying and dying, of giving birth, of getting drunk, of laughing and crying, which culminated in that successful test at Alamogordo bombing range' (Wilson and Serber 1988: xi). For these white middle-class women, accompanying their husbands to Los Alamos was an adventure. From a life of middle-class respectability as an academic wife, Ruth Marshak says, she now 'felt akin to the pioneer women accompanying their husbands across the uncharted plains westward, alert to danger' (in Wilson and Serber 1988: 1–2).

The Los Alamos women too see themselves as community builders, fitting Jean Elshtain's (1987) notion of women as 'civic cheerleaders', not flag-wavers exactly, but creating and maintaining civic life:

> There was much that was amiss in the ugly town where the bomb was born. Yet I have only to think of the neighborliness and warmth and esprit de corps of Los Alamos to be heartily glad for the chance that took me there … Los Alamos was our town, our own creation. To no other community will we ever give so much of ourselves.
>
> (Serber and Wilson 1988: 19)

Nuclear families

The view of Oak Ridge and the other communities as creative clearly parallels the then general definition of the making of the bomb as a creative scientific act, rather than an act of destructive violence. This was a gendered discourse in which the bombs had nicknames like 'Big Boy' and 'Fat Boy' (later, 'Fat Man'). Winston Churchill was informed of the success of the Trinity Test with the words 'Babies satisfactorily born' (Easlea 1983). Klaus Theweleit (1993) suggests parallels to the actual control of childbirth by male American doctors, who announced the successful delivery to husband and relatives.

This 'birth of the bomb' discourse was incorporated by women into their own life stories. For instance, Joanne Gailar's chapter on early Oak Ridge, written in 1947 while pregnant with her first child, is called 'A Man, A Woman, A-Bomb' and Charlotte Serber's account of women's paid employment is called 'Labour Pains' (in Wilson and Serber 1988). Laura Fermi's autobiography, *Atoms in the Family*, presents the inventors of the bomb as family men. Children, she says, became aware that their 'ordinary fathers', who 'scolded and explained how to use a chemistry set … who took too long shaving in the bathroom, who wore white badges on their coats, who ate their meals and went off to work … those men were important people' (1954: 258–259).

These images of domesticated masculinity are not about patriarchal authority but about fathers reduced to squabbling with their children. Fermi goes on to domesticate atomic bombs and their inventors still further, quoting from the alphabet Edward Teller concocted for his son Paul:

> A stands for atom; it is so small
> No one has ever seen it at all.
>
> B stands for bomb; the bombs are much bigger,
> So brother, do not be too fast on the trigger.
>
> S stands for secret; you can keep it forever
> Provided there's no one abroad who is clever.
>
> (1954: 238)

Divisions of 'race' and class

From the evidence of the few academic studies of Los Alamos and Oak Ridge residents, it appears that inequalities of 'race' and class were an integral part of the way the army recruited labour and planned the sites, both of which reflected the priority given to attracting white, middle-class scientists. The 'community' to which the narratives refer was a partial one. Social relations were usually much less close between the middle class narrators' families and the families of skilled, white, male workers, who were sometimes allocated flats in the four-apartment blocks where many of the Los Alamos scientists were housed, than between the scientists' families, and the hutment neighbourhoods and trailer camps were practically another world.

To build Oak Ridge the army had purchased the land cheaply, displacing hill farmers, who were forced to leave their crops standing in the fields, and were usually unable to purchase a new home or farm with what they had been paid (Johnson and Jackson 1981; Overholt 1987). Few of these families from the immediate environs of Oak Ridge became part of the new town, although it was working-class white women from rural Tennessee who were employed to monitor the calutrons which separated the U-235 from raw uranium. The main division was between the white military administrators, scientists, and Army technicians and their families, on the one hand, and African-American manual workers on the other. Racial segregation was intense and degrading. Valeria Steele, in the 1980s a young Oak Ridge playwright and historian looking back on Oak Ridge history, comments:

> The black men and women who came to Oak Ridge believed that it was a city of opportunity. They came by the hundreds from Alabama, Mississippi, Georgia, and Tennessee. They arrived with great anticipation of how life could be improved and how they could make a new start. But soon, they realized the hollowness of such a dream. For coming to Oak Ridge only reaffirmed one rude fact: that they still lived in America, in the country that had always denied them freedom and equality. In Oak Ridge, as in other places, segregation would continue to play a central role in their lives.
>
> (in Overholt 1987: 199)

African-Americans were allocated only menial physical work and lived in segregated hutment neighbourhoods; even the proposed 'Negro village' was axed in order to provide more housing for whites. African-American married couples were not allowed to live together; the men and women's hutments were apparently separated by a five-foot barbed wire fence. A woman was not permitted to bring her children with her and, if she became pregnant, she was evicted from the reservation. These hutments were primitive frame buildings shared by four workers, without bath or toilet, fourteen by fourteen feet, with dirt floor, coal stove, and simple shutters instead of glass windows. In summer, the removal of the stove made room for a fifth occupant. (White male construction workers also had poor housing, often barracks or caravans, but in separate areas.) While the hutments disappeared at the end of the war, schools remained segregated, as in the rest of the South, until a 1955 directive from the national Atomic Energy Commission, and restaurants, cafeterias, 'Laundromats' and barbershops for even longer (Johnson and Jackson 1981).

In Los Alamos, there was a division between the white manual and professional workers' families, as well as, among the latter, a pecking order based on the men's prestige as scientists. The machinists, those who worked for outside contractors, the hutment and Nissan hut dwellers are mentioned in very few of the earlier personal narratives (Smith 1965 is an exception). Although these illustrate mainly divisions between army personnel and scientists, recent interviews with the now adult children of the 'pioneers' suggest that, because all the children attended the same schools, they found class differences in the town more difficult to avoid (Mason 1995). The main ethnic groups were the white incomers, the Spanish Americans and the Native American inhabitants of the Parajito plateau. In order to free the scientists' wives for work in the Technical Area and elsewhere, Native American women – called 'girls' in the narratives – were bussed in daily as domestic cleaners and childminders. Their working hours were allocated by the administrators in order of priorities worked out by the white, working mothers themselves (women teachers and those with the youngest children had priority). Stories about the Native American domestic workers form part of many of the white women's narratives, but because the focus is on their dances, costumes and pottery they tend to be portrayed as exotic 'others' rather than as part of the core community; the exceptions were a well-known potter and her husband and other artists with a reputation in the USA.

The husbands' bomb

The women's narratives concentrate mostly on gender relations of their communities. The most striking aspect of these narratives is the taken-for-granted organisation of the communities around 'husbands' and 'wives' as the key social categories, and the way that this inflects many women's relationship to the bomb. For instance, the Wilson and Serber volume is 'affectionately dedicated to our husbands, and to all the men who made the atomic bomb a reality' (1988: ix). Told there was a chance that their husbands would be 'blown to bits', Elsie McMillan stood vigil, with her woman neighbour through the night (McMillan in Badash 1980). Jane Wilson watched from her front porch, thinking of her husband at the 'desert proving ground':

> The Test was scheduled for four in the morning. The air seemed empty and bitterly cold, although it was July … Four fifteen, and nothing yet one could see, maybe it had failed. At least, then the husbands were safe. God only knew what this strange thing could do to its creators. The men down there, standing before the unknown, might never come home.
>
> (1988: xi)

She continues:

> Something happened all right, for good or ill. Something wonderful. Something terrible. The women waiting there in the cold are a part of it. The atomic bomb had been born …

> (1988: xi)

Susan Griffin's (1994) book on the 'private life of war' draws on Laura Fermi's account of her husband's involvement in the Manhattan Project to show how psychological denial and the epistemology of scientific detachment blight the lives of scientists like Fermi (see also the discussion by Myers (1996)). But Fermi's account is also interesting for how it constructs her own relationship to the bomb, as wife: 'The men in the squash court [where the first atomic pile was erected] knew that their research might make possible the development of atomic weapons … My husband was their leader' (1954: ix).

Fermi seems to have set herself against knowing or learning anything about her husband's work, despite the hints of his colleagues, who even gave her books to read, a denial she maintains, against their implicit scepticism, in a later account (in Badash 1980). In one of the few accounts by a woman scientist involved in the project, Leona Marshall Libby (1979) seems to make fun of the way Fermi holds on to the identification of wife, seeing it as an abdication of responsibility. Telling of a visit with Fermi, now widowed, in 1975, when she and another scientist's wife, Freda Utley, supported the Nuclear Initiative referendum in California, which sought to prevent the building of any more nuclear power plants:

> I was shocked by their action, which required any new nuclear power plant to have two thirds vote in the state legislature. I said that it would make it impossible for any new plants to be built in California … I asked her how she, the author of *Atoms for the World* … Laura replied that because her husband and Freda's husband were no longer running the nuclear power industry it was no longer in safe hands and therefore, the United States would have to get along without it ….

> (1979: 130)

When Libby argues with them about the safety of nuclear plants, they say only: 'We'll ask Harold when he comes home' (1979: 130). While this story reflects on the longstanding antagonism between Leona Libby and Laura Fermi, and relates to a later period, Fermi's comment is reminiscent of research on perceptions of industrial safety in Oak Ridge (Wolfe in Overholt 1987) which found that long-term residents' sense of security rested mainly on trust between colleagues and personal acquaintances.

However, the husbands' work was as much a source of tension as pride. As Marshak says in her contribution to the Wilson and Serber volume:

The Tech[nical] Area was a great pit which swallowed our scientist husbands out of sight, almost out of our lives … They worked as they had never worked before … Few women understood what the men were seeking there or comprehended the magnitude of the search. The loneliness and heartache of some scientists' wives during the years before the atomic bomb was born were very real.

(1988: 10–11)

Most of these women were also connected with the actual work of the Manhattan Project through their own jobs, which they were allocated after arrival. Given their responsibilities in the community and almost total responsibility for families, their jobs were subordinate to their identity as wives and mothers. For example, Fermi talks slightingly of her own job and tells how impressed her children were that their teachers 'were no less than the wives of great scientists, Mrs Robert Wilson and Mrs Cyril [Alice Kimball] Smith' (1954: 259). Charlotte Serber had a very visible role in the Technical Area as the Scientific Librarian who kept track of secret documents, but she suggests that most of the married women saw their jobs as temporary aberrations. Indeed, a few of the middle-class women refused to accept paid work at all, arguing that their husbands' long hours left women with sole responsibility for the care and schooling of children, whose lives they felt had been disrupted enough by the move to Los Alamos (Jette 1977).

However, most of the women scientists recall the period as one in which they felt 'terribly alive and vitally involved with their work' (Howes and Herzenberg 1993: 109). Like Leona Marshall Libby (1979), they were often the only woman in a group. For instance, when Marshall became pregnant she told only Enrico Fermi, because otherwise they would probably have insisted on 'kicking me out' of the reactor building. Her work clothes – coveralls and a blue denim jacket – concealed the bulge, and the 'pockets, containing cutters, tape measure, slide rule, micrometer, and pencil, needle-nose pliers … produced other bulges'. She spent her days on top of the thermal column at Argonne '[riding] to work on a bus without springs for the 9 months, with me arriving each morning barely in time to vomit before starting the day's work' (1979: 165).

Two women

Virginia Woolf suggests in *Three Guineas* (1943) that it is only when women have economic independence that they will be able to resist incorporation into men's culture of war. As detailed above there would seem to be evidence for Woolf's pessimism in the accounts written by the wives of scientists and technicians who, though through affection as much as dependency, frame the building of the bomb in terms of the joys and tensions of personal relations. What I term 'the domestication of the bomb' refers to the narrowness of the writers' framework as much as to its familial content. But I would not want to assume that the wife's narrative was the only version of the story put forward by women. There is at least one woman writer of the time whose point of departure lies in resistance to and alienation from Los Alamos personnel, and her account is framed within a somewhat different discourse, one which centres on the relationship between two women, and one which links nuclear power with the superhuman.

The narrative by Peggy Pond Church (1960) centres on the friendship between two women. The daughter of the founder of the Los Alamos Ranch School for Boys, Church was married to a schoolmaster at the school. She and her husband and sons were thrown out of their home when the school was taken over as the site for the Los Alamos scientific installation. In 1951 she 'was still bitter at having been exiled from the plateau' (1960: 114) and her different relationship to the Project gives her a kind of critical distance from it.

Church's *The House on Otowi Bridge* (1960) takes the form of a biography of Edith Warner, a single schoolteacher from Philadelphia who rented a house not far from Los Alamos and made her life among the Native Americans of the nearby pueblo of Ildefonso. It details Warner's early attempt to stretch her earnings from a small job for the school by using her house first as a tea room and home for paying guests and, later, after the creation of the Project, as a restaurant for senior staff and their families. It is based partly on the annual Christmas letters which Edith Warner sent to her friends over nearly seventeen years and, to a lesser extent, on conversations between the two women before 1943, when Church used to escape to Warner's house from her small children and her husband's all-male school, with its 'disparagement of everything feminine' (1960: 66).

Although Warner herself drew the worlds together: her unfinished autobiography apparently began, 'This is the story of a house … a house that stood for many years beside a bridge between two worlds' (Church 1960: 5). However, Church frequently invokes the violence of the bomb, and perceives an incongruity between, on the one hand, Edith's fellowship with the incoming scientists and, on the other, her rootedness in nature and her ties with the Native American pueblo community, which in Church's narrative signifies the elemental and the primitive. She imagines Warner thinking:

> How gaily these men had talked of their children, of mountain climbing and of music. It was hard to believe that they had been working day and night to split the atom and release its energy for the use of man, the violent use of man. In the days after Hiroshima she had seen many of these men recoil at the implications of what they had done … How strange it seemed that the bomb which had created such waste and such suffering had been made on the plateau where the ancient people for so long invoked their gods in beauty. In the smallest atoms of dust the forces that hold the worlds together lay slumbering … Had men forgotten the wisdom of the heart, the knowledge that all men everywhere are of one substance?
>
> (Church 1960: 111)

Ultimately Church too comes to accept rather than reject the nuclear age, integrating it into her life as vines grow over a house, a recurring image in the book.

In terms which prefigure ecologists' respect for natural forces, as if she herself is tired of railing against the world, Church speaks 'through' Edith Warner of the 'one-ness' of the world, here understood both as a cry against science *and* as the way through which both women implicitly come to accept the inevitable: 'The energy in the atom – was it really different from that which slept in the waiting seed, in the sunlight released from blazing pine knots, in the stone that pulsed under the fingers that touched it rightly … ' (1960: 111). Perhaps because the idea of the assumed inevitability of the bomb is also, as Lifton and Mitchell (1995) argue, one aspect of the official discourse legitimating the bombing of Hiroshima and Nagasaki, Church's paean to natural forces never quite evokes resistance to it, whether or not that had been her intention.

Conclusions

In her scholarly history of the postwar atomic scientists' movement for international control, Alice Kimball Smith, who had been a Los Alamos teacher, wife and mother, comments that while the general public might imagine the bomb as 'the genie in the bottle' and wonder why scientists worked on it in the first place (Smith 1965: 13), during the war this was not an issue for the scientists (or, by implication, for their wives). There was the fear of Hitler's Germany developing its own bomb, non-military factors, including curiosity, the desire to be part of history, the belief in peaceful uses of atomic energy which might come afterwards. Things might look different in hindsight, she says, when we tend to assume the assurance of 'victory', but in the midst of the fears and uncertainties of wartime such rationalisations were 'telling' (1965: 5).

In addition to these more general points, the authors of the narratives I have examined were attached to the Manhattan Project by what they perceived to be their finer qualities: loyalty to and concern for their husbands, their sense of civic virtue, their commitment to the immediate communities which they helped build, the cooperative networks women built among themselves. These women's attachment to the Project clearly reflected also many aspects of their structural position, which made the development of an independent vantage point difficult. Their roles were defined by the army, who designated 'Tech Area' and 'Townsite' as distinct (and gendered) social worlds; even those whose husbands had told them what kind of weapon was being made experienced life in these communities 'outside the inner wall' (McMillan in Badash 1980: 41). Moreover, censorship and the travel restrictions on scientists' families made it impossible to discuss what was going on with outsiders. Such was the social isolation of these communities that when the Los Alamos High School principal, on a short trip to California, reported the organisation of a prayer service for the victims of the Hiroshima bombing and the (presumed to be guilt-ridden) 'unfortunate people' who had constructed it, the Los Alamos community was astonished (Brode 1997: 66). None the less, there is a sense in which the narratives seem to hold very tightly to the wartime viewpoint, as if refusing awareness of other possible readings of the making of the atomic bombs. Nor do the narratives deal adequately with the different experiences of white working-class women or black women, nor even with the tensions between husbands and wives which occasionally surface in the narrative. Before we assume that the only language of denial is masculine, abstract and technical, we need to recognise the domestication of the bomb one sees in these narratives as an important variation on the official narrative and to recognise the disjunctions between women which form part of the private life of war.

Notes

1   Although they may disagree with my conclusions, I would like to thank Lisa Adkins, Lynda Birke, Joanne Gailar, Terry Lovell, Nicole Vitellone and Judy Wajcman for their encouragement.
2   There are also two recent publications by Los Alamos working-class women (Downs 1997; Roensch 1993). Although their narratives differ in some respects from those examined here, neither questions the making or use of the bomb. The same seems to be true of the women employed as scientists (Howes and Herzenberg 1993). I have found no published contemporary accounts by women from Hanford, or by African-American or Native American women, although according to Boyer (1994) the pride expressed by the contemporary black press in the participation of black scientists and workers in the Project was soon replaced by hostile scepticism about US government motives. There is also an interesting collection of contemporary photographs published by Laura and Enrico Fermi's granddaughter (Fermi and Samra 1995), which hints at the contradictions of life in the Manhattan Project communities.
3   Most later official and unofficial histories concentrate on the careers of and networks between key Army and corporate players and the organisational feats involved in redirecting resources on such an enormous scale (for example Jones 1985). In Oak Ridge alone, 40,000 people were employed in the plants, excluding military personnel, and 80,000 in the immediate area. The many biographies and collections of scientists' reminiscences are too numerous to list.
    Women flit in and out of this literature, although as one Oak Ridge woman seems to have complained at the time they were not mentioned in the Smyth Report (Larsen in Overholt 1987: 193). The European women physicists who contributed to the earliest theoretical discoveries, such as Lise Meitner and Ida Noddack, are mentioned, and women's memories occasionally provide material for the 'human-interest' angle a few accounts incorporate, especially Szasz (1992). Most comprehensive is Howes and Herzenberg's (1993) identification of over seventy women who held scientific or technical jobs in the Manhattan Project, including thirty at Los Alamos and twenty-four in Oak Ridge. About sixteen of these women had PhDs; the rest were more junior staff. One was a future Nobel-laureate. Although in response to a questionnaire distributed by Howes and Herzenberg some of these women expressed concern about the consequences of their work, only one is said to have actually regretted her involvement.
    Women also participated in what became known as the atomic scientists' movement, the organisations formed by scientists at the University of Chicago, Oak Ridge and Los Alamos which petitioned against the use of the bombs against civilian targets and, after the war, tried to use their new status to limit the US military control over nuclear power (Smith 1965).

References

Alperovitz, G. (1995) *The Decision to Use the Atomic Bomb and an American Myth*, London: Harper Collins.

Badash, L. Hirschfelder, J.O. and Broida, H. (eds) (1980) *Reminiscences of Los Alamos 1943–1945*, Dordrecht, Holland, Boston, Mass., and London: D. Reidel.

Boyer, P. (1994, first published 1985) *By the Bomb's Early Light: American Thought and Culture at the Dawn of the Atomic Age*, Chapel Hill and London: University of North Carolina Press.

Brode, B. (1997) *Tales of Los Alamos: Life on the Mesa 1943–1945*, New Mexico: Los Alamos Historical Society.

Brown, A.C. and MacDonald, C.B. (1977) *The Secret History of the Atomic Bomb*, New York: Delta.

Caldicott, H. (1984) *Missile Envy: The Arms Race and Nuclear War*, New York: William Morrow.

Caputi, J. (1996) 'Unthinkable Fathering: Connecting Incest and Nuclearism', in K.J. Warren and D.L. Cady (eds) *Bringing Peace Home: Feminism, Violence and Nature*, Bloomington and Indianapolis: Indiana University Press.

Church, P. Pond (1960) *The House at Otowi Bridge: The Story of Edith Warner and Los Alamos*, Albuquerque: University of New Mexico Press.

Cohn, C. (1989) 'Sex and Death in the Rational World of Defence Intellectuals', in R. Cooke and A. Woollacott (eds) (1993) *Gendering War Talk*, Princeton, N.J.: Princeton University Press.

—— (1993) 'Wars, Wimps and Women', in R. Cooke and A. Woollacott (eds) *Gendering War Talk*, Princeton, N.J.: Princeton University Press.

Cooking behind the Fence: Recipes and Recollections from the Oak Ridge '43 Club (1992), Olathe, Kans.: Cookbook Publishers.

Cooke, R. and Woollacott, A. (eds) (1993) *Gendering War Talk*, Princeton, N.J.: Princeton University Press.

Downs, M.B. (1997) *Lest I Forget*, Santa Fe, N.Mex: Sun Books.

Easlea, B. (1983) *Fathering the Unthinkable: Masculinity. Scientists and the Nuclear Arms Race*, London: Pluto.

Elshtain, J. Bethke (1987) *Women and War*, New York: Basic Books.

Fermi, L. (1954) *Atoms in the Family: My Life with Enrico Fermi*, Chicago, Ill.: University of Chicago Press.

Fermi, R. and Samra, E. (1995) *Picturing the Bomb: Photographs from the Secret World of the Manhattan Project*, New York: Harry N. Abrams.

Freedland, J. (1995) 'Memories Deaden Enola Gay's Lustre', *Guardian*, 30 June.

Gailar, J. Stern (1991) *Oak Ridge and Me: From Youth to Maturity*, Oak Ridge, Tenn.: Children's Museum of Oak Ridge.

Gallagher, C. (1993) *American Ground Zero: The Secret Nuclear War*, Boston: MIT Press.

Goldberg, S. (1995) 'Smithsonian Suffers Legionnaire's Disease', *Bulletin of the Atomic Scientists* 51, 3 (May/June): 28–33.

Griffin, S. (1994) *A Chorus of Stones: The Private Life of War*, London: Women's Press.

Howes, R.H. and Herzenberg, C.L. (1993) 'Women in Weapons Development: The Manhattan Project', in R.H. Howes and M.R. Stevenson (eds) *Woman and the Use of Military Force*, Boulder, Colo., and London: Lynne Rienner.

Jette, E. (1977) *Inside Box 1663*, Los Alamos, N.Mex: Los Alamos Historical Society.

Johnson, C.W. and Jackson, C.O (1981) *City Behind a Fence: Oak Ridge, Tennessee, 1942–1946*, Knoxville: University of Tennessee Press.

Jones, V. (1985) *Manhattan: The Army and the Atomic Bomb*, Washington, D.C.: Center of Military History, United States Army.

Jungk, R. (1958) *Brighter than a Thousand Suns: The Moral and Political History of the Atomic Scientists*, trans. J. Cleugh, London: Victor Gollancz in association with Rupert Hart-Davies.

Kaplan, L.D. (1996) 'Women as Caretakers: An Archetype that Supports Patriarchal Militarism', in K.J. Warren and D.L. Cady (eds) *Bringing Peace Home: Feminism, Violence and Nature*, Bloomington and Indianapolis: Indiana University Press.

Libby, L. Marshall (1979) *The Uranium People*, New York: Crane Russak.

Lifton, R.J. and Mitchell, G. (1995) *Hiroshima in America: A Half Century of Denial*, New York: Avon Books.

Mason, K.R. (1995) *Children of Los Alamos*, New York and London: Twayne Publishers/Prentice Hall International.

Myers, W. A. (1996) '"Severed Heads": Susan Griffin's Account of War, Detachment and Denial', in K.J. Warren and D.L. Cady (eds) *Bringing Peace Home: Feminism, Violence and Nature*, Bloomington and Indianapolis: Indiana University Press.

Overholt, J. (ed.) (1987) *These Are Our Voices: The Story of Oak Ridge 1942–1970*, Oak Ridge, Tenn.: Children's Museum.

Roensch, E. Stone (1993) *Life within Limits*, Los Alamos, N.Mex: Los Alamos Historical Society.

Rosenberg, S. (1993) 'The Threshold of Thrill: Life Stories in the Skies over Southeast Asia', in R. Cooke and A. Woollacott (eds) *Gendering War Talk*, Princeton, N.J.: Princeton University Press.

Ruddick, S. (1989) *Maternal Thinking*, New York: Ballantine Books.

Russell, D.E.H. (ed.) (1989) *Exposing Nuclear Phallacies*, New York: Pergamon Press.

Smith, A.K. (1965) *A Peril and a Hope*, Chicago, Ill.:University of Chicago Press.

Szasz, F.M. (1992) *British Scientists and the Manhattan Project: The Los Alamos Years*, Basingstoke, England: Macmillan.

Theweleit, K. (1993) 'The Bomb's Womb and the Genders of War (War Goes on Preventing Women from Becoming the Mothers of Invention)', in R. Cooke and A. Woollacott (eds) *Gendering War Talk*, Princeton, N.J.: Princeton University Press.

Tredici, R. del (1987) *At Work in the Fields of the Bomb*, London: Harrap.

Wajcman, J. (1991) *Feminism Confronts Technology*, Cambridge: Polity Press.

Wilson, J. and Serber, C. (eds) (1988) *Standing By and Making Do: Women of Wartime Los Alamos*, Los Alamos, N.Mex: Los Alamos Historical Society.

Woolf, V. (1943) *Three Guineas*, London: Hogarth Press.

Part IV

Subject matters

Introduction

Jane Kilby and Celia Lury

Subject matters are fundamental to feminist theory and practice. Feminists have been much concerned with the question of whether and how women might be subjects, although what is meant by 'the subject' has been an issue of debate. The question of whether and how women might be subjects has no easy answers. On the one hand, feminists have made significant contributions to a critique of the ethnocentric and liberal model of the autonomous subject within Western discourse (Spivak 1987; Butler 1990; Barrett and Phillips 1992). Indeed, feminism has shown how this universalising model of the subject is actually very particular, both culturally and historically: it sets limits as to whose thought is recognised, who can act in the world, and whose rights are guaranteed as a form of self-possession. Women, as well as, for example, gays and lesbians and the working classes, are categorically excluded from such a definition of the subject; simply put, they do not matter. It is perhaps no surprise then, given this critique, that subjectivity has become a fraught and complex issue for feminism (as indeed, feminism is a difficult and complicated political terrain for subjects to inhabit). Nevertheless, it is recognised in these critiques that the ways in which the self-same, autonomous individual is constructed through the expulsion of difference leaves a trace, a remainder, the abject. Feminism has offered numerous accounts of marginalised subjectivity, many of which emphasise the body, relationality, contingence, and an inescapable intimacy or mutual imbrication between self and other (although here questions of asymmetry are never far away).

On the other hand, feminists have also been concerned with questions of the subject and of identity at what might be called a categorical level, that is, with the ideal of Woman and of biological and social understandings of women as a group or type (Pateman 1988; Riley 1988; hooks 1989; Nicholson 1990). Thus feminists have developed critiques of biologically essentialist constructions of the category of women, through, for example, challenges to the notion of a maternal instinct, or the naturalness of heterosexual desire, and with challenging the ways in which women are denied recognition – as, for example, agents – through their social positioning. Yet since biology was typically seen as fixed in many such accounts, and the social was understood as a sphere for intervention, it sometimes appeared as if it was sufficient for feminism to propose a form of social constructionism to bring about transformation. At the same time, however, as the advocacy of an understanding of gender as a social construction was being elaborated, there developed an internally directed critique of feminist understandings of women as a social group. Here, black, post-colonial and post-structuralist perspectives highlighted the ways in which simplistic uses of social constructionism to explain gender inequalities could display the characteristics of essentialism, ahistoricism and universalism – and thus frequently displayed the very same political implications of exclusion and the denial, marginalisation and pathologisation of difference that had been the object of feminist critiques of biological essentialism.

One consequence of this internal critique has been that the heuristic of culture was taken up as an alternative to society (and biology), in order to facilitate a more nuanced, particularistic and processual understanding of gender.[1] This has gone along with a concern with gender as *doing*, rather than *being*, a shift in emphasis that is especially associated with the work of Judith Butler (1993). There has also been an increasing concern with the effects of gender, or, rather, with gender as an effect, rather than with its causes. This concern has been largely expressed through an elaboration of gender and sexual identities as a performance or an enactment. In some respects, this can be seen as a shift in feminist agendas – a shift which parallels a more widespread lack of interest in asking the question 'why?' and a growing concern with 'how?' questions that are associated with a culture of simulation (Turkle 1996). However, it is sometimes suggested that one consequence of the turn to culture, of the concern with effects, rather than causes, is that it becomes difficult to intervene in specific situations or bring about 'real' political change. But the implications of such a shift in thinking for understandings of transformation are not clear. On the one hand, as Turkle notes, it may encourage an acceptance of opacity and lead to a willingness to abdicate any commitment to political change; on the other hand, it can 'confront us with the dependency on opaque simulations we accept in the real world' (1996: 71). This confrontation, she points out, can feed into either 'simulation resignation' or 'simulation denial'; then again, it can pose a challenge 'to develop a more sophisticated social criticism' (1996: 71).

In this section, the authors take up – and extend – feminist critiques of the abstract autonomous subject of Western thought and political life. However, the challenges they offer are very different as they trace the matter of the subject across a number of sites including the workplace, modern consumerism, maternity, monstrosity and visual representations. Moreover, these writers seek to develop 'a more sophisticated social criticism' which ignores neither the social nor the biological, and does not presume the fixity or changeability of either. Rather the concern is to open up – and identify the possibility of intervening in – the enactment of gender. Thus, in the first chapter in this section, Lisa Adkins considers the thesis that contemporary modernisation involves the increasing potential for self-reflexivity and the apparent freeing of agency from social structure, and hence the release of individuals from the ascriptive economies of modernity (where they would have been identified, for example, by categories of class, race and gender). However, Adkins problematises such a thesis by examining how the desegregation and restructuring of the workplace involves less a transformation of identities than the re-traditionalisation or, indeed, 'revival' of gender relations. As such, modern subjects, even in the seemingly democratic post-occupational and post-segregational workplace, are not free to 'be' whatever gender they like, but remain constrained by social relations which produce women workers as a social group and men as individuals, and which thus, in the absence of formal economic structures, continue to determine the organisation of production according to gendering processes.

This is not to suggest that the gender identity of women workers is pre-given; rather it is to show how gender is done in the workplace. Moreover, Adkins suggests that since they are – continually and through a series of ongoing processes – positioned as members of a social group with a fixed identity rather than as individuals who perform an identity, the agency and autonomy of women workers is limited by the social category of gender. Despite the prevalent conditions of reflexivity under late modernity, then, there is not a simple detachment or disembedding of individuals from social categories, but rather a continual, processual re-embedding in circuits and networks in which re-traditionalised rules, norms and expectations are at stake.

Anne M. Cronin also examines the apparent shifts in subject formation of modernity, but focuses on contemporary consumerist discourses of self-actualisation, self-transformation, willpower and choice. Cronin suggests that the modern self who can will itself to be (through consumption) is not freely accessible to all, and that women, as well as other marginalised groups, remain excluded from this reinvention of the liberal subject. Via a reading of Nike's ubiquitous imperative *Just Do It*, Cronin argues that the space of advertising images as an imagined ideal zone of pure voluntarity, in which interpretative freedom becomes expressive, and performatively productive of individuality, is one which is not open to all subjects. Moreover, its address is exclusionary. In short, the gendering address of consumerist imagery restricts the access of women to the contemporary forms of individuality it offers.

The question of women's exclusion from a model of subjectivity predicated on autonomy and the practice of free will is taken up in a different way by Imogen Tyler. By exposing and yet refusing the disavowal of maternal origin in individualist models of the self, Tyler argues that pregnant women's subjectivity cannot be theorised in conventional terms. Indeed, drawing on the work of Luce Irigaray she suggests that such individualist models posit an abstracted, disembodied norm: the privileged and supposedly contained morphology of white, middle-class and heterosexual masculinity. Moreover, she argues that the generative potential embodied by the transitional concept and fleshy reality of pregnancy speaks to a different subjectivity. Thus her analysis asks us to reconsider how pregnant women's subjectivity is lived in a significantly excessive corporeality.

This project of thinking the power of the maternal body is also continued in the final two chapters in this section (although necessarily transformed as the question of maternity moves into different domains). By identifying 'monsters' from the archival texts of the early history of teratology through to modern filmic representations, Margrit Shildrick argues in her chapter that the anxiety generated by monstrous bodies – which historically includes the fecund bodies of pregnant women – suggests that they have a power to unsettle the bounded identity of the masculine subject. Indeed, set against the exclusion of the monster as the absolute other is the fear that monsters might overflow the boundaries of the self, that they might be 'half us, half something else'. And what is at stake, Shildrick argues, is the incomplete abjection of the monstrous which threatens the breakdown of distinctions that underpin the ideal of the masculine self. By mapping the meta-history of monstrous and feminine bodies, then, Shildrick offers an analysis of the relationship between self and other in which there is excess, overflow and leakage wherein lies the possibility of the recognition that the monstrous is always already within.

Maggie Humm provides a close textual analysis of Virginia Woolf's extensive photograph albums in order to examine how subjects are constituted through identification and desire. In this, the first full study of the collection, Humm argues that the albums' distinctive and unusual visual sequences are a stylised representation of Woolf's identification with her 'fantasmatic' mother. Once again, then, we find the spectre of the mother is of particular interest to understandings of the female subject, and here Humm introduces Bracha Lichtenberg-Ettinger's concept of the matrixial gaze to examine the intimate relationship between daughter and mother. Indeed, Humm's analysis of photographic sequences as forms of belonging and unbelonging allows us to rethink the function of matrixial/maternal memory in the constitution of subjects and others outside the Oedipal frame provided by other feminist work on subjectivity.

This section makes clear the importance of feminist challenges to the liberal and masculine model of the subject predicated on autonomy and separation from the social world. And at the same time, it clears the way for a transformative vision of subjectivity which recognises that subjects are always embodied and embedded in relationships with others. The papers here thus begin to offer an understanding of women as a social group which is neither essentialist nor universalist, and also acknowledges the significance of subjectivity without reducing it to notions of individual agency. However, in bringing these pieces together, it also becomes clear that the matter of the subject – or perhaps it may be more useful to use the notion of the person here – is a complex, multifaceted phenomenon. Indeed, juxtaposing these accounts indicates the importance for feminism of refusing the conventional understandings of, for example, the relationship between interiority and exteriority, whereby subjectivity is located on the inside, and subjectification on the outside, as if it were something imposed from the exterior, by 'social' forces. There is also here a recognition of the need to question the morphological limits of the body, and an acknowledgement not only of the inter- as well as the intra- subjective and biological mechanisms of personhood, but of their complex interrelationship.

It is clear that all feminists do not agree on, for example, the place of the psyche in the development of the self, or on the usefulness of existing models of social or biological constructionism for understanding what it means to be 'women'. Clearly, not only is there no such agreement, but there is also widespread debate. However, in addition to the turn to culture discussed above – which is, of course, by no means the only approach present in contemporary feminist thinking – it is possible to identify a number of tendencies in this debate. First, much of feminism has been concerned to challenge the universalism of the liberal, autonomous subject, and, second, in the context of this critique, feminists have sought to develop understandings of the person which move beyond the terms and assumptions on which the notion of the autonomous subject is predicated. It is also clear that just as the notion of the liberal autonomous subject is not some fixed ideal, but is rather the ever-shifting result of a complex set of practices and knowledges, so feminist critiques have shifted focus and tactics. Thus both Adkins and Cronin explore some of the unexpected implications of the gendering of contemporary individualism for contemporary politics.

In different ways, both authors problematise the notion of progress that persists not only in common sense but also in many social scientific accounts of social change. They problematise the notion implicit in such accounts that the subject is the agent of change, as well as pointing out that women are still denied agency in their positioning as a social group. More controversially, Shildrick's chapter seeks to explore how the category of the monstrous might be analysed across historical time, outlining gender as a principle of classification which once again reminds feminists of the necessity of thinking through a notion of the self which is both more and less than the embodied individual. In these ways, then, all these pieces show how it is both that the subject is constituted in relation to understandings of (natural and social) history and vice versa. The subject is not simply the progressive agent of history, and neither is history simply the context in which subjects emerge.

Here and elsewhere, as feminists have sought to understand the specificity of subjects, they have investigated both the difficulties and the possibilities of transformation. Indeed, what is clear from all the chapters in this section – but perhaps especially those by Humm and Tyler – is that the relationships between belonging, recognition and identification are the source of intense ambivalence and antagonism, setting up resistances to and enabling tactics for change at both personal and collective levels. Both the pieces by Humm and Tyler explore aspects of the maternal, a category which has itself been the source of some considerable debate within feminism because of anxieties concerning its possible universalist and (biologically) essentialist uses. What is interesting in these pieces, however, is the way in which an understanding of the possibilities of the maternal is shown to be mediated through culturally and historically specific forms of knowledge and representation: philosophy and photography. Nevertheless, in both these cases, a (partially) biological notion of the maternal is not simply dismissed, but is rather explored for its transformative possibilities. Moreover, there is an elaboration of some of the ways in which personhood and agency may, in the vocabulary developed by Marilyn Strathern (1992) among others, be said to be distributed or extended between subjects.

At the beginning of this introduction, we suggested that gender is increasingly being understood as doing – as an enactment – rather than as being. What such an understanding makes it possible to see is that gender is neither simply a cause nor only an effect. Perhaps, then, it is both. Or, perhaps, as the chapters in this section suggest, the reduction of the possibility of change to the subject of a process of cause and effect is what makes it difficult to think transformation *for* feminism. There is thus an incitement to develop more adequate models of change together with a demonstration of the complexity of subject matters. In the acknowledgement of gender as doing, there is a recognition that feminism is already thinking *through* transformation.

Note

1   See Barrett (1992) and de Groot and Maynard (1993) for further discussion of the turn to culture.

References

Barrett, M. and Phillips, A. (eds) (1992) *Destablizing Theory: Contemporary Feminist Debates*, Cambridge: Polity Press.

Butler, J. (1990) *Gender Trouble: Feminism and the Subversion of Identity*, London and New York: Routledge.

—— (1993) *Bodies That Matter: The Discursive Limits of Sex*, London and New York: Routledge.

de Groot, J. and Maynard, M. (eds) (1993) *Women's Studies in the 1990's: Doing it Differently?*, London: Macmillan.

hooks, b. (1989) *Talking Back: Thinking Feminist, Thinking Black*, London: Sheba Feminist Publishers.

Nicholson, L. (ed.) (1990) *Feminism/Postmodernism*, London and New York: Routledge.

Pateman, C. (1988) *Sexual Contract*, Cambridge: Polity Press.

Riley, D. (1988) *Am I That Name: Feminism and the Category of 'Women' in History*, Basingstoke, England: Macmillan.

Spivak, G. (1987) *In Other Worlds: Essays on Cultural Politics*, London: Methuen.

Strathern, M. (1992) *After Nature: English Kinship in the Late Twentieth Century*, Cambridge: Cambridge University Press.

Turkle, S. (1996) *Life on the Screen: Identity in the Age of the Internet*, London: Weidenfeld and Nicolson.

15 Objects of innovation

Post-occupational reflexivity and re-traditionalisations of gender

Lisa Adkins

My concern in this chapter is with recent analyses of late modernity, especially those which stress that the contemporary condition may be characterised by an increased capacity for reflexivity. While there is some disagreement regarding the exact meaning of reflexivity (see for example Beck, Giddens and Lash 1994; Alexander 1996), Lash (1994) has usefully defined two forms of reflexivity generally at issue in such analyses. First, he refers to 'structural reflexivity' whereby agency reflects both on the rules and resources of social structure and on the conditions of existence of agency itself: 'the more societies are modernised, the more agents (subjects) acquire the ability to reflect on the social conditions of their existence and to change them in that way' (Beck 1994b: 174). Second, he writes of self-reflexivity in which agency reflects on itself and there is increasing self-monitoring: 'we are, not what we are, but what we make of ourselves' (Giddens 1991: 75). Such intensified tendencies towards reflexivity are often understood to be constituted by a destabilisation of the significance of structural forms of determination, a destabilisation which is progressively 'freeing' or 'unleashing' agency from structure. 'Reflexive modernity' is therefore, 'a theory of the ever-increasing powers of social actors, or "agency" in regard to structure' (Lash 1994: 111). So thoroughgoing is this process that reflexivity is now understood to characterise a range of domains including the economic (Beck 1992; Lash and Urry 1994; Lash 1994), the political (Beck 1994a, 1997), the aesthetic (Lash 1994; Lash and Urry 1994), the intimate and the personal (Giddens 1992; Beck and Beck-Gernsheim 1995). Indeed, reflexivity is now understood to be central to the formation of the contemporary subject (Giddens 1991).

But the freeing of agency from structure means a great deal more than intensified reflexivity, for also at issue are powerful processes of de-traditionalisation and individualisation. Through the freeing of agency from structure, individuals are increasingly untied from the rules, norms, expectations and traditions of modernity such as those of class and gender. For example, in relation to gender, Beck has suggested that, 'people are being removed from the constraints of gender … men and women are released from traditional forms and ascribed roles' (Beck 1992: 105).[1] In such commentaries, the social is now increasingly constituted by and through the individual, instead of through traditional forms and ascribed roles. Thus external, traditional forms of authority are giving way to the authority of the individual: 'individual subjects are themselves called upon to exercise authority in the face of ... disorder and contingency' (Heelas 1996: 2). Beyond this, individuals are increasingly compelled to create and invent their own self-identities and themselves as individuals (Giddens 1991, 1992; Beck 1992; Beck and Beck-Gernsheim 1996). Reflexive modernity therefore signals a thoroughly new constitution of ways of life. For example, 'family' ties are now to be understood less in terms of obligations constituted by fixed 'ties of blood' and more in terms of negotiated commitments and bonds (Finch 1989; Giddens 1992; Beck and Beck-Gernsheim 1995); and labour market positions are constituted less by determinants such as gender and class location and more by self-design, self-creation and individual performances (Beck 1992).

In this chapter I aim to question the radical de-traditionalisation thesis found in analyses of reflexive modernity. In particular, I suggest that reflexive modernity, while certainly signalling new modes of interaction, involves not a simple detachment or disembedding of individuals from social categories such as those of class and gender, but also re-embedding process in circuits and networks in which new, yet traditional – or re-traditionalised – rules, norms and expectations are at issue. To address such re-traditionalising tendencies, I concentrate here on the economic domain, since it has been suggested that many of the changes associated with the freeing of agency from structure are most marked in economic life (Lash 1994). Specifically, I will focus on gender in relation to the economic, for here, as I shall go on to show, both de- and re-traditionalising tendencies are at play.

De-segregation and de-traditionalisation: gender as an object of workplace innovation

Recent research and analyses of gender in relation to economic life provide plenty of evidence that some of the shifts suggested in theories of reflexive modernity are at issue. For instance, there is evidence of processes of de-segregation of occupations in terms of gender, a loosening of the boundaries between 'men's work' and 'women's work'. So rather than being segregated within a limited range of jobs, women are now found in a wider range of occupations, are increasingly working in the same jobs as men, and are moving into high status occupations (see, for example, Savage 1992; Crompton 1997).[2] These forms of de-segregation are of some significance since processes of gendered occupational structuring have long been understood to be key in the creation of the sexual division of labour, that is, in constituting men's advantage at work in terms of wages, workplace status and other workplace resources (see, for example, Cockburn 1981, 1985; Game and Pringle 1984; Walby 1986, 1990; Bradley 1989).

Processes of de-segregation in relation to gender therefore certainly seem to add fuel to the argument that there is current destabilisation of modernity's traditional structures. For if occupational structuring was key to the constitution of gender within modernity, then perhaps, as theorists of reflexive modernity might suggest, what is at issue in such processes of de-segregation is a de-traditionalisation of gender, that is, an untying and disembedding of individuals from modernity's rules, norms and expectations in relation to gender at work. Indeed, such de-traditionalising tendencies have been made explicit in recent analyses of shifts in organisational structuring. For instance, in a recent study of organisational change in banking, nursing and local government in the UK, Halford, Savage and Witz (1997) report that the substructure of organisations and careers is shifting away from hierarchies informed by a traditional ascriptive gender order based on familial and gendered ideals, towards one based on performance in which there is 'an undeniable decoupling of gender (as well as age) from organisational position' (Halford, Savage and Witz 1997: 262).[3]

But it is not only processes of de-segregation and de-traditionalisation in relation to gender which are at issue in such transformations in the organisation of the economic. Similar processes have also been noted in relation to other traditional categories of modernity. For example, in a study of a multinational corporation engaged in the manufacture and use of advanced technological products based in the US, Casey (1995) has documented the breakdown of traditional boundaries between occupations and professions and the emergence of what she terms a 'post-occupational condition' in organisations. Given that occupation has been key for a range of forms of social organisation (for example class and status and indeed for social cohesion and self-identification) the post-occupational condition marks a major shift in the organisation of the social. Casey suggests that replacing occupation as a primary locus of class and self-identification in workplaces are teams in which people share knowledge, skills and resources and where identification lies not with occupation but with team members, product and companies. Here Casey is identifying a major de-traditionalisation of class, status, social cohesion and identity at work through the decline of processes of occupational structuring. What is at issue in the undoing of occupational structuring – the destabilisation of the traditional structures of modern workplaces – is the disembedding of individuals, not only from rules, expectations and norms in relation to gender, but also from a range of social categories and identifications.

Such processes of disembedding appear to be creating a range of interesting new moves at work. For example, in a discussion of some current elements of organisational change, including the breakdown of traditional workplace hierarchies and moves to flexible, adaptive, learning teams, Martin (1994) has noted the ways in which men are increasingly being rewarded for performing acts traditionally associated with femininity and women for acts associated with masculinity. Moreover, she observes how such 'reversals' are increasingly being called for in today's business environment (Martin 1994: 281). Thus, although Martin does not quite put it in this way, there seems to be evidence that the undoing of traditional workplace structures means that gender is increasingly constituted as a matter of flexibility at work. Rather than being a marker of essential sexes (or a fixed characteristic workers possess by virtue of 'social' determination) gender is now established as mobile, fluid, and indeterminate. Furthermore, gender may now be performed, mobilised and contested by workers in a variety of ways in order to innovate and succeed at work.

McDowell (1997) provides further evidence of such a shift. Reporting on a study of professional financial sector workers in the City of London she argues that recent workplace restructuring (including the entry of less elite men and more women into financial sector jobs, and a recognition of embodied performances as workplace resources) is leading to 'the disruption of conventional dichotomised gender divisions and the acceptance, albeit limited, of "complex and generative subject positions" for men and for women' (McDowell 1997: 207). For example, McDowell reports on how men are increasingly performing various forms of body work and argues that such bodily performances may transgress conventional gender divisions. Following Grace (1991), McDowell suggests that men may now be the new sex-objects at work with desire and pleasure being displaced from women to men workers, thus disrupting the long-standing ideal of a disembodied, rational male worker. Similarly, she argues that women financial traders who perform traditionally masculine acts such as authoritative, empathic gestures 'challenge traditional images of feminine passivity' and create anxiety, in that they disrupt the traditional representation of women as objects of male desire and pleasure.

On this kind of evidence it would seem that the de-traditionalising tendencies associated with the retreat of social structure – in this case the breaking down of gendered occupational structuring – certainly appear to disembed and release men and women from modernity's traditions in relation to gender at work. Gender at work may now not simply be represented as an ascribed 'role' or set of determined characteristics, but as a performable set of options, as 'decidable down to the small print' (Beck and Beck Gernsheim 1996: 29). Moreover, gender may now be performed and mobilised in a variety of ways to innovate and succeed at work. Hence the untying of actors from structure or the disembedding of workers from the rules and norms of gender means that, rather than controlling and regulating workers ('trapping' workers in particular roles and positions), gender now seems to constitute an object of workplace agency. In this sense it seems that Pringle may have cause to celebrate: the current de-traditionalising tendencies of gender appear so strong that her vision of establishing women's rights to be choosing subjects, rather than over-determined objects, at work appears to becoming rapidly realised (Pringle 1989: 100).

The traditionalisation of the economic

Yet while there is plenty of evidence pointing to a thesis stressing radical forms of de-traditionalisation, disembedding and individualisation, along with other commentators I want to emphasise the importance of considering the production of tradition in relation to the freeing of agency from structure (see also Adam 1996; Alexander 1996). In his analysis of the emergence and increasing significance of knowledge-intensive production, Lash (1994) gives us an example of this view. Such production, Lash stresses is reflexive in that accumulation can only take place on the condition that agency can free itself from rule-bound 'Fordist' structures:

It entails self-reflexivity in that heteronomous monitoring of workers by rules is displaced by self-monitoring. It involves ... structural reflexivity in that the rules and resources ... no longer controlling workers, become the object of reflection for agency. That is, agents can reformulate and use such rules and resources in a variety of combinations in order chronically to innovate.

(Lash 1994: 119)

Lash also stresses that rather than involving radically de-traditionalised forms, the freeing of agency from structure involves the formation of traditional or what at times he refers to as 'pre-modern' relations: 'pre-modern and communal-traditional forms ... can be conducive to information flow and acquisition which are the structural conditions of reflexive production ... communal regulation is optimal for the scope and power of information and communication structures' (Lash 1994: 127). Here, then, 'tradition' is seen not as outmoded for or undone by reflexive workers or economies, but rather as conducive to and incited by new forms of production.

Lash looks to Germany and Japan for examples of reflexive production and, in particular, to demonstrate the significance of traditional or pre-modern forms. He shows how promotion incentives in large firms in Japan are often tightly linked to the acquisition of knowledge or information, and that flows of information are optimised through personalised trust relations. Employment contracting is therefore often 'relational' where exchange relationships involve not only straightforwardly cash-nexus exchanges, but also symbolic exchanges of, for example, shared identities. All such forms are key to reflexive accumulation: they all optimise information flow. This emphasis on the significance of non-market exchanges for reflexive production is also stressed in relation to the German case. Here inclusive information structures and highly reflexive production are achieved through a traditionalist corporate governance of production systems. For instance, information flow and knowledge acquisition are facilitated by the circulation of personnel through technical colleges and firms and status equality between, for example, professionals, technicians and skilled workers. In both cases Lash stresses that what is at issue is an ethics of commitment and obligation not to the self but to a community, 'this community being the firm in the Japanese case and the Beruf in the German case' (Lash 1994: 126). Practices in such communities are not simply a matter of the acquisition of money, power, or status but are motivated towards 'workmanship [*sic*] or the good of the firm' (Lash 1994: 126). The freeing of agency from structure for Lash is, therefore, not a simple matter of the destruction of tradition, but rather is constitutive of new traditional forms. It is in the largest and most modern firms in Germany and Japan that it is suggested that such non-market, traditional structures are to be found, structures which Anglo-Saxon firms are now attempting to develop.

But Lash is also interested in what he terms the 'structural conditions of reflexivity', especially 'reflexivity winners' and 'reflexivity losers'. And amongst the latter, he places women because of their exclusion from the new labour market spaces of reflexive production:

> In countries like Germany this exclusion of women (and minorities) is exacerbated by the corporatist institutions of the apprenticeship, the welfare state and the education system, in which women perform welfare services, not in firms operating through the market, not by working in jobs in the welfare state, but (as excluded from labour markets) in the home. Hence the very low labour-force participation rate of women in Germany.
>
> (Lash 1994: 133)

In the Japanese case such exclusion in relation to reflexive production takes on a different character. For example, Saso has shown that while women's employment rates in Japan are relatively high, 'a substantial portion of women's economic activity has been outside the large companies – especially in small companies or in family enterprises including farms' (Saso 1990: 7). In addition, she shows that a high proportion of women work in manufacturing as production workers and that 'long serving women are usually found in small companies where wages are considerably lower than in larger companies' (Saso 1990: 69). In other words, Saso's evidence suggests that women may be excluded from precisely those spaces which Lash argues are those of reflexive production: large companies involved with the production of information and knowledge, where work is de-materialised and culturalised.

Reflexive production: a re-traditionalisation of gender?

This tendency towards the exclusion of women from knowledge-intensive forms of work in reflexive economies is striking in that 'rule bound' Fordist modes of accumulation have been characterised not by the exclusion, but by the segregation and marginalisation of women within employment (see, for example, Walby 1986, 1990; McDowell 1991). Indeed, accepting the terms of analyses of reflexive modernity, it seems rather ironic that in regimes where actors are 'trapped' in structure, where individuals are embedded in the norms and expectations of categories such as class and gender, employment prospects for women may be better than those in reflexive modes of accumulation where there has been a freeing of agency from structure.

Reflecting on exclusions from the reflexive classes, Lash suggests that women may be part of a new lower class or underclass. Although Lash defines this as a new class category, he also contends that 'the personnel filling these class positions are typically determined by more particularistic, "ascribed" characteristics – by race, country of origin and gender' (Lash 1994: 134). Yet Lash does not attend to the processes of ascription. He does not consider, for example, if there is a relationship between these processes and the practices of reflexive economies themselves, nor does he interrogate the nature of exclusion from reflexive

economies. Indeed, given that the processes of the freeing of agency from structure are generally understood to disembed individuals from 'ascribed
characteristics', norms and expectations, we might ask how such processes of
ascription are taking place.

However, Lash does go on to suggest that 'civil society could be said to be built on
the back of the labour of the new lower class today' (1994: 134). This idea of the
formation of social spheres through the appropriation of the labour of others is, of
course, a familiar one in feminist analyses of modernity. Indeed, Pateman (1988)
has argued that the gender division of labour was key for the historical emergence of
the public sphere, suggesting, along with Acker (1990), that modern subjects came
into being through a gendered division of labour. For instance, she notes that the
notion of a 'worker' presupposes that he is a man who has a woman, a (house)wife,
to take care of his daily needs. In this sense, both Acker and Pateman maintain that
women can never be 'workers' in the same way as men because they are not free to
exchange their labour on the same terms as men. For Pateman this explains why
'most women can find paid employment only in a narrow range of low-status low-
paid occupations, where they work alongside other women and are managed by
men' (Pateman 1988: 132).

In relation to reflexive forms of production, it seems that women may not
even have the opportunity to be labour market 'workers' at all, let alone be
workers in the same way as men. This assessment, together with the observation
that there has been an intensification of women's domestic and welfare servicing
in relation to reflexive economies, suggests that as well as constituting traditional–communal economic forms (such as those identified by Lash), the freeing
of agency from structure seems also to involve a re-traditionalisation of gender.
Indeed, women's exclusion from labour market positions, together with an intensification of domestic and welfare servicing, suggests not a process of
individualisation – involving the disembedding of 'people from the constraints of
gender' – but more a re-embedding of 'women' in circuits and networks of
exchange where there is an intensification of traditional norms, expectations and
rules in relation to gender. Indeed, this eerily echoes the classic sexual contract of
modernity. So it seems that, rather than becoming self-determining individuals
in the space of reflexive economies, women are increasingly being embedded in
re-traditionalising socialities.

Although, on the one hand, new forms of exclusion appear to be emerging
which may be connected to a re-traditionalisation of gender, on the other, as I
have made clear, post-occupational and post-segregational conditions appear to
signal de-traditionalising processes. But examining the post-occupational socialities of contemporary workplaces more closely may call into question the
narrative of progressive de-traditionalisation. Not only do these de-segregated,
post-occupational socialities seem to involve some of the traditional forms identified by Lash, but they involve also re-traditionalising processes in relation to
gender.

Post-occupational socialities: simulated families and reflexivity

Lash has characterised the socialities of reflexive accumulation as involving traditional relations including personalised trust relations and motivations not towards power or status, but to 'workmanship' and the good of the firm. Similarly, Casey emphasises that post-occupational team socialities may be characterised not by identification in terms of status or class, but rather with team members, product and company. In addition, Casey identifies these socialities as being organised in terms of family relations. Indeed these post-occupational teams are characterised by Casey as 'workplace family forms' or 'simulated corporate families'. So thoroughgoing is this organisation that employees identify their position in the workplace in familial terms and 'treat each other at work like family. They believe, or at least act out an effort to believe, their ascribed roles and corporate identities' (Casey 1995: 193). Indeed, employees become workplace subjects through their performance of a team-family role. Post-occupational employees therefore assume family-type roles and bonds with each other and are governed by family rules and processes. For instance, teammate-siblings compete for the attention and favour of manager-fathers, and manager-fathers protect their family-teams from hostile external environments.

Casey stresses that in post-occupational settings family-teams provide a key source of cohesion necessary for corporate production: 'To be effective, the team requires the deliberate creation of a substitute discursive cohesion that is necessary for production to occur. A social cohesion without the primary element of occupation is provided by the corporation's simulated family' (Casey 1995: 109). The simulated corporate family is, therefore, the everyday organising principle of production, ensuring that employees carry out their assigned tasks, organisational principles and procedures are adhered to, and authority obeyed. Beyond this, Casey's findings show (although she does not discuss them in these terms) how the shift from occupations to family-teams entails reflexivity. Employees assume family-like roles and are managed by family rules and processes; external forms of monitoring are no longer necessary as 'members are disciplined and constrained by internalised rules of acceptable group behaviour ... A culture of discipline is established and the employees police themselves' (Casey 1995: 123).

What is so interesting about these post-industrial, simulated workplace families is that, as with Lash's workplace communities, reflexivity clearly involves the formation of traditional relations, in this case a simulation of traditional familial relations. Indeed, Casey identifies the simulated corporate family as a metaphoric bourgeois family, the very family form which was central to the project of industrialism: 'The new culture manifests a revival of an old form of social life ... upon which modern industrialism was socially structured' (Casey 1995: 194). The bourgeois family of industrialisation has itself been shown to be a distinctively gendered social form, which was crucial to the organisation of industrial society. Davidoff and Hall (1987), for example, have argued that the bourgeois family was organised around the idea of the housewife and homemaker and have linked the emergence of the bourgeoisie with the development of a distinction between the (male) public realm of work and (female) private realm of home (see, also, Weeks 1981). In contrast to this historical research, Casey is curiously silent on the issue of gender. She does not, for example, consider if the family roles that employees perform and assume are new work-place positions which are somehow simulations of the gendered roles of the traditional bourgeois family. She does note, however, that workplace families are governed by paternalism and hierarchy (Casey 1995: 113). In this sense, we might ask if reflexivity involves the formation, or as Casey would term it a 'revival', of traditional gendered family forms.

To consider this issue, I now turn to a further example of post-occupational workplace socialities, married management teams (consisting of team-wives and team-husbands) employed in the tourist industry in the UK (Adkins 1995).[4] Such teams have replaced clearly demarcated, externally regulated management occu-pations and, like Casey's simulated corporate families, are autonomous and internally monitoring. Here what is also clearly at issue is a 'revival' of a patriar-chal family-team form of labour organisation, where everyday production, cohesion and regulation are organised in terms of the direct rule of the father, that is, in terms of direct patriarchal control.[5] In such teams often only manager-husbands hold employment contracts (and therefore receive wages) since companies assume that team husbands 'own' the labour of team-wives. In addi-tion, companies assume manager-husbands will directly control the work of team-wives. Thus, in contrast to all other employees including team-husbands, team-wives are given no job description by companies. Like companies, team-husbands also do not regard wives as 'regular' employees. For example, they stress the range of 'duties' performed by team-wives which go far beyond those performed by standard employees. These include, for instance, working indefi-nite hours and taking 'extra care' with customers and with the appearance of establishments. Team-husbands also stress the autonomy and control afforded to them by the married-team form. There is a relative lack of external monitoring and direct control in terms of production over the ways in which they perform the work they want to do and when they want to do it. They also stress how they can rely on team-wives to cover for them. In these ways, team-wives seem to be employed less as 'workers' and more as patriarchally ruled wives, their employ-ment contract being less of a wage-labour and more of a workplace family-marriage contract.

This organisation of post-occupational work through patriarchal governance clearly adds further weight to the broad argument presented here that forms of traditionalisation are being constituted by processes of reflexive modernisation. More specifically, this case seems to suggest that there may well be a 'revivalism' or re-traditionalisation of gender involved in the constitution of workplace reflexivity. For example, in these workplace teams manager-husbands are rela-tively free of external regulation in their employment situation and are self-regulating workplace agents, that is, self-reflexive workers. This reflexivity of manager-husbands is constituted in the organisation of post-occupational workplace socialities through traditional patriarchal relations. Thus, team-husbands can perform flexibly in terms of task and time, and moreover, be self-determining, individualised workplace agents because of their direct control of the married team. Indeed, such degrees of workplace agency would not be available if team-wives were 'regular' employees. For example, this would not be possible if this work was organised by occupation rather than through decen-tralised patriarchal teams.

While for team-husbands, married-team socialities constitute workplace agency, this does not seem to be the case for team-wives. Indeed, the freeing of agency from structure for team-wives looks more like a re-embedding in a new re-traditionalised field of rules, expectations and norms. What appears to be at play is a new kind of social domination at work, not the indirect distant regula-tion of Fordism, but direct, localised patriarchal rule. Interestingly, Casey also notes that simulated corporate families are characterised by immediate, everyday rule, and she comments that, 'employees are not as afraid of the corporate bureaucracy as they are their own team or "family"' (Casey 1995: 122–123). This, together with her observations regarding the power of manager-fathers in family-teams, and the governance of these socialities in terms of principles of 'paternalism and hierarchy', indicates that these corporate families are organised in terms of a traditionalised gendered hierarchy. Moreover, as we have seen, Casey's simulated corporate families also entail the constitution of reflexive workers. So if, as I have suggested, these post-industrial and post-occupational socialities involve both a re-traditionalisation of gender and an untying of agents from structure, then we might ask which members of these simulated corporate families are emerging as reflexive, self-determining workers.

Conclusions

One of the main arguments of this chapter has been that the tradition-alisation associated by writers such as Lash and Casey with post-industrial reflexive economies entails a re-traditionalisation of gender. Such forms of re-traditionalisation are evidenced in the reflexive traditional forms of production considered by Lash (especially the exclusion of women from these forms of production and intensified domestic and welfare servicing in the private sphere), and in the organisation of post-occupational workplace socialities in terms of familial relations. I have questioned the radical de-traditionalisation thesis often found in analyses of reflexive modernity especially since, rather than a simple progressive disembedding of individuals from the norms, rules and expectations of social categories, reflexivity appears to involve the creation of new socialities in which new but re-traditionalised norms may be at play. I am not suggesting, as Casey does, that there is a simple revivalism or rehabilitation of traditional social structures; that these new traditions are copies, or metaphors of an original, but now past, social form. Rather, the re-traditionalised norms, rules and expectations discussed in this chapter concern new positions and new traditionalised socialities.

I also take issue with the distinction that Casey tends to make between workplace 'simulated' families and more literal 'private' families. As a number of commentators have argued, family relations are themselves now being constituted in a range of ways. For instance, the operation of familial relations no longer depends on being 'related' through, for example, marriage or blood lines (Finch 1989; Giddens 1992; Beck and Beck-Gernsheim 1995). Rather, family relations may now be invoked across a range of domains where there are no such linkages. Hence corporate workplace families cannot simply be understood to be metaphoric, or simulated with a 'real' family lurking elsewhere. Such socialities are familial; the family may now be constituted in and through work. Indeed, even 'patriarchal' rule in the case of married-teams cannot be understood to derive from the literal marriage contract as some kind of effect of an essential pre-given. For the positioning of employees as (subordinated) wives and (patriarchal) husbands is clearly being constituted by and through the conditions of employment of these 'married' teams.

Husbands, in these workplace teams, clearly occupy a post-occupational position and, in this sense, their location may be said to be characteristic of the shifts outlined by theorists of reflexive modernity. Here, in these literally post-structural married workplace teams, gender has become the object of their workplace agency. The reflexivity of team-husbands depends on, and moreover is constituted by, the family-work relations of the patriarchal team. In this sense, gender may now become an object of what Lash terms structural reflexivity, where workplace rules and resources – for instance, of patriarchal-teams and of the corporate family – may be used to innovate at work.

This leads me back to some of my introductory comments, about the ways in which gender seems to be increasingly constituted as an object of workplace innovation and success. In my reading of McDowell's body work and Martin's flexibility theses, gender reversals appear to be equally available to all workers to perform for rewards. However, in the workplace socialities considered in this chapter, access to gender as a workplace resource appears unevenly distributed. For instance, in married workplace teams the mobilisation of the rules and resources of gender are only available to manager-husbands. If, as I am suggesting here, workplace reflexivity is unevenly realised amongst workers, then, in terms of the 'reversal' thesis of de-traditionalisation, it is perhaps worth bearing in mind, as Illouz (1997) points out, that reversals usually demand reflexivity. Therefore, it is only post-occupational workers (the most reflexively charged) who are likely to occupy a position in which they can perform reversals and achieve success. Finally, perhaps what can be said about reversals and indeed de-traditionalisation is best left to Haraway: 'reversals and substitutions never just substitute for or reverse the values of the original. Rather, reversals and substitutions undo the original, opening the story up in unexpected ways' (1997: 35).

Notes

1   For Beck, this untying of individuals from modernity's rules and norms in relation to gender is located as the consequence of a number of shifts or turning points. For

instance, women are understood as being liberated from the 'traditional traits ascribed by femininity' (Beck 1992: 110) through the equalisation of participation in education and occupations, the de-skilling of housework, the growing number of divorces, contraception, and demographic liberation, that is, an increase in life expectancy beyond the period required for children (Beck 1992: 110–111).

2   It is important to note that writers commenting on processes of de-segregation also stress the need to recognise an increasingly bifurcated employment structure. For instance, while Crompton notes that 'women are increasing their share of employment in managerial and professional jobs', she goes on to stress, 'but opportunities for the unskilled and/or unqualified are declining (as they are, indeed, for men)' (Crompton 1997: 47).

3   While Halford, Savage and Witz provide extensive documentation of this shift, they also find evidence to suggest that it should not be read unproblematically. For instance, they find evidence of the emergence of new divisions between full-time and part-time workers, a clustering of women in senior jobs which are removed from centres of organisational power, and the emergence of new forms of organisational masculinity based on macho competitiveness.

4   Although such teams are not involved in the knowledge- and design-intensive work which Lash characterises as being that of reflexive production, nevertheless, tourist production has been connected to some cutting-edge shifts in terms of the economic, especially the emergence of what are sometimes referred to as culturalised forms of production (see, for example, Urry 1990; Rojek and Urry 1997).

5   For a historical account of the patriarchal family-team systems of labour see Witz and Mark-Lawson (1990), who discuss this form of labour organisation in relation to nineteenth-century coal mining.

References

Acker, J. (1990) 'Hierarchies, Jobs and Bodies: A Theory of Gendered Organizations', *Gender and Society* 4, 2: 139–158.

Adam, B. (1996) 'Detraditionalization and the Certainty of Uncertain Futures', in P. Heelas, S. Lash, and P. Morris (eds) *Detraditionalization: Critical Reflections on Authority and Identity*, Oxford: Blackwell.

Adkins, L. (1995) *Gendered Work: Sexuality, Family and the Labour Market*, Buckingham, England: Open University Press.

Alexander, J.C. (1996) 'Critical Reflections on "Reflexive Modernization"', *Theory, Culture and Society* 13, 4: 133–138.

Beck, U. (1992) *Risk Society: Towards a New Modernity*, London: Sage.

—— (1994a) 'The Reinvention of Politics: Towards a Theory of Reflexive Modernization', in U. Beck, A. Giddens and S. Lash, *Reflexive Modernization: Politics, Tradition and Aesthetics in the Modern Social Order*, Cambridge: Polity Press.

—— (1994b) 'Self-Dissolution and Self-Endangerment of Industrial Society: What Does This Mean?', in U. Beck, A. Giddens and S. Lash, *Reflexive Modernization: Politics, Tradition and Aesthetics in the Modern Social Order*, Cambridge: Polity Press.

—— (1997) *The Reinvention of Politics*, Cambridge: Polity Press.

Beck, U. and Beck-Gernsheim, E. (1995) *The Normal Chaos of Love*, Cambridge: Polity Press.

—— (1996) 'Individualization and "Precarious Freedoms": Perspectives and Controversies of a Subject-orientated Sociology', in P. Heelas, S. Lash and P. Morris (eds) *Detraditionalization: Critical Reflections on Authority and Identity*, Oxford: Blackwell.

Beck, U., Giddens, A. and Lash, S. (1994) *Reflexive Modernization: Politics, Tradition and Aesthetics in the Modern Social Order*, Cambridge: Polity Press.

Bradley, H. (1989) *Men's Work, Women's Work*, Cambridge: Polity Press.

Casey, C. (1995) *Work, Self and Society: After Industrialism*, London: Routledge.

Cockburn, C. (1981) 'The Material of Male Power', *Feminist Review* 9: 41–58.

—— (1985) *Machinery of Dominance: Women, Men and Technical Know-How*, London: Pluto.

Crompton, R. (1997) *Women and Work in Modern Britain*, Oxford: Oxford University Press.

Davidoff, L. and Hall, C. (1987) *Family Fortunes: Men and Women of the English Middle Classes*, London: Hutchinson.

Finch, J. (1989) *Family Obligations and Social Change*, Cambridge: Polity Press.

Game, A. and Pringle, R. (1984) *Gender at Work*, London: Pluto.

Giddens, A. (1991) *Modernity and Self-Identity: Self and Society in the Late Modern Age*, Cambridge: Polity Press.

—— (1992) *The Transformation of Intimacy: Sexuality, Love and Eroticism in Modern Societies*, Cambridge: Polity Press.

Grace, H. (1991) 'Business, Pleasure, Narrative: The Folktale in Our Times', in R. Diprose and R. Ferrell (eds) *Cartographies: Poststructuralism and the Mapping of Bodies and Spaces*, Sydney: Allen and Unwin.

Halford, S., Savage, M. and Witz, A. (1997) *Gender, Careers and Organisations: Current Developments in Banking, Nursing and Local Government*, Basingstoke, England: Macmillan.

Haraway, D. (1997) 'The Virtual Speculum in the New World Order', *Feminist Review* 55: 22–72.

Heelas, P. (1996) 'Detraditionalization and Its Rivals', in P. Heelas, S. Lash and S.P. Morris (eds) *Detraditionalization: Critical Reflections on Authority and Identity*, Oxford: Blackwell.

Illouz, E. (1997) 'Who Will Care for the Caretaker's Daughter?: Toward a Sociology of Happiness in the Era of Reflexive Modernity', *Theory, Culture and Society* 14, 4: 31–66.

Lash, S. (1994) 'Reflexivity and Its Doubles: Structure, Aesthetics, Community', in U. Beck, A. Giddens and S. Lash (eds) *Reflexive Modernization: Politics, Tradition and Aesthetics in the Modern Social Order*, Cambridge: Polity Press.

Lash, S. and Urry, J. (1994) *Economies of Signs and Space*, London: Sage.

McDowell, L. (1991) 'Life without Father and Ford: The New Gender Order of Post-Fordism', *Transactions*, Institute of British Geographers 16, 4: 400–419.

—— (1997) *Capital Culture: Gender at Work in the City*, Oxford: Blackwell.

Martin, E. (1994) *Flexible Bodies: Tracking Immunity in American Culture – From the Days of Polio to the Age of AIDS*, Boston, Mass.: Beacon.

Pateman, C. (1988) *The Sexual Contract*, Cambridge: Polity Press.

Pringle, R. (1989) *Secretaries Talk: Sexuality, Power and Work*, London: Verso.

Rojek, C. and Urry, J. (eds) (1997) *Touring Cultures: Transformations of Travel and Theory*, London and New York: Routledge.

Saso, M. (1990) *Women in the Japanese Workplace*, London: Shipman.

Savage, M. (1992) 'Women's Expertise, Men's Authority: Gendered Organisation and the Contemporary Middle Classes', in M. Savage and A. Witz (eds) *Gender and Bureaucracy*, Oxford: Blackwell.

Urry, J. (1990) *The Tourist Gaze: Leisure and Travel in Contemporary Societies*, London: Sage.

Walby, S. (1986) *Patriarchy at Work: Patriarchal and Capitalist Relations in Employment*, Cambridge: Polity Press.

—— (1990) *Theorizing Patriarchy*, Oxford: Blackwell.

Weeks, J. (1981) *Sex, Politics and Society: The Regulation of Sexuality Since 1800*, London: Longman.

Witz, A. and Mark-Lawson, J. (1990) 'Familial Control or Patriarchal Domination?: The Case of the Family System of Labour in Nineteenth Century Coal Mining', in H. Corr and L. Jamieson (eds) *Politics of Everyday Life*, Basingstoke, England: Macmillan.

16 Consumerism and 'compulsory individuality'

Women, will and potential

Anne M. Cronin

Nike's ubiquitous imperative *Just Do It* crystallises a range of cultural ideals emblematic of contemporary Western consumerism; individual autonomy, self-expression, 'healthy free will' and the ultimate goal of achieving individual potential. This is an individualised *project* in which the self is both subject and object. In this chapter, I explore the relationship between women and these contemporary consumerist discourses of self-actualisation, self-transformation, will-power and choice. I focus on the role of advertising images as an imagined ideal zone of pure voluntarity in which interpretive freedom becomes expressive, and performative, of individuality. This leads me to ask about the shifting gendered discourses of consumerism and transformations in the ways in which women have discursive access to forms of individuality.

Women and consumerism

Women and Western consumerism have long had an ambiguous relation in which women have been seen as both the subject and object of consumerism, both agents and a commodified currency in capitalist exchange. Rachel Bowlby (1985) notes that in Walter Benjamin's influential work, 'Paris, capital of the nineteenth century', female prostitutes represented the essence of growing consumerism in their role as the embodiment of both the saleswoman and the commodity. This, Bowlby argues, distilled the logic of early consumer capitalism which projected its appeal to women as primary purchasers by offering them sexually attractive images of femininity. In effect, potential female consumers were addressed as seductees in heterosexual fantasy narratives in which their role was to lose self-control and passively yield to powerful male persuasion (Bowlby 1985). Yet these logics of female passivity and lack of control were set against a projected ideal of consumerism as the emblem of growing female freedom in which 'women's consumption could be advocated unequivocally as a means towards the easing of their domestic lot and a token of their growing emancipation' (Bowlby 1985: 20).

The gendered ambiguity and tensions in the growth of Western consumerism are mirrored in some contemporary academic studies. These studies simultaneously mobilise the sign 'Woman' as a passive cipher for the essence of consumerism whilst highlighting women's agency in the distinctively feminine arena of consumption. Don Slater (1997) notes that his attempts to address issues of gender consistently in his study of consumerism fail equally consistently. He argues that his aims to *factor in* gender become systematically *structured out* because the field of consumption is always already figured simultaneously as 'neutral' (although, in effect, masculine) *and* as the emblematic site and sign of femininity. On the one hand, studies of the creative, romantic self of consumerism, or the ideal of Man as producer, emphasizing capitalist 'labour' rather than the labour of reproduction, take the male subject as their generic model from which general statements about consumerism are extrapolated (Slater 1997). On the other hand, the majority of domestic consumption practices such as shopping are carried out by women and the area of consumerism has historically been characterised as feminine (Slater 1997).[1] Indeed, in the development of modern consumerism in the West, 'the feminine is inscribed as the prototypical consumer' (Radner 1995: 3) and consumerism has long been associated with the 'feminine' traits of 'capriciousness and hedonism' (Bowlby 1993: 99). So, whilst the successful targeting of the lucrative market of female consumers is a primary commercial aim and important economic arena, the field of consumption is frequently seen in derogatory terms as feminised, superficial and frivolous.

As Slater (1997) recognises, the generic model of 'the individual' which forms the basis for conceptualisations of the consumer is founded on discourses of Enlightenment rationality which exclude women. As feminist theorists have rigorously argued, gender and what are seen as other 'particularities' such as 'race' have been 'structured out' of the historically embedded epistemological pedigree of 'the individual'. 'The individual' is an exclusive and politically privileged category, access to which is restricted for the overlapping groups of women, lesbians and gay men, black people, working classes, children, and the disabled (see Cornell 1993; Diprose 1994; Fraser 1989; Pateman 1988, 1989; Yeatman 1994). The very exclusion of these intra-categorical 'differences' forms the boundaries for the interiority of 'the individual'. 'He' is self-present in that 'he' has discursive access to the ideal of a unitary, temporally and spatially bounded selfhood: a coherent, 'rational' biographical account of privileged 'identity' defined against 'others' (Diprose 1994). 'Rational Man' as the ideal of self-possessed[2] self-control is set against frivolous, consuming 'Woman' lacking in self-control. This is a complementary gendered structure which is an

> opposition between control and its absence, between behaviour that is knowing and conscious of its aims and behaviour that is imposed on a mind incapable of, or uninterested in, resistance. A perfect accord, which is also a ready-made, and a custom-built, tension, existing between the passive and the active, the victim and the agent, the impressionable and the rational, the feminine and the masculine, the infantile and the adult, the impulsive and the restrained.
>
> (Bowlby 1993: 99)

I would suggest that the 'structuring out' of gender in accounts of consumerism, which is simultaneously the very structuring of the possibility of the self-present identity of 'the individual', can also be seen as *a structuring of will and self-control*. I will return to concepts of will in later sections of the chapter, but at present I want to emphasize the ambiguous position of women in discourses of consumerism. As Hilary Radner (1995) suggests, consumerism offers women the opportunity of acting, but in terms which simultaneously affirm and deny certain forms of feminine identity. In the following section, I examine how the acting out of identities runs alongside discourses of inner potential, self-expression and authenticity in the politics of identity.

Identity politics and Do-It-Yourself culture

The exclusions which constitute the category 'the individual' impact upon the very terms of 'individuality' as an available form of unique selfhood. Contemporary popular discourses of individuality and identity in consumerism take as their centre ideals of an authentic inner self which can be expressed through consumption practices as technologies of the self (see Cole and Hribar 1995).[3] Yet consumption practices include not only material decisions and economic exchange, but also an engagement with images within consumerist discourses of desire, acquisition and pleasures of looking. As I will go on to discuss, advertising images draw on and re-present the ideals of individuality and inner authenticity within contemporary discourses of selfhood. This introspective search for the essence of individuality, in which the self is seen as having *inner depths* (Foucault 1988), is situated within more general rhetoric of identity politics. This is an explicit politicising of individual self-definition in which discourses position individuals as having a *right* to self-expression (Miller 1993). 'Finding yourself' and expressing this discovery as the truth of individual identity is lauded as the ultimate authentic goal of selfhood. This search for the self is played out in one form through an engagement with images and, indeed, access to media images has become codified within certain media policy discourses as an important *right* (Murdoch 1992).

Charles Taylor (1994) locates these identity politics through a discussion of individual 'potential' and the cultural imperative to express this potential. Here, the self is directed to embark on processes of self-monitoring through the production of 'authentic self-knowledge' of the self's interiority whilst being encouraged to engage reflexively with the self as 'project'. Taylor argues that contact with this inner self takes on a moral accent or form of 'duty' to oneself. Added to this morally inscribed interrogation of interiority is the idea that each person has a unique, original inner essence which is considered as individualised 'potential' (Taylor 1994). The realisation of this potential as a form of 'self-actualisation' becomes a duty in the imperative to live one's life 'authentically', that is, in touch with one's inner, or true, self: 'Being true to myself means being true to my own originality, which is something only I can articulate and discover. In articulating it, I am also defining myself. I am realizing a potentiality that is properly my own' (Taylor 1994: 78).

The long-running series of advertising campaigns for Nike provide an apt illustration of these politics of interiority and individuality. These campaigns abstract the advertising message to such a degree that we are presented only with the imperative *Just Do It*. The advertisements draw on ubiquitous discourses of self-transformation, exercise regimes, free will and self-expressive individuality (Cole and Hribar 1995). In the following, I will argue that in the presentation of *self as project*, these discourses mobilise (at least) two distinct, yet mutually implicated, forms of temporality. The self is presented as a project, venture, or goal to be aimed at. This is a casting forward of a promise of potential and transformation. Yet, the project also implies a projecting forward of an already-established identity which makes possible the search for transformation in the first place.

In the first sense, the self is framed as a future-oriented goal to be achieved, a potentiality that sets forth an aim for the self that will be. Here, a specific notion of individuality is invoked in which only that self may know what it must do in the imperative to *Just Do It*. It is a search for the inner depths and potential of the self, and one which the advertising campaigns attempt to brand. Nike appears to promise self-transformation through exercise, yet the true exercise that Nike is proposing is the branded search for individuality and authenticity in the exploration of potential. Yet this search for the self, or actualisation of potential, can never be finally realised as the very discourse of potentiality is future-oriented; it forever looks forward to what it may be (or what it may buy). In this sense, the self as project is a journey which does not depart from a located self-present identity; it projects an ideal of identity towards which it aims.

In the second form of temporality, the framing of potential does not so much set forth an aim as project that which already exists. The self as project paradoxically requires the very capacities of actualised selfhood for which it is searching in order to initiate that same search. In this second sense, it is less a formulation of *self as project* yet to be achieved, more a *projecting* of a pre-constituted self. The imperative to *Just Do It* in the Nike advertisements temporally projects the status of established selfhood which awaits the moment of self-expression through a branded commodity in consumerist discourses. So here, Nike is accessing a second level of potential and proposes that you 'just be yourself' through the medium of its brand. The promise of the brand is that it taps into and expresses the essence of who you are in ways which you can barely articulate yourself.

In these multiple temporalities, the potential of the self is always already located in the inner depths of the self, or unique individuality of that person. Yet simultaneously, the self's potential is located beyond the imagined interiority of the self as a future projection which always shifts out of reach. As in Taylor's (1994) account, each person is posited as *innately* original and unique, and yet cannot be named as such until that person articulates their inner essence or potential. However, the particular form that this originality will take, that which defines the very 'individuality' of the person, can only be articulated by that same person. Yet they are authorised and enabled to search for it only by the very qualities of unitary and unique personhood for which they are searching.

This selfhood will only be realised, materialised or recognisable as such in the *Just Do It* moment of articulation and definition.

These temporalities coincide to produce an ideal of the self that shifts uneasily between the unique and the universal, what exists and what will exist, the potential and the actual. The imperative *Just Do It* invokes a tension between spontaneity and calculated goal-orientation, and between will or self-control and the material of the body. This materiality of the body is framed as the raw material in the processes of self-transformation in which the body is a site of potentiality in non-specified aims of self-materialisation or transformation. This is a body of projected potentiality in which regimes of self-control release that self-expressive potential of the body-to-be. Such a body-to-be can be described as harder, slimmer and more disciplined. Self-control and will-power shape the future body. Yet within the same discursive frame, the materiality of the body is presented as a pre-existent material base from which to project an ideal of self-control or will; here the body shapes the will.

This fusion of seemingly contradictory temporalities can be said to operate *performatively* in a 'reiterative and citational practice by which discourse produces the effects it names' (Butler 1993: 2). As I will explore in later sections, the will or self-control that threads through this process cannot be seen as a voluntaristic self-expression which calls the self into being. The ideal of the voluntaristic will of the individual is paradoxically framed through 'compulsory individuality'. As I will argue, this is compulsory in the sense that the expression of selfhood is framed as both a right and a duty, and the ambiguous terms of 'authentic individuality' within consumerist identity politics become one of the few ways to access a legitimised selfhood.

Yet, as I have discussed, certain overlapping groups have suffered *compulsory exclusion* from these very terms of individuality. Those excluded from the white, Western, male, heterosexual, middle class, able-bodied model of 'the individual' do not have this privileged access to the discursive status of individuality. They are not located from a position of ideal, unitary identity from which to depart and return, and so do not hold the same relation to potential. If excluded groups cannot fully access the terms of individuality, in what ways may they be potentially unique? In what ways may they search for their imagined 'authentic' inner selves if they have historically been located beyond the borders of 'the authentic' self-present individual? These 'non-locations' in relation to ideal selfhood may be thought as forms of *inter-temporality* which may not be legible in conventional terms. That is, certain groups may be positioned in multiple and shifting relations to 'the self that is' and 'the self to be'. These positionings may criss-cross over and through the categories of race, gender, sexuality, class, and forms of experiencing the body in ways which may not be easily read or easily seen through images. In the following section, I explore how Drucilla Cornell's (1993) formulation of 'recollective imagination' may be used to think through these disjunctive temporalities.

Recollective imagination: anticipating the past and reviewing the future

Cornell's (1993) conceptual framework of 'recollective imagination' provides a way of understanding the relations between time, knowledge and the possibilities of the self. It can help to imagine how the 'authentic uniqueness' of individuals in identity politics is proposed to exist or develop over time. 'Recollective imagination' insists on the mutual implication of the past, present and future in any one moment of interpretation. Cornell developed this schema primarily to explore the temporalities of legal interpretation, but here I want to use the framework to address performativity as an interpretive and visual process. 'The self as project' invokes this interpretive process of seeking self-knowledge in the imagined depths of the self through the medium of advertising images. These are interpretive moments in which the self draws on its potential in order to imagine what that potential may be through discourses of self-presence and authenticity which are particularly prevalent in consumerism.

In this schema, Cornell argues for a recognition of the importance of the conjectural as a future-oriented exercise in interpretation, in the form of the 'would be' or 'as if'. This projection of meaning is crucial for understanding processes of interpretation, yet is also interwoven with accessing understandings of the past and present:

> Interpretation ... is retrospective in the sense that we always begin the process of interpretation from within a pregiven context. The process is also prospective, because it involves the elaboration of the 'would be's' inherent in the context itself ... The 'as if' is oriented toward the future in that we project the proposition onto a future situation to draw out its meaning. The future is implicit in the act of interpretation.
>
> (Cornell 1993: 27–28)

In the context of viewers' interpretations of advertising images such as the Nike campaigns, this projection of potential in the search for the meaning of the self draws on the past, present and future. The ideal self in the temporal present attempts to authorise itself by drawing on a coherent biographical sense of past-self. This past-self, in turn, can only be understood through projecting the present-self onto the future through conjectures of 'would be' or 'as if'. The interpretation of the imperative *Just Do It* in the Nike advert involves the departure from, and the return to, an ideal of unitary identity which frames that self's potential. *Just Do It* is the ideal of consumer choice as the route to the paradoxical identification and expression of the self's potential. This is a meeting of a temporalised politics of interpretation and a politics of choice in which consumerist discourses of self-actualisation frame the self's potential.

A politics of choice and compulsory individuality

Marilyn Strathern (1992) has explored how discourses of choice have come to form a crucial site in the Western production of ideas of 'individuality'. The mechanisms of choice do not necessarily function through external control, for example the persuasion of advertising. Rather, such mechanisms provide what Strathern calls a 'prescriptive individualism' (1992: 152). That is, forms of control are manifested in inner-directed technologies of the self which in consumerism are expressed as technologies of choice. An individual is defined by the 'innate' capacity of 'free choice' and this choice expresses the inner authentic individuality of that person. The abstracted notion of 'choice' becomes an inherent ideal as well as the route to the expression of individuality. Yet, within this politics of choice, we have *no choice but to choose* if we are to express ourselves as individuals, and self-expression is the cornerstone of the politics of identity described by Taylor (1994). This self-expressive choice installs what I would call a *compulsory individuality*. The expression and enactment of choice (and the capacity of choosing) is framed as a compulsory choice: individuality is not an option but rather the compulsory route to selfhood. In these politics of choice *Just Do It* is not an invitation, but an imperative.

Choice does not merely *represent* a pre-formed self imbued with potential. Rather, it is a performative enactment of self, invoking the category of selfhood, or the potential of individual selfhood, in the temporality of interpretation and agentic choice (or search for self-knowledge). This model of choice produces the self, in Nikolas Rose's terms, as 'an entrepreneur of itself' (1992: 150), in which consumerist work upon the self is a project or enterprise. This self-management through choice, Rose argues, is framed as an ethical duty to the self and to society. Yet, as I have argued, the self is not a pre-constituted category, but must be performatively produced through those very discourses of choice. *Just Do It* as the anthem for a kind of *Do It Yourself* culture draws on the twin ideals of 'just be yourself' and 'just do yourself'. You can 'Just be who you are' by searching for your inner essence and potential; 'just do yourself' as the performative, reiterative series of acts which constitutes that very self in the moment of acting.

On the one hand, the (white, classed, heterosexual) category 'Woman' is the epitome of this politics of choice and self-actualisation in which the self is 'an entrepreneur of itself' (Rose 1992: 150). In Bowlby's (1985) account of Benjamin's work on Paris, turn-of-the century prostitutes were saleswomen and product in one and encapsulated the growing consumerist ethos. More generally, the category 'Woman' is caught in this tension through a historical positioning of being both subject and object of consumerism. Consumerism promises women self-transformation and appears to validate women's choices. Yet, even as subjects, women have faced an impossible imperative 'to be ourselves' through 'doing ourselves' mediated by 'doing' make-up (making yourself up), fashion (fashioning yourself), dieting and exercise (re-forming yourself) (Evans and Thornton 1989; Radner 1995). This Do-It-Yourself culture revolves around an expression of will and 'free choice' in the actualisation and transformation of the self. Yet, despite the often skilful ways that women negotiate these tensions, the epistemological status of self-present identity is denied to women because of compulsory exclusion from the category of individuality.[4] This crystallises the impossible imperative to 'be yourself' in the identity politics of consumerism. Women have never inhabited a self-present identity in order to return to it in interpretive processes of self-knowledge.

In these politics of individuality, agency or will is foregrounded and is focused through an ideal of self-expression, for example in the exercise of the body and the will required in the regimes of the *Just Do It* campaign. Yet, if self-expressive individuality is compulsory yet exclusive, the terms of 'will' or agency become problematised. In the following section, I explore Sedgwick's (1994) work on discourses of free will and how they have developed through ubiquitous contemporary discourses of addiction.

Maladies of the will and compulsive individuality

The paradoxical discourse of *compulsory* choice restates the terms of so-called 'free will' or agency and points to the possibly compulsive nature of such choice. Eve K. Sedgwick (1994) has explored how the histories of the concepts of 'free will' and compulsion or addiction have been unevenly intertwined such that individual acts come to gel into identities. Sedgwick traces the history of how drug-users came to be redefined discursively as *addicts* and so displaced the locus of addictiveness from the substance (as in 'substance abuse') to the compromised 'will free' or self-control of the addict. This, she argues, radically expanded the potential for addiction attribution such that individual's *relation* to substances was emphasised rather than the imagined addictive properties of substances themselves. For example, the pathologising of food consumption (as in Overeaters Anonymous) coexists with the pathologising of food refusal (anorexia) and the pathologising of highly controlled intermittent food consumption (bulimia) (Sedgwick 1994). Here, the food itself is not seen as the site from which is produced addictive compulsion, but rather, it is the exercise of will or self-control that defines the addiction: 'Addiction, under this definition, resides only in the *structure* of a will that is always somehow insufficiently free, a choice whose voluntarity is insufficiently pure' (Sedgwick 1994: 132). Indeed, Sedgwick argues, contemporary formulations of addiction (as lack of the capacity of choice) are focused on any object or site, including work ('workaholism'), shopping ('shopaholism'), relationships ('co-dependency'), or even self-help groups for addicts.

This 'structuring of the will' should be seen as a fundamentally gendered discourse, interweaving ideals of class, race, respectability and sexuality.[5] Indeed, Sedgwick's description of the shift in how pathological addiction is constructed can be compared with the seductive effect of the extravagant display of commodities on women shoppers in early Western consumerism. In particular, the department stores' visual display of luxurious goods was accused of 'unleashing passions' and causing 'intoxication' amongst women shoppers who were seen as vulnerable to this powerful influence (Nava 1997: 76). In this scenario, the voluptuousness of the commodities and the dizzyingly extravagant experience of the department store were the sites/objects of compulsion which could release such compelling forces and destroy women's self-control. This destruction of self-control was seen to be manifested in one form through such 'aberrant' behaviour as shoplifting.

Understandings of the site of compulsion, particularly in relation to consumerism, shifted with the development of psychological models for conceptualising shoplifting in department stores. Cecilia Fredriksson (1997) describes how discourses of kleptomania grew in the inter-war period in Europe and became strongly associated with women. Kleptomania was seen as a form of irrational behaviour and the feminine lack of self-control was seen to be exacerbated by the temptations of the department store. Social order was disrupted and middle class women suddenly became 'common thieves' (Fredriksson 1997: 120). Significantly, the growth of kleptomania as an explanatory framework shifted the locus of compulsion from the stores themselves (which came to be seen as an aggravation rather than a primary cause) to within the self; the kleptomaniac became a specific classed and gendered taxonomy whose addiction was considered to be caused by a pathological lack of self-control (Fredriksson 1997).

In these 'maladies of the will', each act of free will or choice problematises the boundaries of voluntarity to the extent that 'the assertion of will itself has come to appear addictive' (Sedgwick 1994: 133). In effect, this expanded potential for attributing addiction scours the frontiers of addiction in the search for a zone of 'natural free will' which is uncontaminated by compulsion. It is compelled, in Sedgwick's words, by its own 'compulsion to isolate some new, receding but absolutized space of *pure* voluntarity' (1994: 134). Sedgwick argues that this space of imagined pure voluntarity is positioned as the imperative *Just Do It* (as in the Nike advert) in antagonism with the imperative *Just Say No* (as in anti-drug campaigns). In effect, there is no choice but to choose to engage the will, and every exercise of will is defined as choice. 'Not choosing' (as differentiated from 'choosing not to') becomes a logical impossibility, a discursive blank space or kind of non-being.

In this scenario, the imagined zone of pure voluntarity is pulled between inner potential and future/exterior potential and is temporally dragged between the past/present/future of self-knowledge and interpretation as described in Cornell's (1993) account. Using Sedgwick's (1994) framework, this is an addictive quest for self-knowledge which impossibly aims for the 'pure voluntaristic self' uncontaminated by addictive compulsion. Sedgwick argues that attempts to manage the impossible binds of these absolutes have been addressed in one form through 'twelve-steps' programmes of addiction therapy. These revolve around what she calls 'the micromanagement of absolutes' (1994: 134) and work through 'a technique of temporal fragmentation, the highly existential "one day at a time" that dislinks every moment of choice (and of course they are infinite) from both the identity-history and the intention-futurity that might be thought to constrain it' (1994: 134).

This, I would argue, can be seen as a redoubling of the temporalities of potential and of interpretation that I discussed in earlier sections. In one sense, this micromanagement of absolutes is an attempt to prise apart the temporalities of identity as project/aim (individual potential as an aim) *and* identity as a pre-constituted, projected selfhood (individual potential as innate). And, in another sense, it is an attempt to isolate and suspend the temporalities of interpretation in Cornell's (1993) 'recollective imagination' such that the interdependence of past-self, present-self and future-self is severed. So here, the ideal zone of pure voluntarity is imagined through the wilful fragmenting of time, choice and inter-pretation. This serves to contract the horizons of the possible and so produce the imagined possibility of action, choice and interpretation divorced from indi-vidual history. In the next section, I will argue that images, and particularly advertising images, have been seen as one form of this ideal space of voluntarity through which 'free interpretive will' is imagined to express the self.

Images as spaces/times of pure voluntarity

Academics and advertising practitioners have long debated the relationship between the interpretation of advertising images, the purchase of goods, the expression of 'informed free choice' and the production of identities (Goldman 1992; Leiss *et al.* 1990; Mattelart 1991; Schudson 1993; Wernick 1991). In one strategy, advertising agencies draw on discourses of free self-expressive choice and interpretation which are prevalent in contemporary identity politics and attempt to *brand* those interpretive movements (see Cronin 1997). This ideal of free *interpretive* choice of advertising images is marked as disconnected from mat-erial and economic constraints and lauded as a zone of free will and pure voluntarity.

Bowlby's (1985) analysis of the concept of the shopper's opt-out clause of 'just looking' encapsulates this ideal of freedom. Bowlby argues that 'just looking' is the time of hesitation, of reflection and of resisting the shop assistant's queries. This could be seen as an attempt at the micromanagement of the contradictory pull from the forces of *Just Buy It* and *Just Say No* in the temporalities of choice. In an adaptation of Sedgwick's (1994) analysis of the 'one day at a time' programmes of addiction management, 'just looking' can become the emblem of the 'one moment at a time' programme of will management. It attempts to dislocate the moments of looking and potential choice from the identity-history and the intention-futurity of the self by a strategy of hesitation and temporal suspension. In the context of visually engaging with advertising images rather than the practice of shopping, 'just looking' abstracts this ideal further. Images become the ultimate imagined zone of 'pure voluntarity' in which potential can be freely expressed and is not temporally confined by identity-history. *Just Do It* does not here refer to the management and re-forming of the body through the will: *Just Do It* is the abstraction of will from the body and the ideal of the pure expression of will and self. In this sense, 'just looking' at images seems at once passive yet wilful.

Yet the ideal of images as the space of pure voluntarity does not only dislocate temporalities of *individual* identity-history and intention-futurity. The *Just Do It* ideal promoted by Nike also disembeds cycles of capitalist consumption and production from their material referents and 'commands "us" to ignore the historical, cultural and structural circumstances and constraints through which "we" make history and history makes "us". Given these erasures, what does Nike (ask us to) imagine?' (Cole and Hribar 1995: 353). What Nike asks us not to imagine (or interpret) through its images are the material circumstances of production of its commodities. Media scandals have exposed how Nike employs extremely low-paid workers in Indonesia, 85 per cent of whom are women, and generates massive profits through large mark-ups.[6] A range of protest groups have been campaigning for better working conditions and pay and have attempted to re-engage the abstraction of Nike's slogan to the materiality of its exploitative practices by producing slogans of their own:[7] 'Boycott Nike. Just Do It!',[8] 'Justice Do It Nike', 'Just Stop It'.

So the ideal of images as a space of pure voluntarity is a utopian gloss on material and discursive constraints in a dual sense. For those workers exploited by Nike, the abstraction of the consumerist ideal of potential and free self-expression is an abstraction from the realities of neo-colonial economic exploitation. For the privileged in the West, the concept of images as the zone of pure voluntarity in interpretation remains a utopian ideal of individual free will. As I have previously argued, discourses of choice, potential and 'compulsory individuality' underwrite this imagined free zone. The self is performatively produced through these discourses in a *compulsory* and reiterative citiational mechanism: the concepts of free will and choice are generated through the very definitions which constrain them. The impossible temporalities of potential and the self as project mean that individuals do not have free access to prise apart those temporalities and suspend definitions of choice and selfhood. In the final section, I explore how women are contradictorily positioned in these shifting discourses of will and choice.

Transformations, choice and will-power

In the discourses I have outlined, the ideal of images as the space of pure voluntarity or will-power is rather ambiguous. This ideal of images as uncontaminated by compulsion or the restriction of choice coexists uneasily with a certain cultural anxiety about the power of images to corrupt or manipulate the will. This anxiety takes many forms including morally inscribed debates over violent images producing violent behaviour (see Seltzer 1993), pornographic images producing objectifying responses from men towards women (see Butler 1997), and advertising images manipulating viewers into identifying with commodities and/or purchasing goods (see Leiss *et al.* 1990).

Within these discourses of anxiety, women are positioned as particularly susceptible to 'manipulation' from images, echoing Bowlby's (1985) analysis of turn-of-the century debates around the feminised domain of consumption. Yet, paradoxically, women are also addressed through consumer discourses which promote the ideal that women can engage in processes of self-transformation through consumption practices. These doublings of images as sites of both voluntarism and compulsion, and women as both agents and passive ciphers or dupes, condense the ideals of certain discourses of identity politics which emphasise will-power as the primary transformative force in an individual's life. However, this is an individualised politics in which women and overlapping subordinated groups have never been granted access to the discursive status of the 'individual'.

This way of approaching contemporary gendered consumer discourses raises several issues which I think require further feminist analysis. First, it may be that there are shifts in the ways in which women can be seen as emblematic of contemporary consumerism. Men, and particularly young men, are increasingly being addressed in marketing and advertising terms as a self-consciously gendered group (Mort 1996). This may alter the terms in which consumer discourses have historically been coded as feminised in ways which may not necessarily 'feminise' the young men being addressed through consumerism. But second, and I think more importantly, the way in which advertising has tapped into and developed self-expressive identity politics changes the terms in which identities are 'imagined' in an epistemological and material sense through visual interpretation.

Cornell's (1993) framework of 'recollective imagination' points to the ways in which 'imagining' is more than an abstract, dream-like realm of self-absorption and reflection.[9] I would suggest that imagining is also a primary means by which a subject draws on epistemological heritages of privilege or subordination and engages these discursive positionings to figure 'itself' as a coherent biographical unity across time, that is, a being with an identity. The meaning-making processes of imagining the connections between the past-self, present-self and future-self draw on and refigure ideals of potential and self-expression. Within the consumerist ethos of advertising imagery, this future-oriented potentiality is positioned as an ideal which can be bought, yet somehow remains elusive, and as an ideal which can never be finally achieved, yet is innate in every individual. The advertising industry attempts to intervene in this imaginative circuitry of potentiality and identity politics and tries to *incorporate* its brand within the individual's biographical imaginative movements.

This incorporation occurs at a material as well as at an epistemological level of biography and discursive heritage. Identities are imagined in a material or corporeal sense in the visual 'acts' of seeing which performatively constitute the self, as I have explored in more depth elsewhere (Cronin 1997). As Butler (1993, 1997) stresses, discourses frame the multiple terms of the materiality of the body. The *Just Do It* terms of the consumerist imperative of self-management and 'compulsory choice' frame the very materiality of the body and effect how those bodies are experienced.

The significance of images within these politics of potentiality and choice cannot be reduced to the expansion of the visual field by technological innovations in image production and new media networks (see Morley and Robins

1995). I would argue that advertising shifts the significance of the visual by the way that certain contemporary advertising abstracts the notion of will and presents ideals of interpretive freedom of images as the ideal of individual voluntarity. This is the ideal of images as the zone of pure voluntarity which promises the ultimate freedom of consumerist self-transformation.

Yet, as I have argued above, this does not produce an egalitarian, abstracted zone of visual interpretation and expression. Approaching images as a zone of pure voluntarity again 'factors out' gender and other 'differences', as in Slater's (1997) account, by the imagined neutrality of the imaginative process of self-constitution. Yet this is not a neutral process, but a structuring of the will and an interpretive wilfulness that draws on the unevenly conferred epistemological status of 'individuality' and reproduces privilege and subordination in new ways. This is an individualised politics of the expression (and the performative production) of 'will-power' and individual potential through the (compulsory) engagement of will in the interpretation of images. This is a 'compulsory individuality' paradoxically produced through interpretive choice and a redoubling of the terms of women's and overlapping groups' exclusion from the social, cultural and epistemological status of 'the individual'.

Acknowledgements

I would like to thank the editors for their help and also Celia Lury and Beverley Skeggs for their insightful comments on earlier forms of this chapter.

Notes

1   Whilst women may predominantly take the role of primary purchaser of goods, the gendered division of decision-making and financial control within marriage points to more complex relations of consumer power (Pahl 1989).
2   This is a reference to 'the possessive individual' of capitalism. See Pateman (1988) for a discussion with specific reference to gender.
3   Elsewhere I have argued that, paradoxically, the terms of this 'authentic individuality' may also be expressed through discourses of a flexible relation to artificiality, dissimulation and irony. This is less an expression of authenticity than a display of the art of artifice (Cronin 1997).
4   This exclusion is differently inflected for overlapping groups of women. See Skeggs (1997) for a discussion of how working-class women use discourses of 'glamour' to negotiate positionings of class and sexuality. See Berlant (1993) on how black women use signs of class and sexuality to 'pass' for white and gain social privilege. See Hermes (1995) on how women read women's magazines and respond to images of femininity.
5   The growth of early department stores occurred in the context of considerable anxiety and upheaval over women's position in society and rhetoric of emancipation. These concerns also focused on class decomposition and shifts in the social order made all the more visible by the social mingling within the stores (Bowlby 1985; Nava 1997).
6   'Nike work at 16p an hour? Just do it', *Observer*, 3 December 1995.
7   'The National Organization for Women' in the USA and 'Community Aid Abroad' (http://www.caa.org.au/campaigns/nike/) have been vigorous in their protests.
8   'Boycott Nike' group's web page is at http://www.saigon.com/~nike/

9   Colin Campbell (1987) has explored the possibility of imaginative pleasures detached from the satisfaction of specific appetites or desires in consumerism. This may be useful in thinking through the implications of visual engagement with advertising imagery detached from the material purchase and consumption of goods or services.

References

Berlant, L. (1993) 'National Brands/National Bodies: *Imitation of Life*', in B. Robbins (ed.) *The Phantom Public Sphere*, Minneapolis: University of Minnesota Press.

Bowlby, R. (1985) *Just Looking: Consumer Culture in Dreisser, Gissing and Zola*, London: Routledge.

—— (1993) *Shopping with Freud*, London: Routledge.

Butler, J. (1993) *Bodies That Matter: On the Discursive Limits of 'Sex'*, London: Routledge.

—— (1997) *Excitable Speech: A Politics of the Performative*, London: Routledge.

Campbell, C. (1987) *The Romantic Ethic and the Spirit of Modern Consumerism*, Oxford: Basil Blackwell.

Cole, C.L. and Hribar, A. (1995) 'Celebrity Feminism: *Nike Style* Post-Fordism, Transcendence, and Consumer Power', *Sociology of Sport Journal* 12, 4: 347–369.

Cornell, D. (1993) *Transformations: Recollective Imagination and Sexual Difference*, London: Routledge.

Cronin, A.M. (1997) 'Temporalities of the Visual and Spaces of Knowledge: Branding 'The Third Dimension' in Advertising', *Space and Culture: The Journal* 1, 1: 85–104.

Diprose, R. (1994) *The Bodies of Women: Ethics, Embodiment and Sexual Difference*, London: Routledge.

Evans, C. and Thornton, M. (1989) *Women and Fashion: A New Look*, London: Routledge.

Foucault, M. (1988) 'Technologies of the Self', in L.H. Martin, H. Gutman and P.H. Hutton (eds) *Technologies of the Self: A Seminar with Michel Foucault*, London: Tavistock.

Fraser, N. (1989) *Unruly Practices: Power, Discourse and Gender in Contemporary Social Theory*, Cambridge: Polity Press (in association with Blackwell).

Fredriksson, C. (1997) 'The Making of a Swedish Department Store Culture', in P. Falk and C. Campbell (eds) *The Shopping Experience*, London: Sage.

Goldman, R. (1992) *Reading Ads Socially*, London: Routledge.

Hermes, J. (1995) *Reading Women's Magazines: An Analysis of Everyday Media Use*, Cambridge and Oxford: Polity Press (in association with Blackwell).

Leiss, W., Kline, S. and Jhally, S. (1990) *Social Communication in Advertising: Persons, Products and Images of Well-Being*, London and New York: Routledge.

Mattelart, A. (1991) *Advertising International: The Privatisation of Public Space*, Baltimore, Md.: Johns Hopkins University Press.

Miller, T. (1993) *The Well-Tempered Self: Citizenship, Culture and the Postmodern Self*, Baltimore, Md.: Johns Hopkins University Press.

Morley, D. and Robins, K. (1995) *Spaces of Identity: Global Media, Electronic Landscapes and Cultural Boundaries*, New York: Routledge.

Mort, F. (1996) *Cultures of Consumption: Masculinities and Social Space in Late Twentieth Century Britain*, New York: Routledge.

Murdoch, G. (1992) 'Citizens, Consumers and Public Culture', in M. Skovmand and K. Schrøder (eds) *Reappraising Transnational Media*, New York: Routledge.

Nava, M. (1997) 'Modernity's Disavowal: Women, the City and the Department Store', in P. Falk and C. Campbell (eds) *The Shopping Experience*, London: Sage.

Pahl, J. (1989) *Money and Marriage*, Basingstoke, England: Macmillan.

Pateman, C. (1988) *The Sexual Contract*, Oxford: Blackwell.

—— (1989) *The Disorder of Women: Democracy, Feminism and Political Theory*, Cambridge: Polity Press (in association with Blackwell).

Radner, H. (1995) *Shopping Around: Feminine Culture and the Pursuit of Pleasure*, London : Routledge.

Rose, N. (1992) 'Governing the Enterprising Self', in P. Heelas and P. Morris (eds) *The Values of Enterprise Culture: The Moral Debate*, London and New York: Routledge.

Schudson, M. (1993) *Advertising, the Uneasy Persuasion: Its Dubious Impact on American Society*, New York: Routledge.

Sedgwick, E.K. (1994) *Tendencies*, New York: Routledge.

Seltzer, M. (1993) 'Serial killers', *Differences*, 5, 1: 92–128.

Skeggs, B. (1997) *Formations of Class and Gender: Becoming Respectable*, London: Sage.

Slater, D. (1997) *Consumer Culture and Modernity*, Cambridge: Polity Press.

Strathern, M. (1992) *After Nature: English Kinship in the Late Twentieth Century*, Cambridge: Cambridge University Press.

Taylor, C. (1994) 'The Politics of Recognition', in D.T. Goldberg (ed.) *Multiculturalism: A Reader*, Oxford: Blackwell.

Wernick, A. (1991) *Promotional Culture: Advertising, Ideology and Symbolic Expression*, London: Sage.

Yeatman, A. (1994) *Postmodern Revisionings of the Political*, London: Routledge.

17 Reframing pregnant embodiment

Imogen Tyler

'I' am not 'I,' I AM not, I am not ONE.

Luce Irigaray

Pregnancies, when they occur, occur in women's bodies. For those who champion 'choice' to lose sight of this simple and obvious, yet profoundly radical fact in a post-1980s struggle for reproductive freedom would be finally to surrender the possibility of freedom.

Valerie Hartouni

We are lacking models that explain how identity might be retained whilst impregnated with otherness, and whilst other selves are generated from within the embodied self.

Christine Battersby

Autobiographical notes on discovering pregnancy: the failure of the cogito

Am I pregnant? Cogito, ergo sum, I think I am, I think, therefore I am. There is no God here though, no certainty. To test my doubt , I turn to science. I get up early. I lock the bathroom door. I pee on a plastic stick. I wait for a lifetime and there it is, a blue line in the window. I am pregnant. I am pregnant, but nothing is assured. The ground shakes. I vomit, once, twice. I get dressed, I go to work. What to think. What to feel. What to do. I am waiting for the train, fingering the notes of my lecture, pregnantly. Today, on my feminist philosophy course, I am teaching Luce Irigaray. What to think, what to feel, what to do. The seminar room is beginning to fill, I write some notes on the blackboard: The concept of … The conception of … She conceives … 'Cells fuse, split, and proliferate; volumes grow, tissues stretch, and body fluids change rhythm, speeding up or slowing down' (Kristeva 1993: 236). The scraping of chairs, laughter, chatting, then quiet. Turning around I look into a sea of faces, all women, all so different, old, young, black, white, mothers, daughters, sisters … I am finding it difficult to concentrate. I pass work sheets around. 'Let us start', I say, 'by reading some quotes together to get a feel for Irigaray's language for her ideas, her work, I'll begin': ' "I" am not "I," I am not, I *am* not *one*' (Irigaray 1985b: 120).

In/out the frame, a philosophy seminar at eight and a half months

> I am a mountain now, among mountainy women.
> The doctors move among us as if our bigness
> Frightened the mind. They smile like fools.
> They are to blame for what I am, and they know it.
> They hug their flatness like a kind of health.
> And what if they found themselves surprised, as I did?
> They would go mad with it.
>
> Sylvia Plath

I walk into a philosophy seminar for postgraduates and staff. There are three women present and fifteen men. I am pregnant. I am heavily pregnant. Indeed, to use an obsolete word, I am 'pregrand', extraordinarily large, gargantuan. I feel like Dog Woman in Jeanette Winterson's *Sexing the Cherry*, 'You are too big Madam' (Winterson 1989: 107). I have arrived late, I had to pee several times before I went in to make sure I would last the course, now there is no sliding into the room unnoticed. Chairs, tables and aspiring philosophers have to be moved to let me through. I manipulate my body as though it is the old me not this mammoth becoming. 'I literally do not have a firm sense of where my body ends and the world begins' (Young 1990: 163). It seems as though I bump against everything, everyone, as I waddle towards an empty seat at the back of the room, 'for my habits retain the old sense of my boundaries' (Young 1990: 164). I ignore the sigh of embarrassment and discomfort initiated by my passage. However, I could not fail to note that men seemed to be 'hugging their flatness' as I squeezed past. Do I frighten the philosophical mind? As de Beauvoir writes, '[the pregnant woman] scares children who are proud of their young, straight bodies and makes young people titter contemptuously because she is a human being, a conscious and free individual, who has become life's passive instrument' (de Beauvoir 1953: 513).

What I clearly recall about this philosophy seminar is not the paper, but the overwhelming sense of difference I had that afternoon. For this experience revealed to me more directly than ever before the way in which masculine principles of individuality, non-contradiction and singular temporality still underpin basic understandings of subjectivity. Can the philosophical body, philosophical bodies, contain, account for, or even imagine, a body, a subject, that reproduces others, not metaphorically, but literally?

The visiting professor delivers his paper. At the end of the philosophy seminar, one of the women in the room asks a question. It goes something like this: 'Do you consider questions of sexual difference, indeed difference, relevant to the formulation of being you have outlined in your paper?' The question is polite but loaded. The answer, 'Interesting', read 'not interesting at all to me'; 'I must think about that', read 'I never will'. The questioner doesn't pursue her point – is there any point? She has undoubtedly asked that question, in variegated forms, in philosophy seminars for years. I hear Irigaray's words echoing from the margins once again: the powerful 'sexual indifference that subtends [philosophical discourse] assures its closure and assurance' (Irigaray 1985b: 72).

That hot day I am overcome with tired rage at this indifference. But I sit quietly in my plastic chair and continue with my gestation, my metamorphosis. There is a foot caught in my ribs, hands and fingers are moving, making tracks on my hard belly. Within these touches there is no possibility of distinguishing what is touching from what is being touched. How can I speak this? 'I/you touch you/me' (Irigaray 1985b: 209). The curve at the bottom of my back aches, ankles are so tumescent that my legs disappear into my feet without distinction. My breasts are heavy and swollen and I do not recognise the feeling of these darkened nipples brushing against my top and leaking colostrum into my bra. And my skin, my skin is ripping apart, veins and stretch marks tattoo me as membranes give way, a dark line runs from navel to crotch where walls of muscle slowly separate. Leaky vessel, I might split apart any moment, pour myself onto the floor in bits. I am not metaphor, but real alien becoming, perpetually modified. My body, my massive pregnant body, wants to stand up, to go to the front of the room, to present *itself* as a question. The dichotomy of subject and object is called into question by this question, as it is already posed by this body, presented, here and now. It dawns on me that my pregnant embodiment is a topology which remains unmapped, unthought, indeed unthinkable, within a philosophical landscape of stable forms. Look: '*She is neither one nor two.* Rigorously speaking, she cannot be identified either as one person, or as two. She resists all adequate definition' (Irigaray 1985b: 26; my emphasis). I am, philosophically, a freak. I embody the loss of self which has always bewitched you, which you have continually romanticised. But I am here, present in the flesh, and I represent 'the ever-present possibility of sliding back into the corporeal abyss from which [you] were formed' (Grosz 1992: 198). Look, look away, quick, there is a knee, an elbow, poking through my skin as you speak. I am fascinating. I want to laugh and laugh as I face the sheer abyss that divides my-self, pregnantly embodied, and the paradigms of self available for me to speak from in the scene of representation in which I find myself and in which I am not for I am not one. I remain silent, busy trying to hold a semblance of self together. Am (I) inappropriate? monstrous? Am (I) obscene? Am I representable as an 'I'? Am I? 'Producing chaos and confusion in a culture of individuals, the pregnant woman has disturbed the conventional categories of subject and object, of self and other' (Stacey 1997: 87).

It is a complex response I am experiencing for it touches on the presuppositions of the scene of representation both in this room, in a university and within the strictures of what constitutes philosophy in a larger institutional and canonical sense. It is in the light of my pregnant embodiment that I was able to discern the absence of any maternal morphology within the real and imaginary spaces of philosophy: that is, in the paper and in the debate I listened to, in the positions taken up, in my feelings of estrangement, in the very structure, the language, the grammar of philosophical discourse. Silence and the desire to laugh, to make a noise, to create disorder, are quite specific reactions to what I perceive as the impossibility of either speaking as or being heard as what I am. I am tongue-tied. Irigaray speaks:

> We are luminous. Neither one nor two. I've never known how to count. Up to you. In their calculations, we make two. Really, two? Doesn't that make you laugh? An odd sort of two. And yet not one. Especially not one. Let's leave one to them: Their oneness, with its prerogatives, its domination, its solipsism.
>
> (Irigaray 1985b: 207)

In that philosophy seminar my pregnant body is a sign of contestation. It defies a certain logic and a present form. 'Am a woman' 'am pregnant', it flashes, but there is no predicate, no I, no model of the subject available, no position, for want of singularity, my monster, myself, can take up to speak this embodiment. For I am both one and the other and I am equally neither one nor the other. Suspended between the one and the other, I experience myself as an 'elusive gap between ... discrete bodies' (Irigaray 1985a: 165). The illusion of the homogeneous body, taking care not to touch, or mingle, but moving carefully along its own straight (but equally solipsistic) line in a continual series of present moments, that body fails me. That imago, that corporeal schema, can not, will not encompass me embodied thus. 'Every utterance, every statement', writes Irigaray, is 'developed and affirmed by covering over the fact that being's unseverable relation to the mother-matter has been buried' (Irigaray 1985a: 162). Is that why the pregnant body is so rigorously surveyed socially, and simultaneously philosophically unrepresentable as anything other than a body/object/space for/against which the subject can become (himself)? My embodiment, my transitional subjectivity is operating in these real and virtual spaces as an 'interpretative lever' (Irigaray 1985b: 72) for the unfolding of the masculinist bias of philosophical discourse.

Feminist contexts

Consider the contradictions of my (non)position. First, I experience myself as radically other(ed), and yet pregnancy is one of the most socially conventional and controlled forms of embodiment which women can, and the majority of women still do, experience. Second, my research reveals just how persistently within its long history philosophy has thrived upon using metaphors of gestation for the renewal of masculine models of being and creativity, while simultaneously and repeatedly disavowing maternal origin in its theories and models of subjectivity.[1] I sat in that particular philosophy seminar not just among Cartesians and Hegelians, but Deleuzians, Derrideans, advocates of deconstruction, lovers of fluidity, dispersal and molecular becoming. It would be easy to write pregnant embodiment into the script of the series of becomings which philosophy currently courts, that is, to privilege the pregnant body as a figure of monstrous body, the body which is already becoming other (see Ahmed 1998). In such a narrative, the specificity of the pregnant body, however ungraspable in the present, would be erased: she would simply signal another of his becomings. In contrast, the encounters I describe above reside at the *interface* between pregnant embodiment and philosophy and aim to capture the displacement that occurs when the pregnant woman is present(ed) as a reproductive subject within a discourse and a culture which increasingly cannot and will not represent her as such. I hence want to argue that it is time to make a pregnant self, to reclaim pregnancy as a transient subjectivity by reframing pregnant women as the active subjects of their own gestation.

First-person narration and visual representations which bear witness to the 'unique temporality' (Young 1990: 160) and transient subjectivity of pregnant existence from an embodied perspective, are largely absent from Western culture. As Young comments, 'We should not be surprised to learn that *discourse on pregnancy omits subjectivity*, for the specific experience of women is absent from our history' (Young 1990: 160; my emphasis). Such an absence has been contested. However, generations of feminists have variously argued that women's reproductive capacity is the lynch pin of female oppression, the anchor which has precluded women from cultural production and its associated value systems (see for example Firestone 1970). As Carol Stabile writes: 'The resistance to theorizing pregnancy, as such, can be understood in terms of the historical trajectory of feminist activism and thought, since an overarching goal was to extricate "woman" from a purely reproductive status' (Stabile 1994: 86). However, I believe that Christine Battersby is right to claim that, whether a woman 'is lesbian, infertile, post-menopausal or childless', she will still be assigned '*a subject-position linked to a body that has perceived potentialities for birth*' (Battersby 1998: 16; my emphasis)

If women are interpellated as subjects with a perceived potentiality for birth, then the theorisation of pregnant embodiment has ramifications for all women. However, the cultural associations between a woman's body, her subjectivity and her potential (or non-potential) for birth can be experienced and lived in innumerable ways. I do not intend to make pregnant embodiment the ultimate sign of sexual difference, suggest sexual difference as the primary or most politically important difference at any given moment or universalize, or homogenize, the myriad pregnant embodiments that women experience.[2]

Indeed, pregnant embodiment highlights the difficulty of making any ontological claims with certainty. The pregnant subject defies the logic of classic ontology and is disruptive when thought as a transitional subjectivity, because it cannot be contained within forms of being constrained by singularity and is at odds with familiar models of the self–other relation – there is an impasse between the 'I' that writes/speaks and pregnant subjectivity, which is the exact antithesis of that I's implied individuality (see Franklin 1991: 203). Simply put, pregnant embodiment 'threatens to collapse a signifying system based on the paternal law of differentiation [as it] automatically throws into question ideas concerning the self, boundaries between self and other, and hence identity' (Doane 1990:170). The mechanisms which place women's experiences of pregnant embodiment outside the frame of representation have serious implications for non-pregnant bodies, in particular for other forms of embodiment which are read as monstrous, are unrepresented or culturally othered.

Between philosophy and pregnancy

Irigaray suggests that the non-position of the *woman–mother*[3] in philosophical discourse can potentially be used as a useful asset for imagining/imaging alternative female subjectivities. As she elusively writes at the end of *Speculum of the Other Woman*, 'as the mute outside that sustains all systematicity; as a maternal and still silent ground that nourishes all foundations – she does not have to conform to the codes theory has set up for itself' (Irigaray 1985a: 365; my emphasis). How does one not 'conform to the codes theory has set up for itself'? To explore pregnant embodiment philosophically as a sex-specific subjectivity is already to risk scripting it back into the context which, Irigaray argues, is dependent upon the disavowal of maternal origin, and therefore on the disavowal of the transitional nature of pregnant embodiment. What is clear is that the pregnant woman, that is, both the idea of the pregnant woman as a transitional concept and lived experiences of pregnancy as transitional embodiment, expose the failure of philosophical models of being, self and subject. It/she contests both, metaphysical (for example Cartesian) and anti-metaphysical (for example psychoanalytic) narratives of the subject, in which the I of enunciation (mis)recognises himself as the foundation of his own becoming. This (mis)recognition involves an erasure or disavowal of the subject's corporeal and maternal roots as it places the speaking subject within a male genealogy, under the law of the father.[4] Writing on/as Aristotle, Irigaray makes the same point, 'the state of existence of the "beginning" from which being will emerge and stand apart is not predicable; being traces its lineage back first to a male parent who already rejoices in a specific form' (Irigaray 1985a: 161).

Picking up the thread of Irigaray's challenge, Battersby (1998) theorises the disavowal of maternal origin within philosophy in terms of the disavowal of birth. As she writes:

> Reading many philosophers we might, indeed, suppose that man experienced himself first in isolation from others; that he never had to learn where the boundaries of his own self, his will and his freedom lie; and that he (or rather she) does not carry within himself (or rather herself) the gradual capacity to become two selves … This lack of theorisation of birth – as if birth was just 'natural', something that simply happened before man 'is' – might be most evident in some continental philosophers (in Heidegger, for

example, whose theorisation starts with an existent who is simply 'thrown' into the world).

(Battersby 1998: 18)

The pregnant woman can be a challenge to this forgetting of origins, for she embodies gestation and is a sign of, or even for, the absence of maternal genealogies of thought. Given that, can pregnant embodiment be theoretically reframed in order to expose how it is always the architecture of masculine corporeal forms which dominate philosophical discourse? If this is the case, it is perhaps not surprising that within 'the patriarchal tradition of metaphysics, birth, growth and differential modes of embodied selfhood remain remarkably untheorised subjects' (Battersby 1998: 15).

How then have feminist philosophers variously confronted the challenge posed by developing models of subjectivity that can account for bodies 'that bleed … with the potentiality of new selves'? (Battersby 1998: 17). There is very little feminist philosophical writing on pregnancy; in this respect the work of Simone de Beauvoir, Iris Marion-Young and Christine Battersby stands out. In focusing on the work of these three philosophers I acknowledge that I inevitably extricate their work from the specific philosophical, feminist and historical contexts in which it was variously produced . In addition, much subsequent feminist philosophy (see for example Grosz 1994; Haraway 1991; Harding 1991) has substantially challenged classic philosophical epistemological and ontological assumptions, and this work implicitly informs my critique. However, the question which concerns me here is: can (a) feminist philosophy address pregnant embodiment within the models of thought available within this tradition without scripting pregnancy back into a history of being which is sustained by its absence?

Simone de Beauvoir's writing on pregnancy in the chapter 'The Mother' from *The Second Sex* (1953) demonstrates well the difficulty involved in trying to adapt existing philosophical models of subjectivity into models which serve the cause of an emancipated female subject. De Beauvoir identifies an absolute breach between maternity and engagement with philosophical, specifically existentialist, projects. Any documented experiences of fulfilment, interest or joy which women have made in pregnancy, de Beauvoir rejects as narcissistic symptoms of a tragic misrecognition of pregnancy as a transcendent creative process. For de Beauvoir, in pregnancy 'the flesh is purely passive and inert, it cannot embody transcendence, even in a degraded form' (1953: 513). Although de Beauvoir recognises the ways in which maternity has served, within Western culture, to enslave women in domestic roles, she also re-enforces the dominant cultural and philosophical conception of pregnancy as a passive, immanent state; 'Ensnared by nature, the pregnant woman is plant and animal, a store-house of colloids, an incubator, an egg' (1953: 513). For de Beauvoir, pregnancy is a condition in which a woman's identity and subjectivity and, in existentialist terms, her freedom, is surrendered to that of her impending child. She has no agency, *she is not the subject of her own proceedings*, but imprisoned by her body. De Beauvoir is writing in the context of exploring prospects for female emancipation, that is, as a feminist, and yet, as she notes:

> Creative acts originating in liberty establish objects of value … whereas the child in the maternal body is not thus justified; it is still only a gratuitous cellular growth, a brute fact of nature as contingent on circumstances as death and corresponding philosophically with it.
>
> (1953: 514)

In this extract, de Beauvoir reinforces the classic legal and medical 'preconditional construction of pregnancy as a hostile relationship between two entities' (Steinberg 1991: 184–185). Indeed, her suggestion that there is a philosophical correspondence between pregnancy and death supports Irigaray's hypothesis that the maternal is that which Western philosophy cannot think because it is dependent upon its absence. In the philosophical development of models of identity and subjectivity, pregnant embodiment is, like death, *a priori* to being itself. Read within this context, it is unsurprising that de Beauvoir goes on to argue that only 'mannish women who are not particularly fascinated by the adventures of their bodies' (1953: 517) can hope to be escape the monstrous immanence and inert non-subjectivity which pregnancy, for her, implies. Indeed within de Beauvoir's strange but familiar philosophical logic, she is even able to assert that miscarriage and morning sickness are *almost exclusively of psychic origin* (1953: 516).

It could be argued in de Beauvoir's defence that what has been offered so far is a very 'straight' reading of her chapter 'The Mother'. It could be argued that the vitriol against maternity and pregnancy in *The Second Sex* is written, in part, ironically. De Beauvoir's style involves a process of describing or mimicking the cultural values ascribed to female forms of experience in order to explore the foundations of such beliefs. Nevertheless, it is impossible to recover a positive account of pregnant embodiment from de Beauvoir's work and she quite clearly is revolted by pregnancy and motherhood, and rejects them as experiences without any philosophical and cultural value. She offers no counter-narratives against the negative inscription of pregnant embodiment she describes and she fails to theorize the revulsion she associates with pregnancy.

The more positive implications of de Beauvoir's writing on motherhood have been explored in more depth elsewhere (Patterson 1989): what concerns me here is why de Beauvoir cannot think pregnant embodiment within the framework of philosophy as a challenging transient subjectivity. The last line of *The Second Sex* reads: 'To gain the supreme victory, it is necessary, for one thing, that by and through their natural differentiation men and women unequivocally affirm their brotherhood' (1953: 741; my emphasis). Here, de Beauvoir reveals the tension that underpins feminist philosophical projects, the desire to be included in the brotherhood and the simultaneous desire to have sexual difference affirmed. De Beauvoir was anxious to adapt an existential model of subjectivity to women (and if necessary to adapt women to fit this masculine model of subjectivity), in order to counter women's status as the second sex. Because only women can be pregnant and suffer socially as a consequence, de Beauvoir has to disavow pregnancy as a creative aspect of an ideal (masculine) existential subjectivity.

Writing fifty years after de Beauvoir, in 'Pregnant Embodiment: Subjectivity and Alienation' (1990), the feminist phenomenologist Iris Marion Young implicitly challenges many of de Beauvoir's assumptions. Young's groundbreaking essay, which has greatly influenced my own work, considers the difficult interface between pregnant embodiment and philosophy. Using her own experience of pregnancy as a starting point, Young explores the challenge pregnant embodiment poses to 'masculine' phenomenological models of self. Yet a close reading of Young's paper reveals a subtle but crucial split between *Young as philosopher* and *Young as pregnant woman*. This is most clearly discernible in the following passage, where she describes her activity, as a philosopher and a researcher, in relation to herself as pregnant:

> To be sure, even in pregnancy there are times when I am so absorbed in my activity that I do not feel myself as a body, but when I move or feel the look of another I am likely to be recalled to the thickness of my body. I walk through the library stacks searching for the *Critique of Dialectical Reason*: I feel the painless pull of false contractions in my back. I put my hand on my belly to notice its hardening, *while my eyes continue their scanning.*
>
> (Young 1990: 163; my emphasis)

On the one hand, it is incidental that Young recalls searching for Immanuel Kant's *Critique of Dialectical Reason* in the library stacks. On the other, through the invocation of this most canonical of texts, Young is able to signify herself *as the philosopher*, an inheritor of a specific and masculine canon of knowledge. In flagging up her philosophical authority Young unwittingly exposes the fissure between the subject who is a philosopher searching for Kant and the subject who is a pregnant woman. As *a philosophical essay on pregnancy*, her essay can be read as an attempt both to bridge this gap and to critique it. However, this paragraph reveals Young's need to be perceived as having philosophical integrity and authority: as Irigaray so forcefully argues in *Speculum of the Other Woman* (1985a), to qualify for this status within the strictures of the Western philosophical tradition, one must appear, within the text, as disembodied. Hence, even as Young is describing her embodiment, she insists 'there are times when I am so absorbed in my activity that I do not feel myself as a body'. What interests me here is not the fact that Young becomes so absorbed in her work, as philosopher, that she can temporarily forget her pregnant embodiment, but rather why she recounts this experience and what this passage of text might reveal about how the relationship between pregnant embodiment and philosophy comes to be lived and written. In effect, Young is stating that she can partake in philosophical projects, *as long as nobody is looking*, so long as nobody is present to signify the enigma of a pregnant philosopher. Young thereby reproduces the classic mind/body dualism that phenomenology has, historically, critiqued and contradicts her own critique of phenomenology from the perspective of pregnancy. 'Alienation' in the title of her essay refers not to the place of women within the institution of philosophy but to the place of pregnant women in the institutions of medical treatment in the USA. In the short final section of this essay, it is philosophy which becomes a vehicle for championing the cause of women, by revealing the assumptions at work in the medicalisation of pregnancy.

Young's essay remains the most important piece of feminist philosophical writing on pregnant embodiment to date not least because it reveals the continual tension between being a philosopher and being a (potentially) pregnant subject. Young demonstrates that this tension can be fruitful and revealing. Such tension is less apparent in Christine Battersby's more recent, *The Phenomenal Woman: Feminist Metaphysics and the Patterns of Identity* (1998). Battersby begins her exploration of female subjectivity with pregnancy and birth. It appears that she, like Young, is engaged in a radically different project from de Beauvoir:

> I am interested in models of identity for 'the object' – and in particular, for a body that is capable of generating a new body from within its 'own' flesh ... I treat 'woman' as 'object', in order to find new models of the self/other relationship and new ways of thinking 'identity' – and, in particular, persistence of an embodied self through mutation, birth and change.
>
> (Battersby 1998: 7)

However, as with *The Second Sex,* this book illustrates the difficulty feminist theorists face when they employ philosophical frameworks to think through pregnancy as subjectivity. Battersby's starting point is similar to my own, in that she is trying to think the reproductive body in relation to the history of Western philosophy – a history which singularly fails to account for the reproductive body. This is despite, as Battersby clearly indicates, the fact that the notion of a history of philosophy is itself a construction, and that within this history there are 'models of mobile identities that work without underlying permanent "object", "substances" or unchanging and universal "forms"' (Battersby 1998: 7).

The extract quoted above indicates the classic and problematic structure of Battersby's approach to pregnant embodiment. The use of inverted commas around the terms 'woman' and 'object' highlights that the categories are under question but simultaneously, I would argue, confirms the position of the philosopher, as one licensed to comment from outside and above as the neutral (non-gendered) observer. This is the same problem which exists, albeit more subtly, in Young's essay. It is the case that Battersby faces the same grammatical problems faced by any theorist who wishes to explore female subjectivity in the context of non-singular models of the self. However, the objective of Battersby's book is to utilise the body that births as 'normal' (Battersby 1998: 3) in order to provide 'a model of identity that ... is more adequate for men (as well as women) than the classic philosophical understandings of the subject, substance and identity' (Battersby 1998: 3).

In contrast to de Beauvoir, who I would argue is anxious to adapt women to a masculine model of subjectivity in order to afford women equal status, Battersby's work could be read as an attempt to propose the object-woman, specifically the potentially pregnant woman, as a subjectivity which can serve as a model for both sexes. The implications of this are extremely disturbing if one considers the ways in which reproduction has historically been employed as a metaphor with which to theorise male creativity and subjectivity (see note 1). Battersby's apparent egalitarianism, like de Beauvoir's, places severe restraints on the possible outcomes of its enquiry. Indeed, although its stated aims are opposed to de Beauvoir's, Battersby's thesis similarly emerges, not out of an assertion of an alternative genealogy of female thought, but from the (re)assertion of a paternal philosophical lineage in which she believes women can find adequate resources for rethinking subjectivity. The last line of her book indicates her commitment to this lineage: 'the way on from postmodernism needs to be looped back through the philosophical past' (Battersby 1998: 210). Of the three feminist philosophical accounts of pregnancy I have focused on, only Young's acknowledges the importance of finding and working with female-authored accounts of subjectivity and pregnant embodiment.

The writings of de Beauvoir, Battersby and to a lesser extent Young highlight the contradictory loyalties which constrict the work of feminist philosophy on the topic of pregnant embodiment and subjectivity. The philosophical egalitarianism to which all these thinkers variously succumb cannot change or seriously challenge the (metaphysical) structures, which have historically given no or little value to women's reproductive capacity. Are feminist philosophical projects limited by their attempts to adapt inherited philosophical models, *the same speech which has rendered women speechless* (Hartouni 1997: 67)?

Arriving at this juncture, it is unclear how one could begin to think pregnant embodiment, as a sex-specific transitional experience of non-singular being, within the context of the available inherited philosophical models of subjectivity. Pregnant subjectivity must be theorised, at least in part, through the analysis of narratives which emerge out of the experiences of pregnant women, even if, or perhaps given, those experiences are themselves not transparent, but mediated. It is time to let the object – the subject matter – speak. Of critical importance to this chapter has been the belief that in order to let the object speak (Irigaray 1985a: 135), pregnant embodiment needs to be thought and written, at least in part, from the embodied position of the subject matter. The autobiographical writing which began this chapter attempted this *mattertalk*. Situated at the interfaces between philosophy and pregnancy, both real and imagined, it both fails and succeeds. Is it possible to express or represent a subjectivity which defies the category subject?

Donna Haraway argues that it is women's 'troubling talent for making other bodies' which accounts for their difficulty in 'counting as individuals in modern Western discourses' (Haraway 1991: 253). I have tried to demonstrate that pregnant embodiment is a state of resistance *par excellence* in respect of the individualism of philosophical models of the self. This is important because these philosophical models of selfhood are not contained within library stacks, but have created the ways we think about our-selves as subjects and individuals in the modern age. In the final part of this chapter, I will outline how foetal narratives demonstrate the need to reframe pregnant embodiment in the context of a subjectivity which is definitely *not one*.

Foetal narratives

The (structural) absence of the pregnant woman as subjectivity, which I identified within philosophical narratives and models for/of subjectivity, is repeated anew within foetal narratives, which operate by the same disavowal of maternal origin. Indeed, the displacement of pregnant embodiment in the foetal narratives of the late twentieth century demonstrates a clear political need to theorise and reframe pregnant embodiment as the subjects of gestation. Like the philosopher, the foetus 'already rejoices in a specific form' (Irigaray 1985a: 161). In fact the foetus is, simply put, the most recent reincarnation of the figure of the philosopher. While pregnant embodiment has historically served as the unacknowledged frame of philosophical models of being, in the late twentieth century 'pregnant women's bodies are erased to make way for the [the other] one true person – the fetus' (Clarke 1995: 147). Pregnant embodiment is thus the unacknowledged frame of both the philosophical and the foetal subject. Both are presented as 'discrete and separate entit[ies], outside of, unconnected to, and, by virtue of its ostensible or visual independence, in an adversarial relationship with the body and life upon which it is nevertheless inextricably dependent' (Hartouni 1997: 67).

As philosophy has provided the template for foetal personhood it is not surprising that the foetus is almost exclusively signified as white and male or that commentators have noted how the foetus appears to have been formed within and by the most traditional narratives of individualised Western selfhood. As Sarah Franklin notes:

> What is significant ... is the extent to which the theme of patriarchal individualism holds together so many different versions of fetal personhood, while at the same time compromising one of the most exclusionary, masculinist perspectives from which to understand the process of reproduction.
>
> (Franklin 1991: 203)

This intertwining of foetal and philosophical narratives indicates that the powerful and coercive politics of foetal narratives and foetal imagery, far from being a contemporary phenomena, is a virulent re-emergence of an old problematic (see Newman 1996). That is, the exclusion of reproductive subjects from philosophical understandings of the self, identity and embodiment underpins the subsequent absence, or lack of cultural value attributed to, pregnant women as subjects of their own gestation in the 'natural sciences'. Such contemporary emergences of this absence within foetal narratives need to be addressed at their source, that is within the context of the disavowal of what could be variously

termed the reproductive subject, woman-mother or maternal within philosophy
– that which Irigaray describes as the concealed and perpetual matricide on
which Western culture is founded (Irigaray 1991, and see Hodge 1994).

In conclusion

In this chapter I have invoked abstract, idealised and yet also subjective experiential narratives of pregnant embodiment to demonstrate how a reconsideration
of pregnancy in the context of feminist philosophical reworkings of subjectivity
can begin to reframe the reproductive body. Feminists working in other disciplines have also undertaken the work of the rethinking and reframing of
pregnancy.[5] I hope this polemical essay contributes to this growing body of
academic work which, alongside a significant increase in popular cultural representations of pregnancy,[6] is shifting the terms of the debate and creating
resources with which to reframe pregnant embodiment and/as subjectivity and
'establish woman centred territory at the centre of reproductive politics'
(Franklin 1991: 204).

Notes

1   A good example of this is the number of phantom pregnancies which can be found
    in the annals of philosophy. Procreation and reproduction are continually dis-
    embodied, (re)incorporated and appropriated, predominantly in the form of
    metaphors, by scientists, philosophers and artists (see for example Hartouni 1997: 62)
2   I am grateful to Jackie Stacey for highlighting some of the difficulties lesbian women
    who wish to be or are mothers face in a homophobic culture which designates lesbian
    bodies as non-reproductive.
3   I read 'woman-mother' as the subject position assigned to women culturally – that is,
    as a position with perceived potentialities for birth (Battersby 1998: 16).
4   For the purposes of this chapter I would argue that it is structurally irrelevant
    whether the law appears in the figure of the Logos, Phallus or God.
5   See, for example, Balsamo (1996), Clarke (1995), Duden (1993), Franklin (1991,
    1995), Martin (1987), McNeil and Franklin (1991), Petchesky (1984), Rothman (1993),
    Stanworth (1987), Stabile (1994).
6   I think that the production of a visual vocabulary of pregnant subjectivity is neces-
    sary to challenge 'the visual discourse of fetal autonomy' (Hartouni 1997: 67). The
    most famous image of pregnancy in contemporary Western culture to date is Annie
    Leibovitz's glamour shot of Demi Moore naked and eight months pregnant on the
    cover of *Vanity Fair* (August 1991). This image provoked outrage, made news head-
    lines and appeared on news-stands in the USA covered by brown paper wrappers.
    This largely negative response to the Demi Moore image supports my hypothesis that
    pregnant embodiment, as a physical sign of maternal origin, is that which is barred
    from representation in Western culture. It is significant that since Demi Moore's
    groundbreaking front cover, there has been an emergence of alternative images of
    pregnant women within (British) popular culture, particularly noticeable in tabloid
    newspapers as I wrote this essay in 1998. (See for example Melanie Blatt – pop star,
    on the front page of the *Sun*, August, 1998). Read positively, such imagery, idealised
    though it may be, could help establish a context which will enable women to 'screen
    out the male-bias embodied in the publicly imaged fetus' (Duden 1993: 52) and
    thereby write new narratives of reproduction for their pregnant selves. Equally, it

would be naïve to suppose that the recent proliferation of pregnant imagery, of pregnant celebrities for instance, is not constrained by the same patriarchal ideology which has historically limited representations of women.

References

Ahmed, S. (1998) *Differences that Matter: Feminist Theory and Postmodernism*, Cambridge: Cambridge University Press.

Balsamo, A. (1996) *Technologies of the Gendered Body: Reading Cyborg Women*, Durham, N.C.: Duke University Press.

Battersby, C. (1998) *The Phenomenal Woman: Feminist Metaphysics and the Patterns of Identity*, Cambridge: Polity Press.

Clark, A. (1995) 'Modernity, Postmodernity and Reproductive Processes, ca. 1890–1990', in C. Gray (ed.) *The Cyborg Handbook*, London: Routledge.

de Beauvoir, S. (1953), *The Second Sex*, ed. H.M. Parshley, London: Penguin.

Doane, M. (1990) 'Technophilia, Technology, Representation, and the Feminine', in M. Jacobus, E. Fox Keller and S. Shuttleworth (eds) *Body/Politics, Women and the Discourse of Science*, New York: Routledge.

Duden, B. (1993) *Disembodying Women: Perspectives on Pregnancy and the Unborn*, Cambridge, Mass.: Harvard University Press.

Firestone, S. (1970) *The Dialectic of Sex : The Case For Feminist Revolution*, New York: Morrow.

Franklin, S. (1991) 'Fetal Fascinations: New Dimensions to the Medical-Scientific Construction of Fetal Personhood' in S. Franklin, C. Lury and J. Stacey (eds) *Off-Centre: Feminism and Cultural Studies*, London: HarperCollins.

—— (1995) 'Postmodern Procreation: A Cultural Account of Assisted Reproduction', in F.D. Ginsberg and R. Rapp (eds) *Conceiving the New World Order: The Global Politics of Reproduction*, Berkeley: University of California Press.

Grosz, E. (1992) 'Julia Kristeva', in E. Wright (ed.) *Feminism and Psychoanalsyis: A Critical Dictionary*, Oxford: Backwell.

—— (1994) *Volatile Bodies: Towards a Corporeal Feminism*, Bloomington: Indiana University Press.

Haraway, D.J. (1991) *Simians, Cyborgs, and Women: The Reinvention of Nature*, London: Free Association Books.

Harding, S. (1991) *Whose Science? Whose Knowledge?: Thinking from Women's Lives*, Milton Keynes, England: Open University Press.

Hartouni, Va. (1997) *Cultural Conceptions: On Reproductive Technologies and the Remaking of Life*, Minneapolis: University of Minnesota Press.

Hodge, J. (1994). 'Irigaray Reading Heidegger', in C. Burke, N. Schor and M. Whitford (eds) *Engaging with Irigaray*, New York: Columbia University Press.

Irigaray, L. (1985a) *Speculum of the Other Woman*, Ithaca, N.Y.: Cornell University Press.

—— (1985b) *This Sex Which Is Not One*, Ithaca, N.Y.: Cornell University Press.

—— (1991) *The Irigaray Reader*, ed. M. Whitford, Oxford: Blackwell.

Kristeva, J. (1993) *Desire in Language: A Semiotic Approach to Literature and Art*, ed. L.S. Roudiez, London: Blackwell.

Leibovitz, A. (1991) photography in *Vanity Fair*, August.

McNeil, M. and Franklin, S. (1991) 'Science and Technology: Questions for Cultural Studies and Feminism', in S. Franklin, C. Lury and J. Stacey (eds) *Off-Centre: Feminism and Cultural Studies*, London: HarperCollins.

Martin, E. (1987) *The Woman in the Body*, Milton Keynes, England: Open University Press.

Newman, K. (1996) *Fetal Positions: Individualism, Science and Visuality*, Stanford, Calif.: Stanford University Press.

Patterson, Y.A. (1989) *Beauvoir and the Demystification of Motherhood*, Ann Arbor, Mich.: UMI Press.

Petchesky, R. (1984) *Abortion and Women's Choice: The State, Sexuality, and Reproductive Freedom*, New York: Longman.

Plath S. (1989) 'Three Women: A Poem for Three Voices', in T. Hughes (ed.) *Sylvia Plath: Collected Poems*, London: Faber and Faber.

Rothman, B.K. (1993) *The Tentative Pregnancy: How Amniocentesis Changes the Experience of Motherhood*, New York: Norton.

Stabile, C.A. (1994) *Feminism and the Technological Fix*, Manchester: Manchester University Press.

Stacey, J. (1997) *Teratologies: A Cultural Study of Cancer*, London and New York: Routledge.

Stanworth, M. (ed.) (1987) *Reproductive Technologies: Gender, Motherhood and Medicine*, Oxford: Polity Press.

Steinberg, D.L. (1991) 'Adversarial Politics: The Legal Construction of Abortion', in S. Franklin, C. Lury and J. Stacey (eds) *Off-Centre: Feminism and Cultural Studies*, London: HarperCollins.

Winterson, J. (1989) *Sexing the Cherry*, London: Vintage.

Young, I.M. (1990) 'Pregnant Embodiment: Subjectivity and Alienation', in *Throwing Like a Girl and Other Essays in Feminist Philosophy and Social Theory*, Bloomington: Indiana University Press.

18 Monsters, marvels and metaphysics

Beyond the powers of horror

Margrit Shildrick

Several months ago, I went to see one of the ubiquitous monster films out on circuit. *Species* is the story of a clinical experiment that goes wrong; of how alien genes mixed with those of a human being produce a voracious, female-identified monster whose sole aim is to mate and reproduce. The band of humans, standing in her way and intent on exterminating her threat, comprises four men representing a variety of masculine stereotypes and a token woman, all of whose appetites are strictly normative. After much predictable carnage, the monster, Sil, is eventually hunted down and destroyed, giving the satisfied survivors a rare moment of reflection and the opportunity to pronounce the epithet: 'She was half us; half something else.' It is precisely this ambiguity that lies at the heart of what makes the monstrous body transhistorically both so fascinating and so disturbing. It is not that the monster represents the threat *of* difference, but that it threatens to interrupt difference – at least in its binary form – so that the comfortable otherness that secures the selfsame is lost. What lies beyond the unproblematic horror of the absolute other is the far more risky perception that the monstrous is not so different after all.

Running through all this are several interwoven strands of special interest, not just to a postmodernist philosophy which calls for the epistemological collapse of binary distinctions, but also to feminism, which, in the last decade, has both mounted a critique of the significance of monstrous corporeality[1] and scanned its own horizons of aspiration. The point is that, like the well-established config-uration of matter and mother to which it is also supplemental in the Derridean sense (Derrida 1976), the monstrous is both excessive to, and yet, as I shall show, embedded in, the structuration of the Western logos. What is at stake is not only the categorical integrity of bodies that matter, but also the hitherto taken for granted presence of the singular human subject as the centre of the logos. Indeed, to be a self at all seems to rely on the certainty of a clearly delineated body, yet one so secure in its morphology that it may simultaneously be brack-eted out of questions of ontology. Against this, the confused and essentially fluid corporeality of monsters makes them an ideal location for an inquiry into the closure of both bodies and subjects that characterises modernist philosophical discourse. The issue, as I have suggested elsewhere, 'is one of leaky boundaries, wherein the leakiness of the logos … is mirrored by the collapse of the human itself as a bounded being' (Shildrick 1996: 1).

Now, if the modernist logos is at best ambivalent about the ontological status of the body, the putative split between mind and body that it puts into play has not resulted in disengagement from issues of corporeal being. The Western imagination is haunted by questions of identity and origin that involve always the 'difficult, even intractable, relations between self and body' (Epstein 1995: 4). What matters is not simply that the boundaries between singular selves should be secure, but that there should be clarity as to which minds and bodies go together. The self-present subject who defines himself against all that is non-self (I will merely note in passing the inherent gendering of the dominant discourse) need scarcely acknowledge his own corporeality. The assumption is that sovereign minds are housed in appropriate bodies, and that those who are 'inappropriate/d others' (to use Haraway's term (1992)) cannot occupy unproblematically the subject position. Now monsters, of course, show themselves in many different and culturally specific ways, but what is monstrous about them is most often the form of their embodiment. I want to be clear from the outset that the 'reality' of various forms is not at issue, and though a descriptive reading of historical texts may yield successive reformulations of inappropriate/d others, what concerns me is that monsters operate primarily in the imaginary. My explicit intention in using archival sources, for example, is to challenge the conventional disciplinary limits set on their intelligibility in order to ask what forms of imaginary are mobilised by their rhetorical devices. The differential interpretations of monstrosity may speak clearly to the mapping of specific socio-historical anxieties and interests, but more importantly what is at stake are the contested relations between self and other, the simultaneous rejection and recognition, horror and fascination, that ground ontological unease. What links the monstrous others, whether those of human birth whose bodies fail to match the normative standard – encephalitic infants, conjoined twins, even Paré's monster of Ravenna,[2] or man-made creations like Sil in the film *Species*, or the replicants in *Blade Runner* – is their unnatural and, often hybrid, corporeality.

But though that differential embodiment might explain the enduring fascination of the monstrous, it does not so easily account for the normative anxiety that they invoke. In any case, the monster is not outside nature, but rather an instance of nature's startling capacity to produce alien forms within, such that identical twins and pregnant women are equally productive of ontological uncertainty. The relationship between monstrosity and what might be deemed the natural was one which greatly exercised the classical mind, and, later, the Church fathers, for whom the problem was how to account for the unnatural within a god-given universe. Unlike many of his contemporaries who posited wholly supernatural explanation, Aristotle concluded that 'Monstrosities belong to the class of things contrary to nature, not any and every kind of nature, but Nature in her usual operations'; the crucial marker for him being that such deformities transgressed the law of generative resemblance (1953: 767b, 5–10). Given, however, that Aristotle regarded any deviation from the morphology of the 'normal' male body as a type of monstrosity, what is at issue is not so much the *unexpected* disruption of corporeal limits, as the putative failure – signalled by both monstrous and female birth – of the male seed to replicate itself, to reproduce paternal likeness.

Such natural science aside, however, it appears from the surviving texts that the important questions for the classical world, the Middle Ages and the early modern period were often the more abstract ones focused on the meaning of the monstrous. The Latin roots of the word are both *monstrare* – to show, and *monere* – to warn, and for the most part it was the commentary offered by Cicero rather than Aristotle which prevailed. In his list of synonyms (*monstra, ostenta, portenta, prodigia* (*De Divinatione*: Vol. 1, para. XLII, pp. 263–264)) Cicero firmly marked out the monstrous as a supranatural signifier of coming social and political calamities, or as a commentary on contemporary mores. Such interpretations were seized upon in Christian Europe as a means of offering social, political and religious comment, and both lay and scholarly texts of the time concur in their understanding of the meaning of monstrosity. Accordingly, gross deviations from the norm were not simply horrifying, but also marvellous, signs both of nature's fecundity and god's power. Thus Paré, writing in 1573, begins his list of the causes of monstrosity: 'The first whereof is the glory of God, that his immense power may be manifested to those which are ignorant of it …. Another cause is, that God may punish men's whickednesse, or show signs of punishment at hand …' (1982: 4). And though in monstrosity, the usual principles of generation might be suspended, the monstrous was not thereby the absolute other, but rather a mirror of humanity: on an individual level, the external manifestation of the sinner within. In a similar way, the longstanding belief in the existence of monstrous races at the outer margins of the habitable world (Pliny's hugely influential *Natural History* lists no fewer than fifty-two such races) is beset by questions as to their human or animal status. This situates them, nevertheless, as ontologically and existentially dependent on the undoubted humanity of the civilised races. What is less obvious, but nonetheless crucial, is that the existential status of that humanity does not stand alone but, by corollary, is dependent on its monstrous other.

Any supposedly monstrous birth could be called upon to support both political and moral exhortations and, for a time, after the invention of the printing press, heavily illustrated popular texts circulated with more or less fantastic versions of monster stories, much as the tabloid newspapers might publish similar stories today. One such English example is Stephen Bateman's *The Doome Warning all Men to the Iudgemente* (1581), which characteristically reiterates both text and pictures already popularised in earlier works. Monstrous births – hermaphrodites, hydrocephalitic infants, hairy men, one-eyed giants, dog-headed humans, human-headed pigs and conjoined twins – and other freak events such as meteorological peculiarities are related with gusto. But where causative explanation is offered, it is invariably overlaid with portentous meaning. Bateman was evidently aware of the doctrine of maternal imagination[3] as his account of twins joined at the head makes clear:

The cause of this Monster was this, two Women spake together, one of whiche was with Child, and the thirde coming upon them sodayne knocked both their Heades together as they were talking, wherewith the Woman with Child being afrayd made a token of the Knock in her Child.

(1581: 287)

But the event flows seamlessly into his reference to a battle between Christians and Turks in the same year. When Bateman turns to the infamous Monster of Cracow, born in 1543 (Figure 18.1), the prodigious nature of the birth is paramount: 'he is said to have lived foure houres after he was borne, and at length (after he had uttered these Wordes, *Vigilate, dominus deus vester adventat*, that is, Watche, youre Lorde is a comming) to have dyed' (1581: 337). What is notable here is that the Latin-spouting infant, a favourite with early modern chroniclers, is as much constructed by the discursive strategies of the political and religious climate as by any account of an actual birth. The monstrosity is materialised in order that it might speak.

That alone should forestall a merely descriptive reading of the historical texts, and, in an acute pun, Derrida urges us to 'interrogate the hierarchives'.[4] Even when popular, monster books and the somewhat later proliferation of street ballads and broadsheets relating similar affronts to nature, operate as much

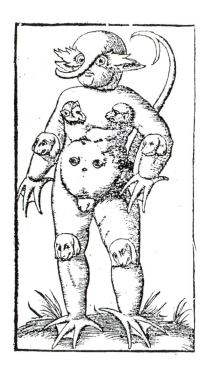

Figure 18.1   The Monster of Cracow

within the realm of entertainment as moral admonition – they always demanded interpretation. Although I am wary of a too simplistic periodisation that lines up the epistemological significance of the monstrous with specific external events, many commentators have claimed that a preoccupation with monstrosity seems to be a regular feature of periods of social and political uncertainty,[5] in which the unnatural otherness of monsters may serve as the focus of abjected fear, anxiety and guilt. For those births attributed to divine or supernatural intervention, the purpose was variously to foretell macro-calamities, to express God's wrath or vengeance on a morally negligent population, or to punish individual immorality such as sodomy, trans-species coupling, consorting with the devil, or intercourse on the Sabbath. In the personally focused cases especially, but not exclusively, both infant and mother might be destroyed, and even when the more naturalistic explanation of maternal imagination was offered, the mother might be held at fault for failing to guard against unwanted influences.

In one sense, the monster functioned as a scapegoat, the *pharmakos*. It was the excluded other which spoke for the *ideal* of a secure, untroubled, natural order. Certainly, monstrosity has taken on very specific cultural and historical forms, but its pertinence, I would argue, is determined, not so much by the contested terrain of a particular historical moment as by the always already problematic ontology of human being. Like Derrida's use of the etymologically linked *pharmakon* as a synonym of *différance*, the monster is neither good nor evil, neither inside nor outside, not self or other. On the contrary, it is always liminal, refusing to stay in place, transgressive and transformative.

Whatever the specifically ascribed meaning, transhistorical horror and fascination with the monstrous seem to centre both on the uncertain aetiology of monsters – which speaks to a more general anxiety about origins, and the relationship between maternal and foetal bodies – and on the disruption of the morphological limits that supposedly mark out the human. The hermeneutics of monstrosity focus, then, on quasi-human beings, for they alone confirm the normalcy and closure of the centred self, though simultaneously unsettling it by being all too human. In his paper 'Monstrosity and the Monstrous', Georges Canguilhem suggests that what gives value to the individual life may be the maintenance of bodily integrity, and the capacity to reproduce it over time. Against such goods, the dissolution of the body by death might seem the greatest threat, but it is one, nonetheless, that Canguilhem dismisses. As he observes: 'It is monstrosity, not death, that is the counter-value to life' (1964: 29). What monstrosity demonstrates is the interior operation of the accidental that renders order doubtful, that thwarts and limits sameness and repetition. And yet, he attests, that precariousness is simultaneously the very thing which bestows value on the normative life that has resisted deformation and fulfilled the principle of generative resemblance. Although what counts as normative, and, indeed, as monstrous, is always caught up in historically and culturally specific determinants, what matters here is that those two concepts remain locked in a mutually constitutive relationship. The monstrous, then, is a necessary signifier of normality, of a self that is constructed discursively against what it is not, and that yet, as I have indicated, remains unstable. The apparent security of the binary self:non-self that guarantees the identity of the selfsame is irrevocably displaced by the necessity that the subject be defined against an other that is never fully or finally excluded. As Judith Butler puts it, that other, the constitutive outside, 'is, after all, "inside" the subject as its own founding repudiation' (1993: 3). The monster, then, is the absent presence whose trace frustrates the Western drive for full self-presence. It is the undecidable signifier that constitutes *différance*, and poses the risk of indifferentiation.

Similar ideas underlie my earlier reference to the monster as the focus of abjected fear, which is intended to put into play the Kristevan notion of the abject as 'something rejected from which one does not part ... Imaginary uncanniness and real threat, it beckons to us and ends up engulfing us' (Kristeva 1982: 4). The abject, moreover, is 'the in-between, the ambiguous, the composite' (*ibid.*). The monstrous fits precisely such a formula. In others words, monsters overturn the distinctions that set out the protective limits of the human subject, and they violate both internal and external order. It is their status as markers of the abject that makes them the focus not simply of the fascination accorded the marvellous, but also of the repulsion directed against that which disturbs integrated identity and presence. For Kristeva, the abject is centred on the maternal body as simultaneously the origin of life and the site of insertion into mortality, the location then of an inherent ambiguity. Hence, the female body just is monstrous in the Western imaginary, the necessary locus of worship and disgust whose corporeality threatens to overflow boundaries and engulf those things which should remain separate. As Rosi Braidotti puts it, the woman's body is 'capable of defeating the notion of fixed *bodily form*, of visible, recognizable, clear and distinct shapes as that which marks the contour of the body. She is morphologically dubious' (Braidotti 1994: 80). And just as the feminine haunts the margins of Western discourses, always out of place in the paradigms of sameness and difference, so too monsters are liminal creatures which cannot be transcribed within the binary, and whose abjection always leaves a trace within.

It is with this inherent ambiguity in mind that we should understand attempts made to fix the epistemology and ontology of monstrosity, to impose order on the disordered. To summarise briefly the empirical parameters of the debate, the history of monstrosity took, during the late seventeenth and eighteenth centuries, a decidedly normative turn. With a reinvigorated interest in practical science, Enlightenment scholars largely abandoned abstract speculations on monstrosity to impose instead a medical discourse – increasingly focused on embryology and comparative anatomy – which served to normalise and domesticate the marvellous and prodigious. The science of teratology seemed to promise the certainty of explanation. As the body in general became an object of intense scrutiny, the monstrous was studied as 'the prototype for a new kind of scientific fact' (Daston 1991: 95), an aberration that would throw light on the normal. The work of Francis Bacon was particularly influential, and his *Novum Organum* (1620) explicitly sets out to categorise 'errors, vagaries, prodigies' and 'deviating instances', the better to understand, and ultimately control, nature. Yet the positivism of science, taken at face value by Daston to signal an epistemological break in the response to monstrosity, tells us little of the enduring and disruptive power of the morphological imaginary. Alongside the work of the learned societies,[6] a sense of wonder remained undisturbed, an indication that the monstrous signified rather more than simple corporeal difference. Far from fitting neatly into the new epistemological categories constructed by the taxonomies of Enlightenment science, the otherness of the monster remains containable neither in its gross materiality, nor as the radically other which sets the limits of the human. Though it resists classification, it does not thereby represent simply what Butler calls 'a domain of unlivability and unintelligibility that bounds the domain of intelligible effects' (Butler 1993: 23). Insofar as neither the attempts to pin down, nor repudiate, the monstrous are ever complete, its disruptive signification persists. It is the marker, then, not of the successful closure of embodied identity, but of the impossibility of securing such boundaries. Even in those historical moments where the issue of monstrous corporeality may seem to be primarily about form, about the difficulty of reconciling in a single body those things which should not go together, what are also thrown up are all sorts of ontological anxieties about what exactly constitutes the human subject. The dislocations of hybridity are, then, the surface manifestations of a much deeper uncertainty. I offer one specific illustration.

The rather charming monster of Ravenna (Figure 18.2) was a familiar figure in monster texts of the early modern period, and counts amongst Paré's examples of those caused by the wrath of God. The images that have survived all show an infant of reputedly human birth, whose body nonetheless displays a variety of transgressive elements, and whose human status was surely complicated by its resemblance to both an angel and a devil. The figure is evidently intersexed, having both penis and pudenda as well as breasts, though the convention refers only to an 'it'. The head bears a single horn, the arms are replaced by feathered, or in some cases, reptilian wings, the legs are fused to form a scaled, sometimes feathered, mermaid-like tail which terminates in a giant avian or reptilian claw. In addition, a third eye peers out at knee level and, in some illustrations, cross-like letters or marks appear on the torso. Despite a startling number of modern attempts to reclaim this creature as the 'real' outcome of several distinct congenital deformities,[7] the monster of Ravenna is a highly symbolic figure constructed at the confluence of a number of discourses – in this instance political, religious and superstitious. The very hybridity of the infant speaks to a series of transgressions with regard to sexuality, species and personhood. If the monster is more than appearance, if it does have an inner life, is it that of the brute animal or does it have a sense of self? More pertinent for its immediate context was the question of whether such a creature should be baptised. If the soul were an attribute of human beings alone, and baptism the necessary gateway to salvation, then the church faced a very real dilemma about the appropriate response to those monstrous births which confounded the putative boundaries of the human. The early seventeenth-century canonist, Alphonzo a Carranza, offered the formula that 'those having human form can and ought to be washed by holy baptism and those truly monstrous, which lack rational souls, not' (quoted in Friedman 1981: 182–183). Nonetheless, the problem of radical hybridity, and what it signifies of inner being, remains. It is not recorded what might have been the fate of the monster of Ravenna.

Perhaps because the qualifier for baptism was, strictly speaking, a rational soul rather than appearance, the turn towards more naturalistic explanations for human monstrosity did not settle the issue of what was appropriate. The Enlightenment interest in natural science inevitably raised questions about birth defects, and the *Philosophical Transactions of the Royal Society* are, from their very start in the mid-seventeenth century, full of reports and discussions on the meaning of monstrosity. A major debate raged around the contentious issue of maternal imagination, the supporters of which saw it as having a direct and natural (rather than mystical) link to foetal development. As the French philosopher Nicolas Malebranche put it: 'there is reason to believe that mothers are capable of imprinting in their unborn children all the same sensations by which they themselves are affected, and all the same passions by which they are agitated' (Malebranche 1980 [1674]: 113).

The principle covered both imagination and affect, and was cited as sufficient cause for all types of deformities from the trivial to the grotesque. A pregnant woman's longing for strawberries, for example, would mark her foetus with a

Figure 18.2   The Monster of Ravenna

characteristic birth stain, while Malebranche gives an account of a congenitally broken-jointed and mad Parisian man whose mother in pregnancy had seen a criminal broken on the wheel. The cause, Malebranche postulates, was that both the mental and the physical agitation experienced by the mother were passed to the child:

> At the sight of this execution, so capable of frightening a woman, the violent flow of the mother's animal spirits passed very forcefully from her brain to all parts of her body corresponding to those of the criminal, and the same thing happened in the child.
>
> (Malebranche 1980 [1674]: 113)

The point about maternal imagination (both to its supporters and to its detractors) and about some other proffered naturalistic causes of monstrosity, such as an ill-formed womb (Maubray 1724) or accidental insults during pregnancy (de Superville 1740), was that the precipitating factor occurred after an otherwise 'normal' conception. It would appear, then, that there could be little question but that the infant at birth must be human and thus the possessor of a soul. Strangely, however, there was still uncertainty, for though an infant might be human in appearance and provenance, there was no guarantee of a rational soul. In a discussion in 1668 of a human-born hairy monster, whose mother had seen an ape during the fifth month of pregnancy, members of the Royal Society debated the power of maternal imagination. The issue, however, was not simply 'whether this creature was endowed with a human soul; [but] if not, what became of the soul of the embryo, that was 5 months old?' (Baldam 1738: Vol. 1, 86). As always, the monster defies explanatory closure.

I want finally to look more closely at the inherent monstrosity of the maternal body, which far exceeds a postnatal retrospective marking of error on the part of the mother. It is not just that the mother is always capable of producing monstrosity, but that she is monstrous in herself. It is above all the very fecundity of the female, the capacity to confound definition *all on their own* that elicits normative anxiety. In the late twentieth century, the disciplinary nature of the clinical encounter, the attempt to regulate and normalise the body, has taken on new forms with the advent of high-technology medicine. But the resulting increase in clinical intervention has both enhanced control in general and undermined it in specific instances. In particular, the new reproductive technologies with their complication of the lines of paternity (and maternity) have opened up anew the horror of indeterminacy. Just at the moment when technological advances have enabled the extension of surveillance to the womb itself, and when sperm and ovum may be processed prior to fertilisation, the fear of what goes on unseen in the recesses of the body may be relocated to uncertainty about origins and foundational narratives. What, we may ask, becomes of the Law of the Father, the symbolic order itself, once the Oedipal scenario is displaced? As Mary Ann Doane suggests: '[t]he story is no longer one of transgression and conflict with the father but of struggle with and against what seems to be an overwhelming extension of the category of the maternal, now assuming monstrous proportions' (Doane 1990: 169).

In Doane's reading of the film *Alien*, the monstrous feminine merges with the environment such that the space of the narrative is the space of the maternal body itself. A similar move characterises the denouement of *Species* where Sil retreats to the sewers to give birth to, literally to pro-ject, her monstrous offspring, leaving the human pursuers to force their way through what amounts to the slime of amniotic/semiotic fluid. *Species* is an altogether less knowing and sophisticated film than *Alien*, but for that reason its motivating anxieties are writ large. As I indicated before, what is directly at issue is the perception that Sil, at the very least, resembles one of 'us', that is, she is recognisably both 'human' and 'woman'. Her surface appearance is that of an attractive and nubile young woman[8] whose devastating drive to procreate serves to remind us that the reproductive identity of all women is similarly out of control. For the human males, the AIDS era link between sex and death is fairly explicit: 'What about protection?' gasps one just before he is overwhelmed by the monstrous embrace. However, it is not sex itself that obliterates the boundaries of selfhood, but the limitless fecundity of the maternal presence.[9]

In the final sewer scene, the fear of the loss of differentiation between self and other, male and female, inside/outside reaches its climax when Dan (whose previous face-to-face encounter with Sil is protected by the speech-act of separation, 'It's you') risks immersion in the metaphorical amniotic fluid. It is a moment of recognition of what is repressed, of the Kristevan abject, of the maternal body that 'disturbs identity, system and order. What does not respect borders, positions, rules' (Kristeva 1982: 4). Significantly, the apparent 'happy ending' of the film where Dan's bodily autonomy is restored relies on a rebirthing scene in which the remaining patriarchal couple haul Dan out of the by now flaming slime to take his place as part of the Oedipal triad. The law of the father is recuperated, and the monstrous mother, blasted by the hunk's gun, disintegrates before the power of the phallus. But that, as the conventions of the genre, and of a more nuanced understanding of monstrosity make clear, is far too simple to effect closure. Despite her sometime human form, the threat of Sil eludes corporeal boundaries and, in opening up to an alarming and engulfing viscosity beneath the skin, she exceeds instantiation as the absolute other. The final gunshot cannot resolve the complicity of the identity and separation that typifies the maternal space. With Sil's extinction, the external threat of the absolute other is vitiated, only for the other within to re-emerge. Her splattered remains produce a tasty snack for a sewer rat which instantly begins its own process of monstrous metamorphosis.

Now if what is at stake for feminism is both the transformation of the masculinist metaphysics of presence – that is, the assurance of a self-complete, self-authorising subject set against the (feminine) other – and the transformation of the categorical fixity of the body, then the analytic of the horror and fascination of the monstrous may indeed be promising. As I have argued throughout, the monster is not simply a signifier of otherness, but an altogether more complex figure that calls to mind not so much the other *per se*, but the trace of the other in the self. And as Derrida reminds us in relation to the similarly uncanny figure of the spectre: 'they are always *there* ... even if they do not exist, even if they are no longer, even if they are not yet' (Derrida 1994: 176). And although the interruption of the oppressive closure of identity that characterises feminism's project must surely profit from Derrida's suggestion that we should learn 'how to let it [the monster] speak, ... or how to give it back speech, even if it is in oneself, in the other, in the other in oneself' (*ibid.*), that should not imply any comfortable assimilation. On the contrary, it is in the very power to disturb and unsettle, to resist final intelligibility, that the monstrous beckons to a more open future. It is not my purpose to suggest that the reading of the monstrous which I propose here is the only one or without risk. The anxieties generated by corporeal difference have most often resulted in a violent policing of boundaries, both practically and metaphorically, and may continue to do so. The task, then, for feminism is to take up the explicit challenge to normative categories of being and to reconceive monstrosity, as would Butler I think, 'not only as an *imaginary* contestation ... but as an enabling disruption, the occasion for a radical rearticu-lation of the symbolic horizon in which bodies come to matter' (Butler 1993: 23). If the monstrous is indeed half human, half something else, then the encounter with the monster need not mark the place of external hazard, but rather the interruption of the dead-end of full presence, and the emergence of the imagi-native *and* embodied complications within. As a move that speaks inevitably to the imperative to reformulate the relations of self and other, it is finally an ethical project.

Notes

1   Notable examples of research on monsters include Grosz (1991), Haraway (1992), Creed (1993), Braidotti (1994), and many of the essays in Thomson (1996).

2   The Renaissance monster of Ravenna, best known today through the work of the French surgeon and writer Ambroise Paré (*c.* 1510–90), is typical of that age's indif-ference to the putative modernist boundaries between reality and fantasy. I look more closely at the figure later in this chapter.

3   As I discuss later in this chapter, the doctrine of maternal imagination was widely accepted in the latter half of the sixteenth century, and was subsequently the subject of rigorous debate for at least another 150 years. Believers held that the pregnant woman might transmit to her foetus a mark both of her own somatic experiences, and of her thoughts and desires. See Huet (1993) for a detailed exposition of the connection between maternal imagination and monstrosity.

4   I am grateful to Janet Price for bringing Derrida's speech 'The State of the Lie; The Lie of the State' (Delhi University, 24 January 1997) to my attention.

5   For historically varying yet situated explanations see, for example, Daston (1991), Pingree (1996), and Thomson (1996).

6   The prestigious Royal Society, chartered in 1660 and operative in Great Britain, was preceded and paralleled by the French institutions of Bureau d'Adresse (1633–42) and the subsequent Académie Royale des Sciences set up in 1666. Other influential groupings of the late seventeenth and eighteenth centuries include the College of Physicians (later the Royal College), The Athenian Society, publishers of *The Athenian Gazette*, and the group around *Le Journal des Savants* in France. Each of these groupings

was concerned to investigate the monstrous from an initially Baconian perspective. See Park and Daston (1981) for further details on the setting up of the Royal Society explicitly in part response to Bacon's tripartite schema for a natural history which gave the investigation of the monstrous co-equal ranking.

7   See Jan Pallister's Appendix to her translation of *On Monsters and Marvels* (Paré 1982), and similar moves in Longo (1995) and Walton *et al.* (1993).

8   Surface resemblance should, of course, never be trusted. Beneath her skin, Sil displays a phallic worm-like writhing structure that complicates the boundaries not just of her putative humanity, but of her femininity.

9   The theme of bodily contamination is in any case neatly turned on its head when the scientists decide that Sil has rejected one would-be mate on the grounds that he has a congenital defect. The monster too appears to have fragile boundaries.

References

Aristotle (1953) *De Generatione Animalium*, trans. A.L. Peck, London: Heinemann.

Bacon, F. (1620) *Novum Organum*, in *The Works of Francis Bacon*, ed. B. Montagu, 1825–34, London.

Baldam, Mr (ed.) (1738) *Memoirs of the Royal Society. Being an Abridgment of the Philosophical Transactions*, London: G. Smith.

Bateman, S. (1581) *The Doome Warning All Men to the Iudgemente*, London: Ralphe Nubery.

Braidotti, R. (1994) 'Mothers, Monsters, and Machines', in *Nomadic Subjects*, New York: Columbia University Press.

Butler, J. (1993) *Bodies That Matter: On the Discursive Limits of 'Sex'*, New York: Routledge.

Canguilhem, G. (1964) 'Monstrosity and the Monstrous', *Diogenes* 40: 27–43.

Cicero, M.T. (1920) *De Divinatione*, Lib. I and II, ed. A.S. Pease, Urbana: University of Illinois Press.

Creed, B. (1993) *The Monstrous-Feminine: Film, Feminism, Psychoanalysis*, New York: Routledge.

Daston, L. (1991) 'Marvellous Facts and Miraculous Evidence in Early Modern Europe', *Critical Inquiry* 18: 93–124.

Derrida, J. (1976) *Of Grammatology*, trans. G. Spivak, Baltimore, Md.: Johns Hopkins University Press.

—— (1994) *Specters of Marx*, trans. P. Kamuf, New York: Routledge.

—— (1997) *The State of the Lie; The Lie of the State*, public lecture, University of Delhi, 24 January 1997.

de Superville, D. (1740) 'Some Reflections on Generation, and on Monsters', in *Transactions of the Royal Philosophical Society* 9: 306–312.

Doane, M.A. (1990) 'Technophilia: Technology, Representation and the Feminine', in M. Jacobus, E. Fox Keller and S. Shuttleworth (eds), *Body/Politics: Women and the Discourses of Science*, New York: Routledge.

Epstein, J. (1995) *Altered Conditions: Disease, Medicine and Storytelling*, New York: Routledge.

Friedman, J.B. (1981) *The Monstrous Races in Medieval Art and Thought*, Cambridge, Mass.: Harvard University Press.

Grosz, E. (1991) 'Freaks', *Social Semiotics* 1, 2: 22–38.

Haraway, D. (1992) 'The Promises of Monsters: A Regenerative Politics for Inappropriate/d Others', in L. Grossberg, C. Nelson and P. Treichler (eds), *Cultural Studies*, New York: Routledge.

Huet, M.H. (1993) *Monstrous Imagination*, Cambridge, Mass.: Harvard University Press.

Kristeva, J. (1982) *The Powers of Horror: An Essay on Abjection*, New York: Columbia University Press.

Longo, L. (1995) 'Classic Pages in Obstetrics and Gynaecology: *De conceptu et generatione hominis*', *American Journal of Obstetrics and Gynaecology*, October: 1349–1350.

Malebranche, N. (1980) *The Search after Truth*, trans. T.M. Lennon and P.J. Olscamp, Columbus: Ohio State University Press.

Maubray, J. (1724) *The Female Physician*, London: James Holland.

Park, K. and Daston, L. (1981) 'Unnatural Conceptions: The Study of Monsters in Sixteenth- and Seventeenth-Century France and England', *Past and Present* 92: 20–54.

Paré, A. (1982) *On Monsters and Marvels*, trans. J.L. Pallister, Chicago, Ill.: University of Chicago Press.

Pingree, A. (1996) 'America's "United Siamese Brothers": Chang and Eng and Nineteenth Century Ideologies of Democracy and Domesticity', in J.J. Cohen (ed.) *Monster Theory: Reading Culture*, Minneapolis: University of Minnesota Press.

Pliny (1961) *The Natural History*, trans. and ed. H. Rackham, Cambridge, Mass.: Harvard University Press.

Shildrick, M. (1996) 'Posthumanism and the Monstrous Body', *Body and Society* 2, 1: 1–15.

Thomson, R.G. (1996) 'Introduction: From Wonder to Error – A Genealogy of Freak Discourse in Modernity', in R.G. Thomson (ed.) *Freakery: Cultural Spectacles of the Extraordinary Body*, New York: New York University Press.

Walton, M.T., Fineman, R.M. and Walton, P.J. (1993) 'Of Monsters and Prodigies: The Interpretation of Birth Defects in the Sixteenth Century', *American Journal of Medical Genetics* 47: 7–13.

19 Belonging and unbelonging

Transformations of memory in the photographs of Virginia Woolf

Maggie Humm

Your films came last night … Two beautiful packets of superfine celluloid. Films! A thousand thanks (as the French say) my dear Herbert for this munificent gift – I shall devote not a few to your remarkable face.

Virginia Woolf, age 15, letter to her brother Thoby (1897)

From the age of 15, photographs framed Woolf's world. Virginia Woolf wrote about photography descriptively in her diaries, letters, fiction and essays, and described her own photographic practice. Before her marriage, and then together with Leonard, Woolf took, developed and preserved photographs in albums. Photography was a continuous part of Virginia and Leonard Woolf's lives even if their photography albums do not tell a coherent life story.

The Frederick Koch collection in Harvard Theatre Library houses Virginia Woolf's seven Monk's House albums, together with four boxes containing over two hundred additional loose photographs. None are catalogued. Although Woolf states in her letters that 'I keep a family album' in the singular and many entries are in her hand, it is impossible to establish, either from their several diaries, letters and autobiographies, or from internal evidence in the albums, who 'authored' each album (Woolf 1980: 169). Just as Leonard and Virginia often shared the taking of photographs, for example for *Orlando*, so it seems that the albums are a joint endeavour. The albums are formally constructed with many sequential and paired matching photographs of friends sitting in armchairs: a striking example of the issue of 'significant form' which so intrigued Bloomsbury art critics (Bell 1914). I will argue that the Monk's House albums are Woolf's unconscious testimony to her childhood past. The albums do not simply provide corroborating evidence for the role of the visual in Woolf's fiction, but, in themselves, richly reveal Woolf's subjective feelings in a visual form. For what is significant in the albums are not the isolated photographs *per se* but the conversations between the photographs and Woolf herself. Woolf's childhood is 'off-screen', but makes the photographs resonate with meaning far beyond the historical moment of their compilation (Pollock 1994). But, in many ways, Woolf's album making also mirrors her aesthetics. In Woolf's fiction a visual image is frequently truth telling. The albums likewise are composed in visual patterns rather than chronologically. Writing to her sister Vanessa Bell, the artist, in 1937, Woolf imagined 'do you think we have the same pair of eyes, only different spectacles' (Woolf 1980: 158). The albums are crucial artefacts, encapsulating and emblematising Woolf's responses to the arts and to her life and friendships. Photographs preserve relationships. Any album's sequencing of photographs creates meaning out of random events. In this respect, albums are memories constructed in the present. The memorial capacity of photographs is self-evident. But where for Freud memory is not the recall of an event but the repetition of a psychic structure in the present, unlike memories, photographs rearranged in albums have a connectedness beyond themselves (Freud and Breuer 1986). The representation of an isolated moment in time means nothing. Meaning depends on how we connect moments. As Henri Bergson argues, a memory only becomes 'actual' by 'borrowing the body of some perception into which it slips' (Bergson 1991: 67).

The principles of selection, montage and tableau in albums are the skeleton of a story. Psychoanalytically speaking, albums, I argue, are often a testimony to our unconscious pasts rather than the pasts we consciously choose to remember.

Memories, or the 'presence without representation', Jean-François Lyotard calls 'the stranger in the house' (Lyotard 1990: 16–17). Where, for Freud, the stranger is 'the scene of seduction perpetrated on the child', for Lyotard, the stranger represents a more general individual incapacity to 'represent and bind a certain something', a something which 'can introduce itself there without being introduced, and would exceed its powers' (Freud and Breuer 1986: 60; Lyotard 1990: 17). For me, it is the 1892 photograph of Woolf's seated mother and father with Woolf in the background mounted as a significant frontispiece in Monk's House Album 3 (Figure 19.1) which 'exceeds its powers' and shapes Woolf's photography. The albums are so unusually anti-chronological because the albums focus on the unrepresentable, on the immemorial; as Lyotard argues, 'the immemorial is always "present"' (Lyotard 1990: 20). The album photographs, through their symbolic organisation, seem to allow Woolf to be in touch with the phantasmatic world of her childhood.

But Woolf's photographs are also a pictorial chain linking childhood with her contemporary world. Woolf, *as* a photographer, skilfully transformed friends and family moments into artful tableaux, and she was surrounded by female friends and family who were also energetic photographers. Lady Ottoline Morrell's photographs 'come out so much better than the professionals'; Vita Sackville-West and the artist Dora Carrington all exchanged photographs with Virginia (Woolf 1977: 46). Julian Bell's girlfriend Lettice Ramsay (whose photographs are in Vanessa Bell's 'Album 7' in the Tate Gallery archives) ran a professional photography agency, Ramsay and Muspratt (Spalding 1983: 263). There is a marked disjunction between Woolf's sometimes dismissive references to photography and her delighted acquisition of friends' photographs. The multiple Monk's House albums reveal how Woolf's photographs were crucial to her sense of identity. Writing to her friend Ethel Smyth in 1940, Woolf compared her own subjective feelings to a photographic process: 'How then do I transfer these images to my sensitive paper brain? Because I have a heart. Yes, and it is the

Figure 19.1   Woolf's mother and father, with Woolf in the background, Talland House
          1892

Source: Frontispiece in Monk's House Album 3. Reprinted by permission of the Harvard Theatre
Collection, The Houghton Library.

heart that makes the paper take, as they say' (Woolf 1980: 393). In an unpublished description of Sophie Farrell, the family servant, Woolf directly connects
family identity with photography: 'Her room is hung with photographs. Her
mind is like a family album. You turn up Uncle George you turn up Aunt Maria.
She has a story about each of them' (Lee 1996: 49).

The essence of photographs lies in the appeal of the experience or the event
portrayed to a viewer. Woolf's letters and diaries describe a constant exchange of
photographs, in which photographs are a meeting-place, a conversation, *aide-
mémoires*, and sometimes mechanisms of survival and enticement. At the age of
16, photographs were 'the best present I can think of' (Woolf 1975a: 18). By the
age of 21, friends' photographs were like erotic emblems: 'I have Marny's
[Madge Vaughan] photograph on my shelf, like a Madonna to which I pray. She
makes my room refined, as lavender in my drawers – (!!)' (Woolf 1975a: 88). The
first volume of Woolf's collected letters ends appropriately with Virginia sending
her photograph to Leonard: 'D'you like this photograph? – rather too noble, I
think. Here's another' (Woolf 1975a: 497).

Through photographs, Woolf invited friends to share their lives with her. She
liked 'very much' to have baby photographs: 'he's an interesting little boy' (of
Katherine Arnold-Forster's son Mark) (Woolf 1976: 495). Barbara Bagenal's
photograph of herself and her son, whom Woolf describes as 'exactly like his
father', is 'stuck in my book'. According to Woolf, this makes an exchange impossible because 'mine all got the foggy dew this summer' (Woolf 1976: 495–496).

After their deaths, photographs of friends were important *memento mori*. After the death of Jacques Raverat, the French painter, in 1924 Woolf wanted to send him 'a picture of me done for a vulgar paper called Vogue' (the photograph in which she is wearing her mother's dress) and desperately needed photographs to continue her mental conversations with him, writing to Gwen Raverat 'for a snapshot or any photograph of him? I go on making up things to tell him' (Woolf 1977: 172–173).

Sharing albums with friends and family helped Woolf to narrativise her friendships. Monk's House 5 contains one of the Woolfs' favourite 'comfy chair' paired sequences of Dorothy Bussy sitting together with her daughter Janie. Magnification revealed that Dorothy was laughing at the very album in which the Bussys would themselves appear. It is as if the album's viewers share the album's narrative construction. Woolf's frequent use of invitational or rhetorical questions in her fiction is matched here by the album's appeal to an active spectator. The album is being observed in the act of memorialising, as if the Bussys see themselves through the photographic gaze of another.

For this reason, Woolf believed that photographs could help her to survive those identity-destroying moments of her own life – her incoherent illnesses. For example, writing to Margaret Llewelyn Davies in 1915, Woolf 'wanted to say that all through that terrible time [a week's attack of apparent insanity] I thought of you, and wanted to look at a picture of you, but was afraid to ask!' (Woolf 1976: 60). Friends' photographs often provide solidly visible autobiographical evidence when feelings of loss of identity become overwhelming.

Mutual image making would also create relationships. Woolf used photographs to entice Vita Sackville-West. Writing to 'Mrs Nicolson' in 1923, Woolf asked Vita to visit in order 'to look at my great aunt's photographs of Tennyson and other people' (Woolf 1977: 4). By 1926, more desperately, Woolf was writing to Vita's mother, Lady Sackville, for the name of Vita's passport photographer so 'that I may write to him myself' for a copy of the photograph (Woolf 1977: 246). Virginia took Vita to London to be photographed for *Orlando* and used the excuse of further illustrations to make additional visits to Knole and more photography sessions: 'You'll lunch here at *one sharp* on Monday won't you: bringing your curls and clothes. Nessa [Vanessa Bell] wants to photograph you at 2' (Woolf 1977: 435). The photograph appears in *Orlando* as 'Orlando about the year 1840'. Angelica Bell posed for the photograph of 'Sasha'. Complimenting Vanessa, Woolf enthused that the photographs were 'most lovely … I'm showing them to Vita, who doesn't want to be accused of raping the under age. My God – I shall rape Angelica one of these days' (Woolf 1977: 497). Perhaps it is not surprising that in her own copy of *Orlando* Lady Sackville pasted a photograph of Virginia alongside the words: 'the awful face of a mad woman whose successful mad desire is to separate people who care for each other. I loathe this woman for having changed my Vita and taken her away from me' (Woolf 1977: 545).

While albums range from nineteenth-century labour scrapbooks to twentieth-century family pictures, most share a predictable format (Spence and Holland 1991). The Woolfs' albums, like others, do not make visible the worlds of politics and work that inhabit letters, diaries and fiction, and memorialise family and friends. But, unlike the numerous typical photos of immaculately happy friends and sunny days, the Woolfs' albums contain out-of-focus photographs alongside perfected takes of the same sitter. Again, Woolf avoids the conventional album long-shot and medium-shot favouring the close-up portrait. The albums do not crudely order friendships into cyclical events, such as weddings. The Woolfs do not construct ideal versions of their lives and friendships and both husband and wife are equally visible. There is no absent, implied male photographer, since in her albums many photographs are evidently taken by Virginia.

It is in Monk's House Album 3 that Woolf's sense of belonging and unbelonging and the power of family memory is most transparent. The album is bound in beautiful 'tumbling-dice' patterned paper with hand-made slits and sixty-eight pages of carefully arranged photographs. Woolf was a knowledgeable bookbinder who personally chose and bound the paper, illustrations and binders for the Hogarth Press books, collaborating with Vanessa's cross-hatched geometric cover designs. Monk's House 3 is not only the richest album in a quantitative sense, but also a very rich example of the Woolf's unusual method of photographing life stories. The past vividly 'narrates' the present. The framing frontispiece is a large $6'' \times 7.5''$ photograph of Julia Stephen immediately followed by the 1892 St Ives photograph of Julia, Leslie and Virginia Stephen. In each subsequent page, the Woolfs photograph each other in similar poses, in similar comfy chairs, and similarly photograph friends in comfy chairs in shots taken on different days, sometimes in different years, but grouped together in the album. Some album pages can have a real gravitas and impact. For example, four $4'' \times 3''$ photographs of Ethel Smyth (probably taken with a 3A Vest Pocket Kodak) resemble cinema stills, each with Smyth in comfy chairs, but with different eye lines (Figure 19.2). Another powerful sequence is the photographs of William Plomer, Vita Nicolson and Charles Siepmann, which are united across time by the chair motive (Figure 19.3). The attraction of the relational, of the monumentally sequential, shapes these photographs. Susan Sontag suggests old photographs can 'transform the present into the past and the past into pastness' (Sontag 1989: 77). Woolf's family past animates the albums. The past processes the present.

But as Stuart Hall points out, there is no such simple unitary thing as 'photography' since the meanings of photographs are inflected by 'the diversity of practices, institutions and historical conjunctions in which the photographic text is produced' (1991: 152). While the precise meaning of the Woolfs' sequential montages will become clearer when I discuss the relevance and the ideas of the artist and psychoanalyst Bracha Lichtenberg-Ettinger, I need briefly to examine 'practices' and 'historical conjectures' in order to be able to show that family memories have a more overriding influence on the Woolfs' albums than contemporary 'practices' (Lichtenberg-Ettinger 1992).

Certainly the Woolfs' skilful intent is not constrained by the limitations of camera technology. Until the acquisition, 'with violent impetuosity', of a Zeiss camera costing twenty pounds in July 1931 ('and said to be unrivalled in the

Figure 19.2   The composer Ethel Smyth

Source: Reprinted by permission of the Harvard Theatre Collection, The Houghton Library.

Figure 19.3   William Plomer, Vita Nicolson and Charles Siepmann

Source: Reprinted by permission of the Harvard Theatre Collection, The Houghton Library.

portrayal of the human – if mine can be said to be human – face' (Woolf 1978: 361)) the Woolfs probably relied on the popular 3A Vest Pocket Kodak which succeeded Virginia's Frena, judging from the size of the album prints. Few options and manipulations were available with these earlier cameras (Spence and Holland 1991). The 3A was introduced to Britain in 1903 with 100,000 sold by 1914 (Coe and Gates 1977). The 3A Kodak took postcard-sized photographs, and many of Woolf's album prints are on cards with pre-printed backs for posting – a standard Kodak feature. The inexpensive, light cameras were particularly popular with women. In September 1905, the *Photographic News* reported that 'thousands of Birmingham girls are scattered about the holiday resorts of Britain this month, and a very large percentage of them are armed with cameras' (Coe and Gates 1977: 28). The Monk's House Albums 3–5 also include $3'' \times 4''$ photographs, the exposure size of the newer 2A Kodak with its superior lens, suggesting that the Woolfs made use of more than one camera. Although Susan Sontag claims that 'a photograph loses much less of its essential quality when reproduced in a book than a painting does', the tonal quality of the original Monk's House prints is often high (Sontag 1989: 5).

Were Woolf's albums shaped by other collections of family photographs or visual memories which Woolf knew well (such as those by Virginia's great-aunt Julia Cameron, her father Leslie Stephen's *Mausoleum Book* and Vanessa Bell's albums now in the Tate Gallery)? Although all three collections favour portraiture there are marked differences between the studies. Using a wet collodian process with glass plates, rather than paper, Julia Cameron took hundreds of photographs of friends and family between 1864 and her death in 1879 (Powell 1973). The portraits of famous men include Tennyson, Carlyle and Darwin, as well as portraits of Virginia's mother and Pre-Raphaelite young girls. Woolf shared Cameron's disregard for sharp images, and *Freshwater*, Woolf's play about the life of her great-aunt, describes Cameron's use of visual metaphors. Just as Vanessa's first act, on leaving the Stephen home, was to decorate 46 Gordon Square with Cameron portraits, so Virginia includes Cameron portraits in her albums, for example the portrait of her mother in Monk's House 3, and, together with Roger Fry, Woolf edited and introduced a book collection of Cameron's photographs. Yet Woolf's devotion to sequential and associative poses differs from Cameron's singular portraits. In Lacanian terms, Woolf's continual photographic repetitions would suggest the 'return' of a visual event which took place outside of her contemporary frames. As Lacan suggests, 'the real is that which always comes back to the same place' (Lacan 1978: 42).

The Monk's House albums also tell a different story of that family past from Leslie Stephen's *Mausoleum Book*, part of which Leslie dictated to Virginia. Immediately following Julia's death, Stephen set out to write an epistolary account of his life as a record for his children of 'two or three little memory pictures' (Stephen 1977: 10). Stephen's surprising intellectual control parallels an exaggerated sentimental portrait of Julia as an abstract, passive Madonna, as she had been depicted in William Burne-Jones's *Annunciation* of 1879 (Lee 1996). In some senses, Stephen's frozen family images are revivified in Woolf's writing.

Both translate family members into characters in similar ways. For example, Stephen's description of Anny Thackeray, his first wife's sister, who 'wrote fragments as thoughts' and stuck these with pins, 'at odd parts of her Ms' resembles Virginia's frequent descriptions of Vanessa's 'shabby, loose, easy clothing attached with pins' (Stephen 1977: 14; Woolf 1981: 246). Both father and daughter loved purple sweet-scented cyclamens, which Woolf transforms into purple anemones in the opening passage of 'Moments of Being', and she curtained the first room of her own in Fitzroy Square with flowing purple. Both believed that the photographs of Julia were also more timelessly affective than painted portraits: 'The beautiful series of portraits taken by Mrs Cameron recall her like nothing else' (Stephen 1977: 32). Julia becomes their 'stranger in the house' since 'she lived in me, in her mother, in her children' (Stephen 1977: 58). More crucially, Stephen explicitly memorialises the exact photograph which Virginia avidly highlights in the opening of Monk's House 3: 'When I look at certain little photographs at one in which I am reading by her side at St. Ives with Virginia … I see as with my bodily eyes the love, the holy and tender love' (Stephen 1977: 58). The connotative power of Julia's image shapes both father's and daughter's 'wider circles of reflection' (Felman and Laub 1992: 71). It is, I will argue, the visual language of this particular photograph, what might be called its 'trauma fragments', that determines Woolf's own photographic constructions.

There are similar quiet connections and discontinuities between the sisters' albums. Both Vanessa and Virginia are drawn to the maternal. When pregnant, Vanessa fantasises to Virginia that 'I shall see you every day and gaze at the most beautiful of Aunt Julia's photographs [that of their mother] incessantly' (Bell 1993: 67). Later, in 1927, she pleads with Virginia 'to write a book about the maternal instinct. In all my wide reading I haven't yet found it properly explored' (Bell 1993: 315). Both shared a Bloomsbury party visit to a film of a caesarean operation: 'Really it is quite the oddest entertainment I've ever been to … Leonard felt very ill' (Bell 1993: 361–362). Yet, although Bell and Woolf mount some of the same photographs in their albums (for example those of the Bell children), Julia Stephen does not haunt Vanessa's albums as a shaping spirit.

Finally, do modernist aesthetics rather than family memories determine Woolf's sequential montages? The modernity of the albums *is* striking and must owe something to Woolf's knowledge of modernism, including Cézanne's painting series and Eisenstein and German cinema. Woolf's use of composite images, the recognition that the process of construction is part of the content of a constructed piece, synchronises with other modernist developments such as John Heartfield's montages in the 1920s and 1930s. Techniques of juxtaposition featured in popular culture, including advertising, as well as in high art (Collecott 1987). Cézanne's still lifes, with their new spatial relation between objects, such as pitchers and fruits, and figures, were the central attraction at Roger Fry's 1910 Post-Impressionist exhibition. Fry claimed that Cézanne sought to express emotion, not mimetically, but through spatial relationships (Watney 1980). It is true that the albums were being constructed in the 1920s, during the period of

Woolf's 'strongest commitment to formalism', its anti-mimetic aesthetic (Reed 1993: 21). Susan Sontag argues that 'photography is the most successful vehicle of modernist taste in its popular version' (1989: 131).

The albums also synchronise with cinema's new range of effects in the 1920s and 1930s. Like other modernist writers and artists, such as James Joyce and the poet H.D., the Woolfs were cinema-goers cognisant of film's stylistic devices such as montage. Virginia's first diary describes her 1915 birthday treat 'at a Picture Palace' as well as the attraction of regular movie going rather than political meetings (Woolf 1979b: 28): 'I went to my Picture Palace, and L. to his Fabians; and he thought, on the whole, that his mind and spirit and body would have profited more by the pictures than by the Webbs' (Woolf 1979b: 18). The Woolfs made eclectic cinema choices. In 1927, Woolf describes seeing a movie with 'a great seduction scene in China' (Woolf 1977: 349). In 1931, she saw 'a very good French one' – *Le Million* – written and directed by René Clair, whose experiments with spatial and temporal dislocations would impact on Woolf's own techniques; as well as being 'given stalls for a night of *Wuthering Heights*' (Woolf 1978: 329). Visiting the Nicolsons in Berlin in 1929, Virginia, together with Vanessa, saw Pudovkin's *Storm Over Asia*, banned in England, and admired its visual landscapes. The accumulation of associations through the composition of montage sequences characteristic of Russian cinema offered a 'new catalytic visual thesis' (Eisenstein 1988: 23). As Eisenstein argues, in cinema, 'the shot merely interprets the object in a setting to use it in juxtaposition to other sequences' (Eisenstein 1988: 80). The Woolfs acknowledged the importance of cinema by publishing film books in the Hogarth Press, such as Eric White's *Parnessus to Let: An Essay About Rhythm in Film* (1928).

As Lyotard claims, cinematography is the 'prime condition of all narration' (Lyotard 1990: 19). Woolf's own writings about cinema, more than most, have a keen-eyed modernist vision. 'The Cinema, the Movies and Reality', first published in *Arts* in New York in 1926, explores relationships between movement and repetition, emotions and spatial organisations (Woolf 1994). As I have argued elsewhere (Humm 1997), 'The Cinema' is perhaps the first British essay to describe cinema as avant-garde, and Woolf's account of film as a space which subverts chronology is very striking:

> The most fantastic contrasts could be flashed before us with a speed which the writer can only toil after in vain; the dream architecture of arches and battlements, of cascades falling and fountains rising, which sometimes visits us in sleep or shapes itself in half-darkened rooms, could be realized before our waking eyes.
>
> (Woolf 1994: 595)

It could be argued that the Woolfs' understanding of the emotional power of spatial arrangements meshed with modernist experiments of the 1920s and 1930s such as Eisenstein's montages.

Yet, while the Monk's House albums, in some respects, reveal Woolf to be an enthusiastic modernist, in other respects they are too repetitious, too obsessive to be defined simply as modernist. The photomontages in the albums suggest that some other preoccupation, whether conscious or unconscious, informs a modernist facade. The page compositions and repeated use of particular objects – the armchairs and vertical flowers and bookcases – seem shaped as much by the psychic as by the formally aesthetic. Like a palimpsest, the album sequences offer a crucial insight into those psychic mechanisms structuring Woolf's aesthetics.

All photographs are a language, and Woolf's language was maternal. Referring to her mother, she claimed that 'She has haunted me' (Woolf 1977: 374). Woolf literally wrote 'through' the maternal: 'Here I am experimenting with the parent of all pens – the black J, *the* pen, as I used to think it, along with other objects, as a child, because mother used it' (Woolf 1979b: 208). Woolf's *To The Lighthouse* visually recreates her mother and father at St Ives in the figures of Mrs and Mr Ramsay. In the novel, Woolf was able to translate abstract metaphysical questions about the meaning of memory into an epistemological question about *how* we can know the meaning of memory by constructing the present time of characters through memories of the past. The publication of *To The Lighthouse* encouraged Woolf's family to remember Julia: 'A voice on the telephone plagued me into the wildest memories – of St. Ives – Gerald … "I am trying to find Cameron photographs of Mama – can you lend me any negatives?"' (Woolf 1977: 380).

Woolf realised that this pictorial enthusiasm raised complex epistemological questions about the psychoanalytic: 'It is a psychological mystery why she should be: how a child could know about her; except that she has always haunted me' (Woolf 1977: 383). Julia Stephen's early death meant that, to Woolf, she became the fantasmatic mother, that is a mother who can exist only as an image, who can be seen or mirrored only in identifications and who might incite the visual imagination (of a photographer) into hallucinatory significations (Jacobus 1995). Hermione Lee argues that the family was Woolf's 'political blueprint' and I would argue that the death of her mother gave Woolf a visual blueprint (Lee 1996: 52). In 'Moments of Being' Woolf describes how it was her mother's death that 'made me suddenly develop perception' (Woolf 1985: 103).

Some developments in recent feminism celebrate this maternal Imaginary. Adrienne Rich's *Of Woman Born* (1976) questions the social construction of motherhood, making a mythical recreation of the psychic pleasures of mothering. In 'Stabat Mater', her essay about the cult of the Virgin Mary, Julia Kristeva (1992) suggests that it is a twentieth-century decline in religious belief, rather than Rich's social constructions, which curtails a maternal language. Kristeva goes on to argue that women need a specular identification with the mother in order to symbolise, that is, to mourn a lost object. In contemporary photographic studies, the phototherapy work of Jo Spence and Rosy Martin offers a vivid example of Rich's and Kristeva's ideas. In phototherapy the camera operator (or phototherapist), through the camera, takes up the gaze of the 'good-enough' mother, one who can mirror the reflection of the other without projecting her distress. As Spence argues, 'after I had been through the pain and pleasure of enacting fragments of my mother's life ... it finally felt safe enough for me to dredge up the traumatic image of the mother I had originally created' (Spence 1991: 236).

This creation of self-identity through maternal memories is the key theme of the work of Bracha Lichtenberg-Ettinger. In *The Matrixial Gaze* (1995) and her essay 'Matrix and Metramorphosis' (1992), Lichtenberg-Ettinger challenges Freud's specular account of Oedipal identity in favour of a matrixial source of identity. The matrixial corresponds, she suggests, to a feminine symbolic discourse derived from the intrauterine coexistence of the maternal 'I' and infant 'Not-I'. Lichtenberg-Ettinger argues that the Oedipal stage/structure, in which masculine development is the norm by which all individuals are measured, is culturally privileged. Hence she contends that according to this framework, we are all trapped in the language of the Phallus, the 'whole symbolic universe is unbalanced' (Lichtenberg-Ettinger 1992: 191). In contrast, Lichtenberg-Ettinger describes matrixial (maternal) representations. Art, she suggests, can 'posit new symbols', a language of margins exploring 'holes in the discourse', perhaps like Woolf's palimpsest photographs (1992: 194).

What this might mean in practice, Lichtenberg-Ettinger goes on to describe, is 'matrixial, *joint* recordings of experience ... emanating from the joint bodily contacts and joint psychic *borderspace*' of mother and infant in the womb (Lichtenberg-Ettinger 1994: 41). She discusses how 'a certain awareness of a borderspace shared with an intimate stranger and of a joint *co-emergence in differ-ence* is a feminine dimension in subjectivity' (1994: 41). 'Metramorphosis is the "becoming threshold" of this activity which alternates between memory and oblivion ... between what has already been created and what has been lost' (1994: 45). The Monk's House albums could be read as a 'becoming threshold', as a 'border space' where Woolf metamorphosised her mother. The albums are matrixial encounters giving meaning 'to a *real* which might otherwise pass by unthinkable, unnoticed and unrecognized' (Lichtenberg-Ettinger 1994: 45). Lichtenberg-Ettinger's belief that phantasies coexist with the earliest instinctual experiences of the maternal offers an explanation of Woolf's obsessive, repetitive photographs and reflections of the maternal.

It is striking that these contemporary understandings of psychoanalytic repre-sentational processes were anticipated in part by Henri Bergson and were very current in Modernism in the 1920s. The aesthetic context in which Woolf worked was shaped by Bergsonian theories of perception. In *Matter and Memory* Bergson points out that we inaccurately 'imagine perception to be a kind of photographic view', when in reality 'the photograph ... is already taken' (Bergson 1991: 38). The past is always present. Every perception is already memory: 'There comes a moment when the recollection thus brought down is capable of blending so well with the present perception that we cannot say where perception ends or where memory begins' (Bergson 1991: 106).

Exploring the ways in which present perceptions interact with memory, Bergson finds 'chains' or relations between discrete perception. Moments are in simultaneous inter-penetration, rather than isolated in time. Bergson argues that objects and forms feature in transitional moments of personal memory and that discrete moments, or perceptions, only possess meaning in relational sequences. Although Woolf claimed in 1932 'I may say that I have never read Bergson', the impact of Bergson's ideas on Bloomsbury's aesthetics is incontrovertible. Simon Watney describes Vanessa's partner Duncan Grant's major painting *Abstract Kinetic Scroll* as a framework of Bergsonian thought (Watney 1980).

Bergson's ideas very much resemble key themes of Lichtenberg-Ettinger *avant la lettre*, and together their critical motifs provide vital clues to Woolf's photographic selections. It could be argued that Woolf's favourite sequences are a form of the matrixial, a return to the maternal photographic memory, in a chain of perceptions. Only occasionally is a photographic image self-sufficient. Photographs belong to a specific life situation. Woolf's photographic tableaux are a psychic construction of her life situation.

As I have described, Monk's House 3 opens with an enlarged 6″ × 7½″ photograph of Julia Stephen immediately followed by the photograph of Julia, Leslie Stephen and Virginia at St Ives in 1892. The treasured 2⅞″ × 2⅞″ photograph, protectively mounted on buff card before insertion in the album, is made larger by a 4″ × 2″ card. What is being constructed before the camera in 1892? At first glance the photograph seems to be a typical domestic interior. But details of this childhood photograph appear again and again in the Woolfs' photo sequences. The photograph's authority stems both from its place, out of chronology, prefacing the subsequent sequences, and from the silent connections between the photograph and sequences. The forty 'comfy chair' photographs in Monk's House 3 were taken on different occasions in different years but are mounted synchronically. The chair is not always placed, as one might suppose, close to a light source, but rather it is a very dominating 'character' in each photograph. The synchronic matching of the St Ives and Monk's House furniture recalls Lichtenberg-Ettinger's idea that the language of the matrixial is a symbolisation of the maternal, childhood home. Following Bergson, the photographic sequences could be a 'chain' of reflections in the present, reflecting the past. There is no chronology. It is as if every close friend sits 'hieratically' in chairs in 'harmony and co-emergence', as Lichtenberg-Ettinger argues (1994: 41), with the Stephen photograph.

Additional details appear in the photographs. Thirteen contain a tall flower, usually a lily, or a tree placed immediately behind the head of the subject, mirroring the flowers behind the Stephens at St Ives. In each photograph the object, like the door panels at St Ives, provides the vertical compositional line of the photograph. In many cases the flower or tree uncomfortably dwarfs the subject, like a residue of the past. Finally, bookcases are prominent objects in the majority of photography in Monk's House 3 with its prefacing Stephen family photograph. The bookcases are not simply the most obvious and convenient background in a writer's home, since objects on them, as well as the books, are moved and regrouped for different photographs, often in the same day (for example, in a photo sequence of E.M. Forster (Monk's House 3: 39)).

In a chapter 'The Dead Mother' (which refers to both depressed and absent mothers) André Green suggests that the 'mirror identification' with the mother 'is almost obligatory' (Green 1993: 151). Green suggestively discusses the history of psychoanalytic concepts in relation to the arts. The mother is a 'framing-structure' for the child, who projects its feelings back onto the mother through 'revivifying repetitions' (Green 1993: 159). Obviously, it is impossible to say how conscious Woolf was of any of these themes, but all photographs are in some way retrospective memories. It is the obsessive repetition of the maternal which brings Woolf into Lichtenberg-Ettinger's matrixial encounter. Just as photographs of dead friends made Woolf 'very glad … how exactly it brings him [Lytton] back!' (Woolf 1979: 16), the Monk's House albums are a matrixial encounter with the dead. Julia Stephen was herself an active memorialist. For example, as Leslie Stephen points out, the memorial erected to James Lowell in the Westminster chapter house (1893) 'was entirely due to her' (Stephen 1977: 81).

The figuration of the dead is a crucial trope in Woolf's novels, famously in the 'Time Passes' section of *To The Lighthouse*, in which Woolf's technique of prosopopoeia, or personification of the dead, keeps Mrs Ramsay alive in the thoughts of others (Hillis Miller 1983: 181). Frances Spalding suggests that Vanessa Bell's paintings similarly revive the maternal. *The Nursery*, inspired by *To The Lighthouse*, has two groups of female figures contained within a circle creating 'a nostalgic evocation of motherhood' (Spalding 1983: 256). Bell evokes the maternal with spatial arrangements of objects, strong verticals and monumental figures of women, very like Virginia's photo sequences. Woolf's albums might be considered to be an artistic reflection of Vanessa's paintings, in that, very unusually, the albums are constructed, not from conventional albums with mounts, but from French artists' sketchbooks (the waterworks were visible with magnification) and with Woolf's experimental coloured end papers.

It could be argued that both sisters 'refuse' their mother's death by constantly revivifying the maternal in art. As Woolf suggested in her first diary, 'I keep thinking of different ways to manage my scenes … seeing life as an immense block of material', and 'in the intervals I've been thinking a good deal about this melancholy state of impending age and death' (Woolf 1979b: 214–215). It is hardly surprising that all of Woolf's work is obsessed with memories. As Lyotard suggests, 'the time of writing does not pass. Every writing [and we could include art] worthy of its name wrestles with the Angel and, at best, comes out limping' (Lyotard 1990: 34). Julia Stephen was Woolf's Angel in the house and becomes her 'stranger in the house' in the album photographs. Woolf continually wrestled with a chain of reflecting memories in photographs which mirror a familial past. The photographs connected Woolf to the past, particularly to the matrixial. The photographs' repeated sequences, spatially organising sitter, chair and flowers, are momentary memories of the past. Her sister's paintings taught Woolf that representations *can* resist death: 'This strange painters world, in which mortality does not enter and psychology is held at bay' (Woolf 1975b: 173).

References

Bell, C. (1914) *Art*, London: Chatto and Windus.

Bell, V. (1993) *Selected Letters of Vanessa Bell*, ed. R. Marler, London: Bloomsbury.

Bergson, H. (1991) *Matter and Memory*, New York: Zone Books.

Coe, B. and Gates, P. (1977) *The Snapshot Photograph*, London: Ash and Grant.

Collecott, D. (1987) 'Images at the Crossroads: The "H.D. Scrapbook"', in M. King (ed.) *H.D. Woman and Poet*, National Poetry Foundation, Orono: University of Maine.

Eisenstein, S.M. (1988) *S.M. Eisenstein: Selected Works: Volume 1 Writings, 1922–34* ed. and trans. R. Taylor, London: British Film Institute.

Felman, S. and Laub, D. (1992) *Testimony: Crises of Witnessing in Literature, Psychoanalysis and History*, London and New York: Routledge.

Freud, S. and Breuer, J. (1986) *Studies in Hysteria*, Harmondsworth, England: Penguin.

Green, A. (1993) *On Private Madness*, Madison, Conn: International Universities.

Hall, S. (1991) 'Reconstruction Work: Images of Post-War Black Settlement', in J. Spence and P. Holland (eds) *Family Snaps*, London: Virago.

Hillis Miller, J. (1983) 'Mr Carmichael and Lily Briscoe: The Rhythm of Creativity in *To The Lighthouse*', in R. Kiely and J. Hildebidle (eds) *Modernism Reconsidered*, Cambridge, Mass.: Harvard University Press.

Humm, M. (1997) *Feminism and Film*, Edinburgh: Edinburgh University Press.

Jacobus, M. (1995) *First Things: The Maternal Imaginary in Literature, Art and Psychoanalysis*, London: Routledge.

Kristeva, J. (1992) 'Stabat Mater', in T. Moi (ed.) *The Kristeva Reader*, London: Blackwell.

Lacan, J. (1978) *The Four Fundamental Concepts of Psychoanalysis*, ed. J.-A. Miller, trans. A. Sheridan, New York: Norton.

Lee, H. (1996) *Virginia Woolf*, London: Chatto and Windus.

Lichtenberg-Ettinger, B. (1992) 'Matrix and Metramorphosis', *Differences* 4, 3: 176–208.

—— (1994) 'The Becoming Threshold of Matrixial Borderlines', in G. Robertson, M. Mash, L. Tickner, J. Bird, B. Curtis and T. Putnam (eds) *Travellers' Tales*, London: Routledge.

—— (1995) *The Matrixial Gaze*, Leeds: University of Leeds.

Lyotard, J.-F. (1990) *Heidegger and 'the jews'*, trans. A. Michel and M.S. Roberts, Minneapolis: University of Minnesota Press.

Pollock, G. (1994) 'Territories of Desire: Reconsiderations of an African Childhood', in G. Robertson, M. Mash, L. Tickner, J. Bird, B. Curtis and T. Putnam (eds) *Travellers' Tales*, London: Routledge.

Powell, T. (1973) Preface to V. Woolf and R. Fry, *Victorian Photographs of Famous Men and Fair Women by Julia Margaret Cameron*, London: Hogarth Press.

Reed, C. (1993) 'Through Formalism: Feminism and Virginia Woolf's Relation to Bloomsbury Aesthetics', in D.F. Gillespie (ed.) *The Multiple Muses of Virginia Woolf*, Columbus, Ohio: University of Missouri Press.

Rich, A. (1976) *Of Woman Born: Motherhood as Experience and Institution*, New York: Norton.

Sontag, S. (1989) *On Photography*, New York: Anchor Books.

Spalding, F. (1983) *Vanessa Bell*, London: Weidenfeld and Nicholson.

Spence, J. (1991) 'Shame-Work: Thoughts on Family Snaps and Fractured Identities', in J. Spence and P. Holland (eds) *Family Snaps*, London: Virago.

Spence, J. and Holland, P. (1991) (eds) *Family Snaps*, London: Virago.

Stephen, L. (1977) *Mausoleum Book*, Oxford: Clarendon Press.

Watney, S. (1980) *English Post-Impressionism*, London: Studio Vista.

Woolf, V. (1927) *To the Lighthouse*, London: Hogarth Press.

—— (1975a) *The Flight of the Mind: The Letters of Virginia Woolf, Vol. I 1888–1912*, ed. N. Nicolson and J. Trautmann, New York: Harcourt Brace Jovanovich.

—— (1975b) 'Vanessa Bell', in *The Bloomsbury Group*, ed. S.P. Rosenbaum, London: Croom Helm.

—— (1976) *The Question of Things Happening: The Letters of Virginia Woolf, Vol. II 1912–1922*, ed. N. Nicolson and J. Trautmann, New York: Harcourt Brace Jovanovich.

—— (1977) *A Change of Perspective: The Letters of Virginia Woolf ,Vol. III 1923–1928*, ed. N. Nicolson and J. Trautmann, London: Hogarth Press.

—— (1978) *A Reflection of the Other Person: The Letters of Virginia Woolf, Vol. IV 1929–31*, ed. N. Nicolson and J. Trautmann, London: Hogarth Press.

—— (1979) *The Diary of Virginia Woolf, Vol. I 1915–19*, ed. A.O. Bell, Harmondsworth, England: Penguin.

—— (1980) *Leave the Letters Till We're Dead: The Letters of Virginia Woolf, Vol. VI 1936–41*, ed. N. Nicolson and J. Trautmann Banks, London: Hogarth Press.

—— (1981) *The Diary of Virginia Woolf, Vol. II 1920–24*, ed. A.O. Bell, Harmondsworth, England: Penguin.

—— (1982) *The Diary of Virginia Woolf, Vol. III 1925–30*, ed. A.O. Bell, Harmondsworth: Penguin.

—— (1985) *Moments of Being*, ed. J. Schulkind, Brighton: Sussex University Press.

—— (1994) 'The Cinema/The Movies and Reality', in A. McNeillie (ed.) *The Essays of Virginia Woolf, Vol. IV 1925–1928*, London: Hogarth Press.

Index

Aboriginal Reconciliation Council 49
abortion 82, 84, 87–8
addiction therapy, 'twelve-steps'
    programmes 281
Adkins, L. 13, 254–5, 257, 267
adultery 37
advertising images, identity politics 284;
    purchase of goods 282
affiliation 171, 184; filiation 168, 170
agency 14, 44, 139, 254, 259, 280; free
    from structure 264–5; legitimating 31;
    linguistic 204; tradition 262; women
    denied 257
ahistoricism 254
Ahmed, S. 10, 112, 187, 292
AIDS 312
Alaskin Inuit 122
Alcoff, L. 137, 215
Alexander, J.C. 259, 262
Alexander, M.J. 114–15
Algren, Nelson 62
'alien consciousness' 138
Alien (film) 312
All-China Women's Federation (ACWF)
    135–6
Allen, P.G., 'Some like Indians Endure'
    53–4
Alperovitz, G. 235, 237
alterity 64–6, 127–8; 'condemned
    passivity' 70, 73; responsibility and 183
American Medical Association, privacy
    and 40
Anglo-American philosophy 196
anti-choice discourses 81–2
anti-Semitism, connectivity 73
anxiety, power of images and 283
aporia 67, 97, 125–6
'argument is war' 199–201
Aristotle 185, 188, 191, 304–5

'Asian' literature 159
Asianness, filiative ethnic identity 166–7
Atomic Energy Commission directive 242
Austin, J. 99, 102–3; How to do Things with
    Words 98, 100
Australia 29, 49–50, 58
Australian Reconciliation Convention 49,
    51, 54–6

Bacon, F., Novum Organum 308
Bakhtinian work on 'dialogism' 132,
    139–40, 142
Balibar, E. 145–6
Bangladesh 124–6
Bateman, S. 306; Doome Warning all Men to
    the Iudgemente 305
Battersby, C. 288, 292–4; Phenomenal
    Woman: Feminist Metaphysics and the
    Patterns of Identity 297
Beck, U. 259–60, 262, 269
Beck-Gernsheim, E. 259–60, 262, 269
Bell, Vanessa 316, 324; Nursery, The 329
Bell, Vikki 15, 27–30, 67, 214
Benhabib, S. 208–9
Benjamin, W., 'Paris, capital of the
    nineteenth century' 273, 279
Bergson, H. 317, 327–8; Matter and Memory
    327
Berlant, L. 12, 27–9, 35, 89
Berlin Wall collapse 228
Bhabha, H. 113, 148, 150
Bill of Rights, Learned Hand essay on 38
bio-engineering, non-biological
    reproduction 194
birth control 84
'Black British' literature 159
black feminism 111–12, 115
Black, Justice Hugo 38
Black Metropolis 71–2

Black Power (USA) 10
Blade Runner (film) 304
body, status of 304
Body Shop, The 125
borderlands 132, 136, 138, 142
boundaries 115, 138, 203; gender 210–11
Bowes v. Hardwick [478 U.S. 186 (1986)] 40
Bowlby, R. 273–4, 279, 282–3
Boyer, P. 235, 237–8
Boyle, Robert, *New Experiments Physico-Mechanical, touching the Spring of the Air* 225
Brah, A. 114; *Cartographies of Diaspora* 167–8
Braidotti, R. 208–9, 308
Brandes-Gratz, Roberta 80, 82
Brewer, R.M. 13, 112
Bringing Them Home 50
Britain 7, 11; apology to Irish 50; imperial policy 122; multicultural and multiracial 160; science and technology 177
British Association for the Advancement of Science 226
Brown, W. 8, 15, 28, 33–4, 42, 51, 61
Burne-Jones, William, *Annunciation* 323
Butler, J., autonomous subject 243–4; consumerism 283–4; declaration of sexuate rights 102–6; gender binarisms 178; identity politics 14, 162; language 202, 204, 208; monsters and 308–9, 313; performativity 99, 277; works: *Bodies That Matter* 162; *Excitable Speech* 201
Buxton, Lee (physician) 36

Cameron, Julia, photographs of 323
Canada 50, 77, 83, 86–7; fetal personhood 87; 'visible minority status' 148
Canguilhem, G., 'Monstrosity and the Monstrous' 307
Cape Canaveral 221, 223
Capitalism, American 223; consumerism and flexible 13; feminism and 7; global 135; labour and 274; neo-liberal framework 31; the personal and 44; technological innovation and 5, 224; transformations wrought by 224; triumphalism of 44
Carrington, Dora 317
Casey, C. 261, 266–8
categorical distinctions/categories 16, 30

categories, sedimentation and ossification 30
Cézanne's painting series 324
Chao, L. 149, 151
Chicago School sociologists 72, 74
China 'Cultural Revolution' 10
Chinese female subject, 'female-ism'(*nuxing zhuyi*) 136
'choice' 279, 283
Church, P. Pond, *House on Otowi Bridge, The* 245–6
Churchill, Winston 240
citizenship 45; definition 34–5; sovereignty of women's 39–40; USA and 34; woman-excluding discourse 28–30
'civil society', new lower class and 265
Clair, René, *Le Million* (film) 325
class 13, 31, 241–2
Clinton, Hillary 116, 131–6, 141
Code, L. 214, 216
Cohn, C. 236, 238
Cole, C.L. 275–6, 283
collectivities 166
Collins, P. Hill 208, 215
colonialism 112–13, 116, 135
Comme des garçons 125
communication, transparency and 203
Complete Works of William Shakespeare 22
compulsory choice 280
compulsory exclusion 277
compulsory individuality 279, 285; maladies of the will and 280–2; politics of choice 279–80
'Condition of England' discourses 160, 163
conditions of possibility 192
connectivity 70
Conrad, J. 162; *Heart of Darkness* 164
Constitutional history, status of privacy 36
consumerism, women and 273–5, 279–81, 284
Cornell, D. 7, 92–3, 95–7, 274, 277–8, 281–2, 284
Council in Foreign Relations (New York) 122
Courier Mail 55
Crenshaw, K. 150, 155
Cronin, A.M. 14, 255, 257, 282, 284
Cruel and Unusual Punishment, state discrimination and 42
Culture, aporia of 125–6; boundaries, identification across 159, 162; difference 145–6, 148; 'ethnic

absolutism' 149, 159; globalisation and
126, 128
cyberfeminism 229–30
cyborg 229

Dalton, Mary 68–9
Darwinian theory 226
Daston, L. 308–9
Davies, Margaret Llewlyn 319
de Beauvoir, Simone 30, 62–7, 69–70,
72–4, 188; identity politics 64; on
pregnancy 289, 294–5, 298; *Second Sex,
The* 64, 73, 295, 297
de-segregation, de-traditionalisation of
gender 260–1
de-traditionalisation 261–3, 265, 268–9
Dean, J. *Solidarity of Strangers: Feminisms after
Identity Politics* 150
Dean, M. 147, 149, 154
Declaration of Independence (USA),
legitimacy of 94–5, 97
deconstruction 10, 97–8, 208, 291;
feminism and 201, 207; metaphor and
philosophy 198; of 'woman' 209;
woman/man 217
Deleuze, G. 48, 51–3, 202
department stores 280–1
deregulation 123
Derrida, J. 44, 179; 'break' and signs 202;
metaphor 198; the monstrous 303,
306–7, 313; performative rights 94–7,
101; sexual difference 182–3, 186, 190,
192; works: *Archive Fever* 185; 'Force of
Law' 95; *Politics of Friendship* 185;
'White Mythology: Metaphor in the
Text of Philosophy' 197
Deutscher, Penelope 19, 27, 30–1
Devi, M., 'Murti' 126, 129
Difference, concept of 52, 138–9, 182,
185, 187, 207; conflict and 3–4;
corporeal 313; cultural 145–6, 148;
feminist debates 132; gendered 216;
multiple female subjects and 136–9;
politics of complexity and 140;
racialisation 145
differential, genealogies and inheritances
193
dis-connections, connections and 52–3, 58
Disney World 223
DNA variations 188
Doane, M. 293, 311–12
Dollard, John, *Class and Castle in the South* 63
domestic violence 209, 213, 216

domination 34
Douglas, Justice William O. 37
drug-users, *addicts* 280
Durga (image of) 126–7

Easlea, B. 176, 225, 240; *Fathering the
Unthinkable* 236
Ecce femina 184, 186
economic literacy 123
Ehrenreich, B. 176, 225
Eisenstein 324
ekla chalo re (walk alone) 126
Elam, D. 10, 151, 208, 212
empathy 57, 70
empowerment, differential 193;
participation in public/international
space 132; strategies 137; subordination
207
ends of enquiry thesis 193
English, D. 176, 225
Enlightenment scholars, monstrosity and
308–310
Enlightenment time–space envelope 131,
134, 141
EPCOT Center 179, 222–5, 228, 231
equal rights 92, 95, 104
essence 189, 193
essentialism 136–7, 142, 150, 254
ethics 3–4, 31, 97
ethnicity 149–50, 159
event 48–9, 51
Everglades, the 231
Experimental Prototype Community of
Tomorrow *see* EPCOT Center

Fairbanks, Dr Charles 224
Felman, S. 43, 324
female, feminist inheritances 191
'female identity' 137
femininity 66–7
feminism, change and 1; culturally and
socially embedded 142; demands
(1970s) 11; epistemic communities
214–17; essentialism and 6, 20, 210;
future possibilities 7; global 122;
'identity politics' 61; learn 'to learn
from below' 115; learning to learn
differently 19; marginalised subjectivity
253; maternal Imaginary 326; new
institutional spaces 13; normative
categories of being and 313; other
intellectual traditions 10; philosophical
9, 191, 193, 207; political and social

injustice 48; politics of *making connections* 117; poststructuralism 178; queer and 51–2; reconciliation 51; reiteration by different 12; standpoint 17–18, 137, 228; status of *objects* and subjects 1, 3; subordination and abuse of women 212; technoscience and 228; traditional ways of knowing 9; transformative practice 7; transforming 14–20; UN-style telecommunicative 125; universalism of the liberal 257; Western 216; 'wounded attachment' 15, 28, 61–2

feminist politics/movements 140, 142; material realities 216

feminists 57; differences of judgement 213; discourse 111; empowerment strategies 137; gender truths and 209, 211; gendered lives and power relations 217; inheritance as transformative 190; Italian 138; knowledge and experience 209, 212; philosophical 187–90; political imagination 62; the psyche and 257; white 215

Fermi, E. 238, 244

Fermi, L. 237–9, 243–4; *Atoms in the Family* 240

fetal subjectivity 81

'Fetishism' 127

fetus/woman dichotomy, pro- and anti-choice subjects 83

filiation, 'organic complicity' 166

Finch, J. 260, 269

Flax, J. 10, 178

Florida 221, 231

Ford Foundation, African artistic traditions and 122

Forster, E.M. 328

Foucault, M. 52–3, 202, 275

foundationalism 3, 207, 212, 214, 216

founding words, 'effect' 101

Franklin, S. 81, 83, 89–90, 292, 299–300

Fraser, M. 15, 31

Fraser, N. 14–15, 27, 274

Frederick Koch collection 316

'free will' or agency 280

French imperial policy 122

Freud, S. 190, 317; essay in 'Fetishism' 127–8

Fromm, Erich, *Art of Loving, The* 222

Fry, Roger 324

Gailar, J. 240; *Oak Ridge and Me* 239

Gandhi 126

Gatens, M. 8, 214

Gates, Bill 5

gays 42, 253

Gemini II launch 222, 224

gender 185; agency and autonomy of women workers 255; de-segregation of occupations 260; discrimination and connectivity 73; enactment 258; feminist and queer theories 53; feminists and 207; international division of labour 114; parallel with race 67; re-traditionalisation 14, 255, 265, 267–8; relational category 111; relations, social transformation 207; structural reflexivity 269; workplace agency 262

'gendered will for globalisation' 115–16

genealogy 44, 184–5, 187–8, 193

General Agreement on Tariffs and Trade (GATT) 121

generation 184

generative thinking, procreative thinking 188

Germany, reflective production 263–4

Giddens, A. 259–60, 269

Global Knowledge '97 conference (Toronto) 119, 122–5

globalisation 114–15, 123, 126

Globe and Mail (Toronto) 231

Goldberg, Justice 37

governance 116, 139–40, 142

Grant, Duncan, *Abstract Kinetic Scroll* 328

Greenham Women's Peace Camp 176, 236

Greer, G. 55, 178

Griffin, S. 235; 'private life of war' 243

Griffiths, M. 176, 215

Grimshaw, J. 9, 176–8

Griswold, Esther 36–8, 40, 43

Griswold v. Connecticut [381 U.S. 479 (1965)] 36

Grosz, E. 290, 294

Guggenheim show 119–20

Guitton, S. 36–7

Gulf War (1991) 177

Gunew, Sneja 13, 17, 20, 116, 148–9

Habermas, J. 28, 141

Hall, C. 8, 52, 266

Hall, S. 48, 51, 162, 320

Hanson, Pauline (Australian MP) 51

Haraway, D. 5, 18, 132, 176; de-traditionalisation 269; difference 134;

feminist knowledge 210, 212, 215;
    monsters 304; pregnant embodiment
    294, 298; science 225–7, 230; situated
    subjects 137–8; work: 'Cyborg
    Manifesto' 228
Harding, S. 5, 175–6, 178, 214, 229
Harlan, Justice (*Poe v. Ullman*) 37
Hartouni, Va. 288, 298–9
Hartsock, N.C.M. 212, 214
Hawke Labour government (Australia) 49
Hawkesworth, M. 214, 216
health care 134
hearing, past feminisms and 6–7
Heartfield, J., montages 324
Heidegger, M. 179, 182–3, 185, 188,
    190–1, 196, 293
Hekman, S.J. 19, 208
Herron, John (Minister of Aboriginal
    Affairs) 55
heterosexuality 38, 40, 44, 134
hijra 210–11
Hiro, D., *Black British, White British* 167
Hiroshima 235, 237, 239, 246
Hitler 71, 246
Hodge, J. 9, 177, 179, 300; 'Forays of a
    philosophical feminist: sexual
    difference, genealogy, teleology' 187
Hogarth press 320, 325
Holland, Janet 10, 14, 178–9, 207, 210,
    214
Holland, P. 319, 323
Holocaust, individual personal trauma 29,
    43
Hom, S.K. 132, 136
homosexuality 37
hooks, b. 13, 112, 134, 253
Howard, John (Australian P.M.) 50, 54–5
Hribar, A. 275–6, 283
'human rights' 19
Humm, Maggie 7, 256–7, 325
Husserl, Edmund 185
Huxley, Thomas Henry 226
hybridic governance 140, 142
hybridity, of the infant 309; migrant
    intellectuals and 164; radical 310
hylomorphic framing, matter and form
    192

identity, Asian as performative 167; belief
    in 6, 17, 27, 137, 139; definitions 159;
    feminists and questions 16; filiative 166;
    gendered 164; metaphor 205; new
    definitions 150; origin and 304;

performance and performative 52, 162;
    self/other 139; subject-centred politics
    142; temporalities of 282
identity politics, do-it-yourself culture
    275–7; feminists and 14–15, 28–9, 32,
    61, 134; global feminism and 150;
    'pitfalls' of 116; politics of complexity
    140; reductionism of 149; *ressentiment*
    tendency 61; signs of subordination 33;
    will-power as transformative force
    284–5
identity-history 281–3
illocutionary infelicity, bill of sexuate rights
    104
illocutionary speech acts 100, 103
image *repetoire* 83
images, beyond the surface 82–4;
    discourses of political struggles 79; fetal
    80–2; interpreting within political
    struggle 84; proof of 80–1;
    spaces/times of pure voluntarity
    282–3; 'taken-for-granteds' 89;
    women's collective experience 88
IMAX cinema 223, 225
inclusion/exclusion meaning 215
Independent Committee on Women and
    Global Knowledge 119
'individual, the' 275, 285
individualisation 262, 265
Indonesia, Nike and workers 283
intention, reception 204
intention-futurity 281–3
inter-organizational relations 140–1
inter-personal networking 140–1
international civil society 123
International Monetary Fund 123
Irigaray, Luce 179; metaphor 202, 205; on
    pregnancy 255, 288–91, 295, 298–300;
    recognition 30–1; rights 19, 92–3,
    94–5, 97–105, 106; sexual difference
    188, 190, 194; works: *Ethics of Sexual
    Difference* 185; *Je, tu nous* 92–3, 101; *Sexes
    and Genealogies* 183; *Speculum of the Other
    Woman* 183, 189, 293, 296; *Thinking the
    Difference* 92, 101
Irish, English and 70
Irons, P. 36–7
Jackson, C.O. 241–2
Japan, apology to 'comfort women' 50;
    reflective production 263–4
John F. Kennedy Space Center 222
Johnson, C.W. 241–2
Joyce, James 325
Jungk, R. 237–8

Just Say No anti-drug campaigns 281–2
justice and fairness 45
'justificatory language of *revolutionary violence*' 95

Kant, Immanuel 184–5; *Analytic* 197; *Critique of Dialectical Reason* 296
Keating, A. 150, 155
Keller, E.F. 225, 230
King, Poppy 55
kleptomania 281
knowing 207
knowledge, feminist claims contested 209; ignorance, gap between 55–7
Knowledge Based Industries of the Royal Bank of Canada 119
Kristeva, J. 288, 308, 312; 'Stabat Mater' 326

Lacan, J. 152, 190, 323
Lacey, N. 93, 99–100, 102, 104
Laha, Kalo Baran (photographer) 126–7
Lake, Ricky 29
Lakoff, G. 198–200
Lancaster University 2–3
language 182, 198–201, 203; performative mode 98
Lash, S. 259–60, 262–6, 268–9
Lau, E. 116, 149, 152; *Oedipal Dreams* 146; *Other Women* 145, 151, 153–5; *Runaway: Diary of a Street Kid* 147–8
Laub, D. 43, 324
Law of the Father 311
Le Doeuff, M. 197; *Hipparchia's Choice* 198; *Philosophical Imaginary, The* 196, 198
Least Developed Countries (LCDs), letters after Toronto conference 124
Lecercle, J.J. 199, 201–2; *Violence of Language, The* 198
Lee, H. 323; 'Moments of Being' 326
legal literacy 123
Leiss, W. 282–3
Leona's Sister Gerri (video 1995) 82
lesbians 42, 57, 134, 253
Leunig 51, 58
Leviathan and the Air-Pump: Hobbes, Boyle, and the Experimental Life 226
Levinas, Emmanuel 179, 182–3, 185
Libby, L. Marshall 237, 243–4
Lichtenberg-Ettinger, Bracha 7, 256, 320, 329; works: *avant la lettre* 328; works: 'Matrix and Metamorphosis' 327; *Matrixial Gaze, The* 327

LIFE magazine 81
Lifton, R.J. 235, 237, 246
listening 17
Loach, Ken, *Land and Freedom* 176
Lorde, A. 9, 111
Los Alamos 235–6, 241, 244
Low, G. 18, 117, 161
Lyotard, J.–F. 5, 10, 43, 317, 325, 329

Mabo and Wik rulings, Aboriginal land rights 50
McClintock, A. 18, 51, 112–13
McDowell, L. 262, 264, 269
MacKinnon, C. 42, 105
McMillan, E. 242, 246
McNeil, M. 8–9, 179
Madama Butterfly 153–4
'maladies of the will' 281
Malebranche, N. 310–11
Manchester Metropolitan University 183
Mandela, Nelson 228
Manhattan Project 235, 243–6
Marshak, R. 239, 243
Martin, E. 230, 261, 269
maternal imagination 310–11
maternal, the, transformative possibilities 257
matrixial encounters, photographs as 7, 327
media companies 29
Merchant, C. 176, 225
metramorphosis, memory and oblivion 327
metanarratives, postmodernism and 10
metaphor 74, 197–205, 298
methodology 207
Michaels, A. 88; *Fugitive Pieces* 77
Midgley, M. 'Philosophical Plumbing' 202
migrant workers 221, 231
migration 114, 117
military, the 175–6, 178–80
minority struggle, self-repetition 34
Mitchell, G. 235, 237, 246
modernism 324
modernity 259; reflexive 260, 264, 268
'modest witness' of science 226–7
Mohanty, C.T. 19, 111, 113–15, 132, 134–5, 138
Molinier, Pierre, *Grande mêlée* 120
Monster of Cracow 306
Monster of Ravenna 304, 309–10
monstrosity 307–8, 310–11
monstrous corporeality 303

monstrous others 304
monstrous, the 307, 313
moral/political stance 215
morphological imaginary, power of 309
Morrell, Lady Ottoline 317
Ms magazine 80, 82
multiculturalism 117, 126–7

(*NAACP v. Alabama* [377 U.S. 288, 307]) 37
Nagasaki 235, 237, 239, 246
Naipaul, V.S. 117, 170; David Cohen
    British Literature Prize 164; *Enigma of
    Arrival, The* 117, 159–65
Narrative, Authority, and Law 41
NASA 179, 222–3, 228, 231
national sentimentality 34–5, 41, 44–5;
    Australian media and 29
nationalism, postcoloniality and 126
Nelson, L. 214, 216
networks, organizational 'intelligence' 141
'new racism' 151
New York's Times Square,
    reterritorialisation 121
Nicholson, L. 10, 253
Nicolson, Vita 320, 322
Nietzsche 15, 28, 61, 68, 184–5, 190; *Ecce
    Homo* 186, 188; *Twilight of the Idols*
    186–7
Nike, *Just Do it* 255, 273, 276–84
Noble, D. 175; *World Without Women* 225
Non-Governmental Organisations (NGOs)
    123–4, 131–2, 141
norms, feminism and 14
North America 7, 11
Nuclear Initiative referendum (California)
    243

Oak Ridge (Tennessee) 235–6, 240–1, 243
'One Nation' party (Australia) 51, 58
Ong, A. 132, 134–5, 138
Orlando 223
O'Sullivan, S. 11–12
'Other' 54, 66, 112, 135, 139, 152–3, 182;
    absolute 303, 312; the colonised 113;
    Native American workers 242;
    pregnancy and 291; women of colour
    111
Otherness 53, 65, 182, 303; of the monster
    309, 312
Overholt, J. 239, 241, 243
owned suffering, image of suffering and 61

pain 33–6

Paré, A. 304–5, 309
Paris is Burning 102
Pateman, C. 28, 253, 265, 274
pathologising of food consumption 280
Pennsylvania Abortion Control Act (1982)
    39–40
performativity 31–2; Austin and 100, 102;
    Butler and 99; concept 18, 21, 30, 98,
    100–1, 146; Irigaray and sexuate rights
    105; irresponsible feminist politics and
    106; political responsibility 98–9; rights
    of 94–5, 103
perlocutionary speech acts 100
'personal is political' 11–12, 28, 43–45
personal responsibility, personal volition 31
Phelan, P. 81, 84, 102
Philosophical Transactions of the Royal Society,
    monstrosity and 310
philosophy 175–6, 178–80, 204; feminist
    views 202–3; metaphors in 201; role of
    196
Photographic News 323
photography, family indentity and 318;
    identity-destroying moments and 319;
    language and 326; meanings in 320;
    modernist taste and 325
Planned Parenthood v. Casey [112 Sup.Ct 2791
    (1992)] 38–40
Plath, S. 289
Plato 198; *Phaedrus* 197
Pliny, *Natural History* 305
Plomer, William 320, 322
Poizat, M. *Angel's Cry, The* 153
political ethnicity 150
politics 40–3; of choice, compulsory
    individuality and 279–80; of identity,
    politics of complexity 139–42; of
    redistribution/recognition 27; of
    trauma 41
polytheism 126–8
positionality 137
post-colonial feminism 19, 51, 111–12,
    131; boundaries 115; 'difference' and
    138; representation 113
'post-deconstructive ethics' 31, 97
post-Enlightenment time–space envelopes,
    'unified sisterhood' 134–5
post-occupational socialities 265–7, 269
postcolonial literature 159, 254
postmodernism 10, 228; and feminism 19,
    207–8
poststructuralism 10, 137, 178, 208, 228,
    254
Potter, E. 215, 225

poverty 134
power relations, oppressive 213
pregnancy 255, 292–3, 297–9
Pringle, R. 260, 262
privacy 28, 36–40
privatisation 123
pro-choice political campaigns 81–2, 84
pro-choice/anti-choice debates 82
Probyn, E. 4, 16, 27–9, 52, 89, 228
procreation 192, 194
psychic pain 42–3
psychoanalysis 10, 151–2

queer codes 57
queers 53, 57

racism 13, 31, 45, 49–50, 52, 64, 73–4;
    black womanhood and 67; connectivity
    with anti-Semitism 73; cultural and
    identity politics 116, 145–6; differential
    148; Los Alamos and Oak Ridge
    241–2; national culture 166; new 151
Radner, H. 274–5, 279
Ramazanoglu, C. 10, 14, 178–9, 210, 213
rape 133–4, 213–14
Rattansi, A. 148, 150–1
Raverat, Jacques (French painter) 319
re-traditionalising tendencies 260, 264–5,
    267–8
recognition 29–31
'recollective imagination' 277–8
Reconciliation 29, 49–52; challenge to *learn*
    for whites 54; event/present 57; queer
    and feminist theories 53; whites' shame
    and 58
'reconstructive', feminist philosophy 179,
    196
reflexive production, re-traditionalisation
    of gender 264–5
reflexivity 13–14, 255, 259; structural
    conditions of 263; traditional relations
    266–7
remetaphorisation 93, 95, 200, 202, 205
reproduction, metaphor for male creativity
    298
reproductive politics, debates 77, 80
ressentiment 51, 53, 58; beyond and modes of
    connectivity 69–74; feminism and 62,
    65, 67–8; feminist politics and 29–30,
    61, 69; Nietzche and 15, 28
Rich, A., *Of Woman Born* 326
rights 135–6
Riley, D. 209–10, 253

Roe v. Wade [410 U.S. 113 (1973)] 39–40
Royal Society, maternal imagination
    debate 311
*Rrose is a Rrose is a Rrose: Gender Performance in
    Photography* 119
rule-bound 'Fordist' structures 262, 264,
    268

Sackville-West, Vita 317, 319
Said, E. 113, 166, 171
Sandlos, Karyn 18, 27, 30, 85–6, 88
Santoro, Gerri (photograph) 30, 77–8, 80,
    82, 84–9
Sartre, J.P. 62; *Being and Nothingness* 201;
    Portrait of the Anti-Semite 63
sati (widow burning) 113
Savage, M. 260–1
Sawhney, S. 210–11
Scalia, Justice 39–40
Schaffer, S. 226–7
science of teratology 308–9
Scott, J.W. 8, 79, 209
second-wave feminism 28, 31, 150, 175–6
Sedgwick, E.K. 53, 57, 280–2
sedimentation 162–3, 201–2, 204
self, body and 304; performative
    enactment 279, 283
Self Employed Women's Association
    (SEWA) 124
self as project 276
'self that is', 'self to be' 277
self-identity, maternal memories 327
self-present subject, non-self 304, 308
self-reflexivity, contemporary
    modernisation 254, 267
self-transformation, exercise and 276
sentimental contract, political optimism
    44–5
Serber, C. 239–40, 242–3
sexual difference 30, 184–5, 194; Derrida
    and 192; effect of legal reform 99–101,
    102; essence 189; the Good and 96; the
    law and 92; paradox of 93;
    performativity and 105; philosophical
    and psychoanalytical tradition 190;
    remetaphorisation 93, 95; traditional
    philosophy and 8
sexual harassment law 42
sexual inequalities 52
sexual orientation, politics of disability 193
sexual privacy 36, 38, 40
sexually undetermined inheritance 191
sexuate rights, basis for legal reform 93–4;

Butler and 102–6; drag performance 102; illocutionary performativity 31; institutional reform 99; Irigarayan bill 95, 97; justifying 95–8
shame 54–8; queer relation to 52
Shapin, S. 226–7
Sheikh, Farhana, *Red Box, The* 117, 159, 165–70
Shildrick, M. 9, 204, 256, 257
shoplifting 281
Siepmann, Charles 320, 322
Silent Scream, The (video) 81
situatedness of knowledges 137
Skeggs, B. 8, 15, 18, 31
Slater, D. 274, 285
Smith, A.K. 242, 244, 246
Smith, D.E. 8, 212, 215
Smithsonian Institute exhibition 237
Smyth, Ethel 317, 321
Socialist Scholars' conference (New York) 122
Sontag, Susan 320, 323, 325
Soper, K. 207, 211–12, 215
Spaceport 228, 231
Spalding, F. 317, 329
Species (film) 303–4, 312
Spelman, E. 67, 111, 214
Spence, J. 319, 323, 326–7
Spinoza 185
Spivak, G.C. 253; essentialism 132, 136–7; gendered colonialism 13, 113, 115–16; unlearning 170–1
Springer, Jerry 29
Squires, J. 229–30
Stabile, C.A. 178, 292
Standing By and Making Do: Women of Wartime Los Alamos 239
stare decisis 37–8
Stephen, Julia, photographs 318, 320, 324, 326, 328
Stephen, Leslie 324, 329; *Mausoleum Book* 323
Stolen Generations 50, 55–6
Storm Over Asia (Pudovkin's film) 325
'strategic essentialism 136–7
strategy 136, 142
Strathern, M. 258, 279
'structural reflexivity' 259, 263
subaltern pain, universally *intelligible* 41
'subaltern woman' 113, 115, 169
subject positions, race and gender 112
'subject, the', debate 253, 257
subject–object relationship, history of the present 123
subjectivities 67, 132, 136–7, 139, 142, 255

subjectivity 255–6; pregnant 292–3, 298–9
subordination 33, 43, 67, 207, 212
'successor science' 229–30
suffering 43, 53
Suleri, S. 163–4
Sum, Ngai-Ling 19, 116, 131, 141
Sun Herald 55
77 Sunset Strip (TV programme) 222
Sydney Morning Herald 51, 55
Szabo, Violetta 176

Tagor (poet) 126
taken-for-granted 44, 89, 202, 242
Taylor, C. 15, 275–6, 279
team-husbands 267–9
team-wives 267–8
technical Darwinism 188
technicity 188
technological change, information technology 230
technoscience 175–6, 178–80, 224–32
telecommunications 13, 115, 121–4
teleology 184–5, 187–9
terra nullius 50–1
third world 10, 13, 114, 122
Thomas, Bigger 65–71, 74
time–space envelopes 131–2; multiple feminisms and 134–6; 'united sisterhood' 136
Tomkins, S. 56–7
tort law 41
Trade Related Intellectual Properties (TRIPS) 121
traditionalisation of the economic 262–4, 268
transformations, choice and will-power 283–5; concept 1, 4, 178; consumerism 273; feminism thinking *through* 7, 258; feminist of global scope 128; political identifications 167; question of 1–4; responding to 10–14; in times of change 4–7
Transformations conference 2–3, 20, 183
transnational literacy 123
'transversal politics' 140
trauma 42, 44; *suffering* 43
'tribalism' 149
Trinity Test 239–40
Tyler, I. 9, 255, 257

United Nations 123
United Nations Conference for Women (Beijing 1995) 19, 116, 124, 131–2

universalism 254
unlearning 170–1
Urry, J. 223, 259
U.S. shuttle Discovery 231
USA 12, 30, 33–4, 43; apology to African-Americans 50; citizenship 40; Civil Rights and Black Power 10; fetal protection issues 83; image of a 'united sisterhood' 134; pregnant women in medical treatment 297; pro-choice and anti-choice movements 77; pro-choice movement (1970s) 81; racism 73; science and technology 177; sex privacy law 38; urban slums 71–2; women of African descent 112

Vancouver magazine 145
Vietnam War 11
virginity 93

Walby, S. 177, 260, 264
Watney, S. 324, 328
West, R. 41–2
Western culture, perpetual matricide 300
Western opera 146, 151, 155
Western philosophical tradition 111, 185, 196, 202
Western scientific medicine 176
White, E., *Parnessus to Let: An Essay About Rhythm in Film* 325
white gays 57
White, Kathryn (Canadian Committee for UNIFEM) 119–21
whites, reconciliation and 58
Whitford, M. 176, 215
Wilberforce, Bishop Samuel 225
Williams, P.J. 38, 42
Williams, R, 'Keywords' 201
Wilson, J. 239–40, 242–3
Winfrey, Oprah 29
Winterson, J., *Sexing the Cherry* 289
WISE (Women into Science and Engineering) 177
'Wolfensohn among the Girls' 120
Wolkowitz, C. 9, 179
Wollstonecraft, M. 18
woman 215; Black feminists and 111–12; development-in-globalism 123
woman/man 210–12, 217
womanhood, subjectivity, connectivity and 73
women 193; agency and 257; antagonistic relationship 111, 114; Black women 67, 111, 114; consumerism and 273–5, 279–81, 284; empowerment and telecommunication 122, 132; female oppression and reproductive capacity 292; femininity and subordination 67; fragmentation amongst 11; Germany and Japan and reflexive production 264; inheritance 184, 187; knowledge-intensive work 264; lineage for rational 188; members of parliament (1997) 6; normative and exclusionary identity 210; philosophical feminists 193; pregnant 255–6, 291–2; privacy and 28; self-transformation 284; subjectivity, dealing with 9, 253; what it means to be 257
women of colour 111, 150
women's rights 18–19
Women's Studies, transformation and 1–2, 4, 8
Women's World Banking 124
Wong, J. 147, 149, 153; *Red China Blues: My Long March from Mao to Now* 149
Woolf, V. 318–19, 324–5, 327, 329; childhood, photographs as link 7, 317; *Monk's House Albums* 316, 317, 320, 323, 325, 327, 329; (3) 317–18, 320, 323, 324, 328; (5) 319; works:'Cinema, 'the Movies and Reality' 325; *Freshwater* 323; *Orlando* 316, 319; *Three Guineas* 244; *To The Lighthouse* 326, 329
Wordsworth 162
World Bank 123–4
World Conference of the International Women's Year (Mexico City 1975) 123
World Trade Organisation 121, 123
Wright, Joseph, *Experiment with a bird in the air pump* 225
Wright, Richard 30, 62–5, 68–74; *Black Boy* 68, 73; 'Long Black Song' 74; *Native Son* 63, 65, 71; *Twelve Million Black Voices* 70–1
Wuthering Heights (film) 325

Young, I.M. 18, 289, 292, 294, 297, 298; 'Pregnant Embodiment: Subjectivity and Alienation' 296
Yugoslavia (former) 149
Yuval-Davis, N. 132, 138–40, 150

Zizek, S. 44, 148, 151–4
'zone of conscience', privacy and 40
zone of privacy 37–8, 45–6
zone of publicity 39